MARIA MONK

THE CONFESSIONAL

AWFUL DISCLOSURES OF

MARIA MONK,

AS EXHIBITED IN A NARRATIVE OF HER SUFFERINGS, DURING
A RESIDENCE OF FIVE YEARS AS A NOVICE, AND TWO YEARS AS
A BLACK NUN, IN THE HOTEL DIEU NUNNERY AT MONTREAL.

WITH ADDITIONAL INFORMATION, AND CONFIRMATION.

TO WHICH IS ADDED, THE NUN; OR,

SIX MONTHS' RESIDENCE IN A CONVENT

BY REBECCA THERESA REED.

"COME OUT OF HER MY PEOPLE, THAT YE BE NOT PARTAKERS
OF HER SINS, AND THAT YE RECEIVE NOT OF HER PLAGUES."
REV. XVIII. 4.

 BooksUlster

Awful Disclosures of Maria Monk first published in 1836. *The Nun; or Six Months' Residence in a Convent* first published in 1835. The text of this new edition is taken from a London republication of c1880 by an unidentified publisher ("Printed for the Booksellers").

Typographical arrangement © Books Ulster 2017

ISBN: 978-1-910375-59-4 (Paperback)

FOREWORD TO THE NEW EDITION

It is now approaching two hundred years since *Awful Disclosures of Maria Monk* made its appearance. The book was first published by Howe & Bates, New York, in January, 1836, and sparked a controversy that continued to rage for more than a century. Monk claimed in her work that she had been a nun at the Hôtel Dieu nunnery in Montreal and that torture, rape, murder and infanticide were practised there. The accusations were hotly contested, and it was stated that Maria Monk had never been a nun at the convent, but the refutations failed to satisfy many of Monk's adherents who continued to believe in the authenticity of her story. The demand for the book was such that numerous editions were produced over the course of the next hundred years.

This edition, originally published (probably) in the 1880s, includes not only the *Awful Disclosures*, but also extracts from public journals, additional information on what happened after Monk's alleged escape, the case in her favour, and testimony of others in confirmation of her claims. Appended to it all is *The Nun; or Six Months' Residence in a Convent*, by Rebecca Theresa Reed, a disputed account of life in an Ursuline convent (subsequently attacked and burned) in Charlestown, Massachusetts, which was first published in 1835, the year before *Awful Disclosures*.

The text in this new edition has been completely reset and a few obvious typographical errors corrected. The 'Description of Nun's Island, and the Buildings on It' has been relocated from the very end of the book to subjoin it with the rest of the material relating to Maria Monk.

April, 2017

CONTENTS

PREFACE.

IT is hoped that the reader of the ensuing narrative will not suppose that it is a fiction, or that the scenes and persons that I have delineated, had not a real existence. It is also desired, that the author of this volume may be regarded not as a voluntary participator in the very guilty transactions which are described; but receive sympathy for the trials which she has endured, and the peculiar situation in which her past experience, and escape from the power of the Superior of the Hotel Dieu Nunnery, at Montreal, and the snares of the Roman Priests in Canada, have left her.

My feelings are frequently distressed and agitated by the recollection of what I have passed through, and by night and day I have little peace of mind, and few periods of calm and pleasing recollection. Futurity also appears uncertain. I know not what reception this little work may meet with, and what will be the effect of its publication here or in Canada, among strangers, friends, or enemies. I have given the world the truth, so far as I have gone, on subjects of which I am told they are generally ignorant; and I feel perfect confidence, that any facts which may yet be discovered, will confirm my words whenever they can be obtained. Whoever shall explore the Hotel Dieu Nunnery at Montreal, will find unquestionable evidence that the descriptions of the interior of that edifice, given in this book, were furnished by one familiar with them; for whatever alterations may be attempted, there are changes which no mason or carpenter can make and effectually conceal; and therefore there must be plentiful evidence in that Institution, of the truth of my description.

There are living witnesses, also, who ought to be made to speak, without fear of penances, tortures, and death, and possibly their testimony at some future time, may be added, to confirm my statements. There are witnesses I should greatly rejoice to see at liberty; or rather there were. Are they living now? or will they be permitted to live after the Priests and Superiors have seen this book? Perhaps the wretched nuns in the cells have already suffered for my sake—perhaps Jane Ray has been silenced for ever, or will be murdered, before she has time to add her most important testimony to mine.

But speedy death in relation only to this world, can be no great calamity to those who lead the life of a nun. The mere recollection of it always makes me miserable. It would distress the reader, should I repeat the dreams with which I am often terrified at night; for I sometimes fancy myself pursued by my worst enemies; frequently I seem as if again shut up in the Convent; often I imagine myself present at the repetition of the worst scenes that I have hinted at or described. Sometimes I stand by the secret place of interment in the cellar; sometimes I think I can hear the shrieks of the helpless females in the hands of atrocious men; and sometimes almost seem actually to look again upon the calm and placid features of St. Frances, as she appeared when surrounded by her murderers.

I cannot banish the scenes and character of this book from my memory. To me it can never appear like an amusing fable, or lose its interest and importance. The story is one which is continually before me, and must return fresh to my mind, with painful emotions, as long as I live. With time, and Christian Instruction, and the sympathy and examples of the wise and good, I hope to learn submissively to bear whatever trials are appointed me, and to improve under them all.

Impressed as I continually am with the frightful reality of the painful communications that I have made in this volume, I can only offer to all persons who may doubt or disbelieve my statements, these two things:

Permit me to go through the Hotel Dieu Nunnery, at Montreal, with some impartial ladies and gentlemen, that they may compare my account with the interior parts of the building, into which no persons but the Roman Bishop and Priests are ever admitted; and if they do not find my description true then discard me as an impostor. Bring me before a court of justice—there I am willing to meet *Latargue, Dufresne, Phelan, Bonin*, and *Richards*, and their wicked companions, with the Superior, and any of the nuns, before a thousand men,

MARIA MONK.

New York, January 11, 1836.

MARIA MONK

CHAPTER I.

EARLY RECOLLECTIONS

EARLY Life—Religious Education Neglected—First School—Entrance into the School of the Congregational Nunnery—Brief Account of the Nunneries in Montreal—The Congregational Nunnery—The Black Nunnery—The Grey Nunnery—Public Respect for these Institutions—Instructions received—The Catechism—The Bible.

MY parents were both from Scotland, but had been resident in Lower Canada some time before their marriage, which took place in Montreal, and in that city I have spent most of my life. I was born at St. John's, where they lived for a short time. My father was an officer under the British Government, and my mother has enjoyed a pension on that account ever since his death.

According to my earliest recollections, he was attentive to his family, and often repeated to us a passage from the Bible, which often occurred to me in after life. I may probably have been taught by him; but after his death I do not recollect to have received any instruction at home, and was not even brought up to read the Scriptures; my mother although nominally a Protestant, did not pay attention to her children. She was inclined to think well of the Catholics, and often attended their churches. To my want of religious instruction at home, and my ignorance of God and my duty, I can trace my introduction to convents, and the scenes I am now to describe.

When about six or seven years of age, I went to school to a Mr. Workman, a Protestant, who taught in Sacrament street, and remained several months. There I learnt to read and write, and arithmetic as far as division. All the progress I ever made in those branches was in that school, as I have never improved in any of them since.

A number of girls of my acquaintance went to school to the nuns of the Congregational Nunnery, or Sisters of Charity. The schools taught by them are perhaps more numerous than my readers may imagine. Nuns are sent out from the convent to many of the towns and villages of Canada to teach small schools; and some of them as instructresses in different parts of the United States. When I was ten years old, my mother asked me one day if I should like to learn to read and write French, and I began to think seriously of attending the school in the Congregational Nunnery. I had already some knowledge of that language, sufficient to speak it a little, and my mother knew something of it.

I have a distinct recollection of my entrance into the Nunnery; the day was an important one in my life, and on it commenced my acquaintance with a convent. I was conducted by some young friends along Notre Dame street, till we reached the gate. Entering, we walked some distance along the side of a building towards a chapel, until we reached a door, stopped, and rung a bell. It was opened, and entering, we proceeded through a covered passage till we took a short turn to the left, and reached the door of the school-room. On my entrance, the Superior met me, and told me that I must dip my fingers into the holy water at the door, cross myself, and say a short prayer; and this she told me was always required of Protestant as well as Catholic children.

There were about fifty girls in the school, and the nuns professed to teach reading, writing, arithmetic, and geography. The methods, however, were very imperfect, and little attention was devoted to them, the time being engrossed with lessons in needle-work, which was performed with much skill. The nuns had no very regular parts assigned them in the management of the schools. They were rather unpolished in their manners, often exclaiming, "O'est un menti," (that's a lie,) and "mon Dieu," (my God,) on the most trivial occasions. Their writing was poor, and they often put a capital letter in the middle of a word. The only book of geography which we studied, was a catechism of geography, from which we learnt by heart a few questions and answers. We were sometimes referred to a map, but it was only to point out Montreal or Quebec, or some other prominent name.

It may be necessary to mention, that there are three Convents in Montreal, founded on different plans, and governed by different rules. Their names are as follows:

I. The Congregational Nunnery. 2. The Black Nunnery, or Convent of Sister Bourgeoise. 3. The Grey Nunnery.

The first of these professes to be devoted entirely to the education of girls. But with the exception of needle-work, hardly anything is taught but prayer and catechism; the instruction in reading, writing, &c., amounting to very little and often to nothing. This Convent is adjacent to the Grey Nunnery, separated from it only by a wall. The second professes to be a charitable institution for the care of the sick, and the supply of bread and medicines to the poor; and something is done in charity, though but little compared with the size of the buildings, and the number of inmates.

The Grey Nunnery, situated in a distant part of the city, is a large edifice, containing departments for the care of insane persons and foundlings. With this I have less acquaintance than with the others. I have often seen two of the Grey nuns, and know their rules; they do not confine them always within their walls, like those of the Black Nunnery. These two Convents have their common names (Black and Grey) from the colours of the dresses worn by their inmates.

In these three Convents there are certain apartments into which strangers can gain admittance, but others from which they are always excluded. In all, large quantities of ornaments are made by the nuns, which are exposed for sale in the *Ornament Rooms*, and afford large pecuniary receipts every year, which contribute much to their income. The nuns of these Convents are devoted to the charitable object appropriated to each, the labour of making different articles known to be manufactured by them, and the religious observances, which occupy much of their time. They are regarded with much respect by the people at large; and when a novice takes the veil, she is supposed to retire from the temptations and troubles of this world into a state of holy seclusion, where, by prayer, self-mortification and good deeds, she prepares herself for heaven. Sometimes the Superior of a Convent obtains the character of working miracles: and when she dies crowds throng the Convent, who think indulgences are to be derived from bits of her clothes and other things she has possessed; and many have sent articles to be touched by her bed or chair, in which virtue is thought to remain. I used to participate in such ideas, and looked upon a nun as the happiest of women, and a Convent as the most holy, and delightful abode. Pains were taken to impress such views upon me. Some of the priests of the Seminary often visited the Congregational Nunnery, and catechised and talked on religion. The Superior of the Black Nunnery also came into the school, and enlarged on the advantage we enjoyed in having such teachers, and dropped something now and then relating to her own convent, calculated to make us entertain the highest ideas of it, and make us sometimes think of the possibility of getting into it.

Among the instructions given us by the priests, some of the most pointed were directed against the Protestant Bible. They often enlarged upon the evil tendency of that book, and told us that but for it many a soul condemned to hell, and suffering eternal punishment might have been in happiness. They could not say anything in its favour; for that would be speaking against religion and against God. They warned us against its woe, and represented it as a thing very dangerous to our souls. In confirmation of this, they would repeat some of the answers taught us at catechism; a few of which I will here give. We had little catechisms, ("Les Petits Catechismes") put into our hands to study; but the priests soon began to teach us a new set of answers, which were not to be found in our books from some of which I received new ideas, and got, as I thought, important light on religious subjects, which confirmed me more in my belief in the Roman Catholic doctrines. Those questions and answers I can still recall with tolerable accuracy, and some of them I will add here. I never have read them as we were taught them only by word of mouth.

"*Question.* Porquoi le bon Dieu n'a pas fait tous les commande-mens?"—"*Response.* Parce que l' homme n'est pas si fort qu'il peut garder tout ses commandemens."

"*Question.* Why did not God make all the commandments?"—"*Answer.* Because man is not strong enough to keep them."

And another; "*Q.* Porquoi l'homme ne lit pas l' Evangile?"—"*R.* Parce que l'esprit de l'homme est trop borne et trop faible pour comprendre qu'est ce que Dieu a écrit."

"*Q.* Why are men not to read the New Testament?"—"*A.* Because the mind of man is too limited and weak to understand what God has written."

These questions and answers are not to be found in the common catechisms in use in Montreal and other places where I have been, but all the children in the Congregational Nunnery were taught them, and many more not found in these books.

CHAPTER II.

CONGREGATIONAL NUNNERY

STORY told by a Fellow Pupil against a Priest—Other Stories—Pretty Mary—Confess to Father Richards—My subsequent Confession—Instructions in the Catechism.

THERE was a girl thirteen years old whom I knew in the School, who resided in the neighbourhood of my mother, and with whom I had been familiar. She told me one day at school, of the conduct of a priest with her at confession, at which I was astonished. It was of so criminal and shameful a nature, I could hardly believe it, and yet I had so much confidence that she spoke the truth, that I could not discredit it.

She was partly persuaded by the priest to believe he could not sin, because he was a priest, and that anything he did to her would sanctify her; and yet she seemed somewhat doubtful how she should act. A priest, she had been told by him, is a holy man, and appointed to a holy office, and therefore what would be wicked in other men, could not be so in him. She told me she had informed her mother of it, who expressed no anger nor disapprobation: but only enjoined it upon her not to speak of it; and remarked to her as priests were not like men, but holy and sent to instruct and save us, whatever they did was right.

I afterwards confessed to the priest that I had heard the story and had a penance to perform for indulging a sinful curiosity in making inquiries; and the girl had another for communicating it. I afterwards learned that other children had been treated in the same manner, and also of similar proceedings.

Indeed it was not long before such language was used to me, and I well remember how my views of right and wrong were shaken by it. Another girl at the school, from a place above Montreal, called the Lac, told me the following story of what had occurred recently in that vicinity. A young squaw, called La Belle Marie, (pretty Mary,) had been seen going to confession at the house of the priest, who lived a little out of the village. La Belle Marie was afterwards missed, and her murdered body was found in the river. A knife was also found bearing the priest's name. Great indignation was excited among the Indians, and the priest immediately absconded, and was never heard from. A note was found on his table addressed to him, telling him to fly, if he was guilty.

It was supposed that the priest was fearful that his conduct might be betrayed by this young female; and he undertook to clear himself by killing her.

These stories struck me with surprise at first, but I gradually began to feel differently, even supposing them true, and to look upon the priests as men incapable of sin; besides, when I first went to confession, which I did to Father Richards in the old French church, since taken down, I heard nothing improper; and it was not until I had been several times that the priests became more and more bold, and were at length indecent in their questions, and even in their conduct when I confessed to them in the Sacristie. This subject, I believe, is not understood nor suspected among Protestants; and it is not my intention to speak of it very particularly, because it is impossible to do so without saying things both shameful and demoralizing.

I will only say here, that when quite a child, I heard from the mouths of the priests at confession, what I cannot repeat, with treatment corresponding; and several females in Canada have assured me that they have repeatedly, and indeed regularly, been required to answer the same and other like questions, many of which present to the mind deeds which the most iniquitous and corrupt heart could hardly invent.

There was a frequent change of teachers in the school of the Nunnery, and no regular system was pursued in our instruction. There were many nuns who came and went while I was there, being frequently called in and out without any perceptible reason. They supply school teachers to many of the country towns, usually two to each of the towns with which I was acquainted, besides sending Sisters of Charity to many parts of the United States. Among those whom I saw most was Saint Patrick, an old woman for a nun, that is about forty, very ignorant and gross in her manners, with quite a beard on her face, and very cross and disagreeable. She was sometimes our teacher in sewing, and was appointed to keep order among us. We were allowed to enter only a few of the rooms in the Congregational Nunnery, although it was not considered one of the secluded Convents.

In the Black Nunnery, which is very near the Congregational, is an hospital for sick people from the city; and sometimes some of our boarders, such as were indisposed, were sent there to be cured. I was once taken ill, and sent there for a few days.

There were beds enough for a number more. A physician attended it, and a number of the veiled nuns of that Convent spent most of their time there.

These would also sometimes read lectures and repeat prayers to us.

After I had been in the Congregational Nunnery two years, I left it, and attended several schools a short time. But I soon became dissatisfied, having many severe trials to endure at home, which my feelings will not allow me to describe; and as my Catholic acquaintances had often spoken to me in favour of their faith, I was inclined to believe it although I knew little of any religion. If I had known anything of true religion I believe I should never have thought of becoming a nun.

CHAPTER III.

BLACK NUNNERY

PREPARATIONS to become a Novice in the Black Nunnery—Entrance—Occupations of the Novices—The apartments to which they had access—First interview with Jane Ray—Reverence for the Superior—A wonderful Nun—Her Reliques—The Holy Good Shepherd, or Nameless Nun—Confession of Novices.

AT length I determined to become a Black Nun, and called upon one of the oldest priests in the Seminary, to whom I made known my intention.

The old priest was Father Rocque. He is still alive. He was at that time the oldest priest in the Seminary, and carried the Bon Dieu, Good God, as the Sacramental wafer is called. When going to administer it in any country place, he used to ride with a man before him, who rang a bell as a signal. When the Canadians heard it, whose habitations he passed, they would prostrate themselves to the earth, worshipping it as God. He was a man of great age, and wore large curls, so that he somewhat resembled his predecessor, Father Roue. He was at that time at the head of the Seminary. This institution is a large edifice, situated near the Congregational and Black Nunneries, being on the east side of Notre Dame street. It is the rendezvous and centre of all the priests in the district of Montreal, and supplies all the country as far down as the Three Rivers, which place, is under the charge of the Seminary of Quebec. About one hundred and fifty priests are connected with that at Montreal, as every small place has one priest, and larger ones have two.

Father Rocque promised to converse with the Superior of the Convent, and proposed my calling again in two weeks, at which time I visited the Seminary again, and was introduced to the Superior of the Black Nunnery. She told me she must make inquiries, before she could give me a decided answer, and proposed to me to take up my abode a few days at the house of a French family in St. Lawrence suburbs.

Here I remained a fortnight; during which time I formed acquaintance with the family, particularly with the mistress of the house, who was a devoted Papist, and had a high respect for the Superior.

On Saturday morning I called, and was admitted into the Black Nunnery as a novice, much to my satisfaction, for I had a high idea of life in a convent, secluded, as I supposed the inmates to be, from the world and all its evil influences, and assured of everlasting happiness in heaven. The Superior received me, and conducted me into a large room, where the novices, who are called in French, Postulantes, were assembled, and engaged in the occupation of sewing.

Here were about forty of them, and they were in groups in different parts of the room, near the windows: but in each group was one of the veiled nuns of the convent, whose abode was in the interior apartments, to which no novice was admitted. As we entered, the Superior informed them that a new novice had come, and desired any present who might have known me in the world to signify it.

Two Miss Feugnees, and a Miss Howard from Vermont, who had been my fellow-pupils in the Congregational Nunnery, immediately recognized me. I was then placed in one of the groups at a distance from them, and furnished by a nun, called Sainte Clotilde, with materials to make a purse, such as priests use to carry the consecrated wafer in, when they administer the sacrament to the sick. I well remember my feelings at that time, sitting among a number of strangers, and expecting with painful anxiety the arrival of the dinner-hour. Then, as I knew, ceremonies were to be performed, for which I was but ill prepared, as I had not yet heard the rules by which I was to be governed, and knew nothing of the forms to be repeated in the daily exercises, except the creed in Latin. This was during the time of recreation, as it is called. The only recreation there allowed, is that of the mind, and of this but little. We were kept at work, and permitted to speak with each other only in hearing of the old nuns. We proceeded to dinner in couples, and ate in silence while a lecture was read.

The novices had access to only eight of the apartments; and whatever else we wished to know, we could only conjecture. The sleeping room was in the second story, at the end of the western wing. The beds were placed in rows, without curtains or anything else, to obstruct the view; and in one corner was a small room partitioned off, in which was the bed of the night-watch, that is, the old nun appointed to oversee us for the night. In each side of the partition were two holes, through which she could look upon us when she pleased. Her bed was a little raised above the others. There was a lamp hung in the middle of our chamber, which showed everything to her distinctly; and as she had no light in her room, we never could perceive whether she was awake or asleep. As we knew that the slightest deviation from the rules would expose us to her observation and that of our companions, in whom it was a virtue to betray one another's faults, as well as to confess our own, I felt myself under a continual exposure to suffer what I disliked, and had my mind occupied in thinking of what I was to do next, and what I must avoid. I soon learned the rules and ceremonies we had to pass, which were many, and we had to be particular in their observance, we were employed in different kinds of work while I was a novice. The most beautiful specimen of the nun's manufacture which I saw, was a rich carpet made of fine worsted, which had been begun before my acquaintance with the Convent, and was finished while I was there. This was sent as a present to the King of England, as an expression of gratitude for the money annually received from the government. It was about forty yards in length, and very handsome. The Convent of the Grey Nuns has also received funds from the government, though on some account or other, they had not for several years.

I was sitting by a window at one time with a girl named Jane M'Coy, when one of the old nuns came up and spoke to us in tones of liveliness and kindness, which seemed strange in a place where everything appeared so cold and reserved. Some remarks which she made were intended to cheer and encourage me, and made me think she felt some interest in me. I do not recollect what she said, but I remember it gave me great pleasure. I also remember that her manners struck me singularly. She was rather old for a nun, probably thirty; her figure large, her face wrinkled, and her dress careless. She seemed also to be under less restraint than the others, and this I afterwards found was the case. She sometimes even set the rules at defiance. She would speak aloud when silence was required, and sometimes walk about when she ought to have kept her place: she would even say and do things on purpose to make us laugh, and, although often blamed for her conduct, had her offences frequently passed over, when others would have been punished with penances.

I learnt that this woman had always been singular. She never would consent to take a saint's name on receiving the veil, and had always been known by her own, which was Jane Ray. Her irregularities were found to be numerous, and penances were of so little use in governing her, that she was pitied by some, who thought her partially insane. She was commonly spoken of as mad Jane Ray; and when she committed a fault, it was often apologized for by the Superior or other nuns, on the ground that she did not know what she did.

The occupations of a novice in the Black Nunnery are not such as some may suppose. They are not employed in studying the higher branches of education: nor offered any advantages for storing their minds, or polishing their manners; they are not taught even reading, writing, or arithmetic; much less any of the more advanced branches of knowledge. My time was chiefly employed, at first, in work and prayers. It is true, during the last year I studied a great deal, and was required to work but very little; but it was the study of prayers in French and Latin, which I had merely to commit to memory, to prepare for the easy repetition of them on my reception, and after I should be admitted as a nun.

Among the wonderful events which had happened in the Convent, that of the sudden conversion of a gay young lady of the city into a nun appeared to me one of the most remarkable. The story which I first heard while a novice, made a deep impression upon my mind. It was nearly as follows:

The daughter of a wealthy citizen of Montreal was passing the Church of Bon Secours one evening, on her way to a ball, when she was suddenly thrown down upon the steps or near the door, and received a severe shock. She was taken up, and removed first, I think, into the church, but soon into the Black Nunnery, which she soon determined to join as a nun; instead, however, of being required to pass through a long novitiate, (which usually occupies about two years and a half, and is abridged only where the character is peculiarly exemplary and devout,) she was permitted to take the veil without delay, being declared by God to a priest to be in a state of sanctity. The meaning of this expression is, that she was a real saint, and already in a great measure raised above the world and its influences, and incapable of sinning; possessing the power of intercession, and a proper object to be addressed in prayer. This remarkable individual, I was further informed, was still in the Convent, though I never was allowed to see her; she did not mingle with the other nuns, either at work, worship, or meals; for she had no need of food, and not only her soul, but her body, was in heaven a great part of her time. What added, if possible, to the reverence and mysterious awe with which I thought of her, was the fact I learned, that she had no name. The titles used in speaking of her were, the holy saint, reverend mother, or saint bon pasteur, (the holy good shepherd.)

It is wonderful that we could have carried our reverence for the Superior so far as we did, although it was the direct tendency of many instructions and regulations, indeed of the whole system, to permit, even to foster, a superstitious regard for her. One of us was occasionally called into her room to cut her nails, or dress her hair; and we would often collect the clippings, and distribute them to each other, or preserve them with the utmost care. I once picked up all her stray hairs I could find after combing her head, bound them together, and kept them until she told me I was not worthy to possess things so sacred. Jane M'Coy and I were once sent to alter a dress for the Superior. I gathered up all the bits of thread, made a little bag, and put them into it for safe preservation. This I wore a long time round my neck, so long, that I wore out a number of strings, which I had replaced with new ones. I believed it to possess the power of removing pain, and often prayed to it to cure the toothache, &c. Jane Ray sometimes professed to outgo us all in devotion to the Superior, and would pick up the feathers after making her bed. These she would distribute among us, saying, "when she dies, relics will begin to grow scarce, and you had better supply yourselves in season." Then she would treat the whole matter in some way to turn it into ridicule. Equally contradictory would she appear, when occasionally she would obtain leave from her Superior to tell her dream. With a serious face, which sometimes imposed upon all of us, and made us half believe she was in a perfect state of sanctity, she would narrate in French some unaccountable vision which she said she had enjoyed; then turning round, would say, "There are some who do not understand me; you all ought to be informed." And then she would say something totally different in English, which put us to the greatest agony for fear of laughing. Sometimes she would say she expected to be Superior herself one of those days.

While I was in the Congregational Nunnery, I had gone to the parish church, to confess, for although the nuns had a private confession-room in the building, the boarders were taken in parties through the streets, by some of the nuns, to confess in the church; but in the Black Nunnery, as we had a chapel, and priests attending in the confessionals, we never left the building.

Our confessions there as novices were always performed in one way. Those of us who were to confess at a particular time, took our places on our knees near the confession-box, and after having repeated a number of prayers, &c., prescribed in our book, came up one at a time and kneeled beside a fine wooden lattice work, which entirely separated the confessor from us, yet permitted us to place our faces almost to his ear, and nearly concealed his countenance from our view. I recollect how the priests used to recline their heads on one side, and often cover their faces with their handkerchiefs, while they heard me confess my sins, and put questions to me, which were often of the most improper and revolting nature, naming crimes both unthought of and inhuman. Still, strange as it may seem, I was persuaded to believe that all this was their duty, or that it was done without sin.

Veiled nuns would often appear in the chapel at confession; though, as I understood, they generally confessed in private. Of the plan of their confession-rooms I had no information; but I supposed the ceremony to be conducted much on the same plan as in the chapel viz., with a lattice interposed between the confessor and the confessing.

Punishments were sometimes resorted to while I was a novice, though but seldom. The first time I ever saw a gag, was one day when a young novice had done something to offend the Superior. This girl I always had compassion for, because she was very young, and an orphan. The Superior sent for a gag, and expressed her regret at being compelled, by the bad conduct of the child, to proceed to such a punishment; after which she put it into her mouth, so far as to keep it open, and then let it remain some time before she took it out. There was a leathern strap fastened to each end, and buckled to the back part of the head.

CHAPTER IV.

DISPLEASED with the Convent—Left it—Residence at St. Denis—Relics—Marriage—Return to the Black Nunnery—Objections made by some Novices.

AFTER I had been a novice four or five years, from the time I commenced school in the Convent, one day I was treated by one of the nuns in a manner which displeased me, and because I expressed some resentment, I was required to beg her pardon. Not being satisfied with this, although I complied with the command, nor with the coldness with which the Superior treated me, I determined to quit the Convent at once, which I did without asking leave. There would have been no obstacle to my departure, novice as I then was, if I had asked permission; but I was too much displeased to wait for that, and went home without speaking to any one.

I soon after visited the Town of St. Denis where I saw two young ladies with whom I had formerly been acquainted in Montreal, and one of them a school-mate at Mr. Workman's School. After some conversation with me, and learning that I had known a lady who kept a school in the place, they advised me to apply to her to be employed as her assistant teacher; for she was then instructing the government school in that place.

I visited her, and found her willing, and I engaged at once as her assistant.

The government society paid her £20 a year: she was obliged to teach ten children gratuitously; might have fifteen pence a month, for each ten scholars more, and then she was at liberty, according to the regulations, to demand as much as she pleased for the other pupils. The course of instruction required by the society embraced only reading, writing, and what was called ciphering. The books used were a spelling book, l' Instruction de la Jeunesse, the Catholic New Testament, and l' Histoire de Canada.

When these had been read through, in regular succession, the children were dismissed as having completed their education. No difficulty is found in making the common French Canadians content with such an amount of instruction as this; on the contrary, it is often found very hard indeed to prevail upon them to send their children at all, for they say it takes too much of the love of God from them to send them to school. The teacher strictly complied with the requisition of the society, and the Roman Catholic catechism was regularly taught in the school, as much from choice, as from submission to authority, as she was a strict Catholic. I had brought with me the little bag in which I had so long kept the clippings of the thread left after making a dress for the Superior. Such was my regard for it, that I continued to wear it constantly round my neck, and to feel the same reverence for it as before. I occasionally had the tooth-ache during my stay at St. Denis, and then always relied on the influence of my little bag. On such occasions I would say—"By the virtue of this bag may I be delivered from the tooth-ache!" and I supposed that when it ceased it was owing to that cause.

While engaged in this manner I became acquainted with a man who soon proposed marriage; and, young and ignorant of the world as I was, I heard his offers with favour. On consulting with my friend, she expressed a friendly interest for me, advised me against taking such a step, and especially as I knew so little about the man, except that a report was circulated unfavourable to his character. Unfortunately, I was not wise enough to listen to her advice, and hastily married. In a few weeks I had occasion to repent of the step I had taken, as the report proved true which I thought justified, and indeed required, our separation. After I had been in St. Denis about three months, finding myself thus situated, and not knowing what else to do, I determined to return to the Convent, and pursue my former intention of becoming a Black Nun, could I admittance. Knowing the inquiries the Superior would make relative to me during my absence, before leaving St Denis I agreed with the lady with whom I had been associated (when she went to Montreal, which she did very frequently) to say to the Lady Superior I had been under her protection during my absence, which would stop further inquiry; as I was sensible, should they know I had been married I should not be admitted.

I soon returned to Montreal, and, on reaching the city, I visited the Seminary, and in another interview with the Superior communicated my wish, and desired her to procure my re-admission as a novice.

After leaving for a short time, she returned and told me that the Superior of the Convent had consented, and I was introduced to her. She blamed me for leaving the nunnery, but told me that I ought to be ever grateful to my guardian angel for taking care of me, and bringing me in safety back. I requested that I might be secured against the reproaches and ridicule of all the novices and nuns, which I thought some might cast upon me, unless prohibited by the Superior; and this she promised me. The money usually required for the admission of novices had not been expected from me. I had been admitted the first time without any such requisition; but now I choose to pay for my re-admission. I knew that she was able to dispense with such a demand, and she knew that I was not in possession of anything like the sum required.

But I was bent on paying to the Nunnery, and accustomed to receive the doctrine often repeated to me before that time, that when the advantage of the church was consulted, the steps taken were justifiable, let them be what they would; I therefore resolved to obtain money on false pretences, confident that if all were known, I should be far from displeasing the Superior. I went to the brigade-major, and asked him to give me the money payable to my mother from her pension, which amounted to about thirty dollars, and without questioning my authority to receive it in her name, he gave it me.

From several of her friends I obtained small sums under the name of loans, so that altogether I had soon raised a number of pounds, with which I hastened to the Nunnery, and deposited a part in the hands of the Superior. She received the money with evident satisfaction, though she must have known that I could not have obtained it honestly; and I was at once re-admitted as a novice.

Much to my gratification, not a word fell from the lips of my old associates in relation to my unceremonious departure, nor my voluntary return. The Superior's orders, I had not a doubt, had been explicitly laid down, and they certainly were carefully obeyed, for I never heard an allusion made to that subject during my subsequent stay in the Convent, except that, when alone, the Superior would sometimes say a little about it.

There were numbers of young ladies who entered awhile as novices, and became weary or disgusted with some things they observed, and remained but a short time. One of my cousins, who lived at Lachine, named Reed spent about a fortnight in the Convent with me. She however, conceived such an antipathy to the priests, that she used expressions which offended the Superior.

The first day that she attended mass, while at dinner with us in full community, she said before us all, "What a rascal that priest was, to preach against his best friend!"

All stared at such an unusual exclamation, and some one enquired what she meant.

"I say," she continued, "he has been preaching against him who has given him his bread. Do you suppose that if there were no devil, there would be any priests?"

This bold young novice was immediately dismissed, and in the afternoon we had a long sermon from the Superior on the subject.

It happened that I one day got a leaf of an English Bible which had been brought into the Convent, wrapped round some sewing silk, purchased at a store in the city. For some reason or other, I determined to commit to memory a chapter it contained, which I soon did. It is the only chapter I ever learnt in the Bible, and I can now repeat it. It is the second of St. Matthew's gospel. "Now when Jesus was born at Bethlehem of Judea," &c. It happened that I was observed reading the paper, and when the nature of it was discovered, I was condemned to do penance for my offence.

Great dislike to the Bible was shown by those who conversed with me about it, and several have remarked to me that if it were not for that book, Catholics would never be led to renounce their own faith.

I have heard passages read from the Evangile, relating to the death of Christ; the conversion of Paul; a few chapters from St. Matthew, and perhaps a few others. The priests would also sometimes take a verse or two, and preach from it. I have read St. Peter's life, but only in the book called the "Lives of the Saints." He, I understood, has the keys of heaven and hell, and has founded our church. As for Saint Paul, I remember, as I was taught to understand it, that he was once a great persecutor of the Roman *Catholics*, until he became convicted, and confessed to one of the *father confessors*, I don't know which. For who can expect to be forgiven, who does not become a Catholic, and confess.

CHAPTER V.

THE day on which I received Confirmation was a distressing one to me. I believed the doctrine of the Roman Catholics, and according to them I was guilty of three mortal sins; concealing something at confession, sacrilege, in putting the body of Christ in the sacrament under my feet, and by receiving it while not in a state of grace! and now I had been led into all those sins in consequence of my marriage, which I never had acknowledged, as it would cut me off from being admitted as a nun.

On the day when I went to the church to be confirmed with a number of others, I suffered extremely from the reproaches of my conscience. I believed, as I had been told, that a person who had been anointed with the holy oil of confirmation on the forehead, and dying in the state in which I was, would go down to hell, and, in the place where the oil had been rubbed, the names of my sins would blaze out of my forehead; these would be a sign by which the devils would know me, and would torment me the worse for them. I was thinking of all this, while I was sitting in the pew, waiting to receive the oil. I felt however some consolation, when my sins came to my mind; which I derived from another doctrine of the church, viz., that a bishop could absolve me from all sins any minute before my death; and I intended to confess them all before leaving the world.

At length the moment for administering the "sacrament" arrived, and a bell was rung. Those who had come to be confirmed had brought tickets from their confessors, which were thrown into a hat, and carried around by a priest, who in turn handed each to a bishop, by which he learned our names and applied a little of the oil to the foreheads. This was immediately rubbed off by a priest with a bit of cloth quite roughly.

I went home with some qualms of conscience, and often thought with dread of the following tale, which I have heard told, to illustrate the sinfulness of conduct like mine.

A priest was once travelling, when he was passing by a house, his horse fell on its knees, and would not rise. His rider dismounted and went in to learn the cause of so extraordinary an occurrence. He found there a woman near death, to whom a priest was trying to administer the sacrament, but without success; for every time she attempted to swallow it, it was thrown back out of her mouth into the chalice. He perceived it was owing to unconfessed sin, and took away the holy water from her; on which his horse rose from its knees, and he pursued his journey.

I also had been told, that we shall have as many devils biting us, if we go to hell, as we have unconfessed sins on our consciences.

I was required to devote myself for a year to the study of the prayers and practice the ceremonies necessary on the reception of a nun. This I found a very tedious duty; but as I was released from the daily labours usually demanded of novices, I felt little disposition to complain.

CHAPTER VI.

I WAS introduced into the Superior's room on the evening preceding the day on which I was to take the veil, to have an interview with the bishop. The Superior was present, and the interview lasted half an hour. The bishop on this as on other occasions appeared to be habitually rough in his manners. His address was by no means prepossessing.

Before I took the veil, I was ornamented for the ceremony, and was clothed in a dress belonging to the Convent, which was used on such occasions; and placed near the altar in the chapel, in the view of a number of spectators, who had assembled. Taking the veil is an affair which occurs so frequently in Montreal, that it has long ceased to be regarded as a novelty; and, although notice had been given in the French parish church as usual, only a small audience assembled.

Being well prepared with a long training, and frequent rehearsals, I stood waiting in my large flowing dress for the appearance of the bishop. He soon presented himself, entering by a door behind the altar: I then threw myself at his feet, and asked him to confer upon me the veil. He expressed his consent; and then turning to the Superior, I threw myself prostrate at her feet, according to my instructions, repeating what I have before done at rehearsals, and made a movement as if to kiss her feet. This she prevented, or appeared to prevent, catching me by a sudden motion of her hand, and granted my request. I then kneeled before the Holy Sacrament, that is a large round wafer held by the Bishop between his forefinger and thumb, and made my vows.

This wafer I had been taught to regard with the utmost veneration as the real body of Jesus Christ, the presence of which made the vows uttered before it binding in the most solemn manner.

After taking the vows, I proceeded to a small apartment behind the altar, accompanied by four nuns, where there was a coffin prepared with my nun's name engraved upon it:

"SAINT EUSTACE."

My companions lifted it by four handles attached to it, while I threw off my dress, and put on that of a nun of Sœur Bourgeoise; and then we all returned to the chapel. I proceeded first, and was followed by four nuns, the Bishop naming a number of worldly pleasures in rapid succession, in reply to which I as rapidly repeated,—

"Je renounce, je renounce, je renounce,"—I renounce, I renounce, I renounce.

The coffin was then placed in front of the altar and I advanced to place myself in it. This coffin was to be deposited, after the ceremony, in an out-house, to be preserved until my death, when it was to receive my corpse. There were reflections which I naturally made at that time, but I stepped in, extended myself, and lay still. A pillow had been placed at the head of the coffin, to support my head in a comfortable position. A thick black cloth was then spread over me, and the chanting of Latin hymns commenced. My thoughts were not the most pleasing during the time I lay in that situation. The pall, or Drap Mortel, as the cloth is called, had a strong smell of incense, which was always disagreeable to me, and then proved almost suffocating. I recollected the story of the novice, who, in taking the veil, lay down in her coffin like me, and was covered in the same manner, but on the removal of the covering was found dead.

When I was uncovered, I rose, stepped out of my coffin, and kneeled. Other ceremonies then followed, of no interest; after which the music commenced, and here the whole was finished. I then returned to the Superior's room, followed by the other nuns, who walked two by two, with their hands folded on their breasts, and their eyes cast down upon the floor. The nun who was to be my companion in future, then walked at the end of the procession. On reaching the Superior's door they all left me, and I entered alone, and found her with the Bishop and two Priests.

The Superior now informed me, that having taken the black veil, it only remained that I should swear the three oaths customary on becoming a nun; and that some explanation would be necessary from her. I was now to have access to every part of the edifice, even to the cellar, where two of the sisters were imprisoned for causes which she did not mention. I must be informed that one of my great duties was to obey the priests in all things; and this I soon learnt, to my astonishment and horror, was to live in the practice of criminal intercourse with them. I expressed some of the feelings which this announcement excited in me, which came upon me like a flash of lightning; but the only effect was to set her arguing with me, in favour of the crime, representing it as a virtue acceptable to God, and honourable to me. The priests, she said, were not situated like other men, being forbidden to marry; while they lived secluded, laborious, and self-denying lives for our salvation. They might, indeed, be considered our saviours, as without their service we could not obtain pardon of sin, and must go to hell. Now it was our solemn duty, on withdrawing from the world to consecrate our lives to religion, to practice every species of self-denial. We could not be too humble, nor mortify our feelings too far; this was to be done by opposing them, and acting contrary to them; and what she proposed was, therefore, pleasing in the sight of God. I now felt how foolish I had been to place myself in their power.

From what she said, I could draw no other conclusions but that I was required to act like the most abandoned of beings, and that my future associates were habitually guilty of the most heinous and detestable crimes. When I repeated my expressions of surprise and horror, she told me that such feelings were very common at first, and that many other nuns had expressed themselves as I did, who had long since changed their minds. She even said, on her entrance into the nunnery, she had felt like me.

Doubts she declared, were among our greatest enemies. They would lead us to question every point of duty, and induce us to waver at every step. They arose only from remaining imperfection, and were always evidences of sin. Our only way was to dismiss them immediately, repent and confess them. They were deadly sins, and would condemn us to hell, if we should die without confessing them. Priests, she insisted, could not sin. It was a thing impossible. Everything that they did, and wished was right. She hoped I would see the reasonableness and duty of the oaths I was then to take, and be faithful to them.

She gave me other information, which excited feelings in me, scarcely less dreadful. Infants were sometimes born in the Convent, but they were always baptised, and immediately strangled! This secured their everlasting happiness; for the baptism purifies them from all sinfulness, and being sent out of the world before they had time to do anything wrong, they were at once admitted into heaven. How happy she exclaimed, are those who secure immortal happiness to such little beings! Their little souls would thank those who kill their bodies, if they had it in their power.

Into what a place, and among what society, had I been admitted! How different did a Convent now appear from what I supposed it to be! The holy women I had always fancied the nuns to be, the venerable Lady Superior, what were they? And the priests of the Seminary adjoining (some of whom, indeed, I had reason to think were base and profligate men,) what were they all? I now learned that they were often admitted into the nunnery, and allowed to indulge in the greatest crimes, which they call virtues.

After having listened to the Superior alone, a number of the nuns were admitted, and took a free part in the conversation. They concurred in everything which she told me, and repeated, without any shame or compunction, things which criminated themselves. I must acknowledge the truth, that all this had an effect upon my mind. I questioned whether I might not be in the wrong, and felt as if their reasoning might have some just foundation. I had been several years under the tuition of Catholics, and was ignorant of the Scriptures, and unaccustomed to the society, example, and conversation of Protestants; had not heard any appeal to the Bible as authority, but had been taught, both by precept and example, to receive as truth everything said by the priests. I had not heard their authority questioned, nor anything said of any other standard of faith. I had long been familiar with the corrupt and licentious expressions used at confessions, and believed that other women were also. I had no standard of duty to refer to, and no judgment of my own which I knew how to use.

All around me insisted that my doubts proved only my own ignorance and sinfulness; that they knew by experience that they would soon give place to true knowledge, and an advance in religion; and I felt something like indecision.

Still there was so much that disgusted me in the debased characters around me, that I would most gladly have escaped from the nunnery, and never returned. But that was a thing not to be thought of. I was in their power, and this I deeply felt, while I thought that there was not one among the whole number of nuns to whom I could look for kindness. There was one, however, who began to speak to me in a tone that gained my confidence,—the nun whom I have mentioned as distinguished by her oddity, Jane Ray, who made us so much amusement when I was a novice. Although there was nothing in her face, form, or manners, to give me any pleasure, she addressed me with apparent friendliness; and while she seemed to concur with some things spoken by them, took an opportunity to whisper a few words in my ear, unheard by them, intimating that I had better comply with everything the Superior desired, if I would save my life. I was somewhat alarmed before, but I now became much more so, and determined to make no further resistance. The Superior then made me repeat the three oaths; and, when I had sworn them, I was shown into the community-rooms, and remained some time with the nuns, who were released from their employments, and enjoyed a recreation day, on account of the admission of a new sister. My feelings during the remainder of the day I shall not describe, but pass on to the ceremonies that took place at dinner.

At eleven o'clock the bell rang for dinner, and the nuns all took their places in a double row, in the same order as they left the chapel in the morning, except that my companion and myself were stationed at the head of the line. Standing thus for a moment, with our hands placed one on the other over the breast, and hidden in our large cuffs, with our heads bent forward, and eyes fixed on the floor; an old nun, who stood at the door, clapped her hands as a signal for us to proceed; and the procession moved on, while we all commenced the repetition of litanies. We walked on in this order, repeating all the way until we reached the dining-room, where we were divided into two lines; those on the right passing down one side of the long table, and those on the left the other; and each stopped in her place. The plates were all arranged, each with a knife, fork, and spoon, rolled up in a napkin, and tied round with a linen band marked with the owner's name. My own were prepared like the rest; and on the band around them I found my new name written—"Saint Eustace."

There we stood till all had concluded the litany, when the old nun who had taken her place at the head of the table, said the prayer before meat, beginning, "Benedicte," and we sat down. I do not remember of what our dinner consisted, but we usually had soup, and some plain dish of meat; the remains of which were served up at supper as fricasee. One of the nuns, who had been appointed to read that day, rose and began a lecture from a book put into her hands by the Superior, while the rest of us ate in perfect silence. The nun who reads during dinner, stays afterwards to dine. As fast as we finished our meals, each rolled up her knife, fork, and spoon, in her napkin, and bound them together with the band, and sat with hands folded. The old nun then said a short prayer, arose, stepped a little aside, clasped her hands, and we marched towards the door, bowing as we passed before a little chapel, or glass box, containing a wax image of the infant Jesus.

Nothing important occurred till late in the afternoon, when, as I was sitting in the community-room, Father Dufresne called me out, saying, he wished to speak with me. I feared what was his intention; but I dared not disobey. In a private apartment, he treated me in a brutal manner; and, from two other priests, I afterwards received similar usage that evening. Father Dufresne afterwards appeared again; and I was compelled to remain in company with him until morning.

I am assured that the conduct of priests in our Convent had never been exposed, and it is not imagined by the people of the United States. This induces me to say what I do, notwithstanding the strong reasons I have to let it remain unknown. Still I cannot force myself to speak on such subjects except in the most brief manner.

CHAPTER VII.

DAILY Ceremonies—Jane Ray among the Nuns.

O N Thursday morning, the bell rang at half-past six to waken us. The old nun who was acting as night-watch immediately spoke aloud:

"Voici le Seignieur qui vient" (Behold the Lord cometh.) The nuns all responded:

"Allons—y pevant lui." (Let us go and meet him.)

We arose immediately, and dressed quickly, stepping into the passage-way, at the foot of our bed, as soon as we were ready, and taking place each beside her opposite companion. Thus we were drawn up in a double row the length of the room, with our hands folded across our breast, and concealed in the broad cuffs of our sleeves. Not a word was uttered. When the signal was given, we all proceeded to the community-room, and took our places in rows facing the entrance, near which the Superior was seated in a vergiere. We first repeated "Au nom du Pere, du Fils, et du Saint Esprit—Ainsi soit il." (In the name of the Father, the Son, and the Holy Ghost,—Amen.) We then kneeled and kissed the floor; then, still kneeling, on our knees, we said a long prayer "Divin Jesus, sauveur de mon ame," (Divine Jesus, Saviour of my soul.) Then the Lord's prayer, three Hail Marys, four creeds, and five confessions, (confesse a Dieu.) the ten commandments; the acts of faith, and a prayer to the Virgin, in Latin, which I never understood a word of. Next we said litanies of the Holy Name of Jesus, in Latin, which were afterwards to be repeated several times in the day. Then came the prayer for the beginning of the day; then bending down, we commenced the Orison Mental, (or Mental Orison,) which lasted about an hour and a half.

This exercise was considered very solemn. We were told in the nunnery that a certain saint was saved by the use of it, as she never omitted it. It consists of several parts: First, the Superior read to us a chapter from a book, which occupied five minutes. Then profound silence prevailed for fifteen minutes, during which we were meditating upon it. Then she read another chapter of equal length on a different subject, and we meditated upon that another quarter of an hour; and after a third reading and meditation, we finished the exercise with a prayer of contrition, in which we asked forgiveness for the sins committed during the Orison. During this hour and a half I became very weary, having before been kneeling for some time, and having then to sit in another position more uncomfortable, with my feet under me, and my hands clasped, and my head bowed down.

When the Orison was over, we all rose to the upright kneeling posture, and repeated several prayers, and the litanies of the providences, "providence de Dieu," &c, then followed a number of Latin prayers, which we repeated on the way to mass, for in the nunnery we had mass daily.

When mass was over, we proceeded in our usual order to breakfast, practising the same forms which I have described at dinner. Having made our meal in silence, we repeated the litanies of the "holy name of Jesus," as we proceeded to the community room; and such as had not finished them on their arrival, threw themselves upon their knees until they had gone through with them and then kissing the floor, rose again. At nine o'clock commenced the lecture which was read by a nun appointed to perform that duty that day: all the rest of us in the room being engaged in work.

The nuns were distributed in different community rooms, at different kinds of work, and each was listening to a lecture. This continued until ten o'clock, when the recreation-bell rang. We still continued our work, but the nuns conversed on subjects permitted by the rules, in the hearing of the old nuns, one of whom was seated in each of the groups. At half-past ten the silence bell rang, and this conversation instantly ceased, and the recitation of some Latin prayers continued half an hour.

At eleven o'clock the dinner-bell rang, and we went through the forms of the preceding day. We proceeded two by two. The old nun clapped her hands as the first couple reached the door, when we stopped. The first two dipped their fingers into the font, touched with the holy water the breast, forehead, and each side, thus forming a cross, said "In the name of the Father, Son, and Holy Ghost, Amen," and then walked to the dining-room repeating the litanies. The rest did the same. On reaching the door the couples divided, and the two rows of nuns marching up, stopped, and faced the table against their plates. There we repeated the close of the litany aloud. The old nun pronounced "Benedicte," and we sat down. One of us read a lecture, during the whole meal: she stays to eat after the rest have retired. When we had dined, each of us folded up her napkin, and again folded her hands. The old nun then repeated a short prayer in French, and stepping from the head of the table, let us pass out as we came in. Each of us bowed in passing the little chapel near the door, which is a glass-case, containing a waxen figure of the infant Jesus. When we reached the community-room we took our places in rows, and kneeled upon the floor, while a nun read aloud. "Doleurs de notre Sainte Marie," (the sorrows of our holy Mary.) At the end of each verse we responded "Ave Maria." We then repeated the litany of the providences and the "Benissante."

Then we kissed the floor, and rising, took our work, to converse on permitted subjects—called *recreation*—till one o'clock. We then repeated litanies, one at a time in succession, still sewing, for an hour.

At two o'clock commenced the afternoon lectures, which lasted till near three. At that hour one of the nuns stood up in the middle of the room, and asked each of us a question out of the catechism; and such as did not answer correctly had to kneel, until that exercise was concluded, upon as many dry peas as there were verses in the chapter out of which they were questioned. I have sometimes kneeled on peas until I suffered great inconvenience and pain. It soon makes one feel as if needles were running through the skin. At four o'clock recreation commenced, when we were allowed to speak to each other while at work. At half-past four we began to repeat prayers in Latin, while we worked till five o'clock, when we repeated the "prayers for the examination of conscience," the "prayer after confession," the "prayer before sacrament," and the "prayer after sacrament." At dark, we laid our work aside, and went over the same prayers which we had repeated in the morning excepting the orison mental: instead of that long exercise, we examined our consciences, to determine whether we had performed the resolution we had made in the morning, and such as had repeated an "acte de joie," or expression of gratitude; such as had not, said an "acte de contrition."

When the prayers were concluded, any nun who had been disobedient in the day, knelt and asked pardon of the Superior and her companions "for the scandal she had caused them," and then requested a penance to perform. When all the penances had been imposed, we all proceeded to the eating-room to supper, repeating litanies on the way. The ceremonies were the same as at dinner, except that no lecture was read. We ate in silence, and went out bowing to the chapelle, and repeating litanies. Returning to the community-room, we had more prayers to repeat, which are called *La couronne*, (crown), which consists of the following parts:—1st. Four Paters. 2nd. Four Ave Marias. 3rd. Four Gloria patris. 4th. Benissez Santeys. At the close we kissed the floor; then had recreation till half-past eight o'clock, conversing on permitted subjects, but closely watched, and not allowed to sit in the corners.

At half-past eight a bell was rung, and a chapter was read to us, in a book of meditations, to employ our minds upon during our waking hours at night. Standing near the door, we dipped our fingers in the holy water, crossed and blessed ourselves and proceeded to the sleeping room two by two. When we had got into bed, we repeated a prayer beginning with,—

> "Mon Dieu, je vous donne mon cœur,"
> "My God I give you my heart;"

and then an old nun, bringing some holy water, sprinkled it on our beds to drive away the devil, while we crossed ourselves with it again. At nine o'clock the bell rang, and all awake repeated a prayer, called the offrande; those who were asleep were considered as excused.

After my admission among the nuns, I had more opportunity to observe the conduct of mad Jane Ray. She behaved quite differently from the rest, and with a degree of levity irreconcileable with the rules. She was a large woman, with nothing beautiful or attractive in her face, form, or manners, careless in her dress, and of a restless disposition, which prevented her from applying herself to anything for any length of time, and kept her roving about, and always talking to somebody or other. She was dressed in the plain garments of the nuns, bound by the same vows, and accustomed to the same life, resembling them in nothing else, and frequently interrupting all their employments. She was apparently always studying, or pursuing some odd fancy; now rising from sewing to walk up and down, or straying in another apartment looking about, addressing some of us, passing out again, or saying something to make us laugh. But what showed she was no novelty, was the little attention paid to her, and the levity with which she was treated by the whole nuns; even the Superior every day passed over irregularities which she would have punished with penances, in any other. I soon perceived that she betrayed two distinct traits of character; a kind disposition towards such as she chose to prefer, and a pleasure in teasing those she disliked, or such as had offended her.

CHAPTER VIII.

I WILL now give from memory a general description of the interior of the Convent of Black Nuns, except the few apartments which I never saw. I may be inaccurate in some things, as the apartments and passages of that spacious building are numerous and various; but I am willing to risk my credit for truth and sincerity on the general correspondence between my description and things as they are. And this would, perhaps, be as good a case as any by which to test the truth of my statements, were it possible to obtain access to the interior. It is well-known, that none but veiled nuns, the bishop and priests, are ever admitted; and, of course that I cannot have seen what I profess to describe, if I had not been a black nun. The priests who read this book will acknowledge to themselves the truth of my description; but will, of course, deny it to the world, and probably exert themselves to destroy my credit. I offer to every reader the following description, knowing that time may possibly throw open those secret recesses, and allow the entrance of those who can satisfy themselves, of its truth. Some of my declarations may be thought deficient in evidence, which must of necessity be in the present state of things. But here is a kind of evidence on which I rely, as I see how unquestionable and satisfactory it must prove, whenever it shall be obtained.

If the interior of the Black Nunnery, whenever it shall be examined, is materially different from the following description, then I shall claim no confidence of my readers. If it resemble it, they will, I presume, place confidence in some of those declarations, on which I may never be corroborated by true and living witnesses.

I am sensible that great changes may be made in the furniture of apartments; that new walls may be constructed, or old ones removed; and I have been informed, that masons have been employed in the Nunnery since I left it. I well know, that entire changes cannot be made, and that enough must remain to substantiate my description, whenever the truth shall be known.

THE FIRST STORY.

Beginning at the extremity of the western wing of the Convent, towards Notre Dame street, on the first story, there is—

1. The Nuns' private chapel, adjoining which is a passage to a small projection of the building extending from the upper story to the ground, with small windows. Into the passage we were required to bring wood from the yard, and pile it for use.

2. A large community-room, with plain benches fixed against the wall to sit, and lower ones in front to place our feet upon. There is a fountain in the passage near the chimney at the further end, for washing the hands and face, with a green curtain sliding on a rod before it. This passage leads to the old nun's sleeping-room on the right, and the Superior's sleeping-room beyond it, as well as to a stair-case which conducts to the nuns' sleeping-room above. At the end of the passage is a door opening into—

3. The dining-room; this is larger than the community-room, and has three long tables for eating, and a collection of little pictures, a crucifix, and an image of the infant Saviour in a glass case. This apartment has four doors, by the first of which we are supposed to have entered, while one opens to a pantry, and the third and fourth to the two next apartments.

4. A large community-room, with tables for sewing, and a stair-case on the opposite left-hand corner.

5. A community-room, for prayer used by both nuns and novices. In the farther right-hand corner is a small-room, partitioned off, called the room for the examination of conscience, which I had visited while a novice by permission of the Superior, and where nuns and novices occasionally resorted to reflect on their character, usually in preparation for the sacrament, or when they had transgressed some of the rules. This little room was hardly large enough to contain half a dozen persons at a time.

6. Next, beyond, is a large community-room for Sundays. A door

leads to the yard, and thence to a gate in the wall on the cross street.

7. Adjoining this is a sitting room, fronting on the cross street, with two windows, and a store room on the side opposite them. There is but little furniture, and that very plain.

8. From this room a door leads into what I call the wax-room, as it contains many figures in wax, not intended for sale. There we sometimes used to pray, or meditate on the Saviour's passion. This room projects from the main building; leaving it, you enter a long passage, with cupboards on the right, in which are stored crockery-ware, knives and forks, and other articles of table furniture, to replace those worn out or broken—all of the plainest description; also, shovels, tongs, &c. This passage leads to—

9. A corner room, with a few benches, &c., and a door leading to a gate in the street. Here some of the medicines were kept, and persons were often admitted on business, or to obtain medicines with tickets from the priests; and waited till the Superior or an old nun could be sent for. Beyond this room we never were allowed to go; and I cannot speak from personal knowledge of what came next.

THE SECOND STORY.

Beginning, as before, at the western extremity of the north wing, but on the second story, the farthest apartment in that direction which I ever entered was—

1. The nuns' sleeping-room, which I have described. Here is an access to the projection mentioned in speaking of the first story. The stairs by which we came up to bed are at the farther end of the room; and near them a crucifix and font of holy water. A door at the end of the rooms opens into a passage, with two small rooms, and closets between them, containing bedclothes. Next you enter,—

2. A small community-room, beyond which is a passage with a narrow staircase, seldom used, which leads into the fourth community-room, in the fourth story. Following the passage just mentioned, you enter by a door,—

3. A little sitting-room furnished in the following manner:—with chairs, a sofa on the north side covered with a red-figured cover and

fringe; a table in the middle, commonly bearing one or two books, an ink-stand, pen, &c. At one corner is a little projection into the room, caused by a staircase leading from above to the floor below, without any communication with the second story. This room has a door opening upon a staircase leading on the yard, on the opposite side is a gate opening into the cross street. By this way the physician is admitted, except when he comes later than usual. When he comes in, he sits a little while, until a nun goes into the adjoining nuns' sick-room, to see if all is ready, and returns to admit him. After prescribing for the patients, he goes no further, but returns by the way he enters; and these are the only rooms into which he is admitted.

4. The nuns' sick-room adjoins the little sitting-room on the east, and has four windows towards the north, with beds ranged in two rows from end to end, and a few more between them, near the opposite extremity. The door to the sitting-room swings to the left, and behind it is a table, while a glass case contains a wax figure of the infant Saviour, with several sheep. Near the north-eastern corner are two doors, one of which opens into a narrow passage, leading to the head of the great staircase that conducts to the cross street. By this passage the physician sometimes finds his way to the sick room, when he comes late. He rings the bell at the gate, which I was told had a concealed pull, known only to him and the priests, proceeds upstairs and through the passage, rapping three times at the door of the sickroom, which is opened by a nun in attendance, after she has given one rap in reply. He returns by the same way.

5. Next beyond the sick-room, is a large unoccupied apartment, half divided by two partitions, which leave an open space in the middle. Here some of the old nuns meet in the day time.

6. A door from this apartment opens into another, not appropriated to any particular use, but containing a table, where medicines are sometimes prepared by an old nun. Passing through this room, you enter a passage, with doors on its four sides: that on the left, which is kept fastened on the inside, leads to the staircase and gate; and that in front to private sickrooms.

7. That on the right leads to another, appropriated to nuns suffering

with the most loathsome disease. There were usually a number of
straw matresses in that room, as I well know, having helped to carry
them in, after the yard-man had filled them. A door beyond enters
into a store-room, which extends also beyond this apartment. On the
right, another door opens into another passage, crossing which, you
enter by a door,

8. A room with a bed and screen in one corner, on which nuns were
laid to be examined, before their introduction into the sick-room last
mentioned. Another door, opposite, opens into a passage, in which is
a staircase leading down.

9. Beyond this is a spare room, sometimes used to store apples,
boxes of different things, &c.

10. Returning now to the passage which opens on one side upon
the stairs to the gate, we enter the only remaining door, which leads
into an apartment usually occupied by some of the old nuns, and
frequently by the Superior.

11. and 12. Beyond this are two more sick-rooms, in one of which
those nuns stay who are waiting their accouchment, and in the other
those who have passed it.

13. The next is a small sitting-room, where a priest waits to baptise
the infants previous to their murder. A passage leads from this room
on the left, by the doors of two succeeding apartments neither of
which have I ever entered.

14. The first of them is the "holy retreat," or room occupied by the
priests, while suffering the penalty of their licentiousness.

15. The other is a sitting-room, to which they have access. Beyond
these, the passage leads to two rooms, containing closets for the storage
of various articles; and two others, where persons are received who
come on business.

The public hospitals succeed, and extend a considerable distance to
the extremity of the building. By a public entrance in that part, priests
often come into the Nunnery; and I have often seen some of them
thereabouts, who must have entered that way. Priests often get into
the "holy retreat," without exposing themselves to the view of other
parts of the Convent, and have been first known to be there, by the

yard-nuns being sent to the Seminary for their clothes.

The congregational Nunnery was founded by a nun, called Sister Bourgeoise. She taught a school in Montreal, and left property for the foundation of a Convent. Her body is buried, and her heart is kept under the Nunnery in an iron chest, which has been shown to me, with the assurance that it continues in perfect preservation, although she has been dead more than one hundred and fifty years. In the chapel is the following inscription:—

"Sœur Bourgeoise, Fondatrice du convent." (Sister Bourgeoise, Founder of the Convent.)

Nothing was more common than for the Superior to step hastily into our community-room, while numbers of us were assembled there, and hastily communicate her wishes in words like these:—

"Here are the parents of such a novice; come with me and bear me out in this story." She would then mention the outlines of a tissue of falsehoods she had just invented that we might be prepared to fabricate circumstances, and throw in whatever else might favour the deception. This was justified and highly commended, by what we were instructed.

It was a common remark at the initiation of a new nun into the Black nunnery to receive the black veil, that the introduction of another novice into the Convent as a veiled nun, always caused the introduction of a veiled nun into heaven as a saint, which was on account of the disappearance of some of the older nuns always at the entrance of new ones.

To witness the scenes which often occurred between us and strangers would have struck a person most powerfully, if he had known how truth was set at nought. The Superior, with a serious and dignified air, and a pleasant voice and aspect, would commence a recital of things most favourable to the character of the absent novice, representing her equally fond of her situation, and beloved by the other inmates. The tale told by the Superior, however unheard before might have been any of her statements, was then attested by us, who in every way we could think of, confirmed her declarations beyond the reach of doubt.

Sometimes the Superior would intrust the management of such a case to the nuns, to habituate us to the practice in which she was so highly accomplished, or to relieve herself of what would have been a serious burden to most other persons, and to ascertain whether she could depend upon us. Often have I seen her throw open a door, and say, in a hurried manner,

"Who can tell the best story?"

One point, on which we had received particular instructions was, the nature of falsehoods. I have heard many a speech, and many a sermon; and I was led to believe that it was of great importance, one on which it was a duty to be well informed, as well as to act.

"What!" exclaimed a priest one day—"what, a nun of your age, and not know the difference between a wicked and a religious lie?" He then went on, as had been done many times in my hearing, to show the essential difference between the two different kinds of falsehoods. A lie told merely for the injury of another, for our own interest alone, or for no object at all, he painted as a sin worthy of penance.—But a lie told for the good of the church or convent, was meritorious, and the telling of it a duty. And of this class of lies there are many varieties and shades. This doctrine had been inculcated on me and my companions, more times than I can enumerate. We often saw the practice of it, and were frequently made to take part in it. Whenever anything which the Superior thought important, could be most conveniently accomplished by falsehood, she resorted to it without scruple.

There was a class of cases, in which she more frequently relied on deception than any other.

The friends of novices frequently applied at the Convent to see them, or to inquire after their welfare. It was common for them to be politely refused an interview, on some account or other, a mere pretext; and then the Superior sought to make as favourable an impression as possible on the visitors. Sometimes she would make up a story on the spot, and tell the strangers; requiring some of us to confirm it in the most convincing way. At other times she would make over to us the task of deceiving, and we were commended in proportion to our ingenuity and success.

Some nun usually showed her submission, by immediately stepping forward. She would then add, that the parents of such a novice, whom she named, were in waiting, and it was necessary that they should be told such and such things. To perform so difficult a task well, was considered a difficult duty, and it was one of the most certain ways to gain the favour of the Superior. Whoever volunteered to make a story on the spot, was sent immediately to tell it, and the other nuns present with her under strict injunctions to uphold her in everything she might state. The Superior, on all such occasions, when she did not herself appear, hastened to the apartment adjoining, there to listen through the thin partition, to hear whether all performed their parts aright. It was not uncommon for her to go rather further, when she wanted to give such explanations as she could have desired.

She would then enter abruptly, ask, "Who can tell a good story this morning?" and hurry us off without a moment's delay, to do our best at a venture, without waiting for instructions. It would be curious, could a stranger from the "wicked world" outside the Convent, witness such a scene. One of the nuns who felt in a favourable humour to undertake the proposed task, would step forward, and signify readiness in the usual way, by a knowing wink of one eye, and a slight toss of the head.

"Well, go and do the best you can," the Superior would say: "and all the rest of you mind and swear to it." The latter part of the order, was always performed; for in every case, all the nuns present appeared as unanimous witnesses of everything that was uttered by the spokeswoman.

We were constantly hearing it repeated, that we must never again look upon ourselves as our own; but must remember, that we were solemnly and irrecoverably devoted to God. I cannot speak to every particular with equal freedom: but I wish my readers to understand the condition in which we were placed, and the means used to reduce us to what we had to submit to. Not only were we required to perform the several tasks imposed upon us at work, prayers and penances, under the idea that we were performing solemn duties to our Maker, but everything else which was required of us, we were constantly told, was indispensable in his sight. The priests, we admitted, were the servants of God, especially appointed by his authority, to teach us our duty, to absolve us from sin, and lead us to heaven. Without their assistance, we had allowed we could never enjoy the favour of God; unless they administered the sacrament to us, we could not enjoy everlasting happiness. Having acknowledged all this, we had no objection to urge against admitting any other demand that might be made by them. If we thought an act ever so criminal, the Superior would tell us that the priests acted under the direct sanction of God, and *could not sin*. Of course, then, it could not be wrong to comply with any of their requests, because they could not demand anything but what was right. On the contrary, to refuse to do anything they asked would necessarily be sinful. Such doctrines admitted, and such practices performed, it will not seem wonderful that we often felt something of their preposterous character.

Sometimes we took pleasure in ridiculing some of the favourite themes of our teachers; and I recollect one subject particularly, that afforded us merriment. It may seem irreverent in me to give the account, but I do it to show how things of a solemn nature were sometimes treated by women bearing the title of saints. A Canadian novice, who spoke very broken English, one day remarked that she was performing some duty "for the God." This peculiar expression had something ridiculous to our ears: and it was soon repeated again and again, in application to various ceremonies which we had to perform. Mad Jane Ray seized upon it with avidity, and with her aid it soon took the place of a by-word in conversation, so that we were constantly reminding each other that we were doing this thing and that thing, "for the God." Nor did we stop here; when the Superior called upon us to bear witness to one of her religious lies, or to fabricate the most spurious one the time would admit; we were sure to be reminded, on our way to the stranger's room, that we were doing it "for the God." And so it was when other things were mentioned—everything which belonged to our condition was spoken of in similar terms.

I have hardly detained the reader long enough to give him a just impression of the stress laid on confession. It is one of the great points to which our attention was constantly directed. We were directed to keep a strict and constant watch over our thoughts; to have continually before our minds, the rules of the Convent, to remember every devotion, and tell all, even the smallest, at confession, either to the Superior or to the priest. My mind was thus kept in a continual state of activity which proved very wearisome; and it required the constant exertion of our teachers, to keep us up to the practice they inculcated.

Another tale recurs to me, of those which were frequently told us, to make us feel the importance of unreserved confession.

A nun of our Convent, who had hidden some sin from her confessor, died suddenly, and without any one to confess her. Her sisters assembled to pray for the peace of her soul, when she appeared and said, that it would be of no use, but rather troublesome to her, as her pardon was impossible. The doctrine is, that prayers made for souls guilty of unconfessed sin, do but sink them deeper in hell; and this is the reason for not praying for Protestants.

The authority of the priest in everything, and the enormity of every act which opposes it, were also impressed upon our minds, by our teachers. A "Father" told us the following story.

A man once died who had failed to pay some money which the priest had asked of him; he was condemned to be burnt in purgatory until he should pay it, but had permission to come back to this world, and take a human body to work in. He came again on earth, and hired himself to a rich man as a labourer. He worked all day, with the fire burning in him, unseen by other people; but while he was in bed that night a girl perceiving the smell of brimstone, looked through a crack in the wall, and saw him covered with flames. She informed his master, who questioned him the next morning, and found that he was secretly suffering the pains of purgatory, for neglecting to pay a sum of money to the priest. He, therefore, furnished him with the amount due; it was paid, and the servant went off immediately to heaven. The priest cannot forgive any debt due unto him, because it is the Lord's estate.

While at confession, I was urged to hide nothing from the priests, they said that they already knew what was in my heart, but would not tell, because it was necessary for me to confess it. I believed that the priests were acquainted with my thoughts; and often stood in awe of them. They often told me, that they had the power to strike me dead at any moment.

CHAPTER IX.

Nuns with similar Names—Squaw Nuns—First visit to the Cellar—Description of it—Shocking Discovery there—Superior's Instructions—Private Signal of the Priests—Books used in the Nunnery—Opinions expressed of the Bible—Specimens of what I know of the Scriptures.

I FOUND that I had several namesakes among the nuns, two others who had already borne away my name, Saint Eustace. This was not a solitary case, for there were five Saint Marys, and three Saint Monros, besides two novices of that name. Of my namesakes, I have little to say, for they resembled most nuns; being so much cut off from intercourse with me and other sisters, that I never saw anything in them, nor learnt anything worth mentioning.

Several of my new companions were squaws, who had taken the veil at different times. They were from the Indian settlements in the country, but were not distinguishable by any striking habits of character from other nuns, and were not very different in their appearance when in their usual dress, and engaged in their occupations. They were treated with much kindness and lenity by the Superior and the old nuns; and this was done in order to render them as contented and happy in their situation as possible: and I should have attributed the motives for this partiality to their wishing, that they might not influence others to keep away, had I not known they were, like ourselves, unable to exert such an influence. And therefore I could not satisfy my mind why this difference was made. Many of the Indians were remarkably devoted to the priests, believing everything they were taught; and as it is represented to be not only a high honour, but a real advantage to a family, to have one of its members become a nun, Indian parents pay large sums of money for the admission of their daughters into a convent. The father of one of the squaws, I was told, paid to the Superior nearly her weight in silver on her reception, although he was obliged to sell nearly all his property to do it. This he did voluntarily, because he thought himself overpaid by having the advantage of her prayers, self-sacrifices, &c., for himself and family. The squaws sometimes served to amuse us; for when we were partially dispirited

THE SUPERIOR GUARDING THE NUNS

THE TORTURE CHAMBER

or gloomy, the Superior would send them to dress themselves in their Indian garments, which usually excited us to merriment.

Among the squaw nuns whom I remember, was one of the Sainte Hypolites, not the one who figured in a dreadful scene, described in another part of this narrative, but a woman of a more mild and humane character.

A few days after my reception, the Superior sent me into the cellar for coals; and after she had given me directions, I proceeded down a staircase with a lamp. I soon found myself on the bare earth, in a spacious place, so dark that I could not at once distinguish its form or size, but I observed that it had very solid stone walls, and was arched overhead, at no great elevation. Following my directions, I proceeded onwards from the foot of the stairs, where appeared to be one end of the cellar. After walking about fifteen paces, I passed three small doors on the right, fastened with large iron bolts on the outside, pushed into posts of stone work, each having a small opening above, covered with a fine grating, secured by a smaller bolt. On my left were three similar doors, resembling these, and opposite them.

Beyond these, the space became broader; the doors evidently closed small compartments, projecting from the outer wall of the cellar. I soon stepped upon a wooden floor, on which were heaps of wood, coarse linen, and other articles, deposited there for occasional use. I crossed the floor, and found the bare earth again under my feet.

A little further on, I found the cellar contracted in size by a row of closets, or smaller compartments, projecting on each side. These were closed by different doors from the first, having a simple fastening, and no opening through them.

Just beyond, on the left side, I passed a staircase leading up, and then three doors, much resembling those first described, standing opposite three more, on the other side of the cellar. Having passed these, I found the cellar again enlarged as before, and here the earth appeared as if mixed with some whitish substance, which attracted my attention.

As I proceeded, I found the whiteness increase, until the surface looked almost like snow, and I observed before me, a hole dug so deep into the earth that I could perceive no bottom. I stopped to observe it—it was circular, twelve or fifteen feet across, in the middle of the cellar, and unprotected by any curb, so that one might easily have walked into it in the dark.

The white substance was spread all over the surface around it; and lay in such quantities on all sides, that it seemed as if a great deal must have been thrown into the hole. It occurred to me that the white substance was lime, and that this was the place where the infants were buried, after being murdered, as the Superior had informed me. I knew that lime is often used by Roman Catholics in burying places; and this accounted for its being about the spot in such quantities.

This was a shocking thought to me; but I can hardly tell how it affected me, as I had been prepared to expect dreadful things, and undergone trials which prevented me from feeling as I should formerly have done in similar circumstances.

I passed the spot, therefore, with dreadful thoughts about the little corpses which might be in that secret burying place, but with recollections also of the declarations about the favour done their souls in sending them direct to heaven, and the necessary virtue accompanying all the actions of the priests.

There is a window or two on each side nearly against the hole, in at which are sometimes thrown articles brought to them from without, for the use of the Convent. Through the window on my right, which opens into the yard, towards the cross street, lime is received from carts; I then saw a large heap of it near the place.

Passing the hole, I came to a spot where was another projection on each side, with three cells like those I first described. Beyond them, in another part of the cellar, were heaps of vegetables, and other things; and on the left, I found the charcoal I was in search of. This was placed in a heap against the wall, near a small high window, like the rest, at which it is thrown in. Beyond this spot, at a short distance, the cellar terminated.

The top, quite to that point, is arched overhead, though at different heights, for the earth on the bottom is uneven, and in some places several feet higher than in others. Not liking to be alone in so spacious and gloomy a part of the Convent, especially after the discovery I had made, I hastened to fill my basket and to return.

Here then I was in a place which I had considered as the nearest imitation of heaven to be found on earth, amongst a society where deeds were perpetrated, which I had believed to be criminal, and had now found the place, in which harmless infants were unfeelingly thrown out of sight, after being murdered. And yet, such is the power of instruction and example, although not satisfied, as many around me seemed to be, that this was all righteous and proper, I sometimes was inclined to believe it, for the priests could do no sin. Among the first instructions I received from the Superior, one was to admit priests into the nunnery, from the street, at irregular hours. It is no secret that priests enter and go out; but if they were to be watched by any person in St Paul's street all day long, no irregularity might be suspected; and they might be supposed to visit the Convent for the performance of religious ceremonies merely.

But if a person were near the gate about midnight, he might form a different opinion; for when a stray priest is shut out of the Seminary, or is put in the need of seeking a lodging, he is sure of being admitted into the Black Nunnery. Nobody but the priest can ring the bell at the sick-room door; much less can any but a priest gain admittance. The pull of the bell is entirely concealed on the outside of the gate.

He makes himself known as a priest by a hissing sound, made by the tongue against the teeth while they are kept closed and the lips open. The nun within, who delays to open the door until informed who is there, immediately recognizes the signal, and replies with two inarticulate sounds, such as are often used instead of yes, with the mouth closed.

The superior considered this part of my instructions important, and taught me the signals. I had often occasion to use them; I have been repeatedly called to the door, in the night, while watching in the sick-room; and on reaching it, heard the hissing sound, then according to my orders, unfastened the door, admitted a priest, who was at liberty to go where he pleased. I will name M. Bierze, from St. Denis.

The books used in the nunnery, such as I recollect of them, were the following. Most of these are lecture books, such as are used by the daily readers, while we were at work and meals. These were all furnished by the Superior, out of her library, to which we never had access. When we had done with the book, it was exchanged for another, as she pleased to select. La Miroir de Chrètien (Christian Mirror,) History of Rome, History of the Church, Life of Sœur Bourgeoise, (the founder of the Convent,) in two volumes, L'Ange Conducteur (the Guardian Angel,) L'Ange Chrètien (the Christian Angel), Les Vies des Saints (Lives of the Saints,) in several volumes, Dialogues, a volume consisting of conversations between a Protestant Doctor, called Dr. D. and a Catholic gentleman, on the articles of faith, in which, after much ingenious reasoning, the former was confuted; one large book, the name I have forgotten, occupied us nine or ten months at our lectures, night and morning, L'Instruction de la Jeunesse (the Instruction of Youth,) containing much about Convents, and the education of persons in the world, with a great deal on confessions, &c. Examen de la Conscience (Examination of Conscience,) is a book frequently used.

I never saw a Bible in the Convent from the day I entered as a novice, until that on which I effected my escape. The Catholic New Testament, commonly called the Evangile, was read to us three or four times a year. The Superior directed the reader what passages to select; but we never had it in our hands to read when we pleased. I often heard the Protestant Bible spoken of, in bitter terms, as a most dangerous book, and which never ought to be in the hands of common people.

CHAPTER X.

MANUFACTURE of Bread and Wax candles, carried on in the Convent—Superstitions—Scapularies—Virgin Mary's Pincushion—Her House—The Bishop's Power over fire—My Instructions to Novices—Jane Ray—Vacillation of Feelings.

LARGE quantities of bread are made in the Black Nunnery every week; for besides what is necessary to feed the nuns, many of the poor are supplied. When a priest wishes to give a loaf of bread to a poor person, he gives him an order, which is presented at the Convent. The making of bread is the most laborious employment in the institution.

The manufacture of wax candles was another important branch of business in the nunnery. It was carried on in a small room, on the first floor, called the ciergerie, or wax room, cierge being the French word for wax. I was sometimes sent to read the daily lecture and catechism, but found it a very unpleasant task, as the smell rising from the melted wax gave me a sickness at the stomach. The employment was considered unhealthy, and those were assigned to it who had the strongest constitutions. The nuns who were more commonly employed in that room, were Saint Maria, Saint Catherine, Saint Charlotte, Saint Frances, Saint Hyacinthe, Saint Hypolite, and others. But with these, as with others in the Convent, I was never allowed to speak, except under circumstances before mentioned. I was sent to read and was not allowed to answer the most trivial question, if one were asked. Should a nun say, "What o'clock is it?" I never dared to reply, but was required to report her to the Superior.

Much stress was laid on the *sainte scapulaire*, or holy scapulary. This is a small band of cloth or silk, formed in a particular manner, to be tied around the neck, by two strings, fastened to the ends. I have made many of them; having been set to make them in the Convent. On one side is marked a double cross (thus, + +) and on the other I. H. S. Such a band is called a scapulary, and many miracles are attributed to its power. Children on first receiving the communion are often presented with scapularies, which they are taught to regard with great reverence. We were told of the wonders effected by their means, in the addresses made to us, by priests, at catechism or lectures. I will repeat one or two of the stories.

A Roman Catholic servant woman, who had concealed some of her sins at confession, acted so hypocritical a part as to make her mistress believe her a *devotee*, or strict observer of her duty. She even imposed upon her confessor so that he gave her a scapulary. After he had given it, however, one of the saints in heaven informed him in a vision, that the holy scapulary must not remain on the neck of so great a sinner, and that it must be restored to the church. She lay down that night with the scapulary round her throat; but in the morning was found dead, with her head cut off, and the scapulary was discovered in the church. The belief was that the devil could not endure to have so holy a thing on one of his servants, and had pulled so hard to get it off, as to draw the silken thread with which it was tied, through her neck; after which, by some divine power, it was restored to the church.

Another story. A poor Roman Catholic was once taken prisoner by the heretics. He had a *Saint scapulaire* on his neck, when God, seeing him in the midst of his foes, took it from the neck by a miracle, and held it up in the air above the throng of heretics; one hundred of whom were converted, by seeing it thus supernaturally suspended.

I had been informed that there was a subterraneous passage, leading from the cellar of our Convent, into the Congregational Nunnery; but, though I had so often visited the cellar, I had never seen it. One day, after I had been received three or four months, I was sent to walk through it on my knees with another nun, as a penance. This, and other penances, were sometimes put upon us by the priests, without any reason assigned. The common way was to tell us of the sin for which a penance was imposed, but we were left many times to conjecture. Now and then the priest would inform us at the subsequent confession, when he happened to recollect something about it, as I thought, and not because he reflected or cared much upon the subject.

The nun who was with me led through the cellar, passing to the right of the secret burial place, and showed me the door of the subterraneous passage, which was towards the Congregational Nunnery. The reasons why I had not noticed it before, were, that it was made to shut close and even with the wall; and that part of the cellar was whitewashed. The door opens with a latch into a passage about four feet and a half high. We got upon our knees, commenced saying the prayers required, and began to move slowly along the dark and narrow passage. It may be fifty or sixty feet in length. When we reached the end, we opened the door, and found ourselves in the cellar of the Congregational Nunnery, at some distance from the outer wall. By the side of the door, was placed a list of names of the Black Nuns, with a slide that might be drawn over any of them. We covered our names in this manner, as evidence of having performed the duty assigned us; and then returned downwards on our knees, by the way we had come. This penance I repeatedly performed afterwards; and by this way, nuns from the Congregational Nunnery sometimes entered our Convent for worse purposes.

We were frequently assured that miracles are still performed; and pains were taken to impress us deeply on this subject. The superior often spoke to us of the Virgin Mary's pincushion, the remains of which are preserved in the Convent, though it has crumbled quite to dust. We regarded this relic with such veneration, that we were afraid even to look at it, and we often heard the following story related, when the subject was introduced.

A priest in Jerusalem had a vision, when he was informed that the house in which the Virgin had lived, should be removed from its foundations, and transported to a distance. He did not think the communication was from God, and disregarded it; but the house was soon after missed, which convinced him that the vision was true, and he told where the house might be found. A picture of the house is preserved in the Nunnery, and was shown us. There are also wax figures of Joseph sawing wood, and Jesus, as a child, picking up the chips. We were taught to sing a song relating to this, the chorus of which I remember:

> "Saint Joseph carpentier,
> Petit Jesus ramassait les copeaux
> Pour faire bouillir la marmite!"

(St Joseph was a carpenter, little Jesus collected chips to make the pot boil!) I recollect a story about a family in Italy saved from shipwreck by a priest, who were in consequence converted, and had two sons honoured with the priest's office.

I had heard, before I entered the Convent, about a great fire which had destroyed a number of houses in the Quebec suburbs, and which some said the Bishop extinguished with holy water. I once heard a Catholic and a Protestant disputing on this subject, and when I went to the Congregational Nunnery, I sometimes heard the children, alluding to the same story, say at an alarm of fire, "Is it a Catholic fire? Then why does not the Bishop run?"

Among the topics on which the Bishop addressed the nuns in the Convent, this was one. He told us the story one day, that he could have sooner interfered and stopped the flames, but that at last, finding they were about to destroy too many Catholic houses, he threw holy water on the fire, and extinguished it. I believed this, and also thought that he was able to put out any fire.

The holy water which the Bishop has consecrated, was considered more efficacious than any blessed by a priest: and this it was which was used in the Convent in sprinkling our beds. It has virtue in it, to keep off any evil spirit.

Now that I was a nun, I was sent to read lectures to the novices, as other nuns had been while I was a novice. There were but few of us who were thought capable of reading English well enough, and, therefore, I was more frequently sent than I might otherwise have been. The Superior often said to me, as I was going: "Try to convert them—save their souls—you know you will have a higher place in heaven for every one you convert."

For whatever reason, Mad Jane Ray seemed to take great delight in crossing and provoking the Superior and old nuns: and often she would cause an interruption when it was most displeasing to them. The preservation of silence was insisted upon most rigidly, and penances of such a nature were imposed for breaking it, that it was a constant source of uneasiness with me, to know that I might infringe the rules in so many ways, and that inattention might at any moment subject me to them. During the periods of meditation, and those of lecture, work, and repose, I kept a strict guard upon myself, to escape penances, as well as to avoid sin: and the silence of the others convinced me that they were equally watchful from the same motives.

My feelings, however, varied at different times, and so did those of many of my companions, excepting the older ones, who took their turns in watching us. We sometimes felt disposed for gaiety, and threw off all idea that talking was sinful, even when required by the rules of the Convent. I even, when I felt that I might perhaps be doing wrong, reflected that confession, and penance, would soon wipe off the guilt.

But I soon found out several things important to be known to a person living under such rules. First, that it was better to confess to a priest a sin committed against the rules, because he would not require the penance I most disliked, viz., those which exposed me to the observation of the nuns, or which demanded self-debasement before them, like begging their pardon, kissing the floor or the Superior's feet, &c., for, as a confessor he was bound to secrecy, and could not inform the Superior against me. My conscience being as effectually unburdened by my confession to the priest, I preferred not to tell my sins to anyone else: and this course was preferred by others for the same good reasons. To Jane Ray, however, it appeared to be a matter of indifference who knew her violations of rule, and to what penance she exposed herself.

Often while perfect silence prevailed among the nuns, at meditation, or while nothing was heard except the voice of the reader for the day, no matter whose life or writings were presented for our contemplation, Jane would break forth with some remark or question, that would attract general attention, and often cause a long and total interruption. Sometimes she would make some harmless remark or inquiry aloud, as if through mere inadvertency, and then her loud and well known voice, would arrest the attention of us all, and incline us to laugh. The Superior usually uttered a hasty remonstrance, or pronounced some penance upon her: but Jane had ever some apology ready, or some reply calculated to irritate more, or to prove that no punishment would be effectual on her. Sometimes she appeared to be actuated by opposite feelings and motives; for though she delighted in drawing others into difficulty, and has thrown severe penances upon her favourites, on other occasions she was regardless of consequences herself, and preferred to take all the blame, to shield others. I have often known her to break silence in the community, as if she had no object beyond that of causing disturbance, or exciting a smile, and as soon as it was noticed, exclaim, "Say it's me, say it's me!" Sometimes she would expose herself to punishment in place of another who was guilty; and thus I found it difficult to understand her. In some cases she seemed out of her wits, as the Superior and priests commonly represented her; but generally I saw in her what prevented me from accounting her insane.

Once she gave me the name of the "Devout English Reader," because I was often appointed to read the lecture to the English girls; and sometimes, sitting near me under pretence of deafness, would whisper it in my hearing, for she knew my want of self-command when excited to laughter. Thus she often exposed me to penances for a breach of decorum, and set me to biting my lips, to avoid laughing outright in the midst of a solemn lecture. "Oh! you devout English reader!" she would say, with something so ludicrous, that I had to exert myself to the utmost to avoid observation.

This came so often at one time, that I grew uneasy, and told her I must confess it, to unburden my conscience. Sometimes she would pass behind us as we stood at dinner ready to sit down, and softly moving back our chairs, leave us to fall down upon the floor, and while we were laughing together, she would spring forward, kneel to the Superior, and beg her pardon and a penance.

CHAPTER XI.

I MUST now come to a deed in which I had some part, and which I look back upon with great horror and pain. In it I was not the principal sufferer. It is not necessary to attempt to excuse myself in this or any other case. Those who judge fairly, will make allowances for me, under the fear and force, the command and examples, before me. It was about five months after I took the veil, the weather was cool, perhaps in October. One day, the Superior sent for me and several other nuns, to receive her commands. We found the Bishop and some priests with her; and speaking in an unusual tone of fierceness and authority, she said, "Go to the room for the Examination of Conscience, and drag St. Frances up stairs." A command so unusual, with her tone and manner, excited in me the most gloomy anticipations. It did not strike me as strange that St. Frances should be in the room to which the Superior directed us; an apartment to which we were often sent to prepare for the communion, and to which we voluntarily went, whenever we felt the compunctions which our ignorance of duty, and the misinstructions we received, inclined us to seek relief from self-reproach. I had seen her there a little before. What terrified me was, first, the Superior's angry manner; second, the expression she used, a French term, whose meaning is rather softened when translated into *drag;* third, the place to which we were directed to take the interesting young nun, and the persons assembled there, as I supposed to condemn her. My fears were such, concerning the fate that awaited her, and my horror at the idea that she was in some way to be sacrificed, that I would have given anything to be allowed to stay where I was. But I feared the effects of disobeying the Superior, and proceeded with the rest towards the room for the examination of conscience.

The room was in the second story, and the place of many a scene of a shameful nature. It is sufficient to say, that things had there occurred which made me regard the place with the greatest disgust. Saint Frances had appeared melancholy for some time. I knew that she had cause, for she had been repeatedly subject to trials which I need not name—our common lot. When we reached her room, I entered the door, my companions standing behind me, as the place was so small as hardly to hold five persons at a time. The young nun was standing alone, near the middle of the room; she was probably about twenty, with light hair, blue eyes, and a very fair complexion. I spoke to her in a compassionate voice, but with such a decided manner, that she comprehended my full meaning. "Saint Frances, we are sent for you."

Several others spoke kindly to her, but two addressed her very harshly. The poor creature turned round with a look of meekness, and without expressing any unwillingness or fear, without even speaking a word, resigned herself to our hands. The tears came into my eyes. I had not a doubt that she considered her fate as sealed, and was already beyond the fear of death. She was conducted to the staircase, and then seized by her limbs and clothes, and almost dragged up stairs. I laid my own hands upon her—I took hold of her, too, more gently indeed than some of the rest; yet I assisted them in carrying her. I could not avoid it. My refusal would not have saved her, nor prevented her being carried up; it would only have exposed me to some severe punishment, as some of my companions would have complained of me. All the way up the staircase, Saint Frances spoke not a word, nor made the slightest resistance. When we entered the room to which she was ordered, my heart sunk within me. The Bishop, the Lady Superior, and five priests, viz.: Bonin, Richards, Savage, and two others, were assembled for trial, on some charge of great importance.

Father Richards questioned her, and she made ready, but calm replies. I cannot give a connected account of what ensued: my feelings were wrought up to such a pitch, that I knew not what I did. I was under a terrible apprehension that, if I betrayed my feelings I should fall under the displeasure of the cold-blooded persecutors of my poor innocent sister; and this fear and the distress I felt for her, rendered me almost frantic. As soon as I entered the room, I stepped into a corner, on the left of the entrance, where I might partially support myself by leaning against the wall. This support prevented me falling to the floor; for the confusion of my thoughts was so great, that only a few of the words I heard made any lasting impression upon me. I felt as if death would not have been more frightful to me. I am inclined to think that Father Richards wished to shield the poor prisoner from the severity of her fate, by drawing from her expressions that might bear a favourable construction. He asked her, among other things, if she was not now sorry for what she had been overheard to say, (she had been betrayed in by a nun,) and if she would not prefer confinement in the cells to the punishment threatened. But the Bishop soon interrupted him, and it was easy to perceive, that he was determined she should not escape. In reply to some of the questions she was silent; to others I heard her reply that she did not repent of the words she had uttered, though they had been reported by some of the nuns who had heard them; that she had firmly resolved to resist every attempt to compel her to the commission of crimes which she detested. She added that she would rather die than cause the murder of harmless babes. "That is enough, finish her!" said the Bishop.

Two nuns instantly fell upon her, and in obedience to directions, given by the Superior, prepared to execute her sentence. She still maintained all the calmness and submission of a lamb. Some of those who took part in this transaction, I believe, were as unwilling as myself; but others delighted in it. Their conduct exhibited a most bloodthirsty spirit. But above all human fiends I ever saw, Saint Hypolite was the most diabolical; she engaged in the horrid task with all alacrity, and assumed from choice the most revolting parts to be performed. She seized a gag, forced it into the mouth of the poor nun, and when it was fixed between her extended jaws, so as to keep them open at their greatest possible distance, took hold of the straps fastened at each end of the stick, crossed them behind the helpless head of the victim, and drew them tight through the loop prepared as a fastening.

The bed which had always stood in one part of the room, still remained there; though the muslin screen, which had been placed before it, with only a crevice through which a person behind might look out, had been folded up on its hinges in the form of a W., and placed in a corner. On the bed the prisoner was laid with her face upward, and then bound with cords so that she could not move. In an instant, another bed was thrown upon her. One of the priests, named Bonin, sprung like a fury first upon it, with all his force. He was speedily followed by the nuns, until there were as many upon the bed as could find room, and all did what they could, not only to smother, but to bruise her. Some stood up and jumped upon the poor girl with their feet, some with their knees: and others, in different ways, seemed to seek how they might best beat the breath out of her body, and mangle it, without coming in direct contact with it, or seeing the effects of their violence. During this time, my feelings were almost too strong to be endured. I felt stupefied, and scarcely was conscious of what I did. Still fear for myself induced me to some exertion; and I attempted to talk to those who stood next, partly that I might have an excuse for turning away from the dreadful scene.

After the lapse of fifteen or twenty minutes, and when it was presumed that the sufferer had been smothered and crushed to death, Father Bonin and the nuns ceased to trample upon her, and stepped from the bed. All was motionless and silent beneath it. They then began to laugh at such inhuman thoughts as occurred to some of them, rallying each other in the most unfeeling manner, and ridiculing me for feelings which I in vain endeavoured to conceal. They alluded to the resignation of our murdered companion; and one of them tauntingly said, "She would have made a good Catholic martyr." Then one of them asked if the corpse should be removed. The Superior said it had better remain a little while. After waiting a short time, the feather-bed was taken off, the cords unloosed, and the body taken by the nuns and dragged down stairs into the cellar, and thrown into the hole which I have already described, covered with a great quantity of lime; and afterwards sprinkled with a liquid, of the properties and name of which I am ignorant. This liquid I have seen poured into the hole from large bottles, after the necks were broken off; and have heard that it is used in France to prevent the effluvia rising from cemeteries.

I did not soon recover from the shock caused by this scene; it still recurs to me, with most gloomy impressions. The next day, there was a melancholy aspect over everything, and recreation time passed in the dullest manner; scarcely anything was said above a whisper. I never heard much said afterwards about Saint Frances.

I spoke with one of the nuns a few words, one day, but we were all cautioned not to expose ourselves very far, and could not place much reliance in each other. The murdered nun had been brought to her shocking end through the treachery of one of our number in whom she confided. I never knew with certainty who had reported her remarks to the Superior, but suspicion fastened on one, and I never could regard her but with detestation. I was more inclined to blame her than some of those employed in the execution; for there could have been no necessity for the betrayal of her feelings.

I was often sent by the Superior to overhear what was said by novices and nuns, when they seemed to shun her: she would say, "Go and listen, they are speaking English;" and though I obeyed her, I never informed her against them. If I wished to clear my conscience, I would go to a priest and confess, knowing that he dared not communicate what I said to any person, and that he would not choose as heavy penances as the Superior.

We were allowed to choose another confessor when we had any sin to confess, which we were unwilling to tell one to whom we should otherwise have done. Not long after this murder a young woman came to the nunnery, and asked for permission to see St. Frances. It was my former friend, with whom I had been an assistant teacher, Miss Louisa Bousquet, of St. Denis. From this, I supposed the murdered nun might have come from that town, or its vicinity. The only answer was, that St. Frances was dead. Afterwards some of St. Frances' friends called to inquire after her, and they were told that she died a glorious death, and had made some heavenly expressions, which were repeated in order to satisfy her friends.

CHAPTER XII.

DESCRIPTION of the Room of the three States, and the Pictures in it—Jane
Ray—ridiculing Priests—their criminal Treatment of us at Confession—
Jane Ray's tricks with the Nuns' Aprons, Handkerchiefs, and Night
Gowns—Apples.

THE pictures in the room of the three States were large, and painted
by an artist who knew how to make horrible ones. They appeared
to be stuck to the walls. The light is admitted from small high windows, curtained, so as to make everything look gloomy. They told us
that they were painted by an artist, to whom God had given power
to represent things exactly as they are in heaven, hell, and purgatory.

In heaven, the picture of which hangs on one side of the apartment,
multitudes of nuns and priests are put in the highest places, with the
Virgin Mary at their head, St. Peter and other saints, far above the great
numbers of good Catholics of other classes, who are crowded in below.

In purgatory are multitudes of people; and in one part, called "*The
place of lambs*," are infants who died unbaptized. "*The place of darkness*"
is that part of purgatory in which adults are collected, there they are
surrounded by flames, waiting to be delivered by the prayers of the
living.

In the picture of hell the faces were the most horrible that can be
imagined. Persons of different descriptions were represented, with
the most distorted features, ghastly complexions, and every variety
of dreadful expression: some with wild beasts gnawing at their heads,
others furiously biting the iron bars which kept them in, with looks
which could not fail to make a spectator shudder.

I could hardly persuade myself, that the figures were not living, and
the impression they made on my feelings was powerful. I was often
shown the place where nuns go who break their vows, as a warning. It
is the hottest place in hell, and worse than that to which Protestants
are assigned; because they are not so much to be blamed, as we were
assured, as their ministers and the Bible, by which they are perverted.
Whenever I was shut in that room, as I was several times, I prayed for
"les âmes des fideles trespasses;" the souls of those faithful ones who

have long been in purgatory, and have no relations living to pray for them. My feelings were of the most painful description, while I was alone with those frightful pictures.

Jane Ray was once put in and uttered the most dreadful shrieks. Some of the old nuns proposed to the Superior to have her gagged; "No," she replied, "go and let out that devil, she makes me sin more than all the rest." Jane could not endure the place; and she gave names to many of the worst figures in the pictures. On catechism-days she took a seat behind a cupboard door where the priest could not see her, while she faced the nuns, and would make us laugh.

"You are not so attentive to your lesson as you used to be," he would say, while we tried to suppress our laughter.

Jane would then hold up the first letter of some priest's name whom she had before compared with one of the faces in "hell," and so look that we could hardly preserve our gravity. I remember she named the wretch who was biting at the bars of hell, with a serpent gnawing his head, with chains and padlocks on, Father Dufresne; and she would say—

"Does he not look like him, when he comes in to catechism with his long solemn face, and begins his speeches with, 'My children, my hope is that you have lived very devout lives?'"

The first time I went to confession after taking the veil, I found abundant evidence that the priests did not treat even that ceremony, which is called a solemn sacrament, with respect enough to lay aside the shameless character they so often showed on other occasions. The confessor sometimes sat in the room for the examination of conscience, and sometimes in the Superior's room, and always alone except the nun who was confessing. He had a common chair placed in the middle of the floor, and instead of being placed behind a grate, or lattice, as in the chapel, had nothing before or around him.

A number of nuns usually confessed on the same day, but only one could be admitted into the room at a time. They took their places just without the door, on their knees, and went through the preparation prescribed by the rules of confession; repeating certain prayers, which occupy a considerable time. When one was ready, she rose from her knees, entered, and closed the door behind her; and no one dared touch the latch until she came out.

I shall not tell what was transacted at such times, under the pretence of confessing, and receiving absolution from sin; far more sin was often incurred than pardon; and crimes of a deep dye were committed, while trifling irregularities in childish ceremonies, were treated as serious offences. I cannot persuade myself to speak plainly on such a subject, as I must offend the virtuous ear. I can only say, that suspicion cannot do any injustice to the priests, because their sins cannot be exaggerated.

Some idea may be formed of the manner in which even such women as many of my sister nuns, regarded the father confessors, when I state that there was often a contest among us, to avoid entering the apartment as long as we could; endeavouring to make each other go first, as that was what most of us dreaded.

During the long and tedious days which filled up the time between the occurrences I have mentioned, nothing or little took place to keep up our spirits. We were fatigued in body with labour, or with sitting, debilitated by the long continuance of our religious exercises, and depressed in feelings by our miserable and hopeless condition. Nothing but the humours of mad Jane Ray could rouse us for a moment from our languor and melancholy.

To mention all her devices, would require more room than is here allowed, and a memory of almost all her words and action for years. I had early become a favourite with her, and had opportunity to learn more of her character than most of the other nuns. As this may be learned from hearing what she did. I will here recount a few of her tricks, just as they happen to present themselves to my memory, without regard to the order of time.

She one day, in an unaccountable humour sprinkled the floor plentifully with holy water, which brought upon her a severe lecture from the Superior, as might have been expected. The Superior said it was a heinous offence: she had wasted holy water enough to save many souls from purgatory: and what would they not give for it! She then ordered Jane to sit in the middle of the floor, and when the priest came, he was informed of her offence. Instead, however, of imposing one of those penances to which she had been subjected, but with so little effect, he said to her,—

"Go to your place, Jane; we forgive you this time."

I was once set to iron aprons with Jane; aprons and pocket hand-kerchiefs are the only articles of dress which are ever ironed in the Convent. As soon as we were alone, she remarked:

"Well, we are free from the rules, while we are at this work;" and, although she knew she had no reason for saying so, she began to sing, and I soon joined her, and thus we spent the time, while we were at work, to the neglect of the prayers we ought to have said.

We had no idea that we were in danger of being overheard, but it happened that the Superior was overhead all the time, with several nuns, who were preparing for confession; she came down and said—

"How is this?"

Jane Ray coolly replied, that we had employed our time in singing hymns, and referred to me. I was afraid to confirm so direct a false-hood, in order to deceive the Superior, though I had often told more injurious ones of her fabrication, or at her orders, and said very little in reply to Jane's request.

The Superior plainly saw the trick that was attempted, and ordered us both to the room for the examination of conscience, where we remained till night, without a mouthful to eat. The time was not, however, unoccupied; I received such a lecture from Jane as I have very seldom heard, and she was so angry with me, that we did not speak to each other for two weeks.

At length she found something to complain of against me, had me subjected to a penance, which led to our begging each other's pardon, and we became perfectly satisfied, reconciled, and as good friends as ever.

One of the most disgusting penances we had ever to submit to, was that of drinking the water in which the Superior had washed her feet. Nobody could ever laugh at this penance except Jane Ray. She would pretend to comfort us, by saying she was sure it was better than mere plain clear water.

Some of the tricks which I remember, were played by Jane with nuns' clothes. It was a rule that the oldest aprons in use should go to the youngest received, and that the old nuns were to wear all the new ones. On four different occasions, Jane stole into the sleeping-room at night, and unobserved by the watch, changed a great part of the aprons, placing them by the beds of nuns to whom they did not belong. The consequence was, that in the morning they dressed themselves in such haste, as never to discover the mistake they made, until they were all ranged at prayers; and then the ridiculous appearance which many of them cut, disturbed the long devotions. I laugh so easy that, on such occasions, I usually incurred a full share of penances. I generally, however, got a new apron, when Jane played this trick; for it was part of her object to give the best aprons to her favourites, and put off the ragged ones on some of the old nuns whom she most hated.

Jane once lost her pocket-handkerchief. The penance for such an offence is, to go without any for five weeks. For this she had no relish, and requested me to pick one from some of the nuns on the way up stairs. I succeeded in getting two; this Jane said was one too many, and she thought it dangerous for either of us to keep it, lest a search should be made. Very soon the two nuns were complaining that they had lost their handkerchiefs, and wondering what could have become of them, as they were sure they had been careful. Jane seized an opportunity, and slipped one into a straw bed, where it remained until the bed was emptied to be filled with new straw.

As the winter was coming on, one year, she complained to me that we were not as well supplied with warm night-clothes, as two of the nuns she named, whom she said she "abominated." She soon after found means to get possession of their fine warm flannel night-gowns, one of which she gave to me, while the other was put on at bedtime. She presumed the owners would have a secret search for them; and in the morning hid them in the stove, after the fire had gone out, which was kindled a little before the hour of rising, and then suffered to burn down.

This she did every morning, taking them out at night through the winter. The poor nuns who owned the garments were afraid to complain of their loss, lest they should have some penance laid on them, and nothing was ever said about them. When the weather began to grow warm in the spring, Jane returned the night-gowns to the beds of the nuns from whom she had borrowed them, and they were probably as much surprised to find them again, as they had been before at losing them.

Jane once found an opportunity to fill her apron with a quantity of fine apples, called *fameuses*, which came in her way, and hastening up to the sleeping room, hid them under my bed. Then coming down, she informed me, and we agreed to apply for leave to make our elevens, as it is called. The meaning of this is, to repeat a certain round of prayers, for nine days in succession, to some saint we choose to address for assistance in becoming more charitable, affectionate, or something else. We easily obtained permission, and hastened up-stairs to begin our nine days' feast on the apples; when, much to our surprise, they had all been taken away, and there was no way to avoid the disagreeable fate we had brought upon ourselves. Jane, therefore, began to search the beds of the other nuns: but not finding any trace of the apples, she became doubly vexed, and stuck pins in those that belonged to her enemies.

When bedtime came, they were much scratched in getting into bed, which made them break silence, and that subjected them to penances.

CHAPTER XIII.

JANE RAY's Tricks continued—The broomstick Ghost—Sleep-walking—Salted Cider—Changing Beds—Objects of some of her tricks—Feigned Humility—Alarm.

ONE night, Jane, who had been sweeping the sleeping-room for a penance, dressed up the broomstick, when she had completed her work, with a white cloth on the end, so tied as to resemble an old woman dressed in white, with long arms sticking out. This she stuck through a broken pane of glass, and placed it so that it appeared to be looking in at the window, by the font of holy water. There it remained till the nuns came up to bed. The first who stopped at the font, to dip the finger in, caught a glimpse of the singular object, and started with terror. The next was equally terrified, as she approached, and the next, and the next.

We all believed in ghosts; and it was not wonderful that such an object should cause alarm, especially as it was but a short time after the death of one of the nuns. Thus they went on, each getting a fright in turn, yet all afraid to speak. At length, one more alarmed, or with less presence of mind than the rest, exclaimed, "Oh, mon Dieu! je ne me coucherais pas!" When the night watch called out "Who's that?" she confessed she had broken silence, but pointed at the cause; and when all the nuns assembled at a distance from the window, Jane offered to advance boldly, and ascertain the nature of the apparition, which they thought a most resolute intention. We all stood looking on, when she stepped to the window, drew in the broomstick, and showed us the ridiculous puppet which had alarmed so many superstitious fears.

Some of her greatest feats she performed as a sleep-walker. Whether she ever walked in her sleep or not, I am unable, with certainty to say. She, however, often, imposed upon the Superior, and old nuns, by making them think so, when I knew she did not; and yet I cannot positively say that she always did. I have remarked that one of the old nuns was always placed in our sleeping-room at night, to watch us. Sometimes she would be inattentive, and sometimes fall into a doze.

Jane Ray often seized such times to rise from her bed, and walk about, occasionally seizing one of the nuns in bed, in order to frighten her. This she generally effected; and many times we have been awakened by screams of terror. In our alarm, some of us frequently broke silence, and gave occasion to the Superior to lay us under penances. Many times, however, we escaped with a mere reprimand, while Jane usually received expressions of compassion: "Poor creature; she would not do so if she were in perfect possession of her reason." And Jane displayed her customary artfulness, in keeping up the false impression. As soon as she perceived that the old nun was likely to observe her, she would throw her arms about, or appear unconscious of what she was doing; falling upon a bed, or standing stock-still, until exertions had been made to rouse her from her supposed lethargy.

We were once allowed to drink cider at dinner, which was quite an extraordinary favour. Jane, however, on account of her negligence of all work, was denied the privilege, which she much resented. The next day, when dinner arrived, we began to taste our new drink, but it was so salt we could not swallow it. Those of us who first discovered it, were as usual afraid to speak; but we set down our cups, and looked around, till the others made the same discovery, which they all soon did, and most of them in the same manner. Some, however at length, taken by surprise, uttered some ludicrous exclamation on tasting the salted cider, and then an old nun, looking across, would cry out—

"Ah tu casses la silence." (Ah! you've broken silence.)

And thus we soon got a laughing, beyond our power of supporting it. At recreation that day, the first question asked by many of us was, "How did you like your cider?"

Jane Ray never had a fixed place to sleep in. When the weather began to grow warm in the spring, she usually pushed some bed out of its place, near a window, and put her own beside it; and when the winter approached, she would choose a spot near the stove, and occupy it with her bed, in spite of all remonstrance. We were all convinced that it was generally best to yield to her.

She was often set to work in different ways: but, whenever she was dissatisfied with doing anything, would devise some trick that would

make the Superior or old nuns drive her off; and whenever any suspicion was expressed of her being in her right mind, she would say
that she did not know what she was doing; and all the difficulty arose
from her repeating prayers too much, which wearied and distracted
her mind.

I was once directed to assist Jane Ray in shifting the beds of the
nuns. When we came to those of some of the sisters whom she most
disliked, she said, now we will pay them for some of the penances we
have suffered on their account; and taking some thistles, she mixed
them with the straw. At night, the first of them that got into bed felt
the thistles, and cried out The night-watch exclaimed as usual "You
are breaking silence there." And then another screamed as she was
scratched by the thistles, and another. The old nun then called on
all who had broken silence to rise, and ordered them to sleep under
their beds as a penance, which they silently complied with. Jane and
I afterwards confessed, when it was all over, and took some trifling
penance which the priest imposed.

Those nuns who fell most under the displeasure of mad Jane Ray, as
I have intimated before, were those who had the reputation of being
most ready to inform of the most trifling faults of others, and especially
those who acted without any regard to honour, by disclosing what they
had pretended to listen to in confidence. Several of the worst-tempered
"saints" she held in abhorrence; and I have heard her say, that such and
such she abominated. Many a trick did she play upon these, some of
which were painful to them in their consequences, and a good number
of them have never been traced to this day.

Of all the nuns, however, none other was regarded by her with so
much detestation as St. Hypolite; for she was always believed to have
betrayed St. Frances, and to have caused her murder. She was looked
upon by us as the voluntary cause of her death, and of the crime which
those of us committed, who unwillingly, took part in her execution.
We, on the contrary, being under the worst of fears for ourselves, in
case of refusing to obey our masters and mistress, thought ourselves
chargeable with less guilt, as unwilling assistants in a scene which it was
impossible for us to prevent or delay. Jane has often spoken with me of

the suspected informer, and always in terms of the greatest bitterness.

The Superior sometimes expressed commiseration for mad Jane Ray, but I never could tell whether she really believed her insane or not. I was always inclined to think, that she was willing to put up with some of her tricks, because they served to divert our minds from the painful and depressing circumstances in which we were placed. I knew the Superior's powers and habits of deception also, and that she would deceive us as willingly as any one else.

Sometimes she proposed to send Jane to St. Anne's, a place near Quebec, celebrated for the pilgrimages made to it by persons differently afflicted. It is supposed that some peculiar virtue exists there, which will restore health to the sick, and I have heard stories told in corroboration of the common belief. Many lame and blind persons, with others, visit St. Anne's every year, some of whom may be seen travelling on foot, and begging their food. The Superior would sometimes say that it was a pity that a woman like Jane Ray, capable of being so useful, should be unable to do her duties, in consequence of a malady which she thought might be cured by a visit to St. Anne's.

Yet to St. Anne's Jane was never sent, and her wild and various tricks continued as before. The rules of silence, which the others were so scrupulous in observing, she set at nought every hour; and as for other rules, she regarded them with as little respect when they stood in her way. She would now and then step out and stop the clock by which our exercises were regulated, and sometimes in this manner lengthened out our recreation till near twelve. At last the old nuns began to watch against such a trick, and would occasionally go out to see if the clock was going.

She once made a request that she might not eat with the other nuns, which was granted, as it seemed to proceed from a spirit of genuine humility, which made her regard herself as unworthy of our society.

It being most convenient, she was sent to the Superior's table, to make her meals after her; and it did not at first occur to the Superior that Jane, in this manner, profited by the change, by getting much better food than the rest of us. Thus there seemed to be always something deeper than any body at first suspected, at the bottom of everything she did.

She was once directed to sweep a community-room, under the sleeping-chamber. This office had before been assigned to the other nuns, as a penance; but the Superior, considering that Jane Ray, did little or nothing, determined thus to furnish her with some employment.

She declared to us that she would not sweep it long, as we might soon be assured. It happened that the stove by which the community-room was warmed in the winter, had its pipe carried through the floor of our sleeping chamber, and thence cross it in a direction opposite that in which the pipe of our stove was carried. It being then warm weather, the hole was left unstopped. After we had all retired to our beds, and while engaged in our silent prayers, we were suddenly alarmed by a bright blaze of fire, which burst from the hole in the floor, and threw sparks all around us. We thought the building was burning, and uttered cries of terror, regardless of the penances, the fear of which generally kept us silent.

The utmost confusion prevailed; for although we had solemnly vowed never to flee from the Convent even if it was on fire, we were extremely alarmed, and could not repress our feelings. We soon learnt the cause, for the flames ceased in a moment or two, and it was found that mad Jane, after sweeping a little in the room beneath, had stuck a quantity of wet powder on the end of her broom, thrust it up through the hole in the ceiling into our apartment, and with a lighted paper set it on fire.

The date of this alarm I must refer to a time soon after that of the election riots; for I recollect that she found means to get possession of some of the powder which was prepared at that time for an emergency to which some thought that the Convent was exposed.

She once asked for pen and paper, and then the Superior told her if she wrote to her friends she must see it. She replied that it was for no such purpose; she wanted to write her confession, and thus make it once for all. She wrote it, handed it to the priest, and he gave it to the Superior, who read it to us. It was full of offences which she had never committed, evidently written to throw ridicule on confessions, and one of the most ludicrous productions I ever saw.

Our bedsteads were made with very narrow boards laid across them, on which the beds were laid. One day, while we were in the bedchambers together, she proposed that we should misplace these boards. This was done, so that at night nearly a dozen nuns fell down upon the floor on getting into bed. A good deal of confusion naturally ensued, but the authors were not discovered. I was so conscience-stricken, however, that a week afterwards, while we were examining our consciences together, I told her I must confess the sin the next day. She replied,—

"Do as you like, but you will be sorry for it."

The next day, when we came before the Superior, I was just going to kneel and confess, when Jane, almost without giving me time to shut the door, threw herself at the Superior's feet and confessed the trick, and a penance was immediately laid upon me for the sin I had concealed.

There was an old nun who was a famous talker, whom we used to call La Mere (Mother). One night, Jane Ray got up, and secretly changed the caps of several of the nuns; and hers among the rest. In the morning there was great confusion, and such a scene seldom occurred. She was severely blamed by La Mere, having been informed against by some of the nuns: and at last became so much enraged, that she attacked the old woman, and even took her by the throat. La Mere called on all present to come to her assistance, and several nuns interfered. Jane seized the opportunity afforded in the confusion, to beat some of her worst enemies quite severely, and then afterward said, that she had intended to kill some of the rascally informers.

For a time Jane made us laugh so much at prayers, that the Superior forbade her going down with us at morning prayers; and she took the opportunity to sleep in the morning. When this was found out, she was forbidden to get into her bed again after leaving it, and then she would creep under it and take a nap on the floor. This she told us of one day, but threatened us if we ever betrayed her. At length she was missed at breakfast, as she would sometimes oversleep herself, and the Superior began to be more strict, and always inquired, in the morning, whether Jane Ray was in her place.

When the question was general none of us answered; but when it was addressed to some nun near her by name, as,—

"Saint Eustace, is Jane Ray in her place?" then we had to reply.

Of all the scenes that occurred during my stay in the Convent, there was none which excited the delight of Jane more than one which took place in the chapel one day at mass, though I never had any particular reason to suppose that she had brought it about.

Some person unknown to me to this day, had put some substance or other, of a most nauseous smell, into the hat of a little boy, who attended at the altar, and he, without observing the trick, put it upon his head. In the midst of the ceremonies he approached some of the nuns, who were almost suffocated with the odour; and as he occasionally moved from place to place, some of them began to beckon to him to stand further off and to hold their noses, with looks of disgust. The boy was quite unconscious of the cause of the difficulty, and paid them no attention, but the confusion soon became so great through the distress of some, and the laughing of others, that the Superior noticed the circumstance, and beckoned the boy to withdraw.

All attempts, however, to engage us in any work, prayer, or meditation, were found ineffectual. Whenever the circumstances in the chapel came to mind, we would laugh out. We had got into such a state, that we could not easily restrain ourselves. The Superior, yielding to necessity, allowed us recreation for the whole day.

The Superior used sometimes to send Jane to instruct the novices in their English prayers. She would proceed to the task with all seriousness; but sometimes chose the most ridiculous, as well as irreverent passages from the songs, and other things, which she had sometimes learned, which would set us, who understood her, laughing. One of her rhymes, I recollect, began with—

> "The Lord of love—look from above,
> Upon this turkey hen!"

Jane for a time slept opposite me, and often in the night would rise, unobserved, and slip into my bed, to talk with me, which she did in a low whisper, and return again with equal caution.

She would tell me of the tricks she had played, and such as she meditated, and sometimes make me laugh so loud, that I had much to do in the morning with begging pardons and doing penances.

One winter's day, she was sent to light a fire; but after she had done so, remarked privately to some of us, "my fingers were so cold—you'll see if I do it again."

The next day there was a great stir in the house, because it was said that mad Jane Ray had been seized with a fit while making a fire, and she was taken up apparently insensible, and conveyed to her bed. She complained to me, who visited her in the course of the day, that she was likely to starve, as food was denied her; and I was persuaded to pin a stocking under my dress, and secretly put food into it from the table. This I afterwards carried to her, and relieved her wants.

One of the things which I had blamed Jane most for, was a disposition to quarrel with any nun who seemed to be winning the favour of the Superior. She would never rest until she had brought such a one into some difficulty.

We were allowed but little soap; and Jane, when she found her supply nearly gone, would take the first piece she could find. One day there was a general search made for a large piece that was missed; when, soon after I had been searched, Jane Ray passed me, and slipped it into my pocket; she soon after was searched herself, and then secretly came for it again.

While I recall these particulars of our Nunnery, and refer so often to the conduct and language of one of the nuns, I cannot speak of some things which I believed or suspected, on account of my want of sufficient knowledge. But it is a pity you have not Jane Ray for a witness: she knew many things of which I am ignorant. She must be in possession of facts that should be known. Her long residence in the Convent, her habits of roaming about it, and of observing everything, must have made her acquainted with things which would be heard with interest. I always felt as if she knew everything. She would often go and listen, or look through the cracks into the Superior's room, while any of the priests were closeted with her, and sometimes would come and tell me what she witnessed. I felt myself bound to confess on such occasions, and always did so.

She knew, however, that I only told it to the priest or to the Superior, and without mentioning the name of my informant, which I was at liberty to withhold, so that she was not found out. I often said to her, "Don't tell me, Jane, for I must confess it." She would reply, "It is better for you to confess it than for me." I thus became, even against my will, informed of scenes supposed by the actors of them to be secret.

Jane Ray once persuaded me to accompany her into the Superior's room, to hide with her under the sofa, and await the appearance of a visitor whom she expected, that we might over-hear what passed between them. We had been long concealed, when the Superior came in alone, and sat for some time; when, fearing she might detect us in the stillness which prevailed, we began to repent of our temerity. At length, however, she suddenly withdrew, and thus afforded us a welcome opportunity to escape.

I was passing one day through a part of the cellar, where I had not often occasion to go, when the toe of my shoe hit something. I tripped and fell down, I rose again, and holding my lamp to see what had caused my fall, I found an iron ring, fastened to a small square trap-door. This I had the curiosity to raise, and saw four or five steps down, but there was not light enough to see more, and I feared to be noticed by somebody and reported to the Superior; so, closing the door again, I left the spot. At first I could not imagine the use of such a passage; but it afterwards occurred to me that it might open to the subterranean passage to the Seminary; for I never could before account for the appearance of many of the priests, who often appeared and disappeared among us, particularly at night, when I knew the gates were closed. They could, as I now saw, come up to the door of the Superior's room at any hour; then up the stairs into our sleeping-room, or where they chose. And often they were in our beds before us.

I afterwards ascertained that my conjectures were correct, and that a secret communication was kept up in this manner between these two institutions, at the end towards Notre Dame street, at a considerable depth under ground. I often afterwards met priests in the cellar, when sent there for coals and other articles, as they had to pass up and down the common cellar stairs on their way.

My wearisome daily prayers and labours, my pain of body and

depression of mind, which were so much increased by penances I have suffered, and those which I constantly feared, and the feelings of shame, remorse, and horror, which sometimes arose, brought me to a state which I cannot describe.

In the first place, my frame was enfeebled by the uneasy postures I was required to keep for so long a time during prayers. This alone, I thought, was sufficient to undermine my health and destroy my life. An hour and a half every morning I had to sit on the floor of the community-room, with my feet under me, my body bent forward, and my head hanging on one side, in a posture expressive of great humility, it is true, but very fatiguing to keep for such an unreasonable length of time. Often I found it impossible to avoid falling asleep in this posture which I could do without detection, by bending a little lower than usual. The signal to rise, or the noise made by the rising of the other nuns, then woke me, and I got up with the rest unobserved.

Before we took the posture just described we had to kneel for a long time without bending the body, keeping quite erect, with the exception of the knees only, with the hands together before the breast. This I found the most distressing attitude for me, and never assumed it without feeling a sharp pain in my chest, which I often thought would soon lead me to my grave—that is, to the great common receptacle for the dead under the chapel. And this upright kneeling posture we were obliged to resume as soon as we rose from the half-sitting posture first mentioned, so that I usually felt myself exhausted and near to fainting before the conclusion of the morning services.

I found the meditations extremely tedious, and often did I sink into sleep, while we were all seated in silence on the floor. When required to tell my meditations, as it was thought to be of no great importance what we said, I sometimes found I had nothing to tell but a dream, and told that, which passed off very well.

Jane Ray appeared to be troubled still more than myself with wandering thoughts; and when blamed for them, would reply, "I begin very well; but directly I begin to think of some old friend of mine, and my thoughts go a wandering from one country to another."

Sometimes I confessed my falling asleep; and often the priests have talked to me about the sin of sleeping in the time of meditation. At last, one of them proposed to me to prick myself with a pin, which is often done, and so rouse myself for a time.

My close confinement in the Convent, and the want of opportunities to breathe the open air, might have proved more injurious to me than they did, had I not been employed a part of my time in more active labours than those of sewing, &c., to which I was chiefly confined. I took part occasionally in some of the heavy work, as washing, &c.

The events which I am am now to relate occurred about five months after my admission into the Convent as a nun; but I cannot fix the time with precision, as I knew not of anything that took place in the world about the same period. The circumstances I clearly remember; but as I have elsewhere remarked, we were not accustomed to keep any account of time.

Information was given to us one day, that another novice was to be admitted among us; and we were required to remember and mention her often in our prayers, that she might have faithfulness in the service of her holy spouse. No information was given us concerning her beyond this fact; not a word about her age, name, or nation. On all similar occasions the same course was pursued, and all that the nuns ever learnt concerning one another was what they might discover by being together, and which usually amounted to little or nothing.

When the day of her admission arrived, though I did not witness the ceremony in the chapel, it was a gratification to us all on one account, because we were always released from labour, and enjoyed a great recreation day.

Our new sister, when she was introduced to the "holy" society of us "saints," proved to be young, of about the middle size, and very good looking for a Canadian: for I soon ascertained that she was one of my own countrywomen. The Canadian females are generally not handsome. I never learnt her name nor anything of her history. She had chosen St. Martin for her nun name. She was admitted in the morning, and appeared melancholy all day. This I observed was always the case; and the remarks made by others, led me to believe that they, and all they had seen, had felt sad and miserable for a longer or shorter time.

Even the Superior, as it may be recollected, confessed to me that she experienced the same feelings when she was received. When bed-time arrived, she proceeded to the chamber with the rest of us, and was assigned a bed on the side of the room opposite my own, and a little beyond. The nuns were all soon in bed, the usual silence ensued, and I was making my customary mental prayer, and composing myself to sleep, when I heard the most piercing and heart-rending shrieks proceed from our new comrade. Every nun seemed to rise as if by one impulse, for no one could hear such sounds, especially in such total silence, without being greatly excited. A general noise succeeded, for many voices spoke together, uttering cries of surprise, compassion or fear. It was in vain for the night-watch to expect silence; for once we forgot rules and gave vent to our feelings, and she could do nothing but call for the Superior.

I heard a man's voice mingled with the cries and shrieks of the nun. Father Quiblier, of the Seminary, I had felt confident, was in the Superior's room at the time when we retired; and several of the nuns afterwards assured me that it was he. The Superior soon made her appearance, and in a harsh manner commanded silence. I heard her threaten gagging her, and then say, "You are no better than anybody else, and if you do not obey, you shall be sent to the cells."

One young girl was taken into the Convent during my abode there, under peculiar circumstances. I was acquainted with the whole affair, as I was employed to act a part in it.

Among the novices was a young lady, of about seventeen, the daughter of an old rich Canadian. She had been remarkable for nothing that I know of, except the liveliness of her disposition. The Superior once expressed to us a wish to have her take the veil, though the girl herself had never any intention that I know of. Why the Superior wished to receive her I could only conjecture. One reason might have been, that she expected to receive a considerable sum from her father. She was, however, strongly desirous of having the girl in our community, and one day said—"Let us take her in by a trick, and tell the old man she felt too humble to take the veil in public."

Our plans then being laid, the unsuspecting girl was induced by us, in sport, as we told her and made her believe, to put on such a splendid robe as I had worn on my admission, and pass through some of the ceremonies of taking the veil. After this she was seriously informed that she was considered as having entered the Convent in earnest, and must henceforth bury herself to the world, as she would never be allowed to leave it. We put her on a nun's dress, though she wept, and refused, and expressed the greatest repugnance. The Superior threatened and promised, and flattered by turns, until the poor girl had to submit; but her appearance long showed that she was a nun only by compulsion.

In obedience to the directions of the Superior we exerted ourselves to make her contented, especially when she was first received, when we got round her and told her we had felt so for a time, but having since become acquainted with the happiness of nun's life, were perfectly content, and would never be willing to leave the Convent. An exception seemed to be made in her favour, in one respect; for I believe no criminal attempt was made upon her, until she had been for some time an inmate of the nunnery.

Soon after her reception, or rather her forcible entry into the Convent, her father called to make inquiries about his daughter. The Superior first spoke with him herself, and then called us to repeat her plausible story, which I did with accuracy. If I had wished to say anything else, I never should have dared.

We told the foolish old man, that his daughter, whom we all affectionately loved, had long desired to become a nun, but had been too humble to wish to appear before spectators, and had, at her own desire, been favoured with a private admission into the community.

The benefit conferred upon himself and his family, by this act of self-consecration, I reminded him, must be truly great and valuable; as every family who furnishes a priest, or a nun, is justly looked upon as receiving the peculiar favour of heaven on that account. The old Canadian, firmly believing every word I was forced to tell him, took the event as a great blessing, and expressed the greatest readiness to pay more than the customary fee to the Convent. After the interview, he withdrew, promising soon to return, and pay a handsome sum to the Convent, which he performed with all despatch and the greatest cheerfulness. The poor girl never heard her father had taken the trouble to call and see her, much less did she know anything of the imposition passed upon him. She remained in the Convent when I left it.

The youngest girl who ever took the veil of our sisterhood, was only fourteen years of age, and considered very pious. She lived but a short time. I was told that she was ill-treated by the priests, and believed her death was in consequence.

CHAPTER XIV.

IT was considered a great duty to exert ourselves to influence novices in favour of the Roman Catholic religion; and different nuns were, at different times charged to do what they could, by conversation, to make favourable impressions on the minds of some, who were, particularly indicated to us by the Superior. I often heard it remarked, that those who were influenced with the greatest difficulty, were young ladies from the United States; and on some of those, great exertions were made.

Cases in which citizens of the States were said to have been converted to the Roman Catholic faith were sometimes spoken of, and always as if they were considered highly important.

The Bishop, as we are told, was in the public square, on the day of an execution, when, as he said, a stranger looked at him in some peculiar manner, which made him confidently believe God intended to have him converted by his means. When he went home he wrote a letter for him, and the next day he found him again in the same place, and gave him the letter, which led to his becoming a Roman Catholic. This man, it was added, proved to be a citizen of the States.

The Bishop, as I have remarked, was not very dignified on all occasions, and sometimes acted in such a manner as would not have appeared well in public.

One day I saw him preparing for mass; and because he had some difficulty in getting on his robes, showed evident signs of anger. One of the nuns remarked: "The Bishop is going to perform a passionate mass." Some of the others exclaimed: "Are you not ashamed to speak thus of my lord?" And she was rewarded with a penance.

But it might be hoped that the Bishop would be free from the crimes of which I have declared so many priests to have been guilty. I am far from entertaining such charitable opinions of him; and I had good reasons, after a time.

I was often required to sleep on a sofa, in the room of the present Superior, as I may have already mentioned.

One night, not long after I was first introduced there for that purpose, and within the first twelve months of my wearing the veil, having retired as usual, at about half-past nine, not long after we had got into bed, the alarm-bell from without, which hangs over the Superior's bed was rung. She told me to see who was there; and going down, I heard the signal given, which I have before mentioned, a peculiar kind of hissing sound made through the teeth. I answered with a low "Hum—hum and then opened the door. It was Bishop Lartique, the present Bishop of Montreal. He said to me, "Are you a Novice or a Received?" meaning a Received nun. I answered, a "Received."

He then requested me to conduct him to the Superior's room, which I did. He went to the bed, drew the curtains behind him, and I lay down again upon the sofa, until morning, when the Superior called me, at an early hour, about daylight, and directed me to show him the door, to which I conducted him, and he took his departure.

I continued to visit the cellar frequently, to carry up coal for the fires, without anything more than a general impression that there were two nuns somewhere imprisoned in it. One day, while there on my usual errand, I saw a nun standing on the right of the cellar, in front of one of the cell doors I had before observed; she was apparently engaged with something within. This attracted my attention. The door appeared to close in a small recess, and was fastened with a stout iron bolt on the outside, the end of which was secured by being let into a hole in the stonework which formed the posts. The door, which was of wood, was sunk a few inches beyond the stonework, which rose and formed an arch overhead. Above the bolt was a small window, supplied with a fine grating, which swung open, a small bolt having been removed from it, on the outside. The nun I had observed seemed to be whispering with some person within, through the little window; but I hastened to get my coal, and left the cellar, presuming that was the prison. When I visited the place again, being alone, I ventured to the spot, determined to learn the truth, presuming that the imprisoned nuns, of whom the Superior had told me on my admission, were confined there. I spoke at the window where I had seen the nun standing, and heard a voice reply in a whisper. The aperture was so small, and the place so dark, that I could see nobody; but I learnt that a poor wretch was confined there a prisoner. I feared that I might be discovered, and after a few words, which I thought could do no harm, withdrew.

My curiosity was now alive to learn everything I could about so mysterious a subject. I made a few enquiries of St. Xavier, who only informed me that they were punished for refusing to obey the Superior, Bishop, and Priests. I afterwards found that the other nuns were acquainted with the fact I had just discovered. All I could learn, however, was that the prisoner in the cell whom I had just spoken with, and another in the cell just beyond, had been confined there several years without having been taken out; but their names, connections, offences, and everything else relating to them, I could never learn, and am still as ignorant of as ever.

Some conjectured that they had refused to comply with some of the rules of the Convent or requisitions of the Superior; others, that they were heiresses whose property was desired for the Convent, and who would not consent to sign deeds of it. Some of the nuns informed me, that the severest of their sufferings arose from fear of supernatural beings.

I often spoke with one of them in passing near their cells, when on errands in the cellar, but never ventured to stop long, or to press my enquiries very far. Besides, I found her reserved, and, little disposed to converse freely, a thing I could not wonder at when I considered her situation, and the character of persons around her. She spoke like a woman in feeble health, and of broken spirits. I occasionally saw other nuns speaking to them, particularly at meal times, when they were regularly furnished with food, which was such as we ourselves ate.

Their cells were occasionally cleaned, and then the doors were opened. I never looked into them, but was informed that the ground was their only floor. I presumed that they were furnished with straw to lie upon, as I always saw a quantity of old straw scattered about that part of the cellar, after the cells had been cleaned. I once inquired of one of them whether they could converse together, and she replied that they could, through a small opening between their cells, which I could not see.

I once inquired of the one I spoke with in passing, whether she wanted anything, and she replied—

"Tell Jane Ray I want to see her a moment if she can slip away."

When I went up I took an opportunity to deliver my message to Jane, who concerted with me a signal to be used in future, in case a similar request should be made through me. This was a sly wink at her with one eye accompanied with a slight toss of the head. She then sought an opportunity to visit the cellar, and was soon able to hold an interview with the poor prisoners, without being noticed by any one but myself. I afterwards learnt that mad Jane Ray was not so mad but she could feel for those miserable beings, and carry through measures for their comfort. She would often visit them with sympathizing words, and when necessary, conceal part of her food while at table, and secretly convey it into their dungeons. Sometimes we would combine for such an object; and have repeatedly aided her in thus obtaining a larger supply of food than they had been able to obtain from others.

I frequently thought of the two nuns confined in the cells, and occasionally heard something said about them but very little. Whenever I visited the cellar, and thought it safe, I went up to the first of them and spoke a word or two, and usually got some brief reply, without ascertaining that any particular change took place with either of them.

The one with whom alone I ever conversed, spoke English perfectly well, and French I thought as well. I supposed she must have been well educated, for I could not tell which was her native language. I remember that she frequently used these words when I wished to say more to her, and which alone showed that she was constantly afraid of punishment,—

"Oh, there's somebody coming—do go away!"

I have been told that the other prisoner also spoke English.

It was impossible for me to form any certain opinion about the size or appearance of those two miserable creatures, for their cells were perfectly dark, and I never caught the slightest glimpse even of their faces. It is probable they were women not above the middle size, and my reason for this presumption is the following: I was sometimes appointed to lay out the clean clothes for all the nuns in the Convent on Saturday evening, and was always directed to lay by two suits for the prisoners. Particular orders were given to select the largest sized garments for several tall nuns; but nothing of the kind was ever said in relation to the clothes for those in the cells.

I had not been long a veiled nun, before I requested of the Superior permission to confess to the "Saint Bon Pasteur," (Holy Good Shepherd) that is, the mysterious and nameless nun whom I had heard of while a novice. I knew of several others who had confessed to her at different times, and of some who had sent their clothes to be touched by her when they were sick; and I felt a desire to unburden my heart of certain things, which I was loath to acknowledge to the Superior, or any of the priests.

The Superior made me wait a little until she could ascertain whether the "Saint Bon Pasteur" was ready to admit me; and, after a time, returned and told me to enter the old nuns' room. That apartment has twelve beds arranged like the berths of a ship by threes; and as each is broad enough to receive two persons, twenty-four may be lodged there, which was about the number of old nuns in the Convent during most of my stay in it. Near an opposite corner of the apartment was a large glass case, with no appearance of a door, or other opening, in any part of it; and in that case stood the venerable nun, in the dress of the community, with her thick veil spread over her face, so as to conceal it entirely. She was standing, for the place did not allow room for sitting, and moved a little, which was the only sign of life, as she did not speak. I fell upon my knees before her, and began to confess some of my imperfections, which lay heavy upon my mind, imploring her aid and intercession, that I might be delivered from them. She appeared to listen to me with patience, but still never returned a word in reply.

I became much affected as I went on; at length began to weep bitterly; and, when I withdrew, was in tears. It seemed to me that my heart was remarkably relieved after this exercise, and all the requests, I had made, I found, as I believed, strictly fulfilled. I often, afterwards, visited the old nuns' room for the same purpose, and with similar results; so that my belief in the sanctity of the nameless nun, and my regard for her intercession, were unbounded.

What is remarkable, though I repeatedly was sent into that room to dust it, or to put it in order, I remarked, that the glass case was vacant and no signs were to be found, either of the nun, or of the way by which she had left it! so that a solemn conclusion rested upon my mind, that she had gone on one of her frequent visits to heaven.

A priest would sometimes come in the day time to teach us to sing, and this was done with some parade or stir, as if it were considered, or meant to be considered, as a thing of importance.

The instructions, however, were entirely repetitions of the words and tunes, nothing being taught even of the first principles of the science. It appeared to me, that although hymns alone were sung, the exercise was chiefly designed for our amusement, to raise our spirits a little, which were apt to become depressed. Mad Jane Ray certainly usually treated the whole thing as a matter of sport, and often excited those of us who understood English, to a great degree of mirth. She had a very fine voice, which was so powerful as generally to be heard above the rest. Sometimes she would be silent when the other nuns began; and the Superior would often call out,—

"Jane Ray, you don't sing."

She always had some trifling excuse ready, and commonly appeared unwilling to join the rest.

After being urged or commanded by the Superior, she would then strike some English song, or profane parody, which was rendered ten times more ridiculous by the ignorance of the lady Superior and the majority of the nuns. I cannot help laughing now when I remember how she used to stand with perfect composure, and sing,

> "I wish I was married and nothing to rue,
> With plenty of money and nothing to do."

"Jane Ray, you don't sing right," the Superior would exclaim.
"Oh," she would reply with perfect coolness, "that is the English for

> 'Seigneur Dieu de clemence,
> Reçois ce grand pecheur!'"

And, as sung by her, a person ignorant of the language would naturally be imposed upon. It was extremely difficult for me to conceal my laughter. I have always had greater exertion to make in repressing it than most other persons, and mad Jane Ray often took advantage of this.

Saturday evening usually brought with it much unpleasant work for some of us. We received Sacrament every Sunday; and in preparation for it, on Saturday evening, we asked pardon of the Superior, and of each other, "for the scandal we had caused them since we last received the Sacrament," and then asked the Superior's permission to receive it on the following day. She enquired of each nun, who necessarily asked her permission, whether she, naming her as Saint somebody had concealed any sin that should hinder her receiving it; and if the answer was in the negative, she granted her permission.

On Saturdays we were catechised by a priest, being assembled in a community-room. He sat on the right of the door, in a chair. He often told us stories, and frequently enlarged on the duty of enticing novices into the nunnery. "Do you not feel happy," he would say, "now that you are safely out of the world, and sure of heaven? But remember how many poor people are yet in the world. Every novice you influence to take the black veil, will add to your honour in heaven. Tell them how happy you are."

The Superior played one trick while I was in the Convent, which always passed for one of the most admirable she ever carried into execution. We were pretty good judges in a case of this kind; for, as may be presumed, we were rendered familiar with the arts of deception under so accomplished a teacher.

There was an ornament on hand in the Nunnery, of an extraordinary kind, which was prized at ten pounds; but it had been made and exposed to view so long, that it became damaged and quite unsaleable. We were one day visited by an old priest from the country, who was evidently somewhat intoxicated; and as he withdrew to go to his lodgings in the Seminary, where the country priests often stay, the Superior conceived a plan for disposing of the old ornament. "Come," said she, "we will send it to the old priest, and swear he has bought it."

We all approved of the ingenious device, for it evidently might be classed among the pious frauds we had so often had recommended to us, both by precept and example; and the ornament was sent to him the next morning, as his property when paid for. He soon came into the Convent, and expressed the greatest surprise that he had been charged with purchasing such a thing, for which he had no need and no desire.

The Superior heard his declaration with patience, but politely insisted that it was a fair bargain; and we then surrounded the old priest, with the strongest assertions that such was the fact, and that nobody would have thought of his purchasing it unless he had expressly engaged to take it. The poor old man was entirely put down. He was certain of the truth; but what could he do to resist or disprove a direct falsehood pronounced by the Superior of a Convent, and sworn to by all her holy nuns? He finally expressed his conviction that we were right; and was compelled to pay his money.

CHAPTER XV.

FREQUENCY of the Priests' Visits to the Nunnery—Their Freedom and Crimes—Difficulty of learning their Names—Their Holy Retreat—Objections in our minds—Means used to counteract Conscience—Ingenious Arguments.

SOME of the priests from the Seminary were in the Nunnery every day and night, and often several at a time. I have seen nearly all of them at different times, though there are about one hundred and fifty in the district of Montreal. There was a difference in their conduct; though I believe every one of them was guilty of licentiousness; while not one did I ever see who maintained a character any way becoming the profession of a priest. Some were gross and degraded in a degree which few of my readers can ever have imagined; and I should be unwilling to offend the eye, and corrupt the heart of any one, by an account of their words and actions. Few imaginations can conceive deeds so abominable as they practised, and often required of some of the poor women, under the fear of severe punishments, and even of death. I do not hesitate to say with the strongest confidence, that although some of the nuns became lost to every sentiment of virtue and honour, especially one of the Congregational Nunnery whom I have before mentioned, Saint Patrick, the greater part of them loathed the practices to which they were compelled to submit, by their Superior and priests, who kept them under so dreadful a bondage.

Some of the priests whom I saw I never knew by name, and the names of others I did not learn for a time, and at last learnt only by accident.

They were always called "Mon Pere," (my father) but sometimes when they had purchased something in the ornament-room, they would give their real names, with directions where it should be sent. Many names, thus learnt, and in other ways, were whispered about from nun to nun, and became pretty generally known. Several of the priests some of us had seen before we entered the Convent.

Many things of which I speak, from the nature of the case, must necessarily rest chiefly upon my own word, until further evidence can be obtained; but there are some facts for which I can appeal to the knowledge of others. It is commonly known in Montreal that some of the priests occasionally withdraw from their customary employments, and are not to be seen for some time; it being understood that they have retired for religious study, meditation, and devotion, for the improvement of their hearts. Sometimes they are thus withdrawn from the world for weeks; but there is no fixed period.

This was a fact I knew before I took the veil; for it is a frequent subject of remark, that such or such a Father is on a "holy retreat." This is a term which conveys the idea of a religious seclusion from the world, for sacred purposes. On the re-appearance of a priest after such a period, in the church or the streets, it is natural to feel a peculiar impression of his devout character—an impression very different from that conveyed to the mind of one who knows matters as they really are. Suspicions have been indulged by some in Canada on this subject, and facts are known by at least a few. I am able to speak from personal knowledge; for I have been a nun of Sœur Bourgeoise.

The priests are liable, by their dissolute habits, to occasional attacks of disease, which render it necessary, or at least prudent, to submit to medical treatment.

In the Black Nunnery they find private accommodation, for they are free to enter one of the private hospitals whenever they please; which is a room set apart on purpose for the accommodation of the priests, and is called a retreat-room. But an excuse is necessary to blind the public, and this they find in the pretence they make of being in a "Holy Retreat." Many such cases have I known; and I can mention the names of priests who have been confined in this Holy Retreat. They are very carefully attended by the Superior and old nuns, and their diet consists mostly of vegetable soups, &c., with but little meat, and that fresh. I have seen an instrument of surgery lying upon the table in that holy room, which is used only for particular purposes.

Father Tombeau, a Roman priest, was on one of his holy retreats about the time when I left the Nunnery. There are sometimes a number confined there at the same time. The victims of these priests frequently share the same fate.

I have often reflected how grievously I had been deceived in my opinion of a nun's condition!—All the holiness of their lives, I now saw was merely pretended. The appearance of sanctity and heaven-ly-mindedness which they had shown among us novices, I found was only a disguise to conceal such practices as would not be tolerated in any decent society in the world; and as for joy and peace like that of heaven, which I had expected to find among them, I learnt too well that they did not exist there.

The only way in which such thoughts were counteracted, was by the constant instructions given us by the Superior and priests, to regard every doubt as a mortal sin. Other faults we might have, as we were told over and over again, which though worthy of penances, were far less sinful than these. For a nun to doubt that she was doing her duty in fulfilling her vows and oaths, was a heinous offence, and we were exhorted always to suppress our doubts, to confess them without re-serve, and cheerfully submit to severe penances on account of them, as the only means of mortifying our evil dispositions, and resisting the temptations of the devil. Thus we learnt in a good degree to resist our minds and consciences, when we felt the rising of a question about the duty of doing anything required of us.

To enforce this upon us, they employed various means. Some of the most striking stories told us at catechism by the priests, were designed for this end. One of these I will repeat. "One day," as a priest assured us, who was hearing us say the catechism on Saturday afternoon, "as one Monsieur * * * *, a well known citizen of Montreal, was walking near the cathedral, he saw Satan giving orders to innumerable evil spirits who were assembled around him. Being afraid of being seen, and yet wishing to observe what was done, he hid himself where he could observe all that passed. Satan despatched his devils to different parts of the city, with directions to do their best for him; and they returned in a short time, bringing in reports of their success in leading persons of different classes to the commission of various sins, which they thought would be agreeable to their master. Satan, however, expressed his dissatisfaction, and ordered them out again; but just then a spirit from the Black Nunnery came, who had not been seen before, and stated that he had been trying for seven years to persuade one of the nuns to doubt, and had just succeeded. Satan received the intelligence with the highest pleasure; and turning to the spirits around him, said: 'You have not half done your work,—he has done much more than all of you.'"

In spite, however, of our instructions and warnings, our fears and penances, such doubts would obtrude; and I have often indulged them for a time, and at length, yielding to the belief that I was wrong in giving place to them, would confess them, and undergo with cheerfulness such new penances as I was loaded with. Others too would occasionally entertain and privately express such doubts; though we all had been most solemnly warned by the cruel murder of Saint Frances. Occasionally some of the nuns would go further, and resist the restraints of punishments imposed upon them; and it was not uncommon to hear screams, sometimes of a most piercing and terrific kind, from nuns suffering under discipline.

Some of my readers may feel disposed to exclaim against me, for believing things which will strike them as so monstrous and abominable. To such, I would say, without pretending to justify myself;—you know little of the position in which I was placed; in the first place, ignorant of any other religious doctrines, and in the second, met at every moment by some ingenious argument, and the example of a large community, who received all the instructions of the priests as of undoubted truth, and practised upon them. Of the variety and speciousness of the arguments used, you cannot have any correct idea. They were often so ready with replies, examples, anecdotes, and authorities, to enforce their doctrines, that it seemed to me as if they could never have learnt it all from books, but must have been taught by wicked spirits.

Indeed, when I reflect upon their conversations, I am astonished at their art and address, and find it difficult to account for their subtlety and success in influencing my mind, and persuading me to anything they pleased. It seems to me that hardly anybody would be safe in their hands. If you were to go to confession twice, I believe you would feel very different from what you do now. They have such a way of avoiding one thing and speaking of another, of affirming this, and doubting and disputing that, of quoting authorities, and speaking of wonders and miracles recently performed, in confirmation of what they teach, as familiarly known to persons whom they call by name, and whom they pretend to offer as witnesses, though they never give you an opportunity to speak with them,—these, and many other means, they use in such a way, that they always blinded my mind, and I should think, would blind the minds of others.

CHAPTER XVI.

IT will be recollected, that I was informed immediately after receiving the veil, that infants were occasionally murdered in the Convent. I was one day in the nuns' private sick room, when I had an opportunity unsought for, of witnessing deeds of such a nature. It was, perhaps, a month after the death of St. Frances.

Two little twin babes, the children of St. Catherine, were brought to a priest, who was in the room, for baptism. I was present while the ceremony was performed, with the Superior and several of the old nuns, whose names I never knew, they being called Ma tant (Aunt.)

The priests took turns in attending to confession and catechism in the Convent, usually three months at a time, though sometimes longer periods. The priest then on duty was Father Larkin. He is a good-looking European, and has a brother who is a Professor in the College. He first put oil upon the heads of the infants, as is the custom before baptism. When he had baptised the children, they were taken, one after another, by one of the old nuns, in the presence of us all. She pressed her hand upon the mouth and nose of the first so tight that it could not breathe, and in a few minutes, when the hand was removed, it was dead. She then took the other, and treated it in the same way. No sound was heard, and both the children were corpses. The greatest indifference was shown by all present during this operation; for all, as I well knew, were long accustomed to such scenes. The little bodies were then taken into the cellar, thrown into the pit I have mentioned, and covered with a quantity of lime.

I afterwards saw a new-born infant treated in the same manner, in the same place; but the actors in this scene I choose not to name, nor the circumstances, as everything connected with it is of a peculiarly trying and painful nature to my own feelings.

These were the only instances of infanticide I witnessed; and it seemed to be merely owing to accident that I was then present. So far as I know there were no pains taken to preserve secrecy on this subject; that is, I saw no attempt made to keep any inmate of the Convent in ignorance of the murder of the children. On the contrary, others were told, as well as myself, on their first admission as veiled nuns, that all infants born in the place were baptised and killed, without loss of time! and I had been called to witness the murder of the three just mentioned, only because I happened to be in the room at the time.

That others were killed in the same manner, during my stay in the nunnery, I am well assured.

How many there were I cannot tell, and having taken no account of those I heard of, I cannot speak with precision; I believe, however, that I learnt through nuns, that at least eighteen or twenty infants were smothered, and secretly buried in the cellar, while I was a nun.

One of the effects of the weariness of our bodies and minds, was our proneness to talk in our sleep. It was both ludicrous and painful to hear the nuns repeat their prayers in the course of the night, as they frequently did in their dreams. Required to keep our minds continually on the stretch, both in watching our conduct, in remembering the rules and our prayers, under the fear of the consequences of any neglect, when we closed our eyes in sleep, we often went over again the scenes of the day; and it was no uncommon thing for me to hear a nun repeat one or two of her long exercises in the dead of the night. Sometimes by the time she had finished, another, in a different part of the room, would happen to take a similar turn, and commence a similar recitation; and I have known cases in which several such unconscious exercises were performed, all within an hour or two.

We had now and then a recreation day, when we were relieved from our customary labour, and from all prayers except those for morning and evening, and the short ones said at every striking of the clock. The greater part of our time was then occupied with different games, particularly backgammon and drafts, and in such conversation as did not relate to our past lives, and the outside of the Convent. Sometimes, however, our sports would be interrupted on such days by the entrance of one of the priests, who would come in and propose that his fete, the birthday of his patron saint, should be kept by "the saints." We saints!

Several nuns died at different times while I was in the Convent; how many, I cannot say, but there was a considerable number. I might rather say many in proportion to the number in the nunnery. The proportion of deaths I am sure was very large. There were always some in the nuns' sick-room, and several interments took place in the chapel.

When a Black Nun is dead, the corpse is dressed as if living, and placed in the chapel in a sitting posture, within the railing round the altar, with a book in the hand as if reading. Persons are then freely admitted from the street, and some of them read and pray before it. No particular notoriety is given, I believe, to this exhibition out of the Convent, but such a case usually excites some attention.

The living nuns are required to say prayers for the delivery of their deceased sister from purgatory, being informed, as in all other such cases, that if she is not there, and has no need of our intercession, our prayers are in no danger of being thrown away, as they will be set down to the account of some of our deceased friends or at least to that of the souls which have no acquaintances to pray for them.

It was customary for us occasionally to kneel before a dead nun thus seated in the chapel, and I have often performed that task. It was always painful, for the ghastly countenance being seen whenever I raised my eyes, and the feeling that the position and dress were entirely opposed to every idea of propriety in such a case, always made me melancholy.

The Superior sometimes left the Convent, and was absent for an hour, or several hours at a time, but we never knew of it until she had returned, and were not informed where she had been. I one day had reason to presume that she had recently paid a visit to the priests' farm, though I had not direct evidence that such was the fact. The priests' farm is a fine tract of land belonging to the Seminary, a little distance from the city, near the Lachine road, with a large old-fashioned edifice upon it. I happened to be in the Superior's room on the day alluded to, when she made some remark on the plainness and poverty of her furniture. I replied that she was not proud, and could not be dissatisfied on that account; she answered:—

"No: but if I was, how much superior is the furniture at the priests' farm; the poorest room there is furnished better than the best of mine."

I was one day mending the fire in the Superior's room, when a priest was conversing with her on the scarcity of money; and I heard him say that very little money was received by the priests for prayers, but that the principal part came with penances and absolutions.

One of the most remarkable and unaccountable things that happened in the Convent, was the disappearance of the old Superior. She had performed her customary part during the day, and had acted and appeared just as usual. She had shown no symptoms of ill health, met with no particular difficulty in conducting business and no agitation, anxiety, or gloom had been noticed in her conduct. We had no reason to suppose that during that day she had expected anything particular to occur, any more than the rest of us.

After the close of our customary labours and evening lectures, she dismissed us to retire to bed, exactly in her usual manner. The next morning the bell rang, we sprang from our beds, hurried on our clothes as usual, and proceeded to the community-room in double line, to commence the morning exercise. There, to our surprise, we found Bishop Lartique; but the Superior was no where to be seen. The Bishop soon addressed us, instead of her, and informed us, that a lady near him, whom he presented to us, was now the Superior of the Convent, and enjoined upon us the same respect and obedience which we paid to her predecessor.

The lady he introduced to us was one of our oldest nuns, Saint Du***, a very large, fleshy woman, with swelled limbs, which rendered her very slow in walking, and often gave her great distress. Not a word was dropped from which we could conjecture the cause of this change, nor of the fate of the old Superior. I took the first opportunity to enquire of one of the nuns, whom I dared to talk to, what had become of her; but I found them as ignorant as myself, though suspicious that she had been murdered by order of the Bishop. Never did I obtain any light on her mysterious disappearance. I am confident, however, that if the Bishop wished to get rid of her privately, and by foul means, he had ample opportunities and power at his command. Jane Ray, as usual, could not allow such an occurrence to pass by without intimating her own suspicions more plainly than any other of the nuns would have dared to do. She spoke out one day in the community-room, and said, "I'm going to have a hunt in the cellar for my old Superior."

"Hush, Jane Ray!" exclaimed some of the nuns, "you'll be punished."

"My mother used to tell me," replied Jane, "never to be afraid of the face of man."

It cannot be thought strange that we were superstitious. Some were more easily terrified than others by unaccountable sights and sounds; but all of us believed in the power and occasional appearance of spirits, and were ready to look for them at almost any time. I have seen several instances of alarm caused by such superstition, and have experienced it myself more than once. I was one day sitting mending aprons, beside one of the old nuns, in the community-room, while the litanies were repeating: as I was very easy to laugh, Saint Ignace or Agnes, came in, walked up to her with much agitation, and began to whisper in her ear. She usually talked but little, and that made me more curious to know what was the matter. I overheard her say to the old nun, in much alarm, that in the cellar from which she had just returned, she had heard the most dreadful groans that ever came from any human being. This was enough to give me uneasiness. I could not account for the appearance of an evil spirit in any part of the Convent, for I had been assured that the only one ever known there was that of the nun who had died with an unconfessed sin; and that others were kept at a distance by the holy water that was rather profusely used in different parts of the nunnery. Still, I presumed that the sounds heard by Saint Ignace must have proceeded from some devil, and I felt great dread at the thought of visiting the cellar again. I determined to seek further information of the terrified nun, but when I addressed her on the subject, at recreation-time, the first opportunity I could find, she replied, that I was always trying to make her break silence, and walked off to another group in the room, so that I could obtain no satisfaction.

It is remarkable that in our nunnery, we were almost entirely cut off from the means of knowing anything even of each other. There were many nuns whom I know nothing of to this day, after having been in the same room with them every day and night for four years. There was a nun, whom I supposed to be in the Convent, and whom I was anxious to learn something about from the time of my entrance as a novice; but I never was able to learn anything concerning her, not even whether she was in the nunnery or not, whether alive or dead. She was the daughter of a rich family, residing at Point aux Trembles, of whom I had heard my mother speak before I entered the Convent. The name of her family I think was Lafayette, and she was thought to be from Europe. She was known to have taken the Black Veil, but as I was not acquainted with the Saint she had assumed, and I could not describe her in "the world," all my enquiries and observations proved entirely in vain.

I had heard before my entrance into the Convent, that one of the nuns had made her escape from it during the last war, and once inquired about her of the Superior. She admitted that such was the fact; but I was never able to learn any particulars concerning her name, origin, or manner of escape.

CHAPTER XVII.

Disappearance of Nuns—St. Pierre—Gags—My temporary Confinement in a Cell—The Cholera Season—How to avoid it—Occupations in the Convent during the Pestilence—Manufacture of Wax Candles—The Election Riots—Alarm among the Nuns—Preparations for Defence—Penances.

I AM unable to say how many nuns disappeared while I was in the Convent. There were several. One was a young lady called St. Pierre, I think, but am not certain of her name. There were two nuns by this name. I had known her as a novice with me. She had been a novice about two years and a half before I became one. She was rather large without being tall, and had rather dark hair and eyes. She disappeared unaccountably, and nothing was said of her except what I heard in whispers from a few of the nuns, as we found moments when we could speak unobserved.

Some told me they thought she must have left the Convent; and I might have supposed so, had I not sometime afterwards found some of her things lying about, which she would, in such a case, doubtless have taken with her. I had never known anything more of her than what I could observe or conjecture. I had always, however, the idea that her parents or friends were wealthy, for she sometimes received clothes and other things which were very rich.

Another nun named St. Paul, died suddenly, but as in other cases, we knew so little, or rather were so entirely ignorant of the cause and circumstances, that we could only conjecture; and being forbidden to speak freely upon that or any other subject, thought little about it. I have mentioned that a number of veiled nuns thus mysteriously disappeared during my residence among them. I cannot perhaps recall them all, but I am confident there were as many as five, and I think more. All that we knew in such cases was, that one of our number who appeared as usual when last observed, was nowhere to be seen, and never was again.—Mad Jane Ray, on several such occasions, would indulge in her bold, and, as we thought, dangerous remarks. She had intimated that some of those, who had been for some time in the

Convent, were by some means removed to make room for new ones; and it was generally the fact, that the disappearance of one and the introduction of another into our community, were nearly at the same time. I have repeatedly heard Jane Ray say, with one of her significant looks, "When you appear, somebody else disappears!"

It is unpleasant enough to distress or torture one's self; but there is sometimes worse in being tormented by others, especially where they resort to force, and show a pleasure in compelling you, and leave you no hope to escape, or opportunity to resist. I had seen the gags repeatedly in use, and sometimes applied with a roughness which seemed rather inhuman; but it is one thing to see and another thing to feel. They were ready to recommend a resort to compulsory measures, and ever ready to run for the gags. These were kept in one of the community-rooms, in a drawer between two closets; and there a stock of about fifty of them were always kept in deposit. Sometimes a number of nuns would prove refractory at a time: and I have seen battles commenced in which several appeared on both sides. The disobedient were, however, soon overpowered: and to prevent their screams from being heard beyond the walls, gagging commenced immediately. I have seen half a dozen lying gagged and bound at once.

I have been subjected to the same state of involuntary silence more than once; for sometimes I became excited to a state of desperation by the measures used against me, and then conducted myself in a manner perhaps not less violent than some others. My hands have been tied behind me, and a gag put into my mouth, sometimes with such force and rudeness as to separate my lips, and cause the blood to flow freely.

Treatment of this kind is apt to teach submission; and many times I have acquiesced under orders received, or wishes expressed, with a fear of a recurrence to some severe measures.

One day I had incurred the anger of the Superior in a greater degree than usual, and it was ordered that I should be taken to one of the cells. I was taken by some of the nuns, bound and gagged, carried down the stairs into the cellar, and laid upon the floor. Not long afterwards I induced one of the nuns to request the Superior to come down and see me: and on making some acknowledgment, I was released. I will, however, relate this story rather more in detail.

On that day I had been engaged with Jane Ray, in carrying into effect a plan of revenge upon another person, when I fell under the vindictive spirit of some of the old nuns, and suffered severely. The Superior ordered me to the cells, and a scene of violence commenced which I will not attempt to describe, nor the precise circumstances which led to it. Suffice it to say, that after I had exhausted all my strength, by resisting as long as I could, against several nuns, I had my hands drawn behind my back, a leathern band passed first round my thumbs, then round my hands, and then round my waist and fastened. This was drawn so tight that it cut through the flesh of my thumbs, making wounds, the scars of which still remain. A gag was then forced into my mouth, not indeed so violently as it sometimes was, but roughly enough; after which I was taken by main force, and carried down into the cellar, across it almost to the opposite extremity and brought to the last of the second range of cells on the left hand. The door was opened, and I was thrown in with violence, and left alone, the door being immediately closed, and bolted on the outside. The bare ground was under me, cold and hard as if it had been beaten even. I lay still in the position in which I had fallen, as it would have been difficult for me to move, confined as I was, and exhausted by my exertions; and the shock of my fall, and my wretched state of desperation and fear disinclined me from any further attempt. I was in almost total darkness, there being nothing perceptible except a slight glimmer of light which came in through the little window far above me.

How long I remained in that condition I can only conjecture. It seemed to me a long time, and must have been two or three hours. I did not move, expecting to die there, and in a state of distress which I cannot describe, from the tight bondage about my hands, and the gag holding my jaws apart at their greatest extension. I am confident I must have died before morning, if, as I then expected, I had been left there all night. By-and-bye, however, the bolt was drawn, the door opened, and Jane Ray spoke to me in a tone of kindness.

She had taken an opportunity to slip into the cellar unnoticed, on purpose to see me. She unbound the gag, took it out of my mouth, and told me she would do anything to get me out of that dungeon. If she had had the bringing of me down she would not have thrust me in so brutally, and she would be resented on those who had. She offered to throw herself upon her knees before the Superior, and beg her forgiveness. To this I would not consent; but told her to ask the Superior to come to me, as I wished to speak to her. This I had no idea she would condescend to do; but Jane had not been gone long before the Superior came, and asked if I repented in the sight of God for what I had done. I replied in the affirmative; and after a lecture of some length on the pain I had given the Virgin Mary by my conduct, she asked whether I was willing to ask pardon of all the nuns for the scandal I had caused them by my behaviour. To this I made no objection; and I was then released from my prison and my bonds, went up to the community-room, and kneeling before all the sisters in succession, begged the forgiveness and prayers of each.

Among the marks which I still bear of the wounds received from penances and violence, are the scars left by the belt with which I repeatedly tortured myself, for the mortification of my spirit. These are most distinct on my side; for although the band, which was four to five inches in breadth, and extended round the waist, was stuck full of sharp iron points in all parts, it was sometimes crowded most against my side, by resting in my chair, and then the wounds were usually deeper there than anywhere else.

My thumbs were several times cut severely by the tight drawing of the band used to confine my arms; and scars are still visible upon them.

The rough gagging which I several times endured wounded my lips very much; for it was common, in that operation, to thrust the gag hard against the teeth, and catch one or both the lips, which were sometimes cruelly cut. The object was to stop the screams made by the offender, as soon as possible; and some of the old nuns delighted in tormenting us. A gag was once forced into my mouth, which had a large splinter upon it; and this cut through my under lip, in front, leaving to this day a scar about half an inch long. The same lip was several times wounded as well as the other; but one day worse than ever, when a narrow piece was cut off from the left side of it, by being pinched between the gag and the under fore-teeth; and this has left an inequality in it which is still very observable.

One of the most shocking stories I heard of events that occurred in the nunnery before my acquaintance with it was the following, which was told me by Jane Ray. What is uncommon, I can date when I heard it. It was on New Year's Day, 1834. The ceremonies, customary in the early part of that day, had been performed; after mass, in the morning, the Superior had shaken hands with all the nuns, and given us her blessing, for she was said to have received power from heaven to do so once a year, and then on the first day of the year. Besides this, cakes, raisins, &c., are distributed to the nuns on that day.

While in the community-room, I had taken a seat just within the cupboard door, where I often found a partial shelter from observation with Jane, when a conversation incidentally began between us. Our practice often was, to take places there beside one of the old nuns, awaiting the time when she would go away for a little while, and leave us partially screened from the observation of others. On that occasion, Jane and I were left for a time alone; when, after some discourse on suicide, she remarked that three nuns once killed themselves in the Convent. This happened, she said, not long after her reception, and I knew, therefore, that it was several years before, for she had been received a considerable time before I became a novice. Three young ladies, she informed me, took the veil together, or very near the same time, I am not certain which. I know they have four robes in the Convent to be worn during the ceremony of taking the veil: but I never have seen more than one of them used at a time.

Two of the new nuns were sisters, and the other their cousin. They had been received but a few days when information was given one morning, that they had been found dead in their beds, amid a profusion of blood. Jane Ray said she saw their corpses, and that they appeared to have killed themselves, by opening veins in their arms with a knife they had obtained, and all had bled together. What was extraordinary, Jane Ray added, that she heard no noise, and she believed nobody had suspected that anything was wrong during the night. St. Hypolite, however, had stated that she had found them in the morning, after the other nuns had gone to prayers, lying lifeless in their beds.

For some reason or other, their death was not made public; but their bodies, instead of being exhibited in full dress, in the chapel, and afterwards interred with solemnity beneath it, were taken unceremoniously into the cellar, and thrown into the hole I have so often mentioned.

There were a few instances, and only a few, in which we knew anything that was happening in the world; and even then our knowledge did not extend out of the city. I can recall but three occasions of this kind. Two of them were when the cholera prevailed in Montreal: and the other was the election riots. The appearance of the cholera, in both seasons of its ravages, gave us abundance of occupation. Indeed, we were more borne down by hard labour at those times, than ever before or afterwards during my stay. The Pope had given early notice that the burning of wax candles could afford protection from the disease, because, so long as any person continued to burn one, the Virgin Mary would intercede for him. No sooner, therefore, had the alarming disease made its appearance in Montreal, than a long wax candle was lighted in the Convent, for each of the inmates, so that all parts of it in use were artificially illuminated day and night. Thus a great many candles were constantly burning, which were to be replaced from those manufactured by the nuns. But this was a trifle. The Pope's message having been promulgated in the Grey Nunnery, and to Catholics at large through the pulpits, an extraordinary demand was created for wax candles, to supply which we were principally depended upon. All who could be employed in making them were therefore set to work, and I, among the rest, assisted in different departments, and witnessed all.

Numbers of the nuns had been long familiar with the business; for a very considerable amount of wax had been annually manufactured in the Convent; but now the works were much extended, and other occupations in a great degree laid aside. Large quantities of wax were received into the building, which was said to have been imported from England: kettles were placed in some of the working-rooms, in which it was clarified by heat over coal fires, and when prepared, the process of dipping commenced. The wicks, which were quite long, were placed, hanging upon a reel, taken up and dipped in succession, until after many slow revolutions of the reel, the candles were of the proper size. They were then taken to a part of the room where tables were prepared for rolling them smooth. This is done by passing a roller over them, until they became even and polished; after which they are laid by for sale. These processes caused a constant bustle in some of the rooms: and the melancholy reports from without, of the ravages of the cholera, with the uncertainty of what might be the result with us, notwithstanding the promised intercession of the Virgin, and brilliant lights constantly burning in such numbers around us, impressed the scenes I used to witness very deeply on my mind. I had very little doubt of the strict truth of the story we had heard of the security conferred upon those who burnt candles, and yet sometimes serious fears arose in my mind. These thoughts I did my utmost to regard as great sins, and evidences of my want of faith.

It was during that period that I formed a partial acquaintance with several Grey Nuns, who used to come frequently for supplies of candles for their Convent. I had no opportunity to converse with them, except so far as the purchase and sale of the articles they required. I became familiar with their countenances and appearances, but was unable to judge of their characters or feelings. Concerning the rules and habits prevailing in the Grey Nunnery, I therefore remained as ignorant as if I had been a thousand miles off: and they had no better opportunity to learn anything of us, beyond what they could see around them in the room where the candles were sold.

We supplied the Congregational Nunnery also with wax candles, as I before remarked; and in both these institutions, it was understood, a constant illumination was kept up. Citizens were also frequently running in to buy candles in great and small quantities, so that the business of store-keeping was far more laborious than common.

We were confirmed in our faith in the intercession of the Virgin, when we found that we remained safe from cholera; and it is a re-markable fact, that not one case of that disease existed in the Nunnery, during either of the seasons in which it proved so fatal in the city.

When the election riots prevailed at Montreal, the city was thrown into general alarm; we heard some reports from day to day, which made us anxious for ourselves. Nothing, however, gave me any serious thoughts, until I saw uncommon movements in some parts of the Nunnery, and ascertained, to my own satisfaction, that there was a large quantity of gunpowder stored in some secret place within the walls, and that some of it was removed, or prepared for use, under the direction of the Superior.

Penances.—I have mentioned several penances in different parts of this narration, which we sometimes had to perform. There are a great variety of them; and, while some, though trifling in appearance became very painful, by long endurance or frequent repetition, others are severe in their nature, and never would be submitted to, unless, through fear of something worse, or a real belief in their efficacy to remove guilt. I will mention here such as I recollect, which can be named without offending a virtuous ear: for some there were, which although I have been compelled to submit to, either by a misled conscience, or the fear of severe punishment, now that I am better able to judge of my duties, and at liberty to act, I would not mention or describe.

Kissing the floor is a very common penance; kneeling and kissing the feet of the other nuns is another; as are kneeling on hard peas, and walking with them in the shoes. We had repeatedly to walk on our knees through the subterranean passage, leading to the Congregational Nunnery; and sometimes to eat our meals with a rope round our necks. Sometimes we were fed only with such things as we most disliked. Garlic was given to me on this account, because I had a strong antipathy against it.

Eels were repeatedly given some of us, because we felt an unconquerable repugnance to them, on account of reports we heard of their feeding on dead carcasses in the river of St. Lawrence. It was no uncommon thing for us to be required to drink the water in which the Superior had washed her feet. Sometimes we were required to brand ourselves with a hot iron, so as to leave scars; at other times, to whip our naked flesh with several small rods, before a private altar, until we drew blood. I can assert with the perfect knowledge of the fact, that many of the nuns bear the scars of these wounds.

One of the penances was to stand for a length of time with our arms extended, in imitation of the Saviour on the Cross. The *Chemin de la croix*, or Road to the Cross, is, in fact, a penance, though it consists of a variety of prostrations, with the repetition of many prayers, occupying two or three hours. This we had to perform frequently going in chapel, and falling before each chapelle in succession, at each time commemorating some particular act or circumstance reported of the Saviour's progress to the place of his crucifixion. Sometimes we were obliged to sleep on the floor in the winter, with nothing over us but a single sheet; and sometimes to chew a piece of window glass to a fine powder, in the presence of the Superior.

We had sometimes to wear a leathern belt stuck full of sharp metallic points, round our waists and the upper part of our arms, bound on so tight that they penetrated the flesh, and drew blood.

Some of the penances were so severe, that they seemed too much to be endured; and when they were imposed, the nuns who were to suffer them showed the most violent repugnance. They would often resist, and still oftener express their opposition by exclamations and screams.

Never, however, was any noise heard from them for a long time, for there was a remedy always ready to be applied in cases of the kind. The gag which was put into the mouth of the unfortunate Saint Frances, had been brought from a place were there were forty or fifty others of different shapes and sizes. These I have seen in their depository, which is a drawer between two closets, in one of the community-rooms. Whenever any loud noise was made, one of these instruments was demanded, and gagging commenced at once. I have known many instances, and sometimes five or six nuns gagged at once. Sometimes, they would become so much excited before they could be bound and gagged, that considerable force was necessary to be exerted; and I have seen the blood flowing from mouths into which the gag had been thrust with violence.

Indeed I ought to know something of this department of nunnery discipline; I have had it tried upon myself, and can bear witness that it is not only most humiliating and oppressive, but often extremely painful. The mouth is kept forced open, and the straining of the jaws at their utmost stretch, for a considerable time, is very distressing.

One of the worst punishments which I ever saw inflicted, was that with the cap; and yet some of the old nuns were permitted to inflict it at their pleasure. I have repeatedly known them to go for a cap when one of our number has transgressed a rule, sometimes though it were a very unimportant one. These caps were kept in a cupboard in the old nuns' room, whence they were brought when wanted.

They were small, made of a reddish looking leather, fitted closely to the head, and fastened under the chin with a kind of buckle. It was the common practice to tie the nun's hands behind, and gag her before the cap was put on, to prevent noise and resistance. I never saw it worn by any one for a moment, without throwing them into severe sufferings. If permitted they would scream in the most shocking manner, and always writhed as much as their confinement would allow. I can speak from personal knowledge of this punishment, as I have endured it more than once; and yet I have no idea of the cause of the pain. I never examined one of the caps, nor saw the inside, for they are always brought and taken away quickly; but although the first sensation was that of coolness it was hardly put on my head before a violent and indescribable sensation began, like that of a blister, only much more insupportable: and this continued until it was removed. It would produce such an acute pain as to throw us into convulsions, and I think no human being could endure it for an hour. After this punishment, we felt its effects through the system for many days. Having once known what it was by experience, I held the cap in dread, and whenever I was condemned to suffer the punishment again, felt ready to do anything to avoid it. But when tied and gagged, with the cap on my head again, I could only sink upon the floor, and roll about in anguish until it was taken off.

This was usually done in about ten minutes, sometimes less, but the pain always continued in my head for several days. I thought that it might take away a person's reason if kept on a much longer time. If I had not been gagged, I am sure I should have uttered awful screams. I have felt the effects for a week. Sometimes fresh cabbage leaves were applied to my head to remove it. Having had no opportunity to examine my head, I cannot say more.

CHAPTER XVIII.

THE punishment of the Cap—The Priests of the District of Montreal have free access to the Black Nunnery—Crimes committed and required by them—The Pope's command to commit indecent Crimes—Characters of the old and New Superiors—The timidity of the latter—I began to be employed in the Hospitals—Some account of them—Warning given me by a sick Nun—Penance of Hanging.

THIS punishment was occasionally resorted to for very trifling offences, such as washing the hands without permission; and it was generally applied on the spot, and before the other nuns in the community-room.

I have mentioned before, that the country, so far down as Three Rivers, is furnished with priests by the Seminary of Montreal; and that these hundred and fifty men are liable to be occasionally transferred from one station to another. Numbers of them are often to be seen in the streets of Montreal, as they may find a home in the Seminary.

They are considered as having an equal right to enter the Black Nunnery whenever they please; and, then, according to our oaths, they have complete control over the nuns. To name all the works of shame of which they are guilty in that retreat, would require much time and space, neither would it be necessary to the accomplishment of my object, which is, the publication of but some of their criminality to the world, and the development in general terms, of scenes thus far carried on in secret within the walls of that Convent where I was so long an inmate.

Secure against detection by the world, they never believed that an eye-witness would ever escape to tell of their crimes, and declare some of their names before the world; but the time has come, and some of their deeds of darkness must come to the day. I have seen in the Nunnery, the priests from more, I presume, than a hundred country places, admitted for shameful and criminal purposes; from St. Charles, St. Denis, St. Mark's, St. Antoine, Chambly, Bertier, St John's, &c.

How unexpected to them will be the disclosures I make! Shut up in a place from which there has been thought to be but one way of egress, and that the passage to the grave, they considered themselves safe in perpetrating crimes in our presence, and in making us share in their criminality as often as they chose, and conducted more shamelessly than even the brutes.

These debauchées would come in without ceremony, concealing their names, both by night and day. Being within the walls of that prison-house of death, where the cries and pains of the injured inno-cence of their victims would never reach the world for relief or redress for their wrongs, without remorse or shame, they would glory, not only in sating their brutal passions, but even in torturing in the most barbarous manner, the feelings of those under their power; telling us at the same time, that this mortifying the flesh was religion, and pleasing to God. The more they could torture us, or make us violate our own feelings, the more pleasure they took in their unclean revelling; and all their brutal obscenity they called meritorious before God.

We were sometimes invited to put ourselves to voluntary sufferings in a variety of ways, not for a penance, but to show our devotion to God. A priest would sometimes say to us—

"Now, which of you have love enough for Jesus Christ to stick a pin through your cheeks?"

Some of us would signify our readiness, and immediately thrust one through up to the head. Sometimes he would propose that we should repeat the operation several times on the spot; and the cheeks of a number of the nuns would be bloody.

There were other acts occasionally proposed and consented to, which I cannot name in a book. Such the Superior would sometimes command us to perform; many of them, things not only useless and unheard of, but loathsome and indecent in the highest possible degree. How they ever could have been invented, I never could conceive. Things were done worse than the entire exposure of the person, though this was occasionally required of several at once in the presence of priests.

The Superior of the Seminary would sometimes come and inform us, that she had received orders from the Pope, to request that those nuns who possessed the greatest devotion and faith, should be requested to perform some particular deeds, which she named or described in our presence, but of which no decent or moral person could ever endure to speak. I cannot speak what would injure any ear, not debased to the lowest possible degree. I am bound by a regard to truth, however, to confess, that deluded women were found amongst us, who would comply with their requests.

There was a great difference between the characters of our old and new Superiors, which soon became obvious. The former used to say she liked to walk, because it would prevent her from becoming corpulent. She was, therefore, very active, and constantly going about from one part of the Nunnery to another overseeing us at our various employments. I never saw in her any appearance of timidity; she seemed, on the contrary, bold and masculine, and sometimes much more than that, cruel and cold-blooded, in scenes calculated to overcome any common person. Such a character she had particularly exhibited at the murder of St. Frances.

The new Superior, on the other hand, was so heavy and lame, that she walked with much difficulty, and consequently exercised a less vigilant oversight of the nuns. She was also of a timid disposition, or else had been overcome by some great fright in her past life; for she was apt to become alarmed in the night, and never liked to be alone in the dark. She had long performed the part of an old nun, which is that of a spy upon the younger ones, and was well known to us in that character, under the name of St. Margarite. Soon after her promotion to the station of Superior, she appointed me to sleep in her apartment, and assigned me a sofa to lie upon. One night, while I was asleep, she suddenly threw herself upon me, and exclaimed in great alarm,—

"Oh! mon Dieu! mon Dieu! qu'estque ca?" ("Oh! my God! my God! what is that?")

I jumped up and looked about the room, but saw nothing, and endeavoured to convince her that there was nothing extraordinary there. But she insisted that a ghost had come and held her bed-curtain, so that she could not draw it. I examined it, and found that the curtain had been caught by a pin in the valence, which had held it back: but it was impossible to tranquillize her for some time. She insisted on my sleeping with her the rest of the night, and I stretched myself across the foot of her bed, and slept there till morning.

During the last part of my stay in the Convent, I was often employed in attending in the hospitals. There are, as I have before mentioned, several apartments devoted to the sick, and there is a physician of Montreal, who attends as physician to the Convent. It must not be supposed, however, that he knows anything concerning the private hospitals. It is a fact of great importance to be distinctly understood, and constantly borne in mind, that he is never, under any circumstances, admitted into the private hospital-rooms. Of those he sees nothing more than any stranger whatever. He is limited to the care of those patients who are admitted from the city into the public hospital, and one of the nuns' hospitals, and these he visits every day.

Sick poor are received for charity by the institution, attended by some of the nuns, and often go away with the highest ideas of our charitable characters and holy lives. The physician himself might, perhaps, in some cases share in the delusion.

I frequently followed Dr. Nelson through the public hospital, at the direction of the Superior, with pen, ink, and paper, in my hands, and wrote down the prescriptions which he ordered for the different patients. These were afterwards prepared and administered by the attendants.

About a year before I left the Convent, I was first appointed to attend the private sick-rooms, and was frequently employed in that duty up to the day of my departure. Of course I had opportunities to observe the number and classes of patients treated there; and in what I am to say on the subject, I appeal, with perfect confidence, to any true and competent witness to confirm my words, whenever such a witness may appear.

It would be in vain for anybody who has merely visited the Convent from curiosity, or resided in it as a novice, to question my declarations. Such a person must necessarily be ignorant of even the existence of the private rooms, unless informed by some one else. Such rooms, however, there are, and I could relate many things which have passed there during the hours I was employed in them, as I have stated.

One night I was called to sit up with an old nun, named St. Clare, who, in going down stairs, had dislocated a limb, and lay in a sickroom adjoining the hospital. She seemed to be a little out of her head a part of the time, but appeared to be quite in possession of her reason most of the night. It was easy to pretend that she was delirious: but I considered her as speaking the truth, though I felt reluctant to repeat what I heard her say, and excused myself from mentioning it even at confession, on the ground that the Superior thought her deranged.

What led her to some of the most remarkable parts of her conversation was, a motion I made, in the course of the night, to take the light out of her little room into the adjoining apartment, to look once more at the sick persons there. She begged me not to leave her a moment in the dark, for she could not bear it.

"I have witnessed so many horrid scenes," said she, "in this Convent, that I want somebody near me constantly, and must always have a light burning in my room. I cannot tell you," she added, "what things I remember, for they would frighten you too much. What you have seen are nothing to them. Many a murder have I witnessed; many a nice young creature has been killed in this Nunnery. I advise you to be very cautious—keep everything to yourself—there are many here ready to betray you."

What it was that induced the old nun to express so much kindness to me I could not tell, unless she was frightened at the recollection of her own crimes, and those of others, and felt grateful for the care I took of her. She had been one of the night watchers, and never before showed me any particular kindness. She did not indeed go into detail concerning the transactions to which she alluded, but told me that some nuns had been murdered under great aggravations of cruelty, by being gagged, and left to starve in the cells, or having their flesh burned off their bones with red hot irons.

It was uncommon to find compunction expressed by any of the nuns. Habit renders us insensible to the sufferings of others, and careless about our own sins. I had become so hardened myself, that I find it difficult to rid myself of many of my former false principles and views of right and wrong.

I was one day set to wash some empty bottles from the cellar, which had contained the liquid that was poured into the cemetery there. A number of these had been brought from the corner where so many of them where always to be seen, and placed at the head of the cellar stairs, and there we were required to take them, and wash them out. We poured in water and rinsed them; a few drops which got upon our clothes soon made holes in them. I think the liquid was called vitriol, or some such name, and I heard some persons say that it would soon destroy the flesh and even the bones of the dead. At another time, we were furnished with a little of the liquid, which was mixed with a quantity of water, and used in dyeing some cloth black which was wanted at funerals in the chapels. Our hands were turned very black by being dipped in it, but a few drops of some other liquid were mixed with fresh water, and given us to wash in, which left our skin of a bright red.

The bottles of which I spoke were made of very thick dark-coloured glass, large at the bottom, and, I should say, held something less than a gallon.

I was once much shocked, on entering the room for the examination of conscience, at seeing a nun hanging by a cord from a ring in the ceiling, with her head downward. Her clothes had been tied round with a leathern strap, to keep them in their place, and then she had been fastened in that situation, with her head some distance from the floor. Her face had a very unpleasant appearance, being dark coloured, and swollen by the rushing in of the blood; her hands were tied, and her mouth stopped with a large gag. This nun proved to be no other than Jane Ray, who for some fault had been condemned to this punishment.

This was not, however, a solitary case; I heard of numbers who were "hung," as it was called, at different times; and I saw St Hypolite and St. Luke undergoing it. This was considered a most distressing pun-ishment; and it was the only one which Jane Ray could not endure, of all she had tried.

Some of the nuns would allude to it in her presence, but it usually made her angry. It was probably practised in the same place while I was a novice, but I never heard or thought of such a thing in those days. Whenever we wished to enter the room for the examination of conscience, we had to ask leave, and, after some delay, were permitted to go, but always under a strict charge to bend the head forward, and keep the eyes fixed upon the floor.

CHAPTER XIX.

I OFTEN seized an opportunity, when I safely could to speak a cheering or friendly word to one of the poor prisoners, in passing their cells, on my errands in the cellars. For a time I supposed them to be sisters; but I afterwards discovered that this was not the case. I found that they were always under the fear of suffering some punishment, in case they should be found talking with a person not commissioned to attend them. They would often ask, "Is not somebody coming?"

I could easily believe what I heard affirmed by others, that fear was the severest of their sufferings. Confined in the dark, in so gloomy a place, with the long arched cellar stretching off this way and that, visited only now and then by a solitary nun, with whom they were afraid to speak their feelings, and with only the miserable society of each other; how gloomy thus to spend day after day, months, and even years, without prospect of liberation, and liable at any moment to another fate to which, the Bishop or Superior might condemn them. But these poor creatures must have known something of the horrors perpetrated in other parts of the building, and could not have been ignorant of the hole in the cellar, which was not far from the cells, and the use to which it was devoted. One of them told me, in confidence, she wished they could get out. They must also have been often disturbed in their sleep, if they ever did sleep, by the numerous priests who passed through the trap door at no great distance. To be subject to such trials for a single day would be dreadful; but these nuns had them to endure for years.

I often felt much compassion for them, and wished to see them released; but at other times yielding to the doctrine perpetually taught us in the Convent, that our future happiness would be proportioned to the sufferings we had to undergo in this world, I would rest satisfied that their imprisonment was a real blessing to them.

Others I presume, participated with me in such feelings. One Sunday afternoon, after we had performed all our ceremonies, and were engaged as usual, at that time, with backgammon and other amusements, one of the young nuns exclaimed, "Oh! how headstrong are those wretches in the cells, they are as bad as the day they were first put in!"

This exclamation was made, as I supposed, in consequence of some recent conversation with them, as I knew her to be particularly acquainted with the older one.

Some of the vacant cells were occasionally used for temporary imprisonment. Three nuns were confined in them, to my knowledge, for disobedience to the Superior, as she called it. They did not join the rest in singing in the evening, being exhausted in the various exertions of the day. The Superior ordered them to sing: and, as they did not comply, after the command had been twice repeated, she ordered them away to the cells.

They were immediately taken down into the cellar, placed in separate dungeons, and the door shut and barred upon them. There they remained through that night, the following day and second night, but were released in time to attend mass on the second morning.

The Superior used occasionally to show something in a glass box, which we were required to regard with the highest degree of reverence. It was made of wax, and called an Agnus Dei. She used to exhibit it to us when we were in a state of grace: that is, after confession and before sacrament. She said it had been blessed *in the very dish in which our Saviour had eaten*. It was brought from Rome. Every time we kissed it, or even looked at it, we were told it gave a hundred days' release from purgatory to ourselves, or if we did not need it, to our next of kin in purgatory, if not a Protestant. If we had no such kinsman, the benefit was to go to the souls in purgatory not prayed for.

Jane Ray would sometimes say to me, "Let's kiss it—some of our friends will thank us for it."

I have been repeatedly employed in carrying dainties of different kinds into the little private room I have mentioned, next beyond the

Superior's sitting-room, in the second story which the priests made their *"Holy Retreat."* That room I never was allowed to enter. I could only go to the door with a waiter of refreshments, set it down upon a little stand near it, give three raps on the door, and then retire to a distance to await orders. When anything was to be taken away, it was placed on the stand by the Superior, who then gave three raps for me, and closed the door.

The Bishop I saw at least once, when he appeared worse for wine, or something of the kind. After partaking of refreshments in the Convent, he sent for all the nuns, and on our appearance, gave us his blessing, and put a piece of pound cake on the shoulder of each of us, in a manner which appeared singular and foolish.

There are three rooms in the Black Nunnery, which I never entered. I had enjoyed much liberty, and had seen, as I supposed, all parts of the building, when one day I observed an old nun go to a corner of an apartment near the northern end of the western wing, push the end of her scissors into a crack in the panelled wall, and pull out a door. I was much surprised, because I never had conjectured that any door was there; and it appeared, when I afterwards examined the place, that no indication of it could be discovered on the closest scrutiny. I stepped forward to see what was within, and saw three rooms opening into each other: but the nun refused to admit me within the door, which she said led to rooms kept as depositories.

She herself entered and closed the door, so that I could not satisfy my curiosity; and no occasion presented itself. I always had a strong desire to know the use of these apartments; for I am sure they must have been designed for some purpose of which I was intentionally kept ignorant, otherwise they never would have remained unknown to me so long. Besides, the old nun evidently had some strong reason for denying me admission, though she endeavoured to quiet my curiosity.

The Superior, after my admission into the Convent, had told me I had access to every room in the building; and I had seen places which bore witness to the cruelties and the crimes committed under her commands or sanction; but here was a succession of rooms which had been concealed from me, and so constructed as if designed to be unknown to all but a few. I am sure that any person, who might be able to examine the wall in that place, would pronounce that secret door a surprising piece of work. I never saw anything of the kind which appeared to me so ingenious and skilfully made. I told Jane Ray what I had seen, and she said at once, "We will get in and see what is there." But I suppose she never found an opportunity.

I naturally felt a good deal of curiosity to learn whether such scenes, as I had witnessed in the death of St. Frances, were common or rare, and took an opportunity to enquire of Jane Ray. Her reply was—

"Oh yes: and there were many murdered while you were a novice, whom you heard nothing about."

This was all I ever learnt on this subject; but although I was told nothing of the manner in which they were killed, I suppose it to be the same which I had seen practised, namely, by smothering.

I went into the Superior's parlour one day for something, and found Jane Ray there alone, looking into a book with an appearance of interest. I asked her what it was, but she made some trifling answer, and laid it by as if unwilling to let me take it. There are two bookcases in the room; one on the right as you enter the door, and the other opposite, near the window and the sofa. The former contains the lecture-books and other printed volumes, the latter seemed to be filled with note and account books. I have often seen the keys in the bookcases while I have been dusting the furniture, and sometimes observed letters stuck up in the room; although I never looked into one, or thought of doing so. We were under strict orders not to touch any of them, and the idea of sins and penances was always present with me.

Some time after the occasion mentioned, I was sent into the Superior's room with Jane, to arrange it; and as the same book was lying out of the case, she said, "Come let us look into it." I immediately consented, and we opened it, and turned over several leaves. It was about a foot and a half long, as nearly as I can remember, a foot wide, and about two inches thick, though I cannot speak with particular precision, as Jane frightened me almost as soon as I touched it, by exclaiming, "There, you have looked into it, and if you tell of me, I will of you."

The thought of being subjected to a severe penance, which I had reason to apprehend, fluttered me very much: and, although I tried to cover my fears, I did not succeed very well. I reflected, however, that the sin was already committed, and that it would not be increased if I examined the book.

I therefore looked a little at several pages, though I still felt a good deal of agitation. I saw at once that the volume was a record of the entrance of nuns and novices into the Convent, and of the births that had taken place in the Convent. Entries of the last description were made in a brief manner, on the following plan; I do not give the names or dates as real, but only to show the form of entering them,

> Saint Mary, delivered of a son, March 16, 1834.
> Saint Clarice   „   daughter, April 2.
> Saint Matilda   „   daughter, April 30, &c.

No mention was made in the book of the death of the children, though I well knew not one of them could be living at that time.

Now I presume that the period the book embraced was about two years, as several names near the beginning I knew: but I can form only a rough conjecture of the number of infants born, and murdered, of course, records of which it contained. I suppose the book contained at least one hundred pages, and one fourth were written upon, and that each page contained fifteen distinct records. Several pages were devoted to the list of births. On this supposition there must have been a large number, which I can easily believe to have been born there in the course of two years.

What were the contents of the other books belonging to the same case with that which I looked into, I have no idea, having never dared to touch one of them; I believe, however, that Jane Ray was well acquainted with them, knowing, as I do, her intelligence and prying disposition. If she could be brought to give her testimony, she would doubtless unfold many curious particulars now unknown.

I am able, in consequence of a circumstance which appeared accidental, to state with confidence the exact number of persons in the Convent one day of the week in which I left it. This may be a point of some interest, as several deaths have occurred since my taking the veil, and many burials had been openly made in the chapel.

I was appointed, at the time mentioned, to lay out the covers for all the inmates of the Convent, including the nuns in the cells. These covers, as I have said before, were linen bands, to be bound around the knives, forks, spoons, and napkins, for eating. These were for all the nuns and novices, and amounted to two hundred and ten. As the number of novices was then about thirty, I know that there must have been at that time about one hundred and eighty veiled nuns.

I was occasionally troubled with a desire of escaping from the Nunnery, and was much distressed whenever I felt so evil an imagination rise in my mind. I believed that it was a sin, a great sin, and did not fail to confess, at every opportunity, that I felt discontented. My confessors informed me that I was beset with evil spirits, and urged me to pray against it. Still, however, every now and then, I would think, "Oh, if I could get out."

At length one of the priests to whom I had confessed this sin, informed me, for my comfort, that he had begun to pray to Saint Anthony, and hoped his intercession would, by-and-by, drive away the evil spirit. My desire of escape was partly excited by the fear of bringing an infant to the murderous hands of my companions, or of taking a potion whose violent effects I too well knew.

One evening, however, I found myself more filled with a desire of escape than ever: and what exertions I made to dismiss the thought proved entirely unavailing. During evening prayers, I became quite occupied with it; and when the time of meditation arrived, instead of falling into a doze, as I often did, though I was a good deal fatigued, I found no difficulty in keeping awake. When this exercise was over, and the other nuns were about to retire to the sleeping-room, my station being in the private sick-room for the night, I withdrew to my post, which was the little sitting-room adjoining it.

Here, then, I threw myself upon the sofa, and being alone, reflected a few moments on the manner of escaping which had occurred to me. The physician had arrived a little before, at half-past eight; and I had to accompany him as usual from bed to bed, with pen, ink, and paper, to write down his prescriptions for the direction of the old nun, who was to see them administered.

What I wrote on that evening, I cannot now recollect, as my mind was uncommonly agitated: but my customary way was to note down briefly his orders, in this manner—

> 1 d. salts, St. Matilda,
> 1 blister, St Genevieve, &c.

I remember that I wrote three orders that evening, and then having finished the rounds, I returned for a few moments to the sitting-room.

There were two ways of access to the street from these rooms; first, the more direct, from the passage adjoining the sick-room down stairs, through a door, into the Nunnery yard, and through a wicker gate: that is the way by which the physician usually enters at night, and he is provided with a key for that purpose.

It would have been unsafe, however, for me to pass out that way, because a man is kept continually in the yard, near the gate, who sleeps at night in a small hut near the door, to escape whose observation would be impossible. My only hope, therefore, was that I might gain my passage through the other way, to do which I must pass through the sick-room, then through a passage, or small room usually occupied by an old nun; another passage and staircase leading down to the yard, and a large gate opening into the cross street. I had no liberty to go beyond the sick-room, and knew that several of the doors might be fastened; still I determined to try; although I have often since been astonished at my boldness in undertaking what would expose me to so many hazards of failure, and to severe punishment if found out.

It seemed as if I acted under some extraordinary impulse, which encouraged me to what I should hardly at any other moment have thought of undertaking. I had sat but a short time upon the sofa, however, before I rose with a desperate determination to make the experiment. I therefore walked hastily across the sick room, passed into the nun's room, walked by in a great hurry, and almost without giving her time to speak or think, said, "A message!" and in an instant was through the door, and in the next passage. I think there was another nun with her at the moment; and it is probable that my hurried manner, and prompt intimation that I was sent on a pressing mission to the Superior, prevented them from entertaining any suspicion of my intention. Besides, I had the written orders of the physician in my hand, which may have tended to mislead them; and it was well known to some of the nuns, that I had twice left the Convent, and returned from choice, so that I was probably more likely to be trusted to remain than many of the others.

The passage which I had now reached had several doors, with all which I was acquainted; that on the opposite side opened into a community-room, where I should probably have found some of the old nuns at that hour, and they would certainly have stopped me. On the left, however, was a large door, both locked and barred: but I gave the door a sudden swing, that it might creak as little as possible, being of iron. Down the stairs I hurried, and making my way through the door into the yard, stepped across it, unbarred the great gate, and was at liberty!

CONCLUSION.

THE following circumstances comprise all that is deemed necessary now to subjoin to the preceding narrative.

After my arrival in New York, I was introduced to the alms-house, where I was attended with kindness and care, and, as I hoped, was entirely unknown. But when I had been some time in that institution, I found that it was reported that I was a fugitive nun; and not long after, an Irish woman, belonging to the house, brought me a secret message, which caused me some agitation.

I was sitting in the room of Mrs. Johnson, the matron, engaged in sewing, when that Irish woman, employed in the institution, came in and told me that Mr. Conroy was below, and had sent to see me. I was informed that he was a Roman Priest, who often visited the house, and he a had particular wish to see me at that time; having come, as I believe, expressly for that purpose. I showed unwillingness to comply with such an invitation, and did not go.

The woman told me, further, that he sent me word that I need not think to avoid him, for it would be impossible for me to do so. I might conceal myself as well as I could, but I should be found and taken. No matter were I went, or what hiding place I might choose, I should be known; and I had better come at once. He knew who I was; and he was authorized to take me to the Sisters of Charity, if I should prefer to join them. He would promise that I might stay with them if I choose, and be permitted to remain in New York. He sent me word further that he had received full power and authority over me from the Superior of the Hotel Dieu Nunnery at Montreal, and was able to do all that she could do; as her right to dispose of me at her will had been imparted to him by a regular writing received from Canada. This was alarming information for me, in the weakness in which I was at that time. The woman added, that the authority had been given to all the priests; so that go where I might I should meet men informed about me and my escape, and fully empowered to seize me whenever they could, and convey me back to the Convent from which I had escaped.

Under these circumstances, it seemed to me that the offer to place me among the Sisters of Charity with permission to remain in New York, was mild and favourable. However, I had resolution enough to refuse to see priest Conroy.

Not long afterwards I was informed, by the same messenger, that the priest was again in the building, and repeated his request. I desired one of the gentlemen connected with the institution, that a stop might be put to such messages, as I wished to receive no more of them. A short time after, however, the woman told me that Mr. Conroy wished to enquire of me, whether my name was not St. Eustace while a nun, and if I had not confessed to Priest Kelly in Montreal. I answered, that it was all true; for I had confessed to him a short time while in the Nunnery. I was then told again that the priest wanted to see me, and I sent back word that I would see him in the presence of Mr. T— or Mr. S—; which, however, was not agreed to; and I was afterwards informed, that Mr. Conroy, the Roman priest, spent an hour in the room and a passage where I had frequently been; but, through the mercy of God, I was employed at another place at that time, and had no occasion to go where I should have met him. I afterwards repeatedly heard, that Mr. Conroy continued to visit the house, and to ask for me; but I never saw him. I once had determined to leave the institution, and go to the Sisters of Charity; but circumstances occurred which gave me time for further reflection: and I was saved from the destruction to which I should have been exposed.

As the period of my accouchment approached, I sometimes thought that I should not survive it; and then the recollection of the dreadful crimes I had witnessed in the Nunnery would come upon me very powerfully, and I would think it a solemn duty to disclose them before I died. To have a knowledge of those things, and leave the world without making them known, appeared to me like a great sin, whenever I could divest myself of the impression made upon me by the declarations and arguments of the Superior, nuns, and priests, of the duty of submitting to everything, and the necessary holiness of whatever they did or required.

The evening but one before the period which I anticipated with so much anxiety, I was sitting alone, and began to indulge in reflections of this kind. It seemed to me that I must be near the close of my life, and I determined to make a disclosure at once. I spoke to Mrs. Ford, a woman whose character I respected, a nurse in the hospital, number twenty-three. I informed her that I had no expectation of living long, and had some things on my mind which I wished to communicate before it should be too late. I added, that I should prefer telling them to Mr. T.—, the chaplain! of which she approved, as she considered it a duty to do so, under those circumstances. I had no opportunity, however, to converse with Mr. T. at that time, and, probably, my purpose of disclosing the facts already given in this book, would never have been executed, but for what subsequently took place.

It was alarm which led me to form such a determination; and when the period of trial had been safely passed, and I had a prospect of recovery, anything appeared to me more unlikely than that I should make this exposure.

I was then a Roman Catholic, at least a great part of my time; and my conduct, in a great measure, was according to the faith and motives of a Roman Catholic. Notwithstanding what I knew of the conduct of so many of the priests and nuns, I thought that it had no effect on the sanctity of the Church, or the authority or effects of the acts performed by the former at the mass, confession, &c. I had such a regard for my vows as a nun, that I considered my hand as well as my heart irrevocably given to Jesus Christ, and could never have allowed any person to take it. Indeed to this day, I feel an instinctive aversion of offering my hand, or taking the hand of another person, even as an expression of friendship.

I also thought that I might soon return to the Catholics, although fear and disgust held me back. I had now that infant to think for, whose life I had happily saved by my timely escape from the Nunnery; what its fate might be, in case it should ever fall into the power of the priests, I could not tell.

I had, however, reason for alarm. Would a child, destined to destruction, like the infants I had seen baptized and smothered, be allowed to go through the world unmolested, a living memorial of the truth of crimes long practised in security, because never exposed? What pledges could I get to satisfy me, that I, on whom her dependence must be, would be spared by those who, I had reason to think, were wishing then to sacrifice me? How could I trust the helpless infant in hands which had hastened the baptism of many such, in order to hurry them into the secret pit in the cellar? Could I suppose that *Father Phelan, Priest of the Parish Church of Montreal*, would see *his own child* growing up in the world, and feel willing to run the risk of having the truth exposed? What could I expect, especially from him, but the utmost rancour, and the most determined enmity, against the innocent child and its abused and defenceless mother?

Yet, my mind would sometimes still incline in the opposite direction, and indulge the thought, that perhaps the only way to secure heaven to us both was to throw ourselves back into the hands of the Church, to be treated as she pleased.—When, therefore, the fear of immediate death was removed, I renounced all thoughts of communicating the substance of the facts of this volume. It happened, however, that my danger was not passed. I was soon seized with very alarming symptoms; then my desire to disclose my story revived.

I had before had an opportunity to speak in private with the chaplain; but, as it was at a time when I supposed myself out of danger, I had deferred for three days my proposed communication, thinking that I might yet avoid it altogether. When my symptoms, however, became more alarming, I was anxious for Saturday to arrive, the day which I had appointed; and when I had not the opportunity, on that day, which I desired, I thought it might be too late. I did not see him till Monday when my prospects of surviving were very gloomy, and I then informed him that I wished to communicate to him a few secrets, which were likely otherwise to die with me. I then told him, that while a nun, in the Convent of Montreal, I had witnessed the murder of a nun, called Saint Frances, and of at least one of the infants which I have spoken of in this book. I added some few circumstances, and I believe disclosed, in general terms, some of the crimes I knew of in that Nunnery.

My anticipations of death proved to be unfounded; for my health afterwards improved, and had I not made the confessions on that occasion, it is very possible I never might have made them. I, however, afterwards, felt more willing to listen to instruction, and experienced friendly attentions from some of the benevolent persons around me, who, taking an interest in me on account of my darkened understanding, furnished me with the Bible, and were ever ready to counsel me when I desired it.

I soon began to believe that God might have intended that his creatures should learn his will by reading his word, and taking upon them the free exercise of their reason, and acting under responsibility to him.

It is difficult for one who has never given way to such arguments and influences as those to which I had been exposed, to realize how hard it is to think aright, after thinking wrong. The Scriptures always affect me powerfully when I read them; but I feel that I have but just begun to learn the great truths, in which I ought to have been early and thoroughly instructed. I realize, in some degree, how it is, that the Scriptures render the people of the United States so strongly opposed to such doctrines as are taught in the Black and Congregational Nunneries of Montreal. The priests and nuns used often to declare that of all heretics, the children from the United States were the most difficult to be converted; and it was thought a great triumph when one of them was brought over to "the true faith." The first passage of Scripture that made any serious impression upon my mind, was the text on which the chaplain preached on the Sabbath after my introduction to the house,—"Search the Scriptures."

EXTRACTS FROM PUBLIC JOURNALS, RELATIVE TO THE TRUTH OF MARIA MONK'S DISCLOSURES.

The following certificate appeared in the Protestant Vindicator, in March, 1836.

WE, the Subscribers, have an acquaintance with Miss Maria Monk, and having considered the evidence of different kinds which has been collected in relation to her case, have no hesitation in declaring our belief in the truth of the Statements she makes in her book, recently published in New York, entitled 'Awful Disclosures,' &c.

"We at the same time declare that the assertion, originally made in the Roman Catholic Newspapers of Boston, that the book was copied from a work entitled 'The Gates of Hell opened,' is wholly destitute of foundation; it being entirely new, and not copied from anything whatsoever.

"And we further declare, that no evidence has been produced which discredits the statements of Miss Monk; while, on the contrary, her story has yet received, and continues to receive, confirmation from various sources.

"During the last week, two important witnesses spontaneously appeared, and offered to give public testimony in her favour. From them the following delineations have been received. The first is an affidavit given by Mr. William Miller, now a resident of this city. The second is a statement received from a young married woman, who, with her husband, also resides here. In the clear and repeated statements made by these two witnesses, we place entire reliance; who are ready to furnish satisfaction to any persons making reasonable enquiries on the subject.

"W. C. BROWNREE," "AMOS BELDEN," "JOHN J. SLOCUM," "DAVID WESSON," "ANDREW BRUCE," "THOMAS HOGAN," "D. FANSHAW."

From the American Protestant Vindicator.

"IT was expected that, after Maria Monk's disclosures, an artful attempt would be made to invalidate her testimony—which was done secretly after her escape from the Hotel Dieu Nunnery, by so altering the appearance of that institution by planking, and bricking, and stoning, as to deceive Col. Stone, who was then requested to examine it for himself and the world. The Col. misrepresented what he saw, he was deceived regarding those alterations by the inmates, who dragged him, as it were, by force through the building during his examination, which was performed in the amazing short space of a few hours. But time is the grand unraveller of mysteries. On the appearance of the book of Miss Monk, the hoodwinked people of Montreal were so surprised and stupefied at finding that the immaculate purity of the Hotel Dieu had been so disparaged, that they *forgot* to think seriously on the subject—but, understanding that the story had gained almost general belief abroad, they, at last, were led to conjecture that perhaps it was partiality that prevented them from believing it at home. General attention, therefore, in Montreal, was directed towards that edifice—and those residing in its immediate vicinity cast a retrospective glance over what they had seen transacted there, between the time at which the 'Disclosures' were published, and the visit of Col. Stone. The result of this investigation has been lately given on the spot to the Rev. Jas. P. Miller, of New York, who visited that city for the purpose of hearing that the truth was gradually coming to light. The neighbours informed Mr. Miller that about the time it was rumoured that she had exposed the institution, a mysterious pile of planks, twenty-five feet in height, had been placed mysteriously in the yard, which were wonderfully and gradually used in progressing some improvements in the building—for they were neither employed outside nor hauled away.

"Whatever may be the fact with regard to Maria Monk's alleged disclosures, those of our people who have read your papers, are satisfied in one point: that Mr. Stone's credibility as a witness has been successfully impeached; that his examination of the Nunnery, was a mere sham; that he was either the dupe of Jesuitical imposture, or that he himself is a fond impostor; that he has been unwillingly or ignorantly befooled; and unless he has had a tangible reward, that he has 'got his labour for his pains.'

"Whatever may be the facts in relation to those 'disclosures,' we needed not your paper to satisfy us either that Jesuits must be as holy as the 'Blessed Virgin Mother' herself, or those conventicles of unprotected females are scenes of the most damning character.—A PROTESTANT."

From the Long Island Star, of Feb. 29th.

"SINCE the publication of our last paper, we have received a communication from Messrs. Howe and Bates, of New York, the publishers of Miss Monk's 'Awful Disclosures.' It appears that some influence has been at work in that city, adverse to the free examination of the case between her and the priests of Canada; for thus far the newspapers have been most entirely closed against everything in her defence, whilst most of them have published false charges against the book, some of a preposterous nature, the contradiction of which is plain and palpable.

"Returning to New York, she then first resolved to publish her story, which she has recently done, after several intelligent disinterested persons had satisfied themselves by much examination that it is true.

"When it became known in Canada that this was her intention, six affidavits were published in some of the newspapers, intended to destroy confidence in her character; but these were found very contradictory in several important points, and in others to afford undesigned confirmation of statements before made by her.

"On the publication of her book, the New York Catholic Diary, the Truth-teller, the Green Banner, and other papers, made virulent attacks upon it, and one of them proposed that the publishers should be 'lynched.' An anonymous handbill was also circulated in New York, declaring the work a malignant libel, got up by Protestant clergymen, and promising an ample refutation of it in a few days. This was re-published in the Catholic Diary, with the old Montreal affidavits, which were distributed through New York and Brooklyn; and on the authority of these, several Protestant newspapers denounced the work as false and malicious.

"Another charge, quite inconsistent with the rest, was made, by the leading Roman Catholic papers and others, viz., that it was a mere copy of an old European work. This had been promptly denied by the publishers with the offer of 100 dollars reward for any book at all resembling it.

"Yet such is the resolution of some, and the unbelief of others, that it is impossible for the publishers to obtain insertions for the replies in the New York papers generally, and they have been unsuccessful in an attempt at Philadelphia.

"This is the ground on which the following article has been offered to us, for publication in the Star. It was offered to Mr. Schneller, a Roman Priest, and Editor of the Catholic Diary, for insertion in his paper of Saturday before last, but refused, although written expressly as an answer to the affidavits and charges his previous number had contained. This article has been refused insertion in a Philadelphia paper, after it had been satisfactorily ascertained that there was no hope of gaining admission for it into any of the New York papers.

"It should be stated in addition, that the authoress of the book, Maria Monk, is in New York, and stands ready to answer any questions, and submit to any enquiries put in a proper manner, and desires nothing so strongly as an opportunity to prove before a court the truth of her story. She has already found persons of respectability who have confirmed some of the facts, important and likely to be attested by concurrent evidence; and much further testimony in her favour may be soon expected.

"With these facts before them, intelligent readers will judge for themselves. She asks for investigation, while her opponents deny her every opportunity to meet the charges made against her. Mr. Schneller, after expressing a wish to see her, to the publishers, refused to meet her anywhere, unless in his own house; while Mr. Quarter, another Roman Catholic priest, called to see her, at ten o'clock one night, accompanied by another man, without giving their names, and under the false pretence of being bearers of a letter from her brother in Montreal.

ADDITIONAL INFORMATION.

CHAPTER I.

AT liberty—Doubtful what to do—Found refuge for the night—Disappointment—My first day out of the Convent—Solitude—Recollections, fears, and plans.

I HAVE but a confused idea of the manner in which I got through some of the doors; several of them, I am confident, were fastened, and one or two I fastened behind me.* But I was now in the street, and what was to be done next? I had got my liberty; but where should I go? It was dark, I was in great danger, go which way I would; and for a moment, I thought I had been unwise to leave the convent. If I could return unobserved, would it not be better? But summoning resolution, I turned to the left, and ran some distance up the street; then reflecting that I had better take the opposite direction, I returned under the same convent walls, and ran as fast down to St. Paul's street, then turning up towards the north, exerted all my strength, and fled for my life. It was a cold evening, but I stopped for nothing, having recollected the house where I had been put to board for a short time, by the priest Roque, when prepared to enter the convent as a novice, and resolved to seek a lodging there for the night. Thither I went. It seemed as if I flew rather than ran. It was by that time so dark, that I was able to see distinctly through the low windows, by the light within; and had the pleasure to find that she was alone with her children. I therefore went boldly to the door, was received with readiness, and entered to take up my lodgings there once more.

Here I changed my nun's dress for one less likely to excite observation; and having received a few dollars in addition to make up the difference, I retired to rest, determined to rise early and take the

---

* Before leaving the nunnery grounds, I ran round the end of the building, stood a moment in hesitation whether I had not better return, then hastening back to the other side, ran to the gate, opened it and went out.

morning steamboat for Quebec. I knew that my hostess was a friend
of the Superior, as I have mentioned before, and presumed that it
would not be long before she would give information against me. I
knew, however, that she could not gain admittance to the convent
very early, and felt safe in remaining in the house through the night.

But after I had retired I found it impossible to sleep, and the night
appeared very long. In the morning early, I requested that the son of
the woman might accompany me to the boat, which he did. At an
early hour, therefore, I walked to the steamboat, but learnt, to my
regret, that it would not go before night. Fearing that I might fall into
the hands of the priests, and be carried back to the nunnery, and not
knowing where to go, I turned away, and determined to seek some
retired spot immediately. I walked through a part of the city, and some
distance on the Lachine road, when finding a solitary place, I seated
myself in much distress of mind, both fearful and anxious, beyond
my power of description. I could not think myself safe anywhere in
the neighbourhood of Montreal; for the priests were numerous, and
almost all the people were entirely devoted to them. They would be
very desirous of finding me, and, as I believed, would make great
exertions to get me again in their hands.

It was a pleasant spot where I now found myself, and as the weather
was not uncomfortable in the day time, I had nothing to trouble me
except my recollections and fears. As for the want of food, that gave
me not the slightest uneasiness, as I felt no inclination whatever to
eat. The uncertainty and doubts I continually felt, kept me in a state
of irresolution the whole day. What should I do? Where should I go?
I had not a friend in the world to whom I could go with confidence;
while my enemies were numerous, and, it seemed to me, all around
me, and ready to seize me. I thought of my uncle, who lived at the
distance of five miles; and sometimes I almost determined to set off
immediately for his house. I had visited it often when a child, and
have been received with the utmost kindness. I remembered that I
had been a great favourite of his; but some considerations would
arise which discouraged me from looking for safety in that direction.
The steamboat was to depart in a few hours. I could venture to pass

through the city once more by twilight; and if once arrived at Quebec, I should be at a great distance from the nunnery, in a large city, and among a larger proportion of Protestant inhabitants. Among them I might find friends, or, at least, some sort of protection; and I had no doubt that I could support myself by labour.

Then I thought again of the place I had left; the kindness and sympathy, small though they were, which I had found in some of my late companions in the convent; the awful mortal sin I had committed in breaking my vows; and the terrible punishments I should receive if taken as a fugitive and carried back. If I should return voluntarily, and ask to be admitted again: what would the Superior say, how would she treat me? Should I be condemned to any very severe penance? Might I not, at least, escape death? But then there was one consideration that would now and then occur to me, which excited the strongest determination never to return. I was to become a mother, and the thought of witnessing the murder of my own child was more than I could bear.

Purgatory was doubtless my portion; and perhaps hell for ever—such a purgatory and hell as are painted in the convent: but there was one hope for me yet.

I might confess all my deadly sins sometime before I died, and a Bishop could pardon the worst of them.

This was good Catholic doctrine, and I rested upon it with so much hope, that I was not quite driven to despair.

In reflections like these, I spent the whole day, afraid to stray from the secluded spot to which I had retreated, though at different times forming momentary plans to leave it, and go in various directions. I ate not a morsel of food, and yet felt no hunger. Had I been well provided, I could have tasted nothing in such a state of mind. The afternoon wasted away, the sun set, and darkness began to come on. I rose and set off again for the city. I passed along the streets unmolested by any one; and reached it a short time before the boat was ready to start.

CHAPTER II.

SOON after we left the shore, the captain, whom I had previously seen, appeared to recognize me.

He came up and inquired if I was not the daughter of my mother, mentioning her name. I had long been taught and accustomed to deceive; and it may be supposed that in such a case, I did not hesitate to deny the truth, hoping that I might avoid being known, and fearing to be defeated in my object. He however persisted that he knew me, and said that he must insist on my returning with him to Montreal, adding that I must not leave his boat to land at Quebec. I said but little to him, but intended to go on shore if possible, at the end of our journey—a thing I had no doubt I might effect.

When we reached Quebec, however, I found, to my chagrin, that the ladies' maid carefully locked the cabin-door while I was in, after the ladies had left it, who were six or eight in number.

I said little, and made no attempts to resist the restriction put upon me; but secretly cherished the hope of being able, by watching an opportunity, to slip on shore at tea-time, and lose myself among the streets of the city. Although a total stranger to Quebec, I longed to be at liberty there, as I thought I could soon place myself among persons who would secure me from the Catholics, each of whom I now looked upon as an enemy.

But I soon found that my last hopes were blighted; the maid, having received, as I presumed, strict orders from the captain, kept me closely confined, so that escape was impossible. I was distressed, it is true, to find myself in this condition; but I had already become accustomed to disappointments, and therefore perhaps sunk less under this new one, than I might otherwise have done. When the hour for departure arrived, I was therefore still confined in the steamboat, and it was not until we had left the shore that I was allowed to leave the cabin. The captain and others treated me with kindness in every respect, except that of permitting me to do what I most desired. I have sometimes suspected, that he had received notice of my escape from some of the priests, with a request to stop my flight, if I should go on board his boat. His wife is a Catholic, and this is the only way in which I can account for his conduct: still I have not sufficient knowledge of his motives and intentions to speak with entire confidence on the subject.

My time passed heavily on board of the steam-boat, particularly on my passage up the river towards Montreal. My mind was too much agitated to allow me to sleep, for I was continually meditating on the scenes I had witnessed in the convent, and anticipating with dread such as I had reason to think I might soon be called to pass through, I bought for a trifle while on board, I hardly know why, a small medallion with a head upon it, and the name of Robertson, which I hung upon my neck. As I sat by day with nothing to do, I occasionally sunk into a doze for a few minutes, when I usually waked with a start from some frightful dream. Sometimes I thought I was running away from the priests, and closely pursued, and sometimes had no hope of escape. But the most distressing of my feelings were those I suffered in the course of the night. We stopped some time at Berthier, where a number of prisoners were taken on board, to be carried up the river; and this caused much confusion, and added to my painful reflections.

My mind became much agitated, worse than it had been before; and what between waking fears, and sleeping visions, I spent a most wretched night. Sometimes I thought the priests and nuns had me shut up in a dungeon: sometimes they were about to make away with me in a most cruel manner. Once I dreamed that I was in some house, and a coach came up to the door, into which I was to be put by force; and the man who seized me, and was putting me in, had no head.

When we reached Montreal on Saturday morning, it was not day-light; and the captain, landing, set off, as I understood, to give my mother information that I was in his boat. He was gone a long time, which led to conjecture that he might have found difficulty in speaking with her; but the delay proved very favourable to me, for perceiving that I was neither locked up nor watched, I hastened on shore, and pursued my way into the city. I felt happy at my escape: but what was I then to do? Whither could I go? Not to my mother; I was certain I could not remain long with her, without being known to the priests. My friendlessness and utter helplessness, with the dread of being murdered in the convent, added to the thoughts of the shame that must await me if I lived a few months, made me take a desperate resolution, and I hurried to put it into effect.

My object was to reach the head of the Lachine canal, which is near the St. Lawrence, beyond the extremity of the southern suburbs. I walked hastily along St Paul's-street, and found all the houses still shut; then turning to the old Recollet Church, I reached Notre-Dame-street, which I followed in the direction I wished to go.

The morning was chilly, as the season was somewhat advanced; but that was of no importance to me. Day had appeared, and I desired to accomplish the object on which I was now bent, before the light should much increase. I walked on therefore, but the morning had broken bright before I arrived at the canal; and then I found to my disappointment, that two Canadians were at work on the bank, getting water, or doing something else.

I was by the great basin where the boats start, and near the large canal storehouse. I had not said what was my design: it was to drown myself.

Fearing the men would rescue me, I hesitated for some time, hoping they would retire: but finding that they would not, I grew impatient. I stood looking on the water; it was nearly on a level with the banks, which shelved away, as I could perceive for some distance, there being no wind to disturb the surface. There was nothing in the sight which seemed frightful or even forbidding to me; I looked upon it as the means of the easiest death, and longed to be buried below. At length finding that the men were not likely to leave the place, I sprang from the bank, and was in an instant in the cold water. The shock was very severe. I felt a sharp freezing sensation run through me, which almost immediately rendered me insensible; and the last thing I can recollect was, that I was sinking in the midst of water almost as cold as ice, which wet my clothes, and covered me all over.

CHAPTER III.

AWAKE among strangers—Dr. Robertson—Imprisoned as a Vargrant—Introduction to my Mother—Stay in her House—Removal from it to Mrs. McDonald's—Return to my Mother's—Desire to get to New York—Arrangements for going.

HOW long I remained in the canal I know not; but in about three minutes, as I conjectured, I felt a severe blow on my right side; and opening my eyes I saw myself surrounded by men who talked a great deal, and expressed much anxiety and curiosity about me. They inquired of me my name, where I lived, and why I had thrown myself into the water; but I would not answer a word. The blow which I had felt, and which was probably the cause of bringing me for a few moments to my senses, I presume was caused by falling, after I was rescued, upon the stones, which lay thickly scattered near the water. I remember that the persons around me continued to press me with questions, and that I still remained silent. Some of them having observed the little medallion on my neck, and being able to read, declared that I was probably a daughter of Dr. Robertson, as it bore the name; but to this, I also gave no answer, and sunk again into a state of unconsciousness.

When my senses once more returned, I found myself lying in a bed covered up warm, in a house, and heard several persons talking of the mass, from which they had just returned. I could not imagine where I was, for my thoughts were not easily collected, and everything seemed strange around me. Some of them on account of the name on the little medallion, had sent to Dr. Robertson, to inform him that a young woman had been prevented from drowning herself in the basin, who had a portrait on her neck, with his family name stamped upon it; and he had sent word, that although she could be no relation of his, they had better bring her to his house, as he possibly might be able to learn who she was. Preparations were therefore made to conduct me thither; and I was soon in his house. This was about midday, or a little later.

The doctor endeavoured to draw from me some confession of my family; but I refused; my feelings would not permit me to give him any satisfaction. He offered to send me to my home if I would tell him where I lived; but at length, thinking me unreasonable and obstinate, began to threaten to send me to jail.

In a short time I found that the latter measure was determined on, and I was soon put into the hands of the jailer, Captain Holland, and placed in a private room in his house.

I had formerly been acquainted with his children, but had such strong reasons for remaining unknown that I hoped they would not recognize me; and, as we had not met for several years, I flattered myself that such would be the case. It was, at first, as I had hoped, they saw me in the evening, but did not appear to suspect who I was.

The next morning, however, one of them asked me if I were not sister of my brother, mentioning his name, and though I denied it, they all insisted that I must be, for the likeness, they said, was surprisingly strong. I still would not admit the truth; but requested they would send for the Rev. Mr. Esson, a Presbyterian clergyman in Montreal, saying I had something to say to him. He soon made his appearance, and I gave him some account of myself, and requested him to procure my release from confinement, as I thought there was no reason why I should be deprived of my liberty.

Contrary to my wishes, however, he went and informed my mother. An unhappy difference had existed between us for many years, concerning which I would not speak, were it not necessary to allude to it, to render some things intelligible which are important to my narrative. I am willing to bear much of the blame, for my drawing part of the pension had justly irritated her. I shall not attempt to justify or explain my own feelings with respect to my mother, whom I still regard, at least in some degree, as I ought. I will merely say, that I thought she indulged in partialities and antipathies in her family during my childhood, and that I attribute my entrance into the nunnery, and the misfortunes I have suffered, to my early estrangement from home, and my separation from the family. I had neither seen her nor heard from her for several years; and knew not whether she had even known of my entrance into the convent, although I now learnt that she still resided where she formerly did.

It was therefore with regret that I heard that my mother had been informed of my condition; and that I saw an Irishwoman, an acquaintance of hers, come to take me to the house. I had no doubt that she would think that I had disgraced her, by being imprisoned, as well as by my attempt to drown myself; and what would be her feelings towards me, I could only conjecture.

I accompanied the woman to my mother's, and found nearly such a reception as I had expected. Notwithstanding our mutual feelings were much as they had been, she wished me to stay with her, and kept me in one of her rooms for several weeks, and with the utmost privacy, fearing that my appearance would lead to questions, and that my imprisonment would become known.

I soon satisfied myself that she knew little of what I had passed through, within the few past years; and did not think it prudent to inform her, for that would greatly have increased the risk of my being discovered by the priests. We were surrounded by those who went frequently to confession, and would have thought me a monster of wickedness, guilty of breaking the most solemn vows, and a fugitive from a retreat which is generally regarded there as a place of great sanctity, and almost like a gate to heaven. I well knew the ignorance and prejudices of the poor Canadians, and understood how such a person as myself must appear in their eyes. They felt as I formerly had, and would think it a service to religion and to God to betray the place of my concealment, if by chance they should find, or even suspect it. As I had become in the eyes of Catholics, "a spouse of Jesus Christ," by taking the veil, my leaving the convent must appear to them a forsaking of the Saviour.

As things were, however, I remained for some time undisturbed. My brother, though he lived in the house, did not know of my being there for a fortnight.

When he learnt it, and came to see me he expressed much kindness towards me: but I had not seen him for several years, and had seen so much evil, that I knew not what secret motives he might have, and thought it prudent to be reserved. I, therefore, communicated to him nothing of my history or intentions, and rather repulsed his advances. The truth is, I had been so long among nuns and priests, that I thought there was no sincerity or virtue on earth.

What were my mother's wishes or intentions towards me, I was not informed: but I found afterwards, that she must have made arrangements to have me removed from her house, for one day a woman came to the door with a carriage, and on being admitted to see me, expressed herself in a friendly manner, spoke of the necessity of air and exercise for my health, and invited me to take a ride. I consented, supposing we should soon return; but when we reached St. Antoine suburbs, she drove up to a house which I had formerly heard to be some kind of refuge, stopped, and requested me to alight. My first thought was, that I should be exposed to certain detection, by some of the priests whom I presumed officiated there; as they had all known me in the nunnery. I could not avoid entering; but I resolved to feign sickness, hoping thus to be placed out of sight of the priests.

The result was according to my wishes: for I was taken to an upper room, which was used as an infirmary and there permitted to remain. There were a large number of women in the house; and a Mrs. M'Donald, who has the management of it, had her daughters in the Ursuline Nunnery at Quebec, and her son in the College. The nature of the establishment I could not fully understand: but it seemed to me designed to become a Nunnery at some future time.

I felt pretty safe in the house, as long as I was certain of remaining in the infirmary; for there was nobody there who had ever seen me before. But I resolved to avoid, if possible, ever making my appearance below, for I felt that I could not do so without hazard of discovery.

Among other appendages of a Convent, which I observed in that place, was a confessional within the building, and I soon learnt, to my dismay, that Father Bonin, one of the murderers of Saint Frances, was in the habit of constant attendance as priest and confessor. The recollections which I often indulged in of scenes in the Hotel Dieu, gave me uneasiness and distress: but not knowing where to go to seek greater seclusion, I remained in the infirmary week after week, still affecting illness in the best manner I could.

At length I found that I was suspected of playing off a deception with regard to the state of my health; and at the close of a few weeks, I became satisfied that I could not remain longer without making my appearance below stairs. I at length complied with the wishes I heard expressed, that I would go into the community-room, where those in health were accustomed to reassemble at work, and then some of the women began to talk of my going to confession.

I merely expressed unwillingness at first: but when they pressed the point, and began to insist, my fear of detection overcame every other feeling, and I plainly declared that I would not go. This led to an altercation, when the mistress of the house pronounced me incorrigible, and said she would not keep me for a hundred pounds a year. She, in fact, became so weary of having me there, that she sent to my mother to take me away.

My mother, in consequence, sent a carriage for me, and took me again into her house; but I became so unhappy in a place where I was secluded and destitute of all agreeable society, that I earnestly requested her to allow me to leave Canada. I believe she felt ready to have me removed to a distance, that she might not be in danger of having my attempt at self-destruction, and my confinement in prison made public.

There was a fact which I had not disclosed, and of which all were ignorant: viz., that which had so much influence in exciting me to leave the convent, and to reject every idea of returning to it.

When conversing with my mother about leaving Canada, I proposed to go to New York. She inquired why I wished to go there. I made no answer to that question; for though I had never been there, and knew scarcely anything about the place, I presumed that I should find protection from my enemies, as I knew it was in a Protestant country. I had not thought of going to the United States before, because I had no one to go with me, nor money enough to pay my expenses; but then a plan presented itself to my mind, by which I thought I might proceed to New York in safety.

There was a man who I presumed would wish to have me leave Canada, on his own account; and that was the man I had so precipitately married while residing at St. Denis. He must have had motives, as I thought, for wishing me at a distance.* I proposed, therefore, that he should be informed that I was in Montreal, and anxious to go to the States, and such a message was sent to him by a woman whom my mother knew. She had a little stand for the sale of some articles, and had a husband who carried on some similar kind of business at the Scotch mountain. Through her husband, as I suppose, she had my message conveyed, and soon informed me that arrangements were made for my commencing my journey, under the care of the person to whom it had been sent.

* He was liable to be prosecuted for bigamy whilst she remained in Canada.—ED.

CHAPTER IV.

SINGULAR concurrence of circumstances, which enabled me to get to the United States—Intentions in going there—Commence my journey—Fears of my companion—Stop at Whitehall—Injury received in a canal boat—Arrival at New York—A solitary retreat.

IT is remarkable that I was able to stay so long in the midst of Catholics without discovery, and at last obtain the aid of some of them in effecting my flight. There is probably not a person in Montreal who would sooner have betrayed me into the power of the priests than that woman, if she had known my history.

She was a frequent visitor at the Convent and the Seminary, and had a ticket which entitled her every Monday to the gift of a loaf of bread from the former. She had an unbounded respect for the Superior and the priests, and seized every opportunity to please them. Now the fact that she was willing to take measures to facilitate my departure from Montreal, afforded sufficient evidence to me of her entire ignorance of myself, in all respects in which I could wish her to be ignorant; and I confided in her, because I perceived that she felt no stronger motive, than a disposition to oblige my mother.

Should anything occur to let her into the secret of my being a fugitive from the Black Nunnery, I knew that I could not trust to her kindness for an instant. The discovery of that fact would transform her into a bitter and deadly enemy. She would at once regard me as guilty of mortal sin, an apostate, and a proper object of persecution. And this was a reflection I had often reason to make, when thinking of the numerous Catholics around me. How important, then, the keeping of my secret, and my escape before the truth should become known, even to a single person near me.

I could realize, from the dangers through which I was brought by the hand of God, how difficult it must be, in most cases, for a fugitive from a nunnery to obtain her final freedom from the power of her enemies. Even if escaped from a convent, so long as she remains among Catholics, she is in constant exposure to be informed against; especially if the news of her escape is made public, which fortunately was not the fact in my case.

If a Catholic comes to the knowledge of any fact calculated to expose such a person, he will think it his duty to disclose it at confession; and then the whole fraternity will be in motion to seize her.

How happy for me that not a suspicion was entertained concerning me, and that not a whisper against me was breathed into the ear of a single priest at confession!

Notwithstanding my frequent appearance in the streets, my removals from place to place, and the various exposures I had to discovery, contrary to my fears, which haunted me even in my dreams, I was preserved; and as I have often thought, for the purpose of making the disclosures contained in this volume. No power but that of God, as I have frequently thought, could ever have led me in safety through so many dangers.

I would not have my readers imagine, however, that I had at that period any thought of making known my history to the world. I wished to plunge into the deepest possible obscurity; and next to the fear of falling into the hands of the priests and Superior, I shrunk most from the idea of having others acquainted with the scenes I had passed through. Such a thought as publishing never entered my mind till months after that time. My desire was, that I might meet with a speedy death in obscurity, and that my name and my shame might perish on earth together. As for my future doom, I still looked forward to it with gloomy apprehensions: for I considered myself as almost, if not quite, removed beyond the reach of mercy. During all the time which had elapsed since I left the convent, I had received no religious instruction, nor even read a word in the scriptures; and, therefore, it is not wonderful that I should still have remained under the delusions in which I had been educated.

The plan arranged for the commencement of my journey was this; I was to cross the St. Lawrence to Longueil, to meet the man who was to accompany me. The woman who had sent my message into the country, went with me to the ferry, and crossed the river, where, according to appointment, we found my companion. He willingly undertook to accompany me to the place of my destination, and at his own expense; but declared, that he was apprehensive we should be pursued. To avoid the priests who, he supposed would follow us, he took an indirect route, and during about twelve days, or nearly that, which we spent on the way, passed over a much greater distance than was necessary. It would be needless, if it were possible, to mention all the places we visited. We crossed Carpenter's ferry, and were at Scotch-mountain and St. Albans; arrived at Champlain by land, and there took the steamboat, leaving it again at Burlington.

As we were riding towards Charlotte, my companion entertained fears, which, to me, appeared ridiculous; but it was impossible for me to reason him out of them, or to hasten our journey. Circumstances which appeared to me of no moment whatever, would often influence, and sometimes make him change his whole plan and direction. As we were one day approaching Charlotte, for instance, on inquiring of a person on the way, whether there were any Canadians there, and being informed that there were not a few, and that there was a Roman Catholic Priest residing there, he immediately determined to avoid the place, and turn back, although we were then only about nine miles distant from it.

During several of the first nights after leaving Montreal, he suffered greatly from fear; and on meeting me in the morning, repeatedly said: "Well, thank God, we are safe so far!" When we arrived at Whitehall, he had an idea that we should run a risk of meeting priests, who, he thought, were in search of us, if we went immediately on; and insisted that we had better stay there a little, until they should have passed. In spite of my anxiety to proceed, we accordingly remained there about a week, when we entered a canal-boat to proceed to Troy.

An unfortunate accident happened to me while on our way. I was in the cabin, when a gun, which had been placed near me, was started from its place by the motion of the boat, caused by another boat running against it, and striking me on my left side, threw me to some distance. The shock was violent, and I thought myself injured, and hoped the effects would soon pass off. I was afterward taken with vomiting blood; and this alarming symptom several times returned: but I was able to keep up.

We came, without any unnecessary delay, from Troy to New York, where we arrived in the morning, either on Thursday or Friday, as I believe: but my companion there disappeared without informing me where he was going, and I saw him no more. Being now, as I presumed, beyond the reach of my enemies, I felt relief from the fear of being carried back to the nunnery, and sentenced to death or the cells; but I was in a large city where I had not a friend. Feeling overwhelmed with my miserable condition, I longed for death; and yet I felt no desire to make another attempt to destroy myself.

On the contrary, I determined to seek some solitary retreat, and await God's time to remove me from a world in which I had found so much trouble, hoping and believing that it would not be long.

Not knowing which way to go to find solitude, I spoke to a little boy whom I saw on the wharf, and told him I would give him some money if he would lead me into the "bush." (This is the common word by which, in Canada, we speak of the woods or forests). When he understood what I meant, he told me that there was no *bush* about New York; but consented to lead me to the most lonely place that he knew of. He accordingly set off, and I followed him, on a long walk to the upper part of the city, and beyond, until we reached the outskirts of it. Turning off from the road, we gained a little hollow, where were a few trees and bushes, a considerable distance from any house; and there he told me, was the loneliest place with which he was acquainted. I paid him for his trouble out of the small stock of money I had in my possession, and let him go home, desiring him to come the next day, and bring me something to eat, with a few pennies which I gave him.

CHAPTER V.

Reflection and sorrows in solitude—Night—Fears—Exposure to rain—
Discovered by Strangers—Their unwelcome kindness—Taken to the Bellevue Almshouse.

THERE I found myself once more alone, and truly it was a great
relief to sit down and feel that I was out of reach of the priests
and nuns, and in a spot where I could patiently wait for death, when
God might please to send it, instead of being abused and tormented
according to the caprices and passions of my persecutors.

But then again returned most bitter anticipations of the future. Life
had no attractions for me, for it must be connected with shame; but
death, under any circumstances, could not be divested of horrors,
so long as I believed in the doctrines relating to it which had been
inculcated upon me.

The place where I had taken up, as I supposed, my last earthly abode,
was pleasant in clear and mild weather; and I spent most of my time
in as much peace as the state of my mind would permit. I saw houses,
but no human beings, except on the side of a little hill near by, where
were some men at work, making sounds like those made in hammering
stone. The shade around me was so thick that I felt assured of being
sufficiently protected from observation if I kept still; and a cluster of
bushes offered me a shelter for the night. As evening approached, I was
somewhat alarmed by the sound of voices near me, and found that a
number of labourers were passing that way from their work. I went
in a fright to the thickest of the bushes, and lay down, until all was
again still, and then ventured out to take my seat again on the turf.

Darkness now came gradually on; and with it, fears of another description. The thought struck me that there might be wild beasts in
that neighbourhood, ignorant as I then was of the country; and the
more I thought of it, the more I became alarmed. I heard no alarming
sound, it is true; but I knew not how soon some prowling ferocious
beast might come upon me in my defenceless condition, and tear me
in pieces. I retired to my bushes, and stretched myself under them

upon the ground: but I found it impossible to sleep; and my mind was continually agitated by thoughts on the future or the past.

In the morning the little boy made his appearance again, and brought me a few cakes which he had purchased for me. He showed much interest in me, inquired why I did not live in a house; and it was with difficulty that I could satisfy him to let me remain in my solitary and exposed condition. Understanding that I wished to continue unknown, he assured me that he had not told even his mother about me; and I had reason to believe that he faithfully kept my secret to the last. Though he lived a considerable distance from my hiding place, and, as I supposed, far down in the city, he visited me almost every day, even when I had not desired him to bring me anything. Several times I received from him some small supplies of food for the money I had given him. I once gave him a half-dollar to get changed; and he brought me back every penny of it, at his next visit.

As I had got my drink from a brook or pool, which was at no great distance, he brought me a little cup one day to drink out of; but this I was not allowed to keep long, for he soon after told me that his mother wanted it, and he must return it. He several times arrived quite out of breath, and when I inquired the reason, calling him as I usually did, "Little Tommy," he said it was necessary for him to run, and to stay but a short time, that he might be at school in good season. Thus he continued to serve me, and keep my secret, at great inconvenience to himself, up to the last day of my stay in that retreat; and I believe he would have done so for three months if I had remained there. I should like to see him again, and hear his broken English.

I had now abundance of time to reflect on my lost condition; and many a bitter thought passed through my mind, as I sat on the ground, or strolled about by day, and lay under the bushes at night.

Sometimes I reflected on the doctrines I had heard at the nunnery, concerning sins and penances, Purgatory and Hell; and sometimes on my late companions, and the crimes I had witnessed in the convent.

Sometimes I would sit and seriously consider how I might best destroy my life; and sometimes would sing a few of the hymns with which I was familiar; but I never felt willing or disposed to pray, as I supposed there was no hope of mercy for me.

One of the first nights I spent in that houseless condition was stormy; and though I crept under the thickest of the bushes, and had more protection against the rain than one might have expected, I was almost entirely wet before morning; and, it may be supposed, passed a more uncomfortable night than usual. The next day I was happy to find the weather clear, and was able to dry my garments by taking off one at a time, and spreading them on the bushes. A night or two after, however, I was again exposed to a heavy rain, and had the same process afterward to go through with: but what is remarkable, I took no cold on either occasion; nor did I suffer any lasting injury from all the exposures I underwent in that place. The inconveniences I had to encounter, also, appeared to me of little importance, not being sufficient to draw off my mind from its own troubles; and I had no intention of seeking a more comfortable abode, still looking forward only to dying as soon as God would permit, alone and in that spot.

One day, however, when I had been there about ten days, I was alarmed at seeing four men approaching me. All of them had guns, as if out on a shooting excursion. They expressed much surprise and pity on finding me there, and pressed me with questions. I would not give them any satisfactory account of myself, my wants, or intentions, being only anxious that they might withdraw. I found them, however, too much interested to render me some service to be easily sent away; and after some time, thinking there would be no other way, I pretended to go away not to return. After going some distance, and remaining some time, thinking they had left the place, I returned; but to my mortification found they had concealed themselves to see whether I would come back. They now, more urgently than before, insisted on my removing to some other place, where I might be comfortable. They continued to question me; but I became distressed in a degree I cannot describe, hardly knowing what I did. At last I called the oldest gentleman aside, and told him something of my history. He expressed great interest for me, offered to take me anywhere I would tell him, and at last insisted that I should go with him to his own house. All these offers I refused; on which one proposed to take me to the Almshouse, and even to carry me by force if I would not go willingly.

To this I at length consented; but some delay took place, and I became unwilling, so that with reluctance I was taken to that institution, which was about half a mile distant.*

---

* See the affidavit of Mr. Hilliker, page 97, "Confirmation of Maria Monk's Disclosures."—ED. [Page 232 in this edition]

CHAPTER VI.

I WAS now at once made comfortable, and attended with kindness and care. It is not to be expected in such a place, where so many poor and suffering people are collected, and duties of a difficult nature are to be daily performed by those engaged in the care of the institution, that petty vexations should not occur to individuals of all descriptions.

But in spite of all, I received kindness and sympathy from several persons around me, to whom I feel thankful.

I was standing one day at the window of the room number twenty-six, which is at the end of the hospital building, when I saw a spot I once visited in a little walk I took from my hiding-place. My feelings were different now in some respects, from what they had been; for, though I suffered much from my fears of my future punishment, for the sin of breaking convent vows, I had given up the intention of destroying my life. (Maria Monk here repeats her confession to the Rev. Mr. Tappin, Chaplain of the Almshouse as in pages 136 to 141.)*

I made some hasty notes of the thoughts to which it gave rise in my mind, and often recurred to the subject. Yet I sometimes questioned the justice of the views I began to entertain, and was ready to condemn myself for giving my mind any liberty to seek for information concerning the foundation of my former faith.

---

* Pages 136–140 in this edition.

CHAPTER VII.

PROPOSITION to go to Montreal and testify against the Priests—Commencement of my journey—Stop at Troy, Whitehall, Burlington, St. Alban's, Plattsburgh, and St. John's—Arrival at Montreal—Reflections on passing the Nunnery, &c.

ABOUT a fortnight after I had made the disclosures mentioned in the last chapter, Mr. Hoyt called at the Hospital to make inquiries about me. I was introduced to him by Mr. Tappin. After some conversation, he asked me if I would consent to visit Montreal, and give my evidence against the priests and nuns before a court. I immediately expressed my willingness to do so, on condition that I should be protected. It immediately occurred to me, that I might enter the Nunnery at night, and bring out the nuns in the cells, and possibly Jane Ray, and that they would confirm my testimony.

In a short time arrangements were made for our journey. I was furnished with clothes; and although my strength was as yet but partially restored, I set off in pretty good spirits.

Our journey was delayed for a little time, by Mr. Hoyt's waiting to get a companion. He had engaged a clergyman to accompany us, as I understood, who was prevented from going by unexpected business. We went to Troy in a steam-boat; and, while there, I had several interviews with some gentlemen who were informed of my history, and wished to see me. They appeared to be deeply impressed with the importance of my testimony; and on their recommendation it was determined that we should go to St. Alban's on our way to Montreal, to get a gentleman to accompany us, whose advice and assistance, as an experienced lawyer, were thought to be desirable to us in prosecuting the plan we had in view: viz., the exposure of the crimes with which I was acquainted.

We travelled from Troy to Whitehall in a canal packet, because the easy motion was best adapted to my state of health. We met, on board, the Rev. Mr. Sprague, of New York, with whom Mr. Hoyt was acquainted, and whom he tried to persuade to accompany us to Montreal.

From Whitehall to Burlington we proceeded in a steamboat; and there I was so much indisposed, that it was necessary to call a physician. After a little rest, we set off in the stage for St. Alban's; and on arriving, found that Judge Turner was out of town. We had to remain a day or two before he returned; and then he said it would be impossible for him to accompany us. After some deliberation, it was decided that Mr. Hunt should go to Montreal with us, and that Judge Turner should follow and join us there as soon as his health and business would permit.*

We therefore crossed the lake by the ferry to Plattsburg, where, after some delay, we embarked in a steamboat, which took us to St. John's. Mr. Hunt, who had not reached the ferry early enough to cross with us, had proceeded on to * * *, and there got on board the steamboat in the night. We went on to Laprairie with little delay, but finding that no boat was to cross the St. Lawrence at that place during the day, we had to take another private carriage to Longueil, whence we were rowed across to Montreal by three men, in a small boat.

I had felt quite bold and resolute when I first consented to go to Montreal, and also during my journey: but when I stepped on shore in the City, I thought of the different scenes I had witnessed there, and of the risks I might run before I should leave it. We got into a caleche, and rode along towards the hotel where we were to stop. We passed up St Paul's street; and, although it was dusk, I recognised everything I had known.

We came at length to the nunnery; and then many recollections crowded upon me. First I saw a window from which I had sometimes looked at some of the distant houses in that street; and I wondered whether some of my old acquaintances were employed as formerly. But I thought that if I were once within those walls, I should soon be in the cells for the remainder of my life, or perhaps be condemned to something still more severe. I remembered the murder of St. Francis, and the whole scene returned to me as if it had just taken place; the appearance, language and conduct of the persons most active in her

---

* Mr. Hunt was recommended as a highly respectable lawyer; to whose kindness, as well as to that of Judge Turner, I feel myself under obligations.

destruction. These persons were now all near me, and would use all exertions they safely might, to get me again into their power.

And certainly they had greater reason to be exasperated against me, than against that poor helpless nun who had only expressed a wish to escape.*

When I found myself safely in Goodenough's hotel, in a retired room, and began to think alone, the most gloomy apprehensions filled my mind. I could not eat, I had no appetite, and I did not sleep all night. Every painful scene I had ever passed through, seemed to return to my mind; and such was my agitation, I could fix my thoughts upon nothing particular. I had left New York when the state of my health was far from being established; and my strength, as may be presumed, was now much reduced by the fatigue of travelling. I shall be able to give but a faint idea of the feelings with which I passed that night,

---

* My gloomy feelings, however, did not always prevail. I had hopes of obtaining evidence to prove my charges. I proposed to my companions to be allowed to proceed that evening to execute the plan I had formed when a journey to Montreal had first been mentioned. This was, to follow the physician into the nunnery, conceal myself under the red calico sofa in the sitting-room, find my way into the cellar after all was still, release the nuns from their cells, and bring them out to confirm my testimony. I was aware that there were hazards of my not succeeding, and that I must forfeit my life if detected—but I was desperate; and feeling as if I could not long live in Montreal, thought I might as well die one way as another, and that I had better die in the performance of a good deed. I thought of attempting to bring out Jane Ray—but that seemed quite out of the question, as an old nun is commonly engaged in cleaning a community-room through which I should have to pass: and how could I hope to get into and out of the sleeping-room unobserved? I could not even determine that the imprisoned nuns would follow me out—for they might be afraid to trust me. However, I determined to try, and, presuming my companions had all along understood and approved my plan, told them I was ready to go at once. I was chagrined and mortified more than I can express, when they objected, and almost refused to permit me. I insisted, and urged the importance of the step—but they represented its extreme rashness. This conduct of theirs, for a time, diminished my confidence in them, although everybody else has approved of it.

but must leave it to the imagination of my readers.

Now once more in the neighbourhood of the convent, and surrounded by the nuns and priests, of whose conduct I had made the first disclosures ever known, surrounded by thousands of persons devoted to them, and ready to proceed to any outrage, as I feared, whenever their interference might be desired, there was abundant reason for my uneasiness.

I now began to realise that I had some attachment to life remaining. When I consented to visit the city, and furnish the evidence necessary to lay open the iniquity of the convent, I had felt, in a measure, indifferent to life; but now, when torture and death seemed at hand, I shrunk from it. For myself, life could not be said to be of much value. How could I be happy with such things to reflect upon as I had passed through? and how could I enter society with gratification? But my infant I could not abandon, for who would care for it if its mother died?

I was left alone in the morning by the gentlemen who had accompanied me, as they went to take immediate measures to open the intended investigation. Being alone, I thought of my own position in every point of view, until I became more agitated than ever. I tried to think what persons I might safely apply to as friends; and, though still undecided what to do, I arose, thinking it would be unsafe to remain any longer exposed, as I imagined myself, to be known and seized by my enemies.

I went from the hotel*, hurried along, feeling as if I were on my way to some asylum, and thinking I would first go to the house where I had several times previously found a temporary refuge. I did not stop to reflect that the woman was a devoted Catholic and friend to the Superior; but thought only of her kindness to me on former occasions,

---

* It occurred to me, that I might have been seen by some person on landing, who might recognize me if I appeared in the streets in the same dress; and I requested one of the female servants to lend me some of hers. I obtained a hat and shawl from her, with which I left the house. When I found myself in Notre Dame street, I felt the utmost indecision what to do, and the thought of my friendless condition almost overpowered me.

and hastened along Notre Dame street. But I was approaching the Seminary; and a resolution was suddenly formed to go and ask the pardon and intercession of the Superior. Then the character of Bishop Lartique seemed to present an impossible obstacle; and the disagreeable aspect and harsh voice of the man, as I recalled him, struck me with horror. I recollected him as I had known him when engaged in scenes concealed from the eye of the world. The thought of him made me decide not to enter the Seminary. I hurried, therefore, by the door; and the great church being at hand, my next thought was to enter there. I reached the steps, walked in, dipped my finger into the holy water, crossed myself, turned to the first image I saw, which was that of Saint Magdalen, threw myself upon my knees, and began to repeat prayers with the utmost fervour. I am certain that I never felt a greater desire to find relief from any of the Saints; but my agitation hardly seemed to subside during my exercise, which continued, perhaps, a quarter of an hour or more. I then rose from my knees, and placed myself under the protection of St. Magdalen and St. Peter by these words: "*Je me mets sous votre protection*"—(I place myself under your protection;) and added, "*Sainte Marie, mere du bon pasteur, prie pour moi*"—(Holy Mary, mother of the good shepherd, pray for me.)

I then resolved to call once more at the house where I had found a retreat after my escape from the nunnery, and proceeded along the streets in that direction. On my way, I had to pass a shop kept by a woman* I formerly had an acquaintance with. She happened to see me passing, and immediately said, "Maria, is that you? Come in."

I entered, and she soon proposed to me to let her go and tell my mother that I had returned to the city. To this I objected. I went with her, however, to the house of one of her acquaintances near by, where I remained some time, during which she went to my mother's and came with a request from her, that I would have an interview with her, proposing to come up and see me, and saying that she had something very particular to say to me. What this was, I could not with any certainty conjecture. I had my suspicions that it might be something from the priests, designed to get me back into their power,

---

* This was Mrs. Tarbert.

or, at least, to suppress my testimony.

I felt an extreme repugnance to seeing my mother, and in the distressing state of apprehension and uncertainty in which I was, could determine on nothing, except to avoid her. I therefore soon left the house, and walked on without any particular object. The weather was then very unpleasant, and it was raining incessantly. To this I was very indifferent, and walked on till I had got through the suburbs, and found myself beyond the windmills. Then I returned, and passed back through the city, still not recognized by anybody.

I once saw one of my brothers, unless I was much mistaken, and thought he knew me. If it was he, I am confident he avoided me, and that was my belief at the time, as he went into the yard with the appearance of much agitation. I continued to walk up and down most of the day, fearful of stopping anywhere, lest I should be recognized by my enemies, or betrayed into their power. I felt all the distress of a feeble, terrified woman, in need of protection, and, as I thought, without a friend in whom I could safely confide. It distressed me extremely to think of my poor babe; and I had now been so long absent from it, as necessarily to suffer much inconvenience.

I recollected to have been told, in the New York Hospital, that laudanum would relieve distress both bodily and mental, by a woman who urged me to make a trial of it. In my despair, I resolved to make an experiment with it, and entering an apothecary's shop, asked for some. The apothecary refused to give me any; but an old man who was there told me to come in, inquired where I had been, and what was the matter with me, seeing that I was quite wet through. I let him know that I had an infant, and on his urging me to tell more, I told him where my mother lived. He went out, and soon after returned, accompanied by my mother, who told me she had my child at home, and pressed me to go to her house and see it, saying she would not insist on my entering, but would bring it out to me.

I consented to accompany her; but on reaching the door, she began to urge me to go in, saying I should not be known to the rest of the family, but might stay there in perfect privacy. I was resolved not to comply with this request, and resisted all her entreaties, though she continued to urge me for a long time, perhaps half an hour. At length she went in, and I walked away, in a state no less desperate than before. Indeed, night was approaching, the rain continued, and I had no prospect of food, rest, or even shelter. I went on till I reached the parade-ground, unnoticed, I believe, by anybody, except one man, who asked where I was going, but to whom I gave no answer. I had told my mother, before she left me that she might find me in the parade-ground. There I stopped, in a part of the open ground where there was no probability of my being observed, and stood thinking of the many distressing things which harrassed me; suffering, indeed, from exposure to wet and cold, but indifferent to them as evils of mere trifling importance, and expecting that death would soon ease me of my present sufferings. I had hoped that my mother would bring my babe to me there; but as it was growing late, I gave up all expectations of seeing her.

At length she came, accompanied by Mr. Hoyt, who, as I afterwards learnt, had called on her after my leaving the hotel, and at her request, had entrusted my child to her care. Calling again after I had left her house, she had informed him that she now knew where I was, and consented to lead him to the spot. I was hardly able to speak or to walk, in consequence of the hardships I had undergone; but being taken to a small inn, and put under the care of several women, I was made comfortable with a change of clothes and a warm bed.

CHAPTER VIII.

RECEIVED into a hospitable family—Fluctuating feelings—Visits from several persons—Father Phelan's declarations against me in his church—Interviews with a Journeyman Carpenter—Arguments with him.

IN the morning I received an invitation to go to the house of a respectable Protestant, an old inhabitant of the city, who had been informed of my situation; and although I felt hardly able to move, I proceeded thither in a carriage, and was received with a degree of kindness, and treated with such care, that I must ever retain a lively gratitude towards the family.

On Saturday I had a visit from Doctor Robertson, to whose house I had been taken soon after my rescue from drowning. He put a few questions to me and soon withdrew.

On Monday, after the close of mass, a Canadian man came in, and entered into conversation with the master of the house in an adjoining room. He was, as I understood, a journeyman carpenter, and a Catholic, and having heard that a fugitive nun was somewhere in the city, began to speak on the subject in French. I was soon informed that Father Phelan had just addressed his congregation with much apparent excitement about myself; and thus the carpenter had received his information. Father Phelan's words, according to what I heard said by numerous witnesses, at different times, must have been much like the following:—

"There is a certain nun now in this city, who has left our faith, and joined the Protestants. She has a child, of which she is ready to swear I am the father. She would be glad in this way to take away my gown from me. If I knew where to find her I would put her in prison. I mention this to guard you against being deceived by what she may say. The devil has such a hold upon people now-a-days, that there is danger that some might believe her story."

Before he concluded his speech, as was declared, he burst into tears, and appeared to be quite overcome. When the congregation had been dismissed, a number of them came round him, and he told some of them that I was Antichrist; I was not a human being, as he was convinced, but an evil spirit, who had got among the Catholics, and being admitted into the nunnery, where I had learnt the rules so that I could repeat them. My appearance, he declared, was a fulfilment of prophecy, as Antichrist is foretold to be coming, in order to break down, if possible, the Catholic religion.

The journeyman carpenter had entered the house, where I lodged under these impressions, and had conversed some time on the subject, without any suspicion that I was near. After he had railed against me with such violence, as I afterwards learned, the master of the house informed him that he knew something of the nun, and mentioned that she charged the priests of the Seminary with crimes of an awful character; in reply to which the carpenter expressed the greatest disbelief.

"You can satisfy yourself," said the master of the house, "if you will take the trouble to step upstairs, for she lives in my family."

"I see her!" he exclaimed—"No, I would not see the wretched creature for anything. I wonder you are not afraid to have her in your house.—She will bewitch you all.—The evil spirit!"

After some persuasion, however, he came into the room where I was sitting, but looked at me with every appearance of dread and curiosity: and his exclamations, and subsequent conversation, in Canadian French, were very ludicrous.

"Eh bin," he began on first seeing me, "c'est ici la malheureuse?" (Well, is this the poor creature?) But he stood at a distance, and looked at me with curiosity and evident fear. I asked him to sit down, and tried to make him feel at his ease, by speaking in a mild and pleasant tone. He soon became so far master of himself, as to enter into conversation.

"I understood," said he, "that she has said very hard things against the priests. How can that be true?" "I can easily convince you," said I, "that they do what they ought not, and commit crimes of the kind I complain of. You are married, I suppose?" He assented. "You confessed, I presume, on the morning of your wedding-day?" He acknowledged that he did. "Then did not the priest tell you at confession, that he had had intercourse with your intended bride, but that it was for her sanctification, and that you must never reproach her with it?"

This question instantly excited him, but he did not hesitate a moment to answer it. "Yes," replied he, "and that looks black enough." I had put the question to him, because I knew the practice to which I alluded had prevailed at St. Denis while I was there, and believed it to be universal, or at least very common in all the Catholic parishes of Canada. I thought I had reason to presume that every Catholic, married in Canada, had had such experience, and that an allusion to the conduct of the priest, in this particular, must compel any of them to admit that my declarations were far from being incredible. This was the effect on the mind of the simple mechanic, and from that moment he made no more serious questions concerning my truth and sincerity during that interview.

Further conversation ensued, in the course of which I expressed the willingness which I have often declared, to go into the convent and point out things which would confirm, to any doubting person, the truth of my heaviest accusations against the priests and nuns. At length he withdrew, and afterward entered, saying, that he had been to the convent to make inquiries concerning me. He assured me that he had been told that, although I had once belonged to the nunnery, I was called St. Jacques, and not St. Eustace; and that now they would not own or recognize me. Then he began to curse me, but yet sat down, as if disposed for further conversation. It seemed as if he was affected by the most contrary feelings, and in rapid succession. One of the things he said, was to persuade me to leave Montreal. "I advise you," said he, "to go away tomorrow." I replied, that I was in no haste, and might stay a month longer.

Then he fell to cursing me once more; but the next moment broke out against the priests, calling them all the names he could think of. His passion became so high against them, that he soon began to rub himself, as the low Canadians, who are apt to be very passionate, sometimes do, to calm their feelings, when they are excited to a painful degree. After this explosion he again became quite tranquil, and turning to me, in a frank and friendly manner, said, "I will help you in your measures against the priests; but tell me, first—you are going to print a book, are you not?" "No," said I, "I have no thoughts of that."

Then he left the house again, and soon returned, saying, he had been at the Seminary, and seen a person who had known me in the nunnery, and said I had been only a novice, and that he would not acknowledge me now. I sent back word by him, that I would show one spot in the nunnery that would prove I spoke the truth. Thus he continued to go and return several times, saying something of the kind every time, until I became tired of him. He was so much enraged once or twice during some of the interviews, that I felt somewhat alarmed; and some of the family heard him swearing as he went down stairs: "Ah, sacre—that is too black!"

He came at last, dressed up like a gentleman, and told me he was ready to wait on me to the nunnery. I expressed my surprise that he should expect me to go with him alone, and told him I had never thought of going without some protector, still assuring him, that, with any person to secure my return, I would cheerfully go all over the nunnery, and show sufficient evidence of the truth of what I alleged.

My feelings continued to vary: I was sometimes fearful, and sometimes so courageous as to think seriously of going into the Recolet church during mass with my child in my arms, and calling upon the priest to own it. And this I am confident I should have done, but for the persuasions used to prevent me.*

---

* I did not make up my mind (so far as I remember), publicly to proclaim who was the father of my child, unless required to do so, until I learned that Father Phelan had denied it.

CHAPTER IX.

A milkman—An Irishwoman—Difficulty of having my Affidavit taken—
Legal objection to it when taken.

ANOTHER person who expressed a desire to see me was an Irish
milkman. He had heard, what had seemed to be pretty generally
reported, that I blamed none but the Irish priests. He put the question, whether it was a fact that I accused nobody but Father Phelan. I
told him it was not so, and this pleased him so well, that he told me,
if I would stay in Montreal, I should have milk for myself and child
as long as I lived. It is well known that strong antipathies have long
existed between French and Irish Catholics in that city.

The next day the poor Irishman returned, but in a very different
state of mind. He was present at church in the morning, he said, when
Father Phelan told the congregation that the nun of whom he had
spoken before, had gone to court and accused him; and that he, by
the power he possessed, had struck her powerless as she stood before
the judge, so that she sunk helpless on the floor. He expressed, by the
motion of his hands the unresisting manner in which she had sunk
under the mysterious influence, and declared that she would have
died on the spot, but that he had chosen to keep her alive that she
might retract her false accusation. This, he said she did, most humbly,
before the court, acknowledging that she had been paid a hundred
pounds as a bribe.

The first words of the poor milkman, on revisiting me, therefore,
were like these: "That's to show you what power the priest has! Didn't
he give it you in the court? It is to be hoped you will leave the city
now." He then stated what he had heard Father Phelan say, and expressed his entire conviction of its truth, and the extreme joy he felt on
discovering, as he supposed he had, that his own priest was innocent,
and had gained such a triumph over me.

A talkative Irishwoman also made her appearance, among those who
called at the house, and urged for permission to see me. Said she, "I
have heard dreadful things are told by a nun you have here, against

the priests; and I have come to convince myself of the truth. I want to see the nun you have got in your house." When informed that I was unwell, and not inclined at present to see any more strangers, she still showed much disposition to obtain an interview. "Well, aint it too bad," she asked, "that there should be any reason for people to say such things against the priests?" At length she obtained admittance to the room where I was, entered with eagerness, and approached me.

"Arrah," she exclaimed, "God bless you—is this you? Now sit down, and let me see the child. And it is Father Phelan's, God bless you? But they say you tell about murders; and I want to know if they are all committed by the Irish priests." "Oh no," replied I, "by no means." "Then God bless you," said she. "If you will live in Montreal, you shall never want. I will see that neither you nor your child ever want, for putting part of the blame upon the French priests. I am going to Father Phelan, and I shall tell him about it. But they say you are an evil spirit. I want to know whether it is so or not." "Come here," said I, "feel me, and satisfy yourself. Besides, did you ever hear of an evil spirit having a child?"

I heard from those about me, that there was great difficulty in finding a magistrate willing to take my affidavit. I am perfectly satisfied that this was owing to the influence of the priests to prevent my accusations against them from being made public. One evening, a lawyer who had been employed for the purpose, accompanied me to a French justice with an affidavit ready prepared in English for his signature, and informed him that he wished him to administer to me the oath. Without any apparent suspicion of me, the justice said, "Have you heard of the nun who ran away from the convent, and has come back to the city, to bear witness against the priests?" "No matter about that now," replied the lawyer hastily; "I have no time to talk with you—will you take this person's oath now or not?" He could not read a word of the document, because it was not in his own language, and soon placed his signature at the bottom. It proved however, that we had gained nothing by this step, for the lawyer afterward informed us, that the laws required the affidavit of a nun and a minor to be taken before a superior magistrate.

CHAPTER X.

INTERVIEW with the Attorney General of the Province—Attempt to abduct me—More interviews—A mob excited against me—Protected by two soldiers—Convinced that an investigation of my charges could not be obtained—Departure from Montreal—Closing reflections.

THOSE who had advised to the course to be pursued, had agreed to lay the subject before the highest authorities. They soon came to the conviction that it would be in vain to look for any favour from the Governor, and resolved to lay it before the Attorney General as soon as he should return from Quebec. After waiting for some time he returned; and I was informed, in a few days that he had appointed an interview on the following morning. I went at the time with a gentleman of the city, to the house of Mr. Grant, a distinguished lawyer. In a short time a servant invited us to walk upstairs, and we went; but after I had entered a small room at the end of a parlour, the door was shut behind me by Mr. Ogden, the Attorney General. A chair was given me, which was placed with the back towards a bookcase, at which a man was standing, apparently looking at the books: and besides the two persons I have mentioned, there was but one more in the room,* Mr. Grant, the master of the house. Of the first part of the interview I shall not particularly speak.

The two legal gentlemen at length began a mock examination of me, in which they seemed to me to be actuated more by a curiosity no way commendable, than a sincere desire to discover the truth, writing down a few of my answers. In this, however, the person behind me took no active part. One of the questions put to me was,—

"What are the colours of the carpet in the Superior's room?"

I told what they were, when they turned to him, and inquired whether I had told the truth. He answered only by a short grunt of assent, as if afraid to speak, or even to utter a natural tone; and at the same time by his hastiness, showed that he was displeased that my answer was correct. I was asked to describe a particular man I had

---

* Unless another was concealed—as I suspected.

seen in the nunnery, and did so. My examiner turned partly round with some remark or question which was answered in a similar spirit. I turned and looked at the stranger, who was evidently skulking to avoid my seeing him, and yet listening to every word that was said. I saw enough in his appearance to become pretty well satisfied that I had seen him before; and something in his form or attitude reminded me strongly of the person whose name had been mentioned. I was then requested to repeat some of the prayers used in the Nunnery, and repeated part of the office of the Virgin, and some others.

At length, after I had been in the little room, as I could judge, nearly an hour, I was informed that the examination had been satisfactory, and that I might go.

I then returned home; but no further step was taken by the Attorney General, and he refused, as I understood, to return my affidavit, which had been left in his hands to act upon.

Besides the persons I have mentioned, I had interviews with numbers of others. I learnt from some, that Father Phelan addressed his congregation a second time concerning me, and expressly forbade them to speak to me if they should have an opportunity, on pain of excommunication. It was also said, that he prayed for the family I lived with, that they might be converted.

I repeated to several different persons my willingness to go into the nunnery, and point out visible evidences of the truth of my statements; and when I was told by one man, who said he had been to the priests, that I had better leave the city, or I would be clapped into prison, I made up my mind that I should like to be imprisoned a little while, because then, I thought, I could not be refused a public examination.

Some Canadians were present one day, when the mistress of the house repeated, in my presence, that I was ready to go into the nunnery if protected, and, if I did not convince others of the truth of my assertions, that I would consent to be burned.

"O yes, I dare say," replied one of the men—"the devil would take her off,—she knows he would. He would take care of her—we should never be able to get her—the evil spirit."

A woman present said—

"I could light the fire to burn you, myself."

A woman of Montreal, who has a niece in the nunnery, on hearing of what I declared about it, said that if it was true she would help to tear it down.

Among those who came to see me, numbers were at first as violent as any I have mentioned, but after a little conversation, became mild and calm. I have heard persons declare, that it would be no harm to kill me, as I had an evil spirit.

One woman told me, that she had seen Father Phelan in the street, talking with a man, to whom he said, that the people were coming to tear down the house in which I stayed, intending afterward to set fire to it in the cellar. This story gave me no serious alarm, for I thought I could see through it evidence of an intention to frighten me, and make me leave the city.*

I was under great apprehensions, however, one day, in consequence of an accidental discovery of a plan laid to take me off by force. I had stepped into the cellar to get an ironholder, when I heard the voices of persons in the street above, and recognised those of my mother and the Irishwoman her friend. There was another woman with them.

"You go in and lay hold of her," said one voice.

"No, you are her mother—you go in and bring her out—we will help you."

I was almost overcome with dread of falling into their hands, believing that they would deliver me up to the Superior. Hastening into a room, I got behind a bed, told the lady of the house the cause of my fear, and calling to a little girl to bring me my child, I stood in the state of violent agitation. Expecting them in the house every instant, and fearing my infant might cry, and lead them to the place of my concealment, I put my hand upon its mouth to keep it quiet.

---

* I felt very confident, from some circumstances, that this woman had been sent to bring such a story by Father Phelan; and such evidence of his timidity rather emboldened me. I was in another room when she came, and heard her talking on and abusing me; then coming out, I said, "How dare you say I do not speak the truth?" "God bless you," said she, "sit down and tell me all."

It was thought desirable to get the testimony of the mistress of the house where I spent the night, after my escape from the nunnery, as one means of substantiating my story. I had been there the day before my visit to the house of Mr. Grant, accompanied by a friend, and on my first inquiring of her about my nunnery dress, she said she had carried it to the Superior; speaking with haste, as if she apprehended I had some object very different from what I actually had. It now being thought best to summon her as a witness before a magistrate, and not knowing her whole name, we set off again towards her house to make inquiry.

On our way we had to pass behind the parade. I suddenly heard an outcry from a little gallery in the rear of a house which fronts another way, which drew my attention.

"There's the nun, there's the nun!" exclaimed a female, after twice clapping her hands smartly together, "There's the nun, there's the nun."

I looked up, and whom should I see but the Irishwoman, who had taken so active a part, on several occasions, in my affairs, on account of her friendship for my mother, the same who had accompanied me to Longeuil in a boat, when I set out for New York, after making arrangements for my journey. She now behaved as if exasperated against me to the utmost; having, as I had no doubt, learnt the object of my journey to Montreal since I had last spoken with her, and having all her Catholic prejudices excited. She screamed out:

"There's the nun that's come to swear against our dear Father Phelan. Arrah, lay hold, lay hold upon her! Catch her, kill her, pull her to pieces."

And so saying she hurried down to the street, while a number of women, children, and some men, came running out, and pursued after me. I immediately took to flight, for I did not know what they might do; and she, with the rest, pursued us, until we reached two soldiers, whom we called upon to protect us. They showed a readiness to do so; and when they learnt that we were merely going to a house beyond, and intended to return peaceably, consented to accompany us. The crowd, might rather be called a mob, thought proper not to offer us any violence in the presence of the soldiers, and after following us a little distance, began to drop off, until all had disappeared. One of the soldiers, however, soon after remarked, that he observed a man following us, whom he had seen in the crowd, and proposed that instead of both of them going before us, one should walk behind, to guard against any design he might have. This was done; and we proceeded to a house near the one where I had found a refuge, and after obtaining the information we sought, returned, still guarded by the soldiers.

All our labour in this case, however, proved unavailing; for we were unable to get the woman to appear in court.

At length it was found impossible to induce the magistrates to do anything in the case; and arrangements were made for my return to New York. While in the ferry-boat crossing from Montreal to Laprairie, I happened to be standing near two little girls, when I overheard the following conversation.

"Why do you leave Montreal so soon?"

"I had gone to spend a week or two; but I heard that Antichrist was in the city, and was afraid to be there. So I am going right home. I would not be in Montreal while Antichrist is there. He has come to destroy the Catholic religion."

I felt quite happy when I found myself once more safe in New York; and it has only been since my return from Montreal, and the conviction I had there formed, that it was in vain for me to attempt to get a fair investigation into the Hotel Dieu Nunnery, that I seriously thought of publishing a book.

CHAPTER XI.

RECOLLECTIONS of several things which happened at different periods—Records made by me of my "disclosures"—My first opinion of Miss Reed's book—Intention to confess while in the Bellevue Asylum—Interview with a New York lady about to become a nun.

SINCE the publication of my first edition, I have had different things brought to my memory, which I had forgotten while reviewing in it the past scenes of my life. Some of these have presented themselves to me while meditating alone, by day or by night; and others have been brought to mind by conversing with others. I have seen a number of my former acquaintances, and in my interviews with them, my memory has often been refreshed on one subject or another. During a conversation I had in March last, with Mr. John Hilliker of New York, who by so kindly persisting in taking me from my exposed retreat, saved my life as I believe, and introduced me to the Almshouse, he recalled to my mind a paper which I held in my hand when he found me in a field. I did not mention that paper in my Sequel, because I did not think of it. He mentions, in his affidavit, that I refused to let him see it, and tore it in pieces, when I found he was resolved to remove me. I had made up my mind that I was soon to die. Indeed, although I have felt unwilling to declare it heretofore, my intention had been to die by starvation, in the lonely place where I had taken my abode. Sometimes this resolution failed me for a time, and I would eat, and even send the little boy who visited me, to buy a cakes. Sometimes, also, I thought of destroying my life by other means; but still thinking it would have some merit in the sight of God, to disclose the worst of the crimes I had witnessed in the Nunnery, I determined to leave behind me a record which might be picked up after my death, whenever and however that event might come upon me. I therefore one day sent Tommy to buy me some paper; and, understanding I wanted to write, he brought me an inkstand and pen, as I believe from his mother's house. I wrote a brief statement of facts upon the paper, and folded it, I believe, in the form of a letter, after signing it, as I think, with my Christian name only, "Maria." This was the paper which Mr. Hilliker endeavoured to obtain, and which I tore, to prevent it from being seen, when I thought death was not so near as I had supposed.

The Sunday before the birth of my child, I again wrote, with similar feelings, and in a similar style, and hid the paper. But I afterwards took it again and burnt it.

While I was in the Asylum, a gentleman who had Miss Reed's book, ("Six Months in a Convent,") read some passages in my presence, which irritated me so much that I spoke to him with passion, and I fear almost insulted him. I had never heard of such a person or such a book before, but I believed everything I heard, because it corresponded with my own experience, so far as it went; but I thought, at that moment, that it was wrong to make known such things to the world, as it was calculated to injure the Church: in such an unsettled state did my mind continue to be for a considerable time. It was perfectly evident to me, however, that the institution where she was, must be materially different from the Black Nunnery, as it was far from being so close, or governed by such strict rules. She also had been in it too short a time to learn all; and besides, being only a novice, it was impossible that she should be fully acquainted with many things which are communicated only to nuns.

While I was in the Asylum, I had once made up my mind to confess to Mr. Conroy, after receiving his invitations and threatening messages, being strongly urged by some of the Catholic women about me. It happened, most fortunately for me, that I was befriended and advised by an excellent woman, Mrs. Neil, who took great pains to instruct and influence me aright. When I had decided on obeying the summons of the priest, Mrs. Neil came in, and having ascertained my intention, urged me to reflect, and impressed it upon my mind, that I was responsible to God, and not to man, for my conduct, and that his power and authority over me were only pretended. I believe I had then sometimes more confidence in priests than in God Almighty. She assured me that I had rights, and had friends there who would protect me. I then determined not to go to confession.

I have generally found it easier to convince Catholics than Protestants of the truth of my story, if they come to me with doubts or even unbelief. Since the first appearance of my book, I have received visits from a great number of persons in consequence of what they had seen or heard of its contents; and among these have been a considerable number of Catholics. While I am able to say that I have had the satisfaction of removing all doubts from the minds of some Protestants whom I have seen, I must confess that in general I have received the greatest satisfaction from interviews with intelligent Catholics. The reason of this is, that I know better how to treat the latter in argument. Having been one myself, I know where their difficulties lie, how to appeal to their own minds, and how to lead them to correct conclusions. Perhaps I can best convey my meaning to my readers, by giving a brief account of some of the interviews alluded to.

There is an interesting little girl whom I have repeatedly conversed with, (the daughter of an ignorant Catholic woman,) who has enjoyed some of the advantages of instruction in the scriptures, and submits with extreme reluctance to the ceremonies which her mother requires her to perform, in compliance with the requisitions of her priest. She believes my book, and she has reason for it. She has acknowledged to me, though with shame and reluctance, that, when compelled by her mother to confess to Father —, in his private room, he has sat with his arms around her, and often kissed her, refusing money for the usual fee, on the plea that he never requires pay for confessing pretty girls. He told her the Virgin Mary would leave her if she told of it. His questions are much the same as I have heard. All this I can believe, and do believe. I need not say that I tremble for her fate.

During the first week in March, 1836, I received a visit at my lodgings in New York, from a young woman, of a Protestant family in this city, who had received a Roman Catholic education. She called, as I understood, at the urgent request of her mother, who was exceedingly distressed at her daughter's intention to enter a Canadian nunnery.

Part of our interview was in private; for she requested me to retire with her a little time, where we might be alone; and I found her intention was, by certain queries, to satisfy herself whether I had ever been a Roman Catholic. She inquired if I could tell any of the questions commonly asked of women in the confession box; and on my answering in the affirmative, she desired me to repeat some, which I did. This satisfied her on that point; and I soon became so far acquainted with the state of her mind, as to perceive that she was prepared to avoid the influence of every argument that I could use against the system to which she had become attached.

She confessed to me, that she had given five hundred dollars to the Cathedral, and a considerable sum to St. Joseph's Church, and that she had decided on entering a nunnery in Canada. I inquired why she did not enter one in the United States. To this she replied, that she had only one objection; her Confessor, Father Pies, having told her that he would by no means recommend the latter, and greatly preferred the former, because the priests had entire control over the Canadian nunneries, which they had not of those in the States. This, and some other parts of our conversation took place in the presence of other persons; and on hearing this declaration of the priest, the motive of which was to us so palpable, a lady present laughed outright.

While we were alone, on her expressing a doubt of the crimes I have charged upon the priests, I said, but you admit that they have said and done such things, (which I do not like to repeat.) She signified assent. Then, said I, how can you pretend that any thing is too bad for them to do? I also said, you admit that they have asked you in the Confession box, whether you ever wished to commit beastiality. She replied, "Yes; but if we have not evil thoughts, there is no harm." "You admit that they have treated you with great familiarity at confession?" She replied, that she confessed to her priest while he sat in a chair, and that he had; "but," said she, "you know a priest is a holy man, and cannot sin." And when I pressed her with another question, she confessed that her priest had told her she could not be sanctified without having performed an act commonly called criminal, and replied in a similar manner.

She was ashamed or afraid to assert her full faith in some of the doctrines she had been taught, when I loudly and emphatically demanded of her whether she did indeed credit them. This was the case with her in regard to the pardon of sins by priests, the existence of purgatory, or a middle place, &c. She spoke of these and other subjects as if she believed in them: but when I said, "Do you believe it really and truly?—you do?" she invariably faltered and denied it.

She spoke of my "Disclosures" as untrue; and I got it out of her, that she had conversed with her priest about me at Confession, who assured her that I was not myself, not Maria Monk, but an evil spirit, in short, the devil in the form of a woman. After considerable conversation, she admitted that my book was undoubtedly true; but still she refused to do, as I told her she ought after saying what she had, come out and be a Protestant.

She informed me that her confessor had a great desire to see me, and inquired if I would consent to an interview. I replied, that I would readily agree to see him in the presence of Dr. Brownlee, but not alone; and she went away without leaving me any reason to hope that she had been released from the power of superstition, or had any intention of gratifying her mother, who was deeply distressed at the prospect of her daughter's ruin.

CHAPTER XII.

WHILE I was a novice, there was a young lady of our number from the Tannery,* named Angelique Duranceau, with whom I was somewhat acquainted, and of whom I had a favourable opinion. She was about eighteen, and at the time of her entrance had every appearance of good health. After she had been there a considerable time, it might be about seven months, (as I know she was not near the period when she could make her general confession, that is, at the end of the first year,) I saw her under circumstances which made a strong impression on my mind.

I had received a summons from the Superior to attend in the Novices' sick-room, with several other novices. When I entered, I found Fathers Savage and Bonin reading a paper, and Miss Duranceau on a bed, with a look so peculiar as quite to shock me. Her complexion was dark, and of an unnatural colour, her look strange, and she occasionally started and conducted very singularly indeed, though she never spoke. Her whole appearance was such as to make me think she had lost her reason, and almost terrified me. The Superior informed us that she wanted us as witnesses; and the priests then coming forward, presented the paper to Miss Duranceau, and asked her if she was willing to give all her property to the church. She replied with a feeble motion of the head and body, and then, having a pen put into her hands, wrote her name to it without reading it, and relapsed into apparent unconsciousness. We were then requested to add our signatures, which being done, we withdrew, as we entered, I believe, without the sick novice having had any knowledge of our presence, or of her own actions.

A few hours afterwards I was called to assist in laying out her corpse, which was the first intimation I had of her being dead. The Superior, myself, and one or two other novices, had the whole of this melancholy

---

* A village a few miles from Montreal.

task to perform, being the only persons admitted into the apartment where the body lay. It was swelled very much. We placed it in a coffin, and screwed on the cover alone. On account of the rapid change taking place in the corpse, it was buried about twenty-four hours after death.

Not long after the burial, two brothers of Miss Duranceau came to the Convent, and were greatly distressed when told that she was dead. They complained of not being informed of her sickness; but the Superior assured them that it was at the urgent request of their sister, who was possessed of so much humility, that she thought herself unworthy of attracting the regard of any one, and not fit to be lamented even by her nearest friends. "What was she," she had said, according to the declarations made by the Superior, "what was she that she should cause pain to her family?"

This was not the only occasion on which I was present at the laying out of the dead. I assisted in three other cases. Two of the subjects died of consumption, or some similar disease; one of whom was an old-country girl, and the other a squaw.—The latter seemed to fall away from the time when she came into the nunnery, until she was reduced almost to a shadow. She left to the Convent a large amount of money.

Several stories were told us at different times, of nuns who had gone into a state of sanctity in the Convent. One, who had excited much attention and wonder by prophesying, was at length found to be in such a condition, and was immediately released from the duty of observing the common rules of the Convent, as the Superior considered her authority over her as having in a manner ceased.

It was affirmed that many priests had been taken to heaven, body and soul, after death.

The following story I was told by some of the nuns and the Superior while I was a novice, and it made a considerable impression upon my mind.—After catechism one day, a dove appeared in the room while the nuns were kneeling and engaged in prayer. It addressed one of the nuns and the Superior, not only in an audible voice, but in a string of French rhymes, which were repeated to me so often that I learnt them almost all by heart, and retain several to this day.

"Un grand honneur je vous confere,
"Aussi a vous, la Superieure."

These were the first two lines. In the sequel the dove informed the audience that in eight days the spirit of the nun should be raised to heaven, to join its own, and that of other souls in that blessed place; and spoke of the honour thus to be conferred upon the nun, and on the Superior too, who had had the training of one to such a grade of holiness.

When the day thus designated arrived, a number of priests assembled, with the Superior, to witness her expected translation; and while they were all standing around her, she disappeared, her body and soul being taken off together to heaven. The windows had been previously fastened, yet these offered no obstacle, and she was seen rising upward like a column moving through the air. The sweetest music, as I was assured, accompanied her exit, and continued to sound the remainder of the day, with such charming and irresistible effect, that the usual occupations of the nuns were interrupted, and all joined in and sang in concert.

CHAPTER XIII.

Story of Ann, the Scotch Novice—Letters of her lover—The Superior's deception—Miss Farnes—Ann's determination to leave the Convent—Means taken to persuade her to stay.

THERE was a young girl, named Ann, who was very stout and rather homely, but not of pleasing manners, though of a good disposition, seventeen or eighteen years of age, to whom I took a liking. She was a novice with me, and the time of which I am to speak, was not long after I returned from St. Denis. The Superior also displayed a partiality for her, and I found she was much in favour of having her received as a nun, if it could be accomplished. She was very handy at different kinds of work; and, what I believe chiefly induced me to regard her with kindness, she was a fatherless and motherless child. She had a beau in town, who one day called to see her at the nunnery, when she was going to confession.

I was with the Superior at the time, who, on being informed that the young man was there, and of his errand, requested me to go into the parlour with her, to meet him. He put into the Superior's hands a parcel and three letters, requesting her to give them to Ann. She took them, with an expression of assent, and he withdrew. Just as he had gone, Ann came hurrying into the parlour, saying that some one had told her that the Superior had sent for her. The Superior rebuked her sharply, and sent her back, without, however, showing her what she had promised to give her. Ann said, that she had understood a young man (mentioning her visitor) had called to see her. This the Superior denied, telling her never to come till she was wanted.

When Ann had gone, the Superior told me to go with her to her room, which I did. She there first made me promise never to tell of what she was going to do, and then produced the letters and package, and began to open them. One of the letters, I remember, was folded in a singular manner, and fastened with three seals. In the parcel was found a miniature of the young man, a pair of ear rings, a breast pin, and something else, what, I have now forgotten. The letters were addressed to her by her lover, who advised her by all means to leave the Convent. He informed her that a cousin of hers, a tailor, had arrived from Scotland, who was in want of a housekeeper; and urged her to live with him, and never renounce the Protestant religion in which she had been brought up.

I was surprised that the Superior should do what I felt to be very wrong and despicable; but she represented it as perfectly justifiable on account of the good which she had in view.

I considered myself as bound to be particularly obedient to the Superior, in order that I might make my conduct correspond with the character given of me to her, by Miss Bousquier, who, as I have mentioned in the sequel of my first volume, had shown me an evidence of her friendship by recommending me to her, and becoming, in some sense, responsible for my good conduct to induce her to receive me back into the nunnery. This was a strong reason for my complying with the Superior's wish in the case of which I am speaking.

Since I have alluded here to the period of my return to the convent, I may remark that the Superior took some pains to ascertain, by her own inquiries, whether there was substantial reason for reliance on the favourable opinion expressed to her of me by Miss Bousquier. I recollect particularly her inquiring of me whom I had conversed with, while at St. Denis, to persuade them to enter the Black Nunnery: for Miss Bousquier, I understood, had informed her that I had shown my attachment to the Hotel Dieu, by making favourable representations of it while with her engaged in keeping school. To the Superior's inquiries I replied, that I had urged little Gueroutte to become a nun. She was the daughter of Jean Richard, as he was familiarly called, to distinguish him from a number of other men of nearly the same name; for he had extensive family connections in that place. He lived opposite Miss Bousquier, so that I had had frequent opportunities to converse with his daughter.

But not to detain my readers longer on this digression, I will return to my story and poor Ann, the Scotch girl. Having received particular instructions from the Superior, I promised to endeavour to get into her confidence, for the purpose of influencing her to take the veil, and to proceed in accordance with the directions given me. The Superior told me by no means to make any approaches to her at once, nor indeed for some time, lest she should suspect our design, but to wait awhile, until she could have no reason to think my movements might have grown out of the circumstances above mentioned: for Ann appeared to be uncommonly penetrating, as the Superior remarked; and of course much caution was necessary in dealing with her. Some time subsequently, therefore, I cannot tell exactly how long, I engaged in conversation with her one day in the course of which she remarked that Miss Farns, a confidential friend of hers, who had spent a short time in the nunnery some time before, was soon coming back.

This Miss Farns had come in on trial, while I was in the Convent, and I had often heard the Superior say, that she must be separated from Ann, because they were so much together, and so often breaking the rules. Ann now told me in confidence, that her friend was coming back, not with any real intention of staying, but only for the purpose of giving her some information favourable to herself, which she had obtained. This she wished to become fully possessed of before she would decide whether to leave the Convent or not.

All this I communicated to the Superior, who then began to look for Miss Farns' return, with a determination to treat her with every appearance of kindness. She often in the meantime, gave me little delicacies, with directions to share them with Ann. Miss Farns soon presented herself for re-admission, and was admitted without any difficulty, not being required even to change her dress. This occurred, as nearly as I can recollect, about six weeks after the affair of intercepting Ann's letters, mentioned a few pages back, and somewhere about the close of summer, or the beginning of autumn.

Being allowed to do pretty much as they choose, Ann and her friend were much together, and generally engaged in deep conversation: so that, as the Superior declared, it was evident they were forming some plan for secret operations. I tried several times to get near and overhear what they were talking about: but I could not learn anything. The next day Miss Farns departed, saying she never intended to return;

which offended the Superior so much, that she said she would have the doors shut if she ever came again.

The same evening Ann requested me to tell the Superior, that she wished to get her clothes, that she might leave the Convent. I went to the Superior's room, where I found Father Bonin sitting on the sofa talking with her. When they were informed of Ann's message, the Superior said, she would let the girl go at once back to the world, and be given up to the devil. Bonin argued a good deal against this. The Superior replied, that she had set the old nuns at work, but without success; they had not been able to influence Ann as she desired; and it was a shame to keep such a creature within holy walls, to make the flock discontented. At length she decided on the course to pursue; and turning to me, said: take her upstairs, give her her clothes, yet argue with her in favour of remaining in the Convent, but at the same time tell her, that I am indifferent about it, and care not whether she goes or stays.

I accordingly returned to Ann, and telling her that she might follow me upstairs and get her clothes, led the way, and delivered them to her. In obedience to my orders, I lost no time in representing her intentions to depart from our holy residence as an insinuation of the devil; and told her that he was trying his best to draw her out into the world, that he might secure her for himself. I told her that he had a strong hold upon her, and she ought to use the greater exertions to resist his temptations; that the Superior thought it might be better on the whole if she departed, because her influence might be very injurious to others if she remained; yet that I felt a deep interest in her, and could not bear to have her perform her intention, because I well knew that her throwing off the holy dress that she then wore, to take her former one, would be the first step towards damnation.

"You need not talk so to me," replied Ann, "you have done the same yourself." I told her that if I had, I had lived to regret it, and was glad to get back to the Convent again. After a while an old nun came up, called me aside, and said the Superior wished me to continue talking to Ann; and, in case I should prevail with her to remain, to make her go down and beg pardon for scandal she had caused by her conduct, and ask to be taken back again into the flock of the good shepherd, as the Superior was often called.

Poor Ann at length began to listen to me; and I got her to repeat to me all that Miss Farns had said to her during her late short visit to the nunnery. The amount of it was, that if Ann would come out at dusk, and go to a particular house she would find her relations waiting for her, who had arrived from Scotland—they were, if I mistake not, her brother and cousin. Having prevailed upon her to break her engagement to meet them, I soon persuaded her to go down stairs as a penitent, and there she humbly kneeled, and in the usual manner kissed the feet of the Superior, and all the novices, and begged and obtained a penance, which was to serve as an atonement for her offence. This was, to fast three mornings, ask forgiveness of all her companions on the same days and perform acts of contrition.

That evening the Superior called me to tea in her own room, when I told her all that I had learnt from the confession of Ann, who I knew was fasting at the time. When the Superior understood the plan proposed by Miss Farns, she spoke of her in very severe terms, and then commended me, saying that I ought to rejoice at having saved a soul from hell, but ought to guard against pride, as I had accomplished what I had undertaken only by the help of the Virgin Mary.

Ann continued to behave as she had promised, and we heard nothing more of any attempt by her friends to get her out of the nunnery. Not long after, however, she was taken sick, and I ascertained, from observation and inquiry, that the cause of it was her discontentment, as she complained of loneliness. I felt compassion for her, and told the Superior that I thought she ought to be treated with more leniency. She said she would get some of the old nuns to talk with her a little more.

Ann was received, in due time, as a nun. I was not present at the ceremony, but I afterwards met with her, and several times had a little conversation with her.

CHAPTER XIV.

Miss Ross—Our early acquaintance—Her request.

THERE was a girl whom I knew from a child, a Miss Ross, the recollection of whom gives me deep pain: for I know too well that I have been the cause of great misfortunes to her. I remember being with her at different times in my early days. After our family removed to Montreal, and had our residence in the Government House, we often had calls from persons of our acquaintance, as many were fond of walking in the garden, or green, as we commonly called it.

Such of my readers as have visited that city will be likely to remember the place of our residence: for the Government House, of which my mother is still the keeper, is of very large size: (I have sometimes heard it spoken of as the most ancient in America.) It was said that the foundation stones of that and the old French church were laid on the same day, as recorded. The gateway is of stone, and it is furnished in a manner becoming the residence of the Governor of the Province. The garden and green are of great extent, and present fine walks and flowers; and as the former overlooks the esplanade, to which it is adjoining, it was a favourite resort on Sunday afternoons, when the troops are on parade.

Miss Ross, I recollect, one evening in particular, paid me a visit with a Miss Robinson; and we amused ourselves together in the green. Her mother lived a little out of the city, near the Lachine road. She was a Scotch lady, and possessed a large property. When Miss Ross grew up, she became attached to a young man of my acquaintance, and indeed a relation of my mother; but when it became known, she found her mother very much opposed to her wishes.

While I was a novice in the Hotel Dieu, Miss Ross came in as one; and we had frequent interviews together, as our acquaintance still continued, and indeed we had always been friends. She became informed of my design of taking the black veil—I presume I must have told her of it myself; and one day she told me, that she had sometimes thought of becoming a nun, but still felt but little inclination that way; yet she requested me to do her the favour to inform her how I was pleased with that mode of life, after I should have been in long enough to form an opinion. If I thought she would be happy as a nun, she desired I would frankly inform her; and if not—as I was acquainted with her disposition—that I would warn her against it. We often conversed on the subject afterwards: and it was repeated, and plainly understood between us, that I was to tell her the exact truth, as she would probably be guided by my opinion in the course she would adopt.

I went through many preparatory steps before my admission, as I have mentioned in my first volume, took the veil, and passed through some of the scenes which I have before spoken of, before I ever particularly reverted to the request of Miss Ross, so far as I now can remember. One thing, however, I here stop to mention, which I omitted to say in my first volume, and which I might forget hereafter, viz.:—that soon after my admission as a "Received," the Superior gave me the charge of her room, that of the old nuns, and the adjoining community-room; and thus kept me for about three months in a degree more separate from the other nuns, than I should otherwise have been. This brought me more into intercourse with the Superior, and in the same proportion made some other nuns regard me with jealousy: for some of them occasionally, in some way or other, would express dislike towards me. Perhaps this state of things the more disposed me to confide in the Superior.

After I had been a nun for some weeks, I cannot tell exactly how long, I recollect that as I lay awake one night, I began to think of Miss Ross, and to recall the conversations we had held together in the novices' apartment. All at once it occurred to me that I might probably do a great benefit to myself, an honour to the nunnery and to true religion, as well as save her, by inducing her to take the black veil, especially as she had so much property to add to the funds. At the same time the thought presented itself to my mind, that by so doing I should gain a very exalted place in heaven for myself: for I had already heard a great deal said, and had repeatedly read the same in our book, that to bring a person into a Convent, was one of the highest kinds of merit. I soon made up my mind to communicate to the Superior all I knew; for although I questioned at once whether it would not be shameful and sinful to betray the confidence of my friend, this was easily got over, by the thought of the vast benefits to result from it, especially to herself.

The next day I told one of the old nuns that I wished to speak to the Superior; for as this was commonly required, and nuns could not go into her room without leave, I conformed to custom. I was soon admitted, when I told her all Miss Ross had said to me, and added, that I wished to get her to take the veil. I apologized for my private conversations. She said they were perfectly justifiable.—I think I never saw the Superior express more satisfaction than she did on the receipt of this intelligence. She appeared overjoyed; listened to all I had to say with great attention and highly approved of my proposition. When I informed her of Miss Ross's attachment to young ———, she replied that that might explain the state of her mind; for the old nuns had for some time spoken of her depressed appearance, and she had mentioned at confession that something lay very heavy on her mind.

The Superior appeared from that moment to devote her whole attention to the consideration of the subject. She seemed for a time almost lost in thought; and remarked to me, "We must consider this matter; we must consider the best way to bring her into the nunnery: for some persons are harder to get out of the devil's power than others. After a little time she told me I should be sent to read the lecture to the novices, and she would tell the old nuns to allow me to converse with Miss Ross, which they would not let me do, as I well knew, without her express orders, as it was contrary to the rules. She then told me many things to say to Miss Ross, and some of her instructions she repeated to me, so that I might not be at a loss when I should converse with her, no matter what objections she might raise.

Among other things which I most distinctly recollect, she told me to assure her, that as to the happiness of a Convent, no person could possibly be more happy than nuns; for there we were assured of the favour of God, and of heavenly enjoyments after death; that while in the world, other young women would draw us off from our duty, and occupy our minds with thoughts that would do us harm: there we were exposed to no such dangers. The sinfulness of vain thoughts might appear to us very trifling, but it was very different in the sight of God; and how could we hope to resist the temptations surrounding us in such a manner in the world? If she made any allusion to her attachment to the young man before mentioned, the Superior told me to declaim against it, as an abomination to think of such a thing in the nunnery; that I could not converse with her if she spoke of it again, as not a proper person. If she appeared to hesitate at my proposition, I was to tell her solemnly, that my offer was a direct invitation from Jesus Christ to become his spouse, which could not be rejected without great guilt.

The Superior told me that I should be richly-rewarded if I succeeded. She thought I would soon be made an old (or confidential) nun: and she would give me a most precious relic, with a piece of the heart of Mary Magdalen, and intercede for me with the Virgin.

After I had listened attentively to all these instructions received from a woman to whom I looked with unbounded respect and veneration, I left her, prepared to put them in practice to the best of my ability, much excited with the hope of accomplishing what I thought a truly great and meritorious act, and one that would ensure the salvation of my friend.

The reader may perhaps recall the disclosures I have heretofore made, of the crimes I had witnessed, and the sufferings I had undergone before this period of my convent life, and wonder how I could possibly have been so far deluded, as really to believe what I was thus prepared to say. Such, however, is indeed the truth; except that I must allow, that my conscience repeatedly disturbed me, and seriously too, with the suggestion that I should be guilty of direct deception, if I said, either that I was happy in the Convent, or that I had at all times unshaken faith in any of the declarations I was about to make. More than once, too, I was shocked at the idea of deceiving my confiding young friend. But as I believed what I had been so often taught, about the virtue of deception, in certain circumstances, I did my best to smother my scruples.

The promised arrangements were made by the Superior; the old nuns were instructed not to interrupt any conversation they might witness between Miss Ross and myself, and I was directed, at the appointed hour, to read the lecture. I thus easily found the opportunity I sought, and was soon with Miss Ross, while the old nuns appeared very busy in another part of the room, and unobserving. Though under a repeated promise to reveal to her the state of my mind, now that I had been long familiar with the secrets of the nunnery, I most cautiously guarded myself, and assumed what did not belong to me—the appearance of one devotedly fond of the institution.

I told her that I had now been long enough a "Received" to be able to express an opinion; and I must inform her that we lived a most happy life within the institution; that I would urge her, as a friend, to take the veil, and withdraw from that world which was so full of temptations. To this she lent a very serious ear; and I saw that my words produced a solemn and saddening effect upon her feelings. She replied that she felt quite undecided what to do. She seemed solicitous to be still farther assured of the happiness I had spoken of as enjoyed by the nuns.

When she touched that subject, I addressed her exactly after the manner directed by the Superior, and speaking rather harshly, inquired of her, "Do you condemn the life of a nun then?" She instantly answered, "No;" and she easily admitted all I said about the attention paid to the comfort of those in the Convent. "But," said she, "my mother is very much opposed to my taking the veil; she is a widow, and you know we are bound to honour and obey our parents—nature teaches us that." The Superior had furnished me, in French, with an answer to this objection; and as we were accustomed to converse in English, I had only to translate her words, which were,

"Les droits de nos parens ne sont pas devant les droits de notre religion."

"The claims of our parents are not before those of our religion."

"I shan't be a nun!" said she, with determination. I talked with her, however, some time, and she began again to listen patiently.

I then added, that Christ had commanded us to "forsake father and mother" to be his disciples, and that we must have trials and tribulations before we could enter the kingdom of heaven. She told me that she felt then less inclined to the world than she had when we had last conversed together; but at length she alluded to Mr. —. "Never mention," I exclaimed, "such abominations! It is sin, it is defilement to speak of such a thing in so holy a place as a convent." This I said very much in the manner and tone which the Superior had used in dictating it to me. I then added, "Now this is the only obstacle which the devil puts in the way of your salvation—and see how he tries more to prevent you, the nearer you are getting to it. All that you have to do, then, is to resist the more."

And the repetition of these expressions, has brought to my mind many others which I often heard, not only about that time, but frequently before and afterwards. One brings up another; and to speak of objections that might be made to any of our nunnery doctrines, or to hear a question asked about our way of life, naturally calls to my memory the replies which were made to them.

"Are you at liberty to buy a farm, and sell it when you please? No—Then how can you give yourself to a young man when you please?"

"Must we not obey our parents?—Quand les droits de la religion sont concerne, les droits de la nature cessent."

["When the rights or claims of religion are concerned, the rights (or claims) of nature cease."]

When the question is put to an old nun—"What made you become a nun?" the regular, fixed answer always is, with a peculiar drawl—"Divine love." But such things as these, although they come up very strongly to my mind, may perhaps appear to be not worth mentioning.

The conversation I held with poor Miss Ross was much longer than I can undertake to give a full account of; but after I had over and over again painted the happiness of a nun's life in the brightest manner I was able, and assured her that I had never known blessedness before I had entered upon it, I told her that I had had some inspirations from heaven, such as I had never enjoyed before, and that she would have the same. I also told her with solemnity, that she had now received, through me, an invitation from Jesus Christ, to become his bride; and that if she rejected it, it would be a sin of deep ingratitude, and he would reject her from the kingdom of heaven: that it was her duty to enter the Convent as a veiled nun, without regarding the feelings of her mother, or any other obstacle; and that she was bound to obtain all the property she could, and put it into the treasury of the institution.

CHAPTER XV.

STORY of Miss Ross continued—Plan to get her into the Nunnery for life—Arrangements—Execution of our design.

IT was very easy for me to see that what I said had a great effect on Miss Ross. I found it impossible however, to make her promise me to take the veil. She persisted that she must see her mother first. I then left her, and went to the Superior's room, where I informed her of all that had passed. She appeared very much delighted, and treated me with great condescension and kindness. She said, however, that we should yet have to do much; for it was plain to her that the novice had very strong scruples to overcome—and she added, that the devil's influence was very powerful over some persons. We must therefore pursue a plan which would require great caution and skill on our part, but which, she had no doubt, would prove successful. This she communicated to me in a few words. That evening the Superior told the nuns that she had been warned in a dream that some one was in great temptations, and desired them to say a Pater and an Ave for her.

We were to disguise ourselves, and appear to Miss Ross, I as Satan, and she as the Holy Mother. Miss Ross must be brought alone, and with solemnity, to some place where we could carry through the deception without interruption, and with the best effect. The whole of her plan she communicated to me; but as we had several rehearsals to go through in preparation, instead of repeating her instructions, I had better relate what was done in conformity with them.

When we were prepared to go through with our parts, in order that we might become familiar with them, she gave me an old robe, which she made me wrap around me, and the devil's cap, head, and horns, which is kept to scare the nuns, few of whom know of it. Thus I was concealed, everything except my eyes, and then approached a spot where we imagined the novice to be lying. I addressed her in a feigned voice, and invited her to become my servant, promising her a happy and easy life. In an instant, at a moment when we supposed her to be making a sign of the cross, I stopped speaking, and hastily withdrew. After a short time, I returned, and made other propositions to her: and then, after flying again from the cross, again came back, and promised her, in case she would comply, to ensure her marriage with the man she loved. I then retired once more; after which, the Superior approached, and with as sweet and winning a voice as she could assume, said that she had listened to what had passed, and had come to assure her of her protection.

After I had become familiar with my part in this sad farce, and acted it to the satisfaction of the Superior, she took measures to have it performed for the last time. In this also I had a principal part to perform: for I was directed to hold another conversation with my deceived friend; and, in obedience to instructions, on Saturday evening took her into the Examination of Conscience room, and informed her, that I had been inspired by the Virgin Mary to tell her, that if she would go into the nuns' private chapel, the Holy Mother would speak with her. I informed her, however, that it would not be at all surprising if the devil should appear to her, and endeavour to prevent her from holding so happy an interview; and that if she should be tempted, she must cross herself, and Satan would instantly leave her, because he could not withstand the power of the sign. Then telling her that she must keep a strict fast on Sunday evening, I informed her, that on Monday morning I would be with her again.

In the meantime, the Superior, with the help of one of the old nuns, Saint Margarite, and myself, had darkened the private chapel as much as we could, by means of black curtains, and placed only a single light in it, and that a taper, burning by the side of the altar. We also took down the cross, and laid it on the floor, with the head turned towards the door, and the foot towards the altar. When all was prepared, I went to Miss Ross, and conducted her into the chapel. I told her to lie down upon the cross, with her arms extended, in the attitude of the crucified Saviour, which she did; and then bound her eyes tight with a bandage, all just as the Superior had ordered, telling her she might otherwise see a horrid sight. I then retired by the door, just outside of which, the Superior was standing; and there I was covered with the old robe; for although it was so dark, the eyes of the poor girl were blinded, and her head purposely so placed, that she could hardly have seen us under any circumstances, yet the Superior said, perhaps she might peep a little and see us. If this plan failed, she said, she must resort to some other.

We were both completely disguised; and I had not only the dress on, and devil's cap, but a slice cut from a potato, and slit in different ways so as to resemble great teeth, which was crowded into my mouth. The front part of my cap had been turned up inside, and I painted my cheeks with some red paint the Superior gave me, and she afterwards put on more paint, thinking I had not enough.

After I had left Miss Ross in the chapel about a quarter of an hour, the Superior signified that it was time to return, and begin my temptation. I therefore approached her, and standing a little distance from her head, repeated some of the words I had been taught, and the circumstances are still most distinctly before me, so that I remember the words as if I had uttered them only yesterday. Perhaps one reason of it is, that every few minutes during the whole time, my conscience stung me severely, so that I could scarcely go on with my part

"Are you a fool," said I, "to be lying there in such a posture, for that God of yours? Had you not better serve me?" She raised her hand, without speaking, and made the sign of the cross, saying, "Jesu, Maria, Joseph, ayez pitie de moi." (Jesus, Mary, Joseph, have pity on me!)

I waited no longer, but immediately retired softly, as if I had vanished. After standing a few minutes beside the Superior, just outside of the door, without either of us speaking, she touched me, and I approached the poor novice again.

"Would you not like to come out of this place," I asked her, "and serve me? You shall have nothing but balls and pleasure of all kinds."

Miss Ross made the sign of the cross again, and I vanished as quickly and silently as before. In a short time I entered again, and told her, "if you will only leave this nunnery, I will do anything for you you wish—I will get you married to the young man you love so much."

Still the poor unsuspecting girl, though doubtless terrified, made the sign of the cross again and again; and at length I left her saying "Jesu, Maria, Joseph, ayez pitie de moi." I then took off my dress, when the

Superior made me sit down, and signified that I must not make the slightest noise. She remarked,—

"Well, if this plan does not succeed, I will try force."

She then went in and addressed her, in French, in this manner:

"I am your Holy Mother, (which means the Virgin Mary,) I have been listening to your faithfulness, and will adopt you as one of my children. Are you willing to become one of my daughters? If you are, you must join the sisters this week, and make your vows before another Sabbath passes over your head; for I am afraid the devil is making great plans to get you. But if you have your vows made, I think you will be safe."

She then asked her if she was willing to give up all she had to the Holy Church, and told her, that unless she would part with all, she could not accept her. She then promised her her protection, if she was willing, and retired saying, "Peace be with you."

In the afternoon I was sent to request her to go into the Superior's room, as she wished to speak with her. On entering it, we found the Superior of the Convent and the Superior of the Seminary both there. The former addressed her, telling her that she had had a vision, in which she was told that the young novice who was doing penance in the chapel, was acceptable in the sight of God. At this, Miss Ross appeared quite overjoyed, but scarcely able to speak.

The Superior then told her, that she ought to listen to any advice I might give her, for she had entire confidence in me, and she ought to be guided by my counsel. She requested her to return to the novices' department, retire into a corner, and determine what she would do. She then whispered to me, and desired me to remain with her until the Superior of the Seminary went away, which I did. She then told me to go to Miss Ross again, and coax her to be received almost immediately.

I went accordingly, and endeavoured to get a promise from her to that effect, but I was unable. She persisted that she must see her mother before she could take the veil. I inquired of her the reason. She replied, that she wished to give to the nunnery all the property her mother could spare her. This I communicated to the Superior, who told me to say that her mother should be sent for the next day.

Her mother came, and had an interview with her, in which she learnt her daughter's intention to become a nun. This was opposed to her utmost; but all the arguments and entreaties she used, were utterly vain—she could make no impression. Her daughter had wished to see her only to tell her that such was her resolution, and to request her to deliver her that afternoon, all the money she intended ever to give her.

The widow retired—the money was sent—Miss Ross took the veil on the Wednesday morning following, and brought a large contribution. I was not present at her reception; and I do not think it necessary to say anything further on the subject, which is, and ever must be, all my life, one of the most painful with which I have had any connection. I will only add, that although I often saw Saint Mary, (as she was called, after her supposed patroness,) I never spoke with her after her reception. Opportunities, it is true, were not very frequent: but, when they were offered, she repeatedly seemed disposed to speak to me. I saw at length, that she was becoming a favourite with Jane Ray, which pleased me, knowing that she would be of some service to her, and befriend her. Many a time she would fix her eyes upon me, and it seemed as if they would pierce through my soul.

CHAPTER XVI.

Mᴏʀᴇ recollections of Jane Ray,—Her confessions of her history.

ONE of the nuns was from St. Mark's, and bore the name of St. Mark. Her father visited the Superior one day, and requested her to have nuns pray for him daily for a short time, leaving with her a considerable sum of money to pay for their intercession. Such things were occasionally done by different persons. He also sent about forty dollars to his daughter, with a desire that they might be distributed among the nuns, to purchase whatever they might wish for. The Superior informed us that it was quite inconsistent with the rules of the nuns to receive such presents, but that, considering the devout character of the giver, she would not entirely forbid the execution of his request.

She therefore furnished us with some molasses to make into candy, and allowed us an unusual degree of liberty during a part of a day. A considerable quantity of molasses was made into candy by some of the most skilled in the process; though by no means as much as forty dollars' worth. The Superior, however, had a trick played on her in consequence of the indulgence: for some of us attributed it to a desire of pleasing the rich contributor, and not to any kindness towards ourselves.

When the time for evening prayers had almost arrived, Jane Ray proposed to drop a little warm candy in the chairs of the Superior and two old nuns. This was soon done; and in a few minutes those seats, as well as the others in the community room, were occupied, and the prayers going on. At the close the Superior attempted to rise, but fell back again into her chair; and at the same moment the two old nuns did the same. After a few unsuccessful attempts, their situation became evident to all the assembly; and there was a great embarrassment at once among us all, arising from a disposition to speak and to laugh, opposed by the endeavour to suppress both. The scene was a very ludicrous one, and Jane enjoyed much amusement before the Superior and the old nuns could be set at liberty.

Jane Ray would sometimes seem to be overcome and lose courage, when detected and exposed for some of her tricks, even though not condemned to any severe penance. I have seen her cry, and even roar, after committing some breach of rules; and then retire to a corner, and after composing herself, begin to meditate a new trick. This she would commonly carry into effect with success; and then laughing aloud, declare that she was satisfied and happy again.

Sometimes she would submit to penances with perfect indifference, though they made her the constant object of observation. To punish her for her habitual negligence in dress, she was once ordered to wear an old nightcap until it fell to pieces; but still she was seen again as usual, with her apron half on and half off, and with stockings of different colours.

She would occasionally slip into the Superior's room, steal pass tickets, and get into the hospital with them; and this she did so boldly, that she was the occasion of the tickets being disused. Sometimes she would bring a Roman Catholic newspaper out of the Superior's room, and give it to the nuns to read; and sometimes repeat to us what she had overheard said in private.

Sometimes scenes of great agitation would occur, and things would be carried to such a state, that one and another of the nuns would become desperate, and resist with violence. For it is to be remembered, that unspeakable practices were sometimes resorted to, at the will of the priests or bishops, countenanced by the Superior; and sometimes, as I have stated in my first volume, required on the authority of the Pope.

Jane Ray sometimes appeared as a loud and violent opposer of what were considered the established rules of the Convent. She would break out in denunciations of the priests, and berate them in a style which it would be difficult to imitate, if it were worth while. Other nuns would sometimes exclaim, "Are you not ashamed to show so little respect for the holy fathers?" "Why are they not ashamed," she would reply, "to show no respect for the holy sisters?"

Some of the best opportunities I ever had for conversing with Jane, were at night; for during a considerable time she had her bed opposite mine, and by watching for a moment, when she could do it without being seen by the night watch, she would slip over to me, and get into my bed. Thus we have often spent hours together, and she found such occasions very convenient for communicating to me such plans as she devised for amusement or revenge. I sometimes lent an ear to her proposals, quite against my will; for I commonly concluded with a solemn confession of the wickedness, as I supposed it, in which she thus induced, and sometimes almost compelled me to engage. Indeed, it often happened that I had nothing to do in the morning, as it were, but to beg pardon; and when I was asked why I had so much of that business to do, I commonly laid it to Jane Ray. She, however, appeared to take much pleasure in the stolen interviews we thus had; and when we were obliged to lie at a distance from each other, she told me that it caused her to weep more than she had ever done in her life.

I naturally felt much curiosity to learn something of the history of Jane Ray, and repeatedly asked her questions intended to lead her to tell me something of her family, her former residence, or life. But, although so communicative on most other subjects, on this she evidently did not like to speak. Repeatedly have I known her to waive my inquiries, and many times, also, when I spoke very plainly, she would become silent, and refuse to speak a word. All this unwillingness, only served to increase my desire to know the truth, but I never was able to draw from her anything more than a very brief and general account of herself; for never, except on a single occasion, did she comply with my wishes so far as even to speak on the subject.

One night, when she had secretly left her bed and entered mine, she happened to be in a very communicative mood, though she appeared more depressed and deeply sunk in melancholy than I had ever known her before. She then informed me, that she had become attached to an officer of the British army in Quebec, in whom she confided to her ruin, believing that he intended to marry her. She left her parents, and after a time proceeded with him to Montreal. There he invited her to visit the Hotel Dieu Nunnery, as a curiosity; but to her surprise, she suddenly found herself deserted by him, and the doors closed upon her. From what she observed or heard, she soon learnt that this was done in consequence of an arrangement made between the officer and the Superiors of the Seminary and Convent, the first having paid a large sum of money to have her shut up from the world.

I understood her to say that the officer was an aid-de-camp of the former governor of Canada, Sir Peregrine Maitland. The priests, she believed, knew her story, but few of the nuns, she thought, had any knowledge of it except myself.

CHAPTER XVII.

My fear of the priests—Arguments used to keep us in subjection—Old nuns.

I WAS kept in great fear of the priests, by pretences they made to various kinds of power. I was once confessing to Father Bedar, who is now dead, and told him I had something on my conscience which I did not like to communicate. He said to me, "I have power to strike you dead this minute, but I will not. I will spare you. Go and examine your conscience, and see if you cannot come back and tell me what it is that you now conceal."

I was much frightened; for I believed what he said, and supposed he could have taken away my life on the spot by only wishing it. I therefore immediately went to the examination of my conscience with fear and trembling.

I have remarked in my first volume, more than once, that we were told it was a duty to submit to the licentious wishes of the priests. This we were urged to on various considerations. We were told, for instance, that being consecrated to God, we were not our own, and even our persons were not to be regarded as at our disposal. Out of considerations of gratitude, too, we were told, it was our duty to suppress the doubts and misgivings which would sometimes arise in our minds, when we allowed our consciences to present the nature of our life in its own proper light. If there were no priests, we were reminded we could never get to heaven; and it would be ungrateful in the extreme, after being insured of eternal life by their kind offices, if we should deny them any wish whatever.

In spite, however, of all that was said, our feelings often revolted, and arguments were renewed. Not only so, but now and then, as I have before remarked, penances of different kinds were often resorted to, to suppress them.

One of the tales told us by the priests, was this—intended to prove the power they exercise by means of sacraments which none but they can administer. I recollect that it was recounted to us one day at catechism, by one of the fathers.

"I was once travelling," said he, "in a desolate region, when I saw something flying like a white dove. Believing it to be the Holy Spirit, I followed it, and it led me to a house, over the door of which it stopped. I went in, and found an old man on his death-bed, who had never been baptized, nor ever heard of any religion. I baptized him; and he went off straight to heaven.*

---

* Among my early recollections, are many anecdotes illustrating the peculiar opinions and ceremonies of the Catholics in and about Montreal. My grandmother, Mrs. Mills, was a Scotch woman, and a firm Protestant. She had a handsome estate about four miles distant from the city, on the Lachine road, where I repeatedly visited her. She was required, like everybody else in the parish who was able, to furnish, in her turn, what is called "holy bread," which is given out in church by the priest before sacrament, but eaten afterwards. The preparation of it was attended with much trouble and some expense; for there were to be eleven loaves made, of different sizes, though they were all of considerable weight. They were made with a good supply of eggs and butter, and took about a bag of flour. They were ornamented on the top with Peter's cock crowing, having on his head a tinsel crown, and were starred over, in a particular manner, which required great painstaking, and often cost many trials before they would be done right. My grandmother used to say that it always cost her ten or twelve dollars to prepare the holy bread; and the sacrifice of her feelings appeared to be still more reluctantly submitted to; for she called it, in her broad Scotch dialect, a service to the Deevil.

She was a regular devout attendant on public worship; notwithstanding her advanced age (above eighty) and the distance from her church, in Montreal, she seldom or never failed to attend, although in consequence of certain unhappy circumstances in her family, she could not for some years command the services of the horses in the barn, and always had to walk. I have lately conversed with a Protestant clergyman residing in Canada, who spoke in high terms of my grandmother, and said he had often overtaken her on the road home from church in the snow, and taken her up in his sleigh.

After her death, the Roman Catholics dwelling in her neighbourhood held her memory in great dislike, and were not allowed to pass over any part of her farm unless they had holy water about them, for fear of being beset by evil spirits.

One reason why I did not like to approach the cells occupied by the imprisoned nuns, was this: the Superior had told me that they were possessed by evil spirits, and that I must always make the sign of the cross on going into the cellar.

There are seven sins, as we were taught, which priests cannot forgive, viz: that of refusing to pay tithes to the church, injuring dumb animals,

---

A man I knew, whose name it is not necessary to mention, the son of a Protestant mother, wished to marry a Catholic woman, but knew he would be disinherited if he did so before she disposed of her property. The priest allowed them to live together as man and wife, with the intention to be married at a future time. When the neighbours began to talk about them, the priest gave the woman permission to turn Protestant for a time, and to be married by a Protestant Clergyman, which was done by Mr. Black. After the death of her mother-in-law, she threw off all disguise and avowed her Catholic sentiments again.

As this worthy couple lived in the house of the parent, in accordance with custom, they had to have the house blessed by a priest, before it was thought to be proper or safe to inhabit it. Accordingly the ceremony was performed, of driving out the devils; and a considerable sum of money was paid to the priest, I believe about a dollar for each window in the house. The man (who appeared to have no real principle) had a priest on his farm as many as seven or eight times to my knowledge, to bless his ground, and to secure his crops from insects; for some of his neighbours had persuaded him that it had been cursed in particular spots where a Protestant minister had trodden, when he visited it during the life of his mother, so that it was unfit to produce the priest's blessed grain.

The ceremony of blessing ground and seeds is one very commonly practised in those places in Canada, where I have been. Before a farmer plants, he takes a handful of seed to his priest, who blesses it, before it is fit to grow; and receives a sum of money for it, commonly, I believe, as many shillings as there are grains. These are to be mixed with the rest of the seed before sowing, and then you are sure of a good crop.—At sowing time the priests have often a good deal to do in this way, and receive much money. The farmers often pay them in grain instead of money, which is commonly the best that is to be had. I know that an uncle of mine commonly bought his seed wheat at the Seminary, because it was the best he could obtain. The priests have in this way a good deal of trade and barter to carry on, as is well known in and about Montreal.

setting a house on fire, hearing a Protestant preach, reading Protestant books, and one more which I do not remember. These, however, can be forgiven by the Bishop or the Grand Vicar.

From what I heard and observed at different times, I had reason to believe that a serious misunderstanding existed between the Bishop and Father Richards. I heard it hinted, in some way, that the former would probably have had his residence in the nunnery but for the latter. But this I state only as what I have been told.

The term "old nun," I did not particularly explain in my first edition. It did not refer entirely to age. None of the nuns, indeed, were old women. For some reason or other, none of them appeared to me to be above forty years of age and few more than thirty. I never knew what made the difference between them and the common veiled nuns, like myself. It was easy to see that they stood on a different footing from the rest of us, but what that footing was I never could thoroughly understand. They had a separate sleeping room, which I have described, and exercised much authority, not merely in overseeing and directing operations in the nuns' and novices' departments, but were allowed to inflict various punishments without consulting the Superior, and sometimes did punish with great severity.

I sometimes imagined that there might be some formal introduction to the dignity and authority of an Old Nun, and that a higher grade existed, above that of the "Received." It has occurred to me as quite possible, (from what I knew of the difference between novices and veiled nuns,) that "Old Nuns" might have taken some peculiar oaths, and submitted to rules of a special nature. All this, however, I inferred only from their conduct, and the concert and understanding which they appeared to have with each other and the Superior. No further light could I obtain on the subject; and I am still as much in the dark as ever, although the Superior once gave me much encouragement to hope that I should become an "Old Nun."

Some of that class, as I began to say, were far from being old; and indeed a number of them were below thirty years of age, according to my judgment. As for their real names, families, or personal history, I knew as little of them as others. We called them, familiarly, Ma Mere (my mother) or Ma Tante, (my aunt), and commonly obeyed them without delay when they laid their commands upon us.

I have no doubt that, whatever was the process by which "Old Nuns" are made, the reason of the elevation of a "Received" to that dignity, is her superior cunning. It was in consequence of my success at imposture, that the Superior told me she hoped I might become one; and the old nuns whom I best knew, were among the greatest adepts at duplicity I ever saw.

CHAPTER XVIII.

AMONG the practices in the nunnery, is that of shaving the hair of the nuns on their admission—This is done to most, but not all; as the hair of some is more easily disposed in a manner thought necessary to the proper arrangement of the headband and veil. My hair was shaved on my reception, and frequently afterwards. At the time of my escape from the convent, it was very short; since when it has been growing, and it is now about six inches long. We used sometimes to shave each other's heads, and I have done it for other nuns.

It is a rule, that no novice shall be received who is not in sound health. Miss Louisa Bousquier, of St. Denis, owed her escape from the life of a nun to an affection of the head, on account of which she was discharged from her noviciate when within about three months of the period when she would have taken the veil.

Sometimes the priests would come to the Superior to borrow money of her, when she would show liberality towards some, but others I have heard her blame for not paying what they already owed her. In several instances I knew difficulties to arise from money affairs.

One day I heard a conversation between the Bishop and the Superior of the Seminary about a quantity of plate which an old lady, on her decease, had bequeathed to the church. The Superior wished to appropriate it to the expenses of the Seminary, but the Bishop claimed it as his own. He said he wanted a set of plate and would have it sent to his house for his own use. The Superior replied, that he could do that as soon as he had paid the price which she could get for it at the silversmith's. The Bishop asked her if she knew whom she was talking to; and things seemed likely to rise to some height, when I left the room.

I heard a conversation, soon after my admission as a nun, between the Bishop and the Superior of the nunnery, in her room. The Bishop was complaining that he could not get his proper dues from the priests; for, as I understood, each priest is required to pay two English shillings out of every dollar he receives, for his support in the Seminary; while the whole of the profits of every high mass for the dead, is considered the property of the Seminary. The Superior of the nunnery replied, that the priests would be better able to pay all their debts if they did not gamble so much; and the state of the country at that time was unfavourable, and little money was to be had. The Bishop said he must preach a sermon to the people, to make them more liberal in their contributions.

I saw a nun one day whose appearance struck me in a singular manner. She was conducting a priest through the sewing room, and had a large bunch of keys, like an old nun. I could hardly tell what to think when I looked on her. It seemed as if I must have seen her before, and yet I could not remember when or where; and I had an impression that she could not be a nun. For some reason or other which I could not understand, I felt a great anxiety to know something about her, and inquired of Jane Ray, but she could tell me but little or nothing. I then asked leave of the Superior to speak with Sainte Thomas,—for that I understood was her name.—She consented, on condition that we should converse in her presence. I accordingly addressed her; but, much to my mortification and surprise, she replied very coldly, and showed at first no disposition to interchange more than a salutation with me. She soon, however, took an opportunity to write something on a bit of paper with a pencil, and to slip it into my hand, which I eagerly read as soon as I could safely do so; and there I found an explanation of her conduct. She intimated that she was unwilling to confide in the Superior, but wished to see me alone the first opportunity.

We soon after had a secret interview, for one night she stole into my bed, and we lay and talked together. She then appeared quite unreserved, and perfectly cordial, and repeated that she believed the Superior was only a spy over us. We soon found that we had been acquaintances in former years, and had been in the Congregational Nunnery together, but after her leaving it, I had met her twice in the street, and heard of her from some one; her family being so wealthy, we had no intercourse in society. She was from a place behind the mountain, where her father, I believe, was a grocer, and a man of wealth. She had an uncle McDonald.

I learnt from her the circumstances under which she entered the nunnery; and they were peculiar. She had not passed a noviciate, but had purchased her admission without such preparation, by the paying of a large sum of money, as she had peculiar reasons for wishing for it.

My restless anxiety was thus in a degree relieved, for I found that my impressions were right, and that St Thomas was not a nun in the common meaning of the word; but, on the other hand, I found I had been deceived in believing that all admitted into the Convent had to pass through the same long trial and training to which I had been subject.

The state of things in the nunnery cannot be fully understood, without a knowledge of the fact, that much jealousy always exists between some of the nuns, on account of their preferences for particular priests. And yet a priest once told me, that there was more wrangling done in the Seminary about nuns, than any thing else.

Saint Clotilde died while I was there, of a natural death; and I heard one of the other nuns say she was glad of it, because she had drawn off the affections of a priest from her. The priests often bring in little delicacies into the nunnery for their favourites, such as fruit, confectionary, &c., and give them without the Superior's knowledge; and sometimes make them much more valuable presents.

There was a nun who entertained a very bitter spirit towards me. This was Sainte Jane; and a cross, disagreeable creature she was as I ever saw. She would sometimes get close by me on purpose, while employed in ironing, or some other kind of work which required us to be up, and in time of silence stand upon my feet, in order to make me speak and get a penance. She once complained to the Superior, that she saw me looking from a place in the nunnery which she mentioned, and heard the voice of some person speaking with me. Although this was utterly false, the Superior thought I might have some intention of escaping, and sentenced me to the most severe penance I ever endured—viz: to live on bread and water for three weeks.

This diet appeared to reduce my strength; and I suffered more severely than usual from the kneeling posture at prayers, which was always peculiarly distressing to me, and made me almost desperate, so that I would sometimes almost as readily die as live.

CHAPTER XIX.

Manners of the Canadian Priests—Confessions of crimes by some of the
Priests—Story told by Aunt Susan, of her visit to a Quebec Nunnery—
Nuns in Priests' dresses—Sister Turcot.

THE priests who are natives of Canada, are generally very clownish
in their manners, and often quite brutish in their vices. The nuns
would sometimes laugh at seeing a Canadian priest from some country
parish, coming in with a large piece of bread in his hand, eating it
as he walked. A large proportion of the priests are foreigners; and a
constant intercourse appears to be kept up with France, as we often
heard of such and such a father just arrived from that country. These
are decidedly the worst class. Most of the wickedness of which I have
any knowledge, I consider as their work.

If I should repeat one half of the stories of wickedness I have heard
from the mouths of some of the priests, I am afraid they would hardly
be believed; and yet I feel bound, since I have undertaken to make
disclosures, not to omit them altogether.

It is not uncommon for priests to recount anecdotes of what they
have seen and done; and several stories which I have heard from some
of them I will briefly repeat.

A country priest said one day, that he knew a priest in a parish better
off than those of the Seminary, for he had seven nuns all to himself.

A priest said to me one day, that he had three daughters in Montreal,
grown up. Their mother was a married woman. One of the daughters,
he added, now occasionally confessed to him, ignorant, however, of
any relationship.

Another said he was once applied to by a man for advice, in consequence of suspicions he had of his wife, and quieted his suspicions by
telling him a falsehood, when he knew the husband was not jealous
without cause, he himself having been her seducer.

It may, it must offend the ear of the modest to hear such exposures
as these, even if made in the most brief and guarded language that
can be used. But I am compelled to declare, that this is not all. I shall

stop here, but lest my readers should infer that it is because there is nothing more that could be said, I must first make the solemn declaration, that *there are crimes committed in the Hotel Dieu Nunnery too abominable to mention.*

I remember a variety of stories relating to confession, which I have heard told in the nunnery by priests; who sometimes become very communicative when intoxicated. One of their favourite topics is Confession. One of them showed a watch, one day, which he said was worth a hundred dollars. He had received it at confession, from a fellow who had stolen it, telling him that he must see it safely restored to the owner, while his intention was to get it into his possession to keep, which he did, and boasted of what he had done.

I have known priests to sit and talk about what they had done in the Confessional, for three or four hours at a time; and I have heard one give another instructions how he might proceed, and what he might do. One priest, I know, paid another fifty dollars, to tell him what was confessed to him by a young woman for whom he had a partiality, or what he called love. Sometimes one will request another to send a particular lady to confess to him, either on account of her beauty or her property, for considerable sums are in such cases obtained from the rich.

In the country the common practice is, so far as I know, to fix the price of confession for the year, at some particular rate: as two bushels of wheat out of twelve; or if the person is not a farmer, a sum of money.

A priest one day said to another in my hearing, You confess such a young lady, mentioning her name. She does not like you, I understand, because you kiss her. She is rich, and you have more rich persons to confess than I think is your share.

I knew a country priest, on a wager, drink a shoe-full of wine. I was once near the priests' parlour, (as I have called it,) when I heard two of them in an altercation, about the speed of two insects; which led to a wager, on the question whether that insect would move quicker over a hot brick or a cold one. They told me to put a brick in the cold, while they heated one on the stove; and when both were prepared, they actually tried the experiment. This scene caused great excitement and loud talking. I have mentioned it to give an idea of the manner in which much time passes in the nunnery.

One day when I was employed in the hospital, Aunt Susan came in, one of the old nuns, who had been absent for several days, and just returned. The circumstances which I am about to relate were brought to my mind the other day, by reading in Rosamond's book about the priests in Cuba taking her into a monastery in disguise.

Aunt Susan was something like Aunt Margaret, in having something the matter with her feet which made her rather lame. I noticed something strange in her appearance when she came into the hospital, and found that she was unable to apply the cup in cupping a patient for whom that remedy had been prescribed, although she had been remarkably skilful before, and now appeared to try her best. I thought she must have taken too much wine, and undertook to perform the operation at her request, which pleased her so well, that she sat down and became very talkative, in a manner little consistent with the rules and practices of the institution.

She told me that she had just returned from Quebec, whither she had gone some days before from our Convent, on a visit to the Hotel Dieu Nunnery of that city. She had gone in the dress of a priest, in company with some father, and had an opportunity to witness the arrangements and habits of that institution. She went on to make remarks on different subjects which had come under her observation, while I was employed in operating on the patient. She represented the rules in the nunnery which she had visited as less strict, or less strictly regarded, than our own; and said there was much less order, peace, and quietness, than we enjoy. The Superior, she said, had less command over the nuns, and they were less orderly, and not so well contented. She had a cousin there, as she informed me, a Miss Duranceau, who was very stubborn, and unmanageable. If she were Superior, she declared she would half murder her for her rebellious conduct.

All that I knew about the story told by Aunt Susan, was what she told me. I did not see her in the dress of a priest, but I had reason to believe that the nuns often left the convent in such a disguise, and that this part of her tale was by no means incredible. Indeed, during my stay in the Hotel Dieu, I personally knew more than one case of the kind.

There was an old nun, notorious in Montreal, known by the name of Sister Turcot, her family name. I was one day employed in the hospital, when I saw her enter dressed like a priest, in company with one or two fathers. She spent a few minutes there, during which she went up to one of the patients' beds, and performed prayers instead of one, and with such address that I should never have suspected any thing irregular, I think, if I had not known her appearance as well as I did. It was with the greatest difficulty that I refrained from laughing at a sight so ludicrous. She was at the time on her way out of the nunnery, in company with the priests, and after a short delay left the hospital, and went, as I supposed, into the street.

But I had still stronger evidence than this, of the departure of nuns in open daylight, in the dress of priests; for I was repeatedly called in to help them to put on their disguise. I have dressed the nun Sainte Felix, three or four times; and a hateful creature she was, in consequence of her jealous disposition. She was always thinking some one else a greater favourite than herself, with some priest.

The place where the change of dress was usually made was the Superior's room; and in the closet in the adjoining passage, at the end nearest the door, were always kept a number of priests' dresses, nearly a shelf full; as well as several black-hooded cloaks, like those worn by the Sisters of Charity.

A priest once told me, that he had three nuns to take out of the Convent that day, and was troubled to know how to do it. He had often taken out one at a time, and had sometimes thought he might lose them if they were disposed to run away. He commonly directed them to limp as they passed along the street;—"for," said he, "many of the priests do so, and they might pass very well for limping priests; and in our dress, how can you tell a man from a woman? But," he added, "now I have got three; and if I should undertake to lead them all out together, the devils of women might start off three different ways at the first corner we come to, and how could I catch them?"

The change made in the dress, when a nun disguises herself as a priest, is complete. All the clothes of the latter are assumed. They pass through the public rooms in going out of the nunnery, and are often absent for several weeks.

CONFIRMATION OF MARIA MONK'S DISCLOSURES.

CHAPTER I.

GENERAL REMARKS.

TRUTH of Miss M.'s having been a nun and of her disclosures blended together—Priests have great advantage—Have Miss M.'s external testimony in their power—Canadian press—Miss M. as a witness—Arguments establishing her truth—From her incapacity to have acted the part of an impostor—From her nunnery knowledge and practice—From her comparative ignorance of everything else—From marks on her person—From the situation in which she was first discovered in New York—From her confession to the Rev. Mr. Tappin—From the consistency of her conduct in the matter—From the simplicity and consistency of her narrative—From the moral character of her mind—Character of the evidence adduced in this chapter.

MARIA MONK affirms that she has been a nun in the Hotel Dieu nunnery of Montreal, and that her statements respecting that establishment are such as she knows, from her own experience and observation, to be true. On the other hand, the priests and their advocates deny that she has ever been an inmate of that convent; and, of course, maintain that her disclosures were so many fictions. The hinge, therefore, on which the whole controversy turns, is the fact, whether or not she has ever been a cloistered nun. And, although this question is distinct from the question of the truth of her statements, in point of fact, yet, in the discussion, they naturally run into each other. The priests, on the one hand, attempt to draw an argument from the character of her disclosures, in support of their position, that she has never been a nun; while on the other hand, the friends of Miss Monk reason from the same source, to prove that she must have been an inmate of the nunnery. The former maintain that the crimes, which she alleges are habitually practised by themselves and

the nuns, are incompatible with human nature; while the latter argue
that they are just what might be expected from the circumstances
of the case—that they are in perfect accordance with the history of
convents, and that a girl in her situation could never have become
as familiar with them as she is, unless she had been associated with a
society addicted to their practice. Hence the question, both as to the
fact of her having been a nun, and as to the truth of her disclosures,
are intimately blended in this discussion.

   In this controversy, aside from truth, the priests have greatly the
advantage. They are a numerous and powerful body of men, skilled in
the arts of controversy. Miss Monk is an inexperienced girl, yet in her
youth, having no friends, except such as she has gained by her apparent
honesty and consistency since the controversy commenced. Moreover,
from a variety of circumstances, the mass of the people in Canada are
prejudiced in favour of the priests and against her, so that they are
disposed to afford them any assistance in their power. This is the case
to a great extent, even with the Protestants, especially in Montreal.
Not only the ordinary relations which bind society together exist
between Catholics and Protestants in Canada, but there are relations
of a special character existing in the present case. The government, it
is true, is nominally Protestant, but then such is the state of parties
there, that it requires, in order to its very existence, the patronage, to
some extent, of the priests. This the wily priests give to it; in order
that they, in their turn, may receive the special smiles of civil officers.
Maria Monk states another circumstance, respecting some few of the
more wealthy and nominal Protestants in and about Montreal, which
is, that they are licentious visitors of the nunnery. If this be true, it
exhibits a reason for the violence of their opposition to her.

   Another thing worthy of special notice is the fact, that the field
of nearly all Miss Monk's external testimony is in the power of the
priests. They have her former associates and companions: nay, they
have her own blood-connexions, so completely under their control
and influence, as to restrain them from uttering anything favourable
to her claims. They also have the nunnery in their possession, and will
not allow it to be impartially examined. Hence the demand for more

external evidence, made by many, is unreasonable. Every subject has evidence appropriate to itself; and that—and that alone ought to be all that should be required.

The public press in Canada is either Catholic or political. Hence it has from the first been violent in its opposition to Miss Monk. It took its stand against her before she had published a single word. Not a single article has ever been published there, so far as I can learn, the design of which has been to exhibit the evidence in support of her truth. The consequence is, that the people of Canada are, in general, profoundly ignorant in respect to the existence of any such evidence; and not only so, but they have been led astray by the numberless misstatements, which have been circulated by the priests, their friends, and the Canadian press. Hence the strong popular prejudices, which are believed to exist to a considerable extent in that province, against Miss Monk.

I might also remark respecting the horrid nature of the crimes, which Miss Monk charges upon the priests and nuns, in connexion with her own character as a professed witness. By her own confession, while in the convent, she lived in impurity, and was taught the arts of deception and hypocrisy. Hence an argument, very properly used to a limited extent, against her as a witness. But, it may be asked, is she not as good a witness as the nature of the case can possibly furnish? If her story be true, are not all the inmates of that convent alike in these respects? The criminal practices which she divulges are of the deepest dye, insomuch that the more virtuous portions of society instinctively recoil at the very thought of believing them. Hence they are predisposed to discard them, without examining the evidence of their truth.

But, notwithstanding all these difficulties, the evidence in support of Miss Monk's claims, when collected and intelligently considered, is irresistible. The argument is cumulative. And I will now proceed, as succinctly as possible, to lay it before my readers.

The character and conduct of Miss Monk furnish the strongest evidence in support of the general truth of her claims, as a professed ex-nun.

1. *Her incapacity to have acted the part of an impostor, is, in the highest degree, evident to all who are personally acquainted with her.*—The cogency of this argument is acknowledged by her opponents. Hence they deny that she is the authoress of the disclosures attributed to her. They maintain that she is a *mere tool*, in the hands of others, who have fabricated and published them in her name. But this, I trust, has been shown to the satisfaction of the reader, to be untrue. It has been shown, that she, and she alone, is the authoress of the dark tale, which she has published to the astonishment of the people of this country.

Miss Monk is young, and possesses a mind altogether undisciplined by study. Her education is inferior to that of ordinary country girls. Habits of study she has none. Her knowledge of books is, or was when she first arrived in New York, next to nothing. And, if the "Awful Exposure" gives us a true history of her life, she has never been either a nun, or a Roman Catholic; but "has led the life of a stroller and a prostitute." If this be true, it is asked, how a girl of her age, character, and attainments, could possibly fabricate such books as her "Disclosures?" The supposition beggars all belief, but that of blindness. If she has fabricated them, Rome, with its numberless saints, may be fearlessly challenged to produce a miracle anything like as great.

Besides, on the supposition, that she had fabricated her "Disclosures," it is impossible that she should have been able to act the part of an impostor, up to the present time, without being detected. Many minds have been at work, for more than a year past, endeavouring to develop her true character. Both friends and foes have been thus employed. Had she been an impostor, it would have been discovered, long before this day. She constitutionally possesses transparency of character, to an uncommon degree. Hence the predominant workings of her mind are very apparent, to a penetrating observer. She has very little of that systematic concealment and forethought, so necessary to a successful impostor. Her openness of character, constitutionally considered, is almost the first thing observed, by an intelligent stranger who may chance to see and converse with her. Hence, if such a person has been sceptically disposed in regard to the general truth of her claims, his scepticism, in perhaps nineteen cases out of twenty, has been removed by a free conversation with her. Such an individual readily perceives, that her mental constitution is such, as totally to disqualify her to act the part of protracted imposture.

The argument, therefore, under this head, is twofold—being founded, 1st, On her incapacity to create her "Disclosures"—2nd, On the supposition that she possessed such ability, her incapacity to have successfully concealed her imposture, up to the present time.

2. *Her minute and extensive nunnery knowledge, connected with the ease and dexterity with which she can perform the many ceremonies of a convent*, can be accounted for, on no other supposition, than that of her having been a nun, as she states. Her practical knowledge of Popery and Jesuitism, of priests and nuns, of the furniture and diversified apartments of the Hotel Dieu, of the ceremonies and practices of that establishment, is such as could have been acquired by her, only by a residence of years in that convent. She is as familiar with the mummery of Popish observances, as a school-boy is with his alphabet—such as penances, hymns, Latin prayers, &c. &c., though she is as ignorant of the meaning of Latin words, as she is of the Chinese language. The same is true with reference to the ease with which she performs the various bodily ceremonies, some of which she speaks of in her book, such as falling upon the knees, and standing erect upon them, &c. &c. With the Romish catechisms, she is perfectly familiar. In a word, she is, in regard to these matters, all that we might suppose her to be, on the supposition that she has, for years, been a resident in the convent. Speaking in the language of common life, "she has learned her trade." And no man, in his senses, can understandingly deny it. How, then, can this evidence be resisted?

3. *Her ignorance of life, disconnected from convents*, can be accounted for, only on the supposition of her having lived a conventual life. I speak now with special reference to what she was, when she first arrived in New York, in the spring of 1835. At that time, her acquaintance with matters and things, as they appear in the domestic circle, and in ordinary life, was very limited. She was evidently a comparative stranger to them; whilst all her movements and manners were such, as bespoke her former life to have been that of a cloistered nun. Says Mr.

Hilliker, in his affidavit:—"We observed also, that she always folded her hands under her apron when she walked, as she has described the nuns as doing, in her "Awful Disclosures."

4. *The marks on her person*, which were produced by suffering penances, and other violent treatment, afford an argument in support of her claims. She has several of these, as she states in her first volume. She speaks of having worn a broad belt around her waist, "stuck full of sharp iron points, for the mortification of her spirit." The writer of this has been informed by a respectable lady, who examined Miss Monk's waist, that the scars produced by this belt, are very manifest. To use her own language, "it looks distressing."

The marks of gagging are seen on her lips; and there are scars also on her thumbs, which were "cut severely by the tight drawing of the band used to confine her arms." These are the signs of Romish penance and violence. But the "Awful Exposure" tells us that she has never been a Roman Catholic!

5. *The circumstances*, in connexion with which she was first discovered by Mr. Hilliker, and his associates, after her arrival in the city of New York, afford an argument in proof of Miss Monk's honesty. She was discovered by Mr. Hilliker and his companions in a retired place, above the city of New York, where she had secreted herself for several days, and where she had evidently made up her mind to die. She was not far from death when thus found; and it was with much difficulty that she was prevailed upon to leave the place of her concealment. Nay, she declined leaving it, until she saw that the gentlemen were determined to remove her by force, unless she would go voluntarily. She had already become so feeble as to need to be supported, by two of the gentlemen, in walking the distance of half a mile, to the almshouse. She was in a strange country, under circumstances peculiarly distressing. After Mr. Hilliker had conversed with her some time alone, and assured her that he was a married man, and that he wished to befriend her in every way he could, she stated to him, that she was an eloped nun, and that she became *enciente* in the convent. He states that he found her in tears, and that she wept for two hours afterwards. He has mentioned several circumstances in his affidavit,

all of which bear the marks of honest sincerity, on the part of Miss Monk. It is impossible to account for them on any other supposition than that she told the truth, as to her elopement from the nunnery. It is impossible, that such circumstances should mislead, for they cannot testify falsely, as guilty man can, and often does, do.

6. *The circumstances* in connexion with which Miss Monk first divulged the principal facts recorded in her book, are such as to afford the strongest evidence in support of her claims to public confidence. These are detailed in the statement of the Rev. Mr. Tappin, on page 167.* She made known these facts to him by way of penitential confession, while sick in the almshouse, and as she supposed, ready to die. Mr. Tappin states that it was perfectly manifest to his mind, that she had no idea of criminating others, or that her statements would ever be made public. She and others thought, that she was on the borders of the grave, and she wished to quiet her troubled conscience, by confessing what she considered to be her grossest sins. She was still a Roman Catholic; it was therefore in perfect accordance with the religion she had been taught, thus to confess. There are two things worthy of special notice in connexion with Miss Monk's confession to the Rev. Mr. Tappin:—1st. *The manifest absence of every sinister motive*, by which she could have been influenced in making these communications to him. What earthly motive could have influenced her? Revenge to the priests? Certainly not; for she had no idea that her confessions would go beyond the mind of him whom she then considered as her confessor. The same reply may be given to the insinuation, that she did it in order to mitigate her unfortunate situation, in being the mother of an illegimate child; or that she did it for the purpose of securing any earthly good whatever.

2nd. The only motives which appeared to be present, at the time, to her mind, were such as arise from the apprehension of speedy dissolution, connected with the solemn retributions of eternity. Was it, then, within the limits of possibility, under such circumstances, for her to acted the part of a diabolical impostor? Is not the supposition utterly incredible? How then can it be otherwise, than that she is

_____
* Page 165 in this edition.

honest in putting forth her claims as an ex-nun? I would only add that the hand of God is extremely manifest in bringing to light Miss Monk's statements respecting the Hotel Dieu Nunnery, in a manner so convincing to every reflecting mind. Let, then, her sad tale be believed; and let it produce the benign effects, in counteracting vice and error, which, under the government of the Supreme disposer of all events, it is adapted to do.

7. *The consistency of Miss Monk's conduct with the demands of truth,* furnishes an argument favourable to her claims. She has acted just as one might suppose she would have done, on the supposition that she was honest in giving her disclosures to the world. Her circumstances have been peculiarly trying, arising in part from her comparative ignorance of the world, connected with the discredit which has been thrown upon her statements, and the consequent violent denunciations which have been heaped upon her by Protestants, especially editors of newspapers, who have taken very little pains to investigate the subject. Often has she felt, as if she had scarcely a real friend on earth—as if all the world was against her, making her the helpless victim of its combined contempt and indignation. Yet amidst all her trials, she has exhibited, to those around her, that she felt an unwavering consciousness of standing upon the truth; and that the God of truth would one day vindicate her honesty. Being possessed naturally of an unusual degree of sensibility, and feeling her forlorn situation, it is true, she has often wept in secret places, for having published her dark story, not because of its untruth, but because of the cruel treatment she has received in consequence of it.

She has invariably manifested a very strong desire that the truth of her charges against the Roman priests and nuns of Lower Canada, might be tested by some equitable tribunal. Hence her visit to Montreal for this purpose, in the August of 1835, and before she ever thought of publishing a book. She then and there solemnly appealed to the civil authorities, to investigate their truth. She was accompanied by two American gentlemen, of the legal profession, who assisted her in presenting her charges in due form, attested on oath, to the Attorney General for prosecution. And after spending some three or four weeks, in fruitless attempts to secure the object of her visit, she returned to New York.

While at Montreal, it was denied by the priests that she had ever been an inmate of the Hotel Dieu. She at once offered a fair test of the fact, which, by a very little trouble, would have settled the point beyond the power of contradiction. She proposed a description of the interior of the convent—its furniture, its inmates and different apartments, and their uses—and staked her all upon its correctness. But the application of it was not allowed by her opponents; on what ground, no mortal can conjecture, unless it were that they were afraid to abide the results.

On the fourteenth day of last July, I received a letter from the Rev. Mr. Perkins of Montreal, informing me, that on the following day a committee of gentlemen were to apply the test, which she had proposed nearly one year before. The thought immediately occurred to me, if she be an impostor I can now discover it, by communicating to her this unexpected intelligence. I applied the test, in the best manner to accomplish the end in view, that I was capable of; and the result was such, as decidedly deepened my convictions of her honesty. Other particulars might be mentioned, were it necessary, all going to show the consistency of her conduct, with the supposition, that she feels herself standing upon the rock of truth.

On the other hand, if she be an impostor, her conduct has been, in the highest degree, preposterous and unaccountable. Suppose that she had described the interior of the Magdalen Asylum of Montreal, instead of the Hotel Dieu nunnery. She certainly must have been sensible of the fact. And if so, is it supposable that she would have gone to Montreal, for the purpose of substantiating crimes, of the darkest hue, against the Hotel Dieu ecclesiastics; and there make oath that she had resided for years in the convent, where she had witnessed their commission; and in proof, that she had thus resided in the convent, offer a description of the persons, furniture, and the interior arrangements of the Montreal Magdalen Asylum? The supposition is absurd, beyond the power of language to express. If she be an impostor, the extremes of unparalleled genius, and the most stupid folly and ignorance, meet in her. Considering her youth and limited opportunities, she has exhibited a talent for invention, in her works, compared with which the powers of Sir Walter Scott are but as a drop to the ocean; while on the other hand, she has evinced stupidity, if possible more remarkable, in staking her all upon the general truth of her description of the interior of a huge building, of which she is as ignorant as she is of the palace of the king of China. And then, to crown her folly, she has urged, with an importunity that would accept of no denial, the application of this test, which she must have known would have procured her inevitable and hopeless ruin. To believe, therefore, that she is an impostor, when the belief implies such an absurdity, I must say for one, I cannot, without a degree of insanity, which it would require, at least, as many as two "*pencils*" in each ear to produce.

8. *The artless manner in which Miss Monk narrates the principal facts in her disclosures,* furnishes a cogent argument in support of her claims. This may be called the internal evidence of the truth of her book. The first ten or fifteen thousand copies of her work were given to the public, accompanied with no other evidence than this. Immense multitudes who read the book, believed it, because they perceived that it bore the internal marks of truth, notwithstanding some of its statements divulged the perpetration of crimes, by priests and nuns, under the cloak of religion, of so horrid a character as to make an honest man shudder at the thought of them. I will mention some two or three things which have been urged as internal marks against the truth of the "disclosures:" but which, it appears to me, afford evidence in its favour. The circumstances connected with the murder of St. Francis, is one of these. It is said "that its comparative publicity, and the number of individuals employed in it, are marks of its falsehood." Thus argues the Rev. Mr. Perkins of Montreal. Now, in the first place, there was no publicity about it, except such as belonged to the convent. It was done within the walls of the nunnery, shut out from all communication with the world. In the second place, the fact, when understandingly considered, that so many were employed in it, is a circumstance corroborative of the truth of the narrative. Two reasons may be assigned for this;—1. It is the policy of such establishments thus to do, for the double purpose of inspiring terror at the thought of disobedience, and

at the same time, implicating all present in the crime committed. It had this effect on Maria Monk. Hence her penitential confession, at the time she thought that she was going to die, to the Rev. Mr. Tappin. The second reason is this, that it was a regular court, or inquisitorial tribunal, the bishop presiding as inquisitor general. The Rev. W. C. Brownlee, D.D. of New York, a gentleman as well versed in the history of popish jurisprudence as any other Protestant in America, mentioned this fact to me, as, affording, to his mind, one of the strongest internal marks in the book, of its truth. Now Maria Monk knows nothing of these reasons; all she knows is the simple fact, that such and such persons were present, and that they did as she states in her narrative. Had she forged the story, undoubtedly she would have made it a more private affair, and would have created reasons for everything connected with it. But as it is, it bears the stamp of simple truth.

Maria Monk, on page 132 of her work,* says that she once saw a book in the superior's room, containing, among other things, a record of births which occur in the convent. Now it is asked, "if infants are immediately baptized and strangled after their birth, what can be the object of such a record? Why expose themselves, by making a record of their own crime?" Now, as in the case above, Miss Monk is incapable of assigning any reason why such a record should be kept. All she knows, or pretends to know, is the simple fact that such a record then existed. Undoubtedly, if she were an impostor, she never would have created the statement, without creating a reason for it at the same time. The same may be said respecting there being no balustrade around the "hole of interment," described by her as existing in the cellar of the Hotel Dieu. Had the description been the work of fancy, fancy would have given us a suitable balustrade.

Were it possible to put my readers in possession of the manuscript notes of the gentleman who arranged and gave form to Miss Monk's disclosures, I am quite confident that they would perceive in them all the artless simplicity of childlike truth. They would exhibit the simple statements of Miss Monk, just as they fell from her lips; and also the fidelity of her amanuensis, in so examining her as to render it

---

* Page 131 in this edition.

impossible for her to have acted the part of an impostor. Miss Monk's mind is undisciplined, and is wholly unaccustomed to connected thought and orderly arrangement. Hence her statements have all the simplicity and want of connexion of those of a child. This circumstance would have enabled her writer to have caused her to contradict herself in her narrations, had she not been based on the truth.

Miss Monk's narrative is consistent with itself and with reason. It is minute and specific in its details, respecting places, persons, and facts. In a word, it has every internal appearance of truth. How can all this be accounted for, if she be an impostor?

9. *The moral character of Miss Monk's mind*, for many months after her arrival in New York, was such as to furnish a high degree of evidence in support of her pretensions. She told us how and where she had lived for several years past. The moral condition of her mind bore its unequivocal testimony to the truth of her narrative. She informed us of the systematic deceptions which were inculcated and practised in the society with which she had been connected. The painful truth of this statement, was easily discovered in the state of her mind. It was seen that for her to speak truth, when a slight temptation to deviate from it, presented itself, required an effort on her part. Truth being the basis of confidence, the latter, as matter of course, cannot exist in the absence of the former. It was, therefore, evident that the inmates of the Hotel Dieu, could place little or no confidence in each other; and that jealousy and suspicion would naturally exist, to a fearful extent, in such a community. Thus it was with Maria Monk; although constitutionally she possesses the opposite qualities. She was suspicious of everybody, and could confide in nobody. To repose full confidence in those around her, was a lesson, which it took her some time to learn. In a word, according to her statements, the character of the community with which she had been living, was peculiar, such as cannot be found in civilized life; but only in a cloistered convent. It was in a high degree selfish, subject to the violent exercise of the darker passions of depraved human nature; such as constant fear, jealousy, want of confidence, suspicions, subjection to absolute authority, not out of respect, but from fear, irritability, growing out of a

forced submission to a code of contemptible ceremonies; in fine, the absence of whatsoever is pure, lovely, and of good report, in the female character. She bore the impress of this wretched community on her soul, thus evincing the character of the education she had received; although, as I had occasion to remark before, the moral texture of her mind, constitutionally considered, is directly the opposite. She is naturally liberal, even to excess, open, frank, affectionate, and confiding; and these traits of character have been, for some time past, rapidly developing themselves.

There can be no stamp without a corresponding seal. But Miss Monk's character furnishes us with a stamp or impress, altogether peculiar; and the question is, where is the seal or counterpart? If it does not now exist, it certainly must have existed at the time the impression was made. I repeat the question, where is it? Miss Monk declares that it was in the Hotel Dieu nunnery. The priests deny it. Let the priests, then, tell the world where it can be found; otherwise the world must believe Maria Monk.

Such is a summary view of the arguments, in confirmation of Miss Monk's claim to public confidence, as deduced from her character, person, conduct, and narrative. They are susceptible of much expansion, as my object has been, rather to suggest thought, than to expand it. The evidence thus derived, is of a character peculiarly strong and convincing. It is of an internal character, such as an enlightened mind loves to confide in. It is the *spontaneous testimony of nature*. And can nature bear false witness? Impossible! It is true, nature may, to some extent, be counterfeited; or we may mistake her voice, and attribute testimony to her, which she does not give, and thus deceive ourselves and others. But it is impossible that she should utter anything, but what is strictly true. Now, it is possible that myself and others, have misinterpreted the language of nature in the present instance; though I declare, that I cannot realize it. Hence, if there were no other evidence in confirmation of Miss Monk's testimony to be found, I should feel that I stood on firm ground, in endeavouring to support the truth of her claims as an ex-nun. For I feel, that the statements and affidavits of interested men, in opposition to the evidence adduced in this chapter, are of no value. In the scales of moral evidence, they are lighter than a breath. They are like chaff to the wheat; fit only to be given to the four winds of heaven. Unbelieving Protestants may hence learn what has been the principal ground, on which the friends of Miss Monk, in New York, have stood, amidst the clamorous denunciation, abuse, and contempt, which have been poured upon them from various quarters. They have felt that they were standing on a solid foundation, against which the waves of prejudice and wrath might beat in vain.

CHAPTER II.

TESTIMONY OF OTHERS IN CONFIRMATION OF MISS MONK'S CLAIMS.

PECULIARITY of Miss Monk's case—Statement of a Montreal lady—State of feeling in and about Montreal—Testimony of Mr. Miller—Of Mrs. Hahn—Opinion of three classes of persons—Of those who have informed themselves upon the subject—Of those around Miss Monk—Of those who know in part—Subterranean passage—Statement of Mr. Sprague—Of a gentleman—Of Mr. Wetmore—Of Mr. Bourne—Of Mr. Hogan.

IT is often asked, why the friends of Miss Monk, provided she has resided for years in the Hotel Dieu, do not produce the testimony of a sufficient number of living witnesses, to establish the fact, beyond the power of contradiction. If a person has lived for years in a given place, it is asked, is it not an easy matter to prove it, by a multitude of witnesses? I answer that it is, in ordinary cases. But the case of Miss Monk is peculiar; perhaps without a parallel on the pages of history. Her residence has been in a cloistered nunnery, shut out from the world. Since she escaped from the convent, she has made known the vile practices of her former associates, the priests and nuns; and they, in self-defence, deny that she was ever one of their number. Moreover, by their management they have sealed the lips of her friends, out of the nunnery, in Canada, who might otherwise testify as to the place of her former abode. Had the matter been otherwise managed at first, doubtless witnesses in abundance could have been found, who would have testified to the fact of her former residence in the Hotel Dieu. But it was not attended to, until the priests had every opportunity they could desire, to arrange matters according to their wishes. Go to Montreal now, and inquire of its older inhabitants, if they ever knew Maria Monk, and many of them will tell you that they used to see her, some six or seven years ago, at her mother's residence and at other places, but that they saw nothing of her during the time in which she alleges herself to have been in the nunnery. They all say, that during this period of time, they have missed her; but as to the fact, whether or no she was in the convent, during this time, they know nothing about it. The following is a specimen of the kind of evidence alluded to. A few days since, I saw a lady from Montreal, who observed, that, a short time ago, she was conversing with a Mrs. **** of Montreal, a respectable and Christian lady, who stated, that she had known Maria Monk from her childhood; and that the last time she ever saw her, was about the time she says that she returned from St. Denis and entered the nunnery—that she (M. M.) then called on her (Mrs. ****) to obtain money from her, for her mother; and that she let her have some, though less than what she asked for. Now it will be recollected that Maria Monk states, on page 24,* that she did obtain money from several individuals, on her mother's account, in order to pay her entrance into the novices' department of the Hotel Dieu.

The following extract of a letter, from a worthy gentleman in Montreal, who has taken some pains to investigate this matter, will enable the reader to understand something of the state of feeling, respecting this subject, in and about that city. After detailing the efforts of himself and another gentleman, in making inquiries of those who ought to know something of Miss Monk's past history, he writes as follows:—"Now the fact is just here, everybody is afraid to *know* anything about this matter: and all her relatives seem backward to say what they might on the subject. Romanism is so far predominant here, that there are only a very few who have correct principle and moral courage enough to *think, speak,* or *act,* aright in the concern. Political, pecuniary, and relative interests and connections, have occasioned such a commingling of Romanism and Protestantism, that it is difficult to reach the *black heart* of the Roman beast, nominal Protestants are so much in the way. A bookseller said to me yesterday, that *he* and all the other booksellers in the town were afraid to keep Maria Monk's book in their stores, lest a mob should attack them."

The subjoined testimony of Mr. Miller and Mrs. Hahn has been some time before the public. That of Mrs. Hahn is the more important.

---

* Page 28 in this edition.

It is that of an old companion, and of course there can be no mistake as to her acquaintance with Miss Monk. Mrs. Hahn described the person of Miss Monk, and stated the substance of her testimony before she saw her; and before Miss Monk knew anything of Mrs. Hahn's residing in New York. Collusion, therefore, between the parties is out of the question. Mr. Jones, while in New York, inquired of me what I should say respecting Mrs. Hahn's testimony, if she herself were to acknowledge that it was false. I replied that it would not in the least shake my confidence in its substantial truth, for such were the circumstances connected with the giving of it, that my reliance was chiefly upon them. Mrs. Hahn, however, remains unchanged as to the truth of her statements.

Mr. William Miller, a resident of New York for several years past, and formerly an old schoolmate of Maria's in Montreal, testifies that, on a visit to the latter city, in the summer of 1833, he called on Mrs. Monk, the mother of Maria, and inquired for Maria; and was informed by her that her daughter Maria was then in the nunnery. The priests, in their work, dispose of this affidavit by exhorting Mr. Miller to *repent!*

Mrs. Hahn, now a resident of New York and formerly a schoolmate of Miss Monk, testifies that she was with Maria in the school of the Congregational nunnery for about two years: that she was present at the time that Maria was received as a novice in the Hotel Dieu; and that she saw her some time after this, while she was yet a novice: and that she saw her a veiled nun, towards the close of the winter of 1833–4, in the hospital of the Hotel Dieu, which she at that time frequently visited, in order to see a sick friend; and that "a short time afterwards," she saw her again in the same place among the veiled nuns. The circumstances connected with the giving of this testimony were such, as to preclude almost the possibility of an error. The reader will see some of these by referring to the whole of her testimony. The authors of the "Awful Exposure" glide over this by a contemptuous sneer! A summary way of disposing of important testimony.

There is also the testimony of three classes of individuals, beside the above; or rather, their opinion formed on evidence more or less conclusive, which ought to have its weight in determining this controversy.

There is the opinion of a large number of individuals, who have taken some considerable pains upon the subject, not only by reading what has appeared in print on both sides of the question, but also by such an examination of Miss Monk, as has been satisfactory to themselves. Among this class are to be found men of the first standing in the different learned professions. I know that this is mere opinion, and as such I give it for what it is worth.—There is another class of persons, whose opinion ought to have still more weight, because their opportunities for forming it have been much greater. Among these are the different families in which Miss Monk has resided, since she came to reside in New York. The celebrated Whitefield, I think it was, was once asked his opinion respecting a certain individual, with whom he had some acquaintance. His reply was, that he did not know him, having never been with him in his family, the only place in which a man's true character can be discovered. Thus it is in regard to Maria Monk; her true character is easily discovered by those with whom she daily associates. And these, I think I may say without a single exception, are thoroughly convinced that she is not an impostor. The affidavits of all Canada could hardly shake their belief.

To these I would add the unwavering opinion of the gentleman who penned her works for her. He is a gentleman of high standing in the community, for literature, integrity, and piety. No man could have felt a deeper solicitude on the subject, than he has felt. He has felt, that not only his own reputation was at stake, but that truth—to him priceless—was to achieve new victories, or receive detriment, according as Miss Monk's testimony should prove true or false. Hence he has spared no pains to get at the simple truth of the case, whatever that might be.

I trust that the reader will not consider it out of place, for the writer of these pages to add his own opinion to the above. It is now some eight or nine months, since Miss Monk came to reside among the people of my pastoral charge. During this time I have seen her in a variety of circumstances; have heard her converse with friends and enemies, Protestants and Catholics, and men of all professions; have improved every opportunity, which God in his providence has given me, to ferret out the truth in relation to her claims—and as the result of the whole, I deliberately say, that I have never seen anything which led me, for any length of time, to doubt the general truth of her story; but on the contrary, the evidence of its truth has been constantly augmenting, so that I could now almost as easily believe any supposable impossibility, as to believe that she has been acting the part of an impostor, in what she has done.

The other class of individuals whose opinion is of some importance on the subject, are those who *know* a part of Miss Monk's statements to be true, and who infer from that, the truth of the remainder. Among these are to be found, those females scattered through the country, who received their education in the Congregational Nunnery of Montreal. A short time since, I heard one of this class speaking on the subject, after the following manner:—"Miss Monk's description of things, persons, and practices, which came under my observation, while a scholar in the Congregational Nunnery of Montreal, are generally so correct, that I cannot but think, that her descriptions of things and practices in the Hotel Dieu, the cloistered part of which I was never permitted to visit, are also generally correct." I have heard gentlemen who have long resided in Montreal, and who were familiar with matters and things without the concealed part of the convent, reason in a similar manner.

It is known to many, that there is a subterranean passage, leading from the priest's Seminary to the Hotel Dieu.

The following, taken from the St. Albans Franklin Journal, is subjoined. Even Mr. Jones, the publisher of the "Awful Exposure," admitted, to several gentlemen in New York, that there was such a passage; but that it was not more than thirty feet long! The existence of this passage is known to many in Montreal. What is the object of such a passage? Can anything virtuous require that a house of priests should be thus united, by a concealed, under-ground passage, to an establishment of secluded women? And I would further ask, how a man, who believes in the existence of such a secret communication, can disbelieve the "Awful Disclosures" of Maria Monk? If the priests are such licentious hypocrites, as to need a dark, under-ground passage to the women of the Hotel Dieu, from the commission of what crime would they abstain, which they considered necessary to conceal their infamy from the public eye? Would they refrain from the murder of infants and nuns? That man has but a slight acquaintance with human depravity, that can believe they would. The following is the communication alluded to.

"As there is some excitement in the community upon the subject of Popish licentiousness and vice from the disclosures of Maria Monk, and as some affect to disbelieve and ridicule her work as totally false, being in possession of some strong evidence that will confirm her statements, I give the public the facts.

"In conversation with a gentleman, who was some months since a Roman Catholic in Montreal, but has renounced their blasphemous dogmas, and is now a professed Christian, he told me, that he had been employed to labour in the cellars of the Priests' Seminary at Montreal, and while there engaged, he discovered a door in the wall of the cellar, which on opening, he found it connected with a passage under ground. He entered the passage and passed through it until he came to some stairs, at the head of which was a trap door. From the direction and distance of the passage, he was perfectly certain that it must be a subterraneous communication between the Seminary and the convent. He further informed me, that from the testimony of many females, his relatives not excepted, that at confession, the priests were in the habit of asking the most licentious and revolting questions that could be propounded, not only to married ladies, but also to girls of thirteen years.

"Likewise from the habiliments of the nuns, and their appearance at times, he was wholly confirmed in the belief that their course in the nunnery was anything but virtuous. At the time of his making these disclosures, I think Maria had not written her book. I think testimony of this kind is powerfully corroborative, and that these things exist, I fully believe. It is truly painful to come before the public with so offensive a subject, but believing the contagion of death to be spreading through the community by Catholicism, leaving putrescence and woe behind, I feel constrained thus to appear.

"E. SPRAGUE."

"St. Albans, July, 1836."

The ensuing statement is from a gentleman who was for many years a resident in Montreal. For reasons satisfactory to himself, his name is withheld. His testimony is undoubtedly true.

"I often heard of a subterranean passage, from the Seminary to the Hotel Dieu nunnery, years ago; and while the cathedral was building, I often saw that part of it which was opened in digging for the foundation. It was near the east corner of the cathedral, where the waterworks were laid along St. Joseph's street. Several years before, I saw the same passage opened in another place by the workmen, who had removed several stones and exposed it to view. I have often heard it spoken of, as a thing very generally known; and never heard any doubt of its existence until the appearance of Mr. Jones' book, and Mr. Stone's pamphlet."

The following documents on the subject of the subterranean passage, are extracted from the American Protestant Vindicator, of November 2, 1836. They have appeared since the above was written:—

"The first witness is the Rev. *Oliver Wetmore*, of Utica. In a late conversation with that beloved minister of the gospel, he thus remarked—

"Mr. Stone says: 'No subterranean passage between the Seminary and the Hotel Dieu nunnery, at Montreal, was ever seen or heard of!' *That is not true!* When I travelled as a missionary in the northern parts of the State of New York, *thirty-three years ago*, I was frequently at the house of Judge Moers, who resided about a mile from the Canada line. That gentleman repeatedly talked with me respecting the Roman priests and Popery, in Montreal, which he had often visited. He spoke of the *subterranean passage between the Seminary and the Nunneries*, as a matter of most public notoriety; and detailed the dissolute lives of the priests, their habitual gambling, intemperance, and profligacy, as well as the licentiousness of the female convents of Montreal; which Judge Moers said, were as open matters of talk at that period, in that city, just as much as the most common affairs of life. Judge Moers also represented to me the priests and nuns of Montreal, from his own personal acquaintance with them, in exactly the same light and character, *thirty-three years ago*, as they have lately been exhibited before the American public. *Mr. Stone, therefore, to my own certain knowledge, has published that which is not true!'"*

It appears, from this statement, that the existence of an underground passage, between the Priests' Seminary and the nunnery, has been a matter of conversation for many years.

The next statement is from the Rev. George Bourne, of New York:— "I most solemnly affirm, that the late Rev. Mr. Christmas, conducted me in the year 1825, I believe, for I have but one criterion by which I can determine the first time that I saw it, to visit the subterranean passage, between the Seminary and the Hotel Dieu convent; and that we frequently afterwards stood over that passage together. At other times, in company with different Christian brethren, I have also examined that underground avenue from the Seminary to the Nunnery; at least, that part of it which was open for common inspection for a considerable period, during the completion of the cathedral in that city.

"GEORGE BOURNE."

The following is the affidavit of Mr. Hogan, now a respectable member of the Methodist church, of New York, but formerly a Roman Catholic student of the Seminary of Montreal:—

"*New York*, October 26, 1836.

"Thomas Hogan, of the city of New York, being duly affirmed, doth say: That in the year 1824, he was a resident of the city of Montreal, Lower Canada—that at that period, the existence of a subterranean passage between the Seminary in Notre-Dame street, and the Hotel Dieu convent, was a matter of the most public notoriety; and that he himself has been in that passage, having entered it from the door in the Seminary—and the said Hogan doth further depose, that to his own personal knowledge, the Roman priests were constantly in the practice of visiting the nuns, for the purpose of licentious intercourse, by that secret passage.

THOMAS HOGAN.

"Affirmed this 26th day of October, 1836.

"Before me, William H. Bogardus, Commissioner of Deeds."

Who, after this, can doubt the existence of such a communication between the two establishments? And the question may be reiterated, what is the object of such a passage? Can it be anything lawful? If so, what is it? The world would be glad to know what it may be.

It is hardly necessary to remind the reader of the fact, that the above testimony furnishes a high degree of evidence, in confirmation of the general truth of the "Awful Disclosures."

CHAPTER III.

THE CONDUCT OF MISS MONK'S OPPONENTS, FURNISHES AN ARGUMENT IN HER SUPPORT.

THEY have expended much labour in vain to disprove her claims—Refusal to have the nunnery examined at first, is evidence against them—Their attempt to prove an Alibi in November, 1835, a failure—Priest Phelan's visit to New York—Attempted abduction of Miss Monk—Failed to destroy her testimony in their attempt to destroy her character—Also in their second attempt to prove an Alibi—Also in their exparte examination of the nunnery—Also in their Magdalen trick—Remarks on this manœuvre—Other failures—Conclusion—Priests found guilty.

"ACTIONS speak louder than words," is a maxim as venerable for age, as it is just and true. According to this maxim, it is evident, that the conduct of Miss Monk's opponents furnishes an argument of great force against themselves, and, of course, in support of her claims. The position, which they have taken, that she is an impostor, and never has been a nun, if true, could have been proved beyond all doubt, with one-thousandth part of the labour, which they have fruitlessly bestowed in their several attempts to prove it. They admit that, until recently, she has always lived in and about Montreal. Could they not then, with very little trouble, have shown us where and with whom she lived, during the time she professes to have been a nun in the Hotel Dieu convent?

But let us look at their conduct a little in the detail. When Miss Monk visited Montreal in the month of August, 1835, and there presented her criminal charges against the priests and nuns, it was denied that she had ever been a nun in the Hotel Dieu nunnery. In proof that she had been an inmate of that convent, Miss Monk offered to furnish a description of its interior—its apartments, its persons, and their occupations, &c.—and urged the examination of the nunnery, with a view to the application of the proposed test. Certainly this was fair on her part. Why, then, did not the priests comply with the proposal? If she had been an impostor, what easier and more ready mode of proving it, to the satisfaction of all concerned, could they have desired? The reply often made, that she and her friends were unworthy of their notice, and that the convent was a sacred place, not to be inspected by men from the world, is not less insulting than it is untrue; for they did notice her, by collecting and publishing affidavits against her; and men from the world, such as they have been pleased to select, have been admitted into the nunnery to inspect it. Does not their conduct in this particular betray guilt?

A short time after Miss Monk returned to New York from Montreal, her opponents made an attempt to prove an alibi—to show that she was elsewhere than in the convent, during the time in which she declares herself to have been in that establishment. They collected and published six or eight affidavits, the import and character of which is known to the public. Five of them refer exclusively to matters subsequent to her arrival in Montreal. The other two are those of Dr. Robertson and her mother, Mrs. Monk. Dr. Robertson states, that on inquiry, he had ascertained that she was at service in Sorel and St. Denis, a portion of the time which she professed to have been in the nunnery; and Mrs. Monk says, that she once told certain persons, that her daughter had not been in the nunnery. This is the amount of their testimony; and, if Maria Monk had been an impostor, can any man believe that the priests and their advocates, would have rested their cause on a foundation, so unsubstantial as this? Does not the weakness of their defence, show the unsoundness of their cause?

The next step worthy of notice in the conduct of the priests, is the visit of father Phelan of Montreal to New York, in order to decoy Miss Monk away from her friends in that city. This was in the winter of 1835–6. As this priest came to New York in disguise, leaving an impression in Montreal that he had gone to spend a few weeks on Nuns' Island, it is presumed, that his visit to this city will be denied. It can, however, be proved that he was in New York at the time specified, and that the impression was made in Montreal that he had gone to the Island. It has been published again and again, without being as yet contradicted, from any reasonable source. Why then should that priest visit New York under such circumstances, unless it were in some way to destroy Miss Monk's testimony? He knew her feelings towards himself as the father of her child; and he knew that a special intimacy had been formed and cherished between himself and her, during her residence in the nunnery; in a word, he knew that if any man could draw her away from her friends in New York, or induce her to withhold her testimony, he was the man. Out of regard to him, Miss Monk was perfectly silent respecting his visit to New York, until after the abduction plot, during the following summer, had been developed. It was, however, noticed by her friends, that her feelings towards him, during this lapse of time, were different from what they were, prior to this visit. Now if Miss Monk were an impostor, is it supposable that this priest would have thus visited her? And does not this visit stamp with the seal of truth her claims as an ex-nun? What stronger evidence can be demanded?

In the present work by Miss Monk, will be found an account of the attempt in May, 1836, to abduct her away from New York. The principal facts in the case are mentioned by her, in her narrative of the attempt. From personal knowledge, I know many of her statements respecting this matter, to be true; and others of them I believe on good authority, to be equally founded in truth. To mention particulars, such as I know to be true, would occupy too much space. They may be seen in her narrative. My object at present, is with the fact, that such an attempt was made; and of this there can be no reasonable doubt in the minds of such as are acquainted with the facts in the case.

It is certain that several individuals were thus engaged; and it is certain that some of them were Canadians. They were prowling about the neighbourhood for a number of days. They were seen again and again, and her uncle, on the Sabbath specified by Miss Monk, was overheard in conversation with her respecting the matter.

The design of the plot was to induce Miss Monk, voluntarily, to leave New York. The plot was well formed, and well conducted; and would have succeeded, had it not been thwarted by the untiring vigilance of Miss Monk's friends. Miss Monk was completely deceived

CONFIRMATION OF DISCLOSURES   253

by her uncle, until the time specified by her in her narrative of the affair, when a gentleman called on her, and made known to her the true nature and design of the plot. I was present at the time when the gentleman called, and I regret that it is not permitted me to mention, at present, particulars as to the betrayal of one of the enemy, by which the ultimate object of the scheme was communicated to her. Now they knew whether or not Miss Monk was an impostor: on this point, they could not possibly be mistaken. Would they then, be at so much trouble and expense, to decoy away a known impostor? The supposition is preposterous in the extreme. It is therefore evident, that she is not an impostor.

The next attempt on the part of the priests to vindicate themselves, worthy of special consideration, is to be found in their book, entitled, "Awful Exposure." The contents of this book have been examined; and it is believed, that the candid reader is prepared to unite in pronouncing the attempt to be an entire failure. Their object has been to destroy Miss Monk's testimony. To do this, they have undertaken:—

1. In the first place, utterly to destroy her character. They have attempted to prove that, besides being insane, she is a compound of all that is infamous in the vilest of women. But in this, they have come short. Their attempt only evinces the weakness of their cause, and the infamy of their witnesses. Their witnesses, as we have seen, are false witnesses, testifying in several instances, in direct opposition to each other.

2. They have repeated their attempt to prove an alibi—that at the time she professes to have been in the nunnery, she was living in Sorel, St. Denis, &c. Here they have failed; and on what ground can their failure be accounted for, unless it be, the falseness of their position? Is it possible rationally to conceive of any other? If so, let it be made known.

3. Being themselves conscious of the incredibility of their testimony to prove an alibi, they have endeavoured to support it, by an exparte examination of the nunnery. But this examination has only helped to expose the unsoundness of their cause. We have seen, that the report of their professed architect furnishes a high degree of evidence of the

fact, that Miss Monk has, as correctly as could have been expected, described the apartments of that portion of the nunnery which she attempted to describe. The priests have, therefore, utterly failed in this effort to mislead and deceive the public. What, then, is the consequence of their failure? Does it not prove them to be false?

4. But, as if sensible of the rottenness of their foundation, they have, as a last desperate resort, taken refuge in Mrs. McDonell's Magdalen Asylum. Why should they go there, if they were satisfied with the evidence which they had collected, to prove Miss Monk to be an impostor? They do not even pretend that she was ever there, prior to the time she professes to have escaped from the convent. If they had satisfactorily proved to the world, that Miss Monk did not obtain the facts, published in her book, from a residence in the Hotel Dieu nunnery, why give themselves any more trouble on the subject? Ah, they knew better; they knew that she had been a nun, and they knew that they could not disprove it.

Respecting this movement of the priests, it is proper to make a few remarks, in order that its character may the better be understood. The idea that Miss Monk and her friends manufactured the "Awful Disclosures," from what she learned in the Asylum, is of recent date. It was never heard of in New York, so far as I can learn, until last summer, nearly a year after she preferred her charges in Montreal, against the priests. After this long period, they wish us to believe that the conventual ceremonies, interior apartments, and persons—themselves excepted, I suppose, though they do not say so—described by Maria Monk, are such as she saw in Mrs. McDonell's Asylum. Miss Monk in her book, speaking of her novitiate state in the Hotel Dieu, mentions the names of four novices, as also that of Jane Ray. The priests, in order to carry forward their novel device, have furnished us with five affidavits, from as many persons, bearing the names mentioned by Miss Monk as inmates of the Hotel Dieu. These women are made to testify that they were inmates of the Asylum at the time Miss Monk was, and that she became acquainted with them there. But who has ever seen these individuals in the Asylum? A gentleman from New York called there twice, but he could find but one out of the five named, and she evidently had never seen Maria Monk, for she described her as having light hair, when in fact her hair is black.

Now, that this whole affair is a mere jesuitical device, designed to mislead the public, is not only manifest from its intrinsic absurdity, but also from the fact that immediately after it was publicly announced, the Asylum was said to be broken up and its inmates dispersed, because no more means could be obtained for their support. How happens it that the streams of benevolence in Montreal should become dry just at that time? And how happens it, that if Maria Monk has described the interior of Mrs. McDonell's establishment, it was not made known at an earlier date? Why especially was it closed from inspection, as soon as the discovery was made? It does appear that, if anything can demonstrate the desperateness of the priest's cause, it is this silly Magdalen trick of theirs. I call it silly, for it does seem to evince a degree of stupidity on the part of the priests, which cannot be accounted for, unless it be on the principle, that those whom the Almighty abandons to destruction for their vices, he often, in his providence, drives to otherwise unaccountable folly and madness.

Thus we have noticed the more prominent attempts, which the priests have made to defend themselves from the charges preferred against them by Maria Monk. Several minor attempts have been passed over; such as their celebrated handbill, which was so extensively circulated in New York and other places, declaring that Miss Monk was a Protestant girl, and had been living for four years with Mr. Hoyt; and also their declaration, that her "book was a translation from an old Portuguese work;" and since then, that it was not her production, but that of "certain individuals who had formed an atrocious plot against the Clergy and Nuns of Lower Canada."

What a mass of untruth and palpable contradictions! Is the supposition possible, that the priests are innocent in this matter, when all their attempts at self-defence have only served to sink them deeper and deeper, in the bottomless abyss of falsehood and infamy? One thing is certain, and that is if they are innocent, their conduct is beyond measure unaccountable. It belies them in a manner that it is truly astonishing. With a voice that cannot be misunderstood, it proclaims them guilty.

In conclusion, I would seriously press the inquiry, whether it is supposable, that, if the priests were innocent they would have borne such a load of reproach and infamy for so long a time, without having demonstrated their innocency to the world. Especially when it could have been done with so much ease, by proving Miss Monk to be an impostor, if she is an impostor as they maintain that she is. The belief of it beggars credulity itself. The reply, "they stand upon their character," and that the "disclosures of Miss Monk are unworthy of their notice," is as preposterous as it is untrue. Stand upon their character! Common sense rebukes so gross an absurdity. The horrid charges, preferred against them by Maria Monk, and believed by thousands and tens of thousands to be sober truth, "unworthy of their notice!" Who can believe this? If it be so, it may be asked what is there on earth, that can arrest their dignified attention?

Finally, it is manifest that the priests have utterly failed, in every attempt they have made in their own defence. What, then, is the legitimate inference, from this fact? Is it not, that they are guilty? That they themselves are impostors, instead of Maria Monk's being an impostor? In reason's name, it is asked, how can it be otherwise? How can it be that they are innocent, and that she is an impostor, when everything that speaks on the subject, proclaims the opposite to be true. This is the voice—not only of her person, character, conduct, narrative, of religion and nature, and of the testimony of others—but it is also the voice of every attempt which they have made in self-vindication.

CHAPTER IV.

REVELATION, REASON, AND NATURE, CONFIRM MISS MONK'S TESTIMONY.

EXTRACT from the New York Observer—Inquiry as to the object of nunneries—Condemned by Christianity—By reason and nature—Their ultimate object not religion—Nor charity to the sick—These are false garbs—Their object priestly indulgence—"Awful Disclosures" confirmed—"Sisters of charity."

THE following is taken from an able article in the New York Observer.

"Popery forbids its priests and ecclesiastics to marry, and encourages the devotion of each sex to a single life. Hence convents are provided both for monks and nuns, to which they may respectively retire from the world, and lead a life of holy seclusion, as it is termed, from the temptations of the flesh. Nature cries out against this unnatural and forced separation of the sexes. Reason condemns it as monstrous and absurd, and religion pronounces upon the unnatural and absurd prohibition its severest denunciations, "forbidding to many," being expressly classed with the "doctrine of devils." We cannot escape from the conclusion that a course which nature, reason, and religion unite to condemn, must be productive of evils of a kind and extent commensurate with the folly, absurdity, and impiety of the parent evil. We here see one of the strongest passions of human nature, a passion implanted in man for the wisest purposes by the God of nature, unnaturally restrained by pains and penalties. What power have unhallowed vows to bind, where God has not required the sacrifice, where he has, in fact, prohibited it? Need I pursue the details of the degenerating process, to see the easy steps by which passion thus restrained, descends to crime? How the nun, at the confessional, must pour into the ear of a man, the secret conflicts of her own breast, with regard to this very passion; how the priest questions; and how he may advise his fair penitent in secret? Need I depict the voluntarily incurred temptations to which both are exposed by this most unnatural intercourse? It can scarcely be otherwise, than that crime should be the result. Both priests and nuns are kept from its commission by no *human* restraint, and certainly by no promise of *divine* assistance, but are left weak and unaided to contend with, and to be vanquished by, this strongest of human passions. Love thus perverted is lust, and every one knows that the secret servant of lust, is Murder."

In reason's name, I would ask, what is the object of female cloistered convents? Why congregate an assembly of youthful females, and then bind them, not only with bolts and bars, but with the most solemn and superstitious vows and oaths, never more to have any communication with the world? Why deprive such of that liberty which the God of nature has given to all mankind? To imprison an individual for life, and thus deprive him of his liberty, is considered to be next to the highest punishment that can be inflicted for crime. But of what crime have the helpless victims of female convents been guilty, prior to their becoming nuns? Can it be said that the religion of the Son of God demands such imprisonment? If so, where is the chapter and verse? I have never been able to find it. But I do find that Christ was *"to proclaim liberty to the captives, and the opening of the prison to them that are bound."* The voice of Christianity, therefore, is that the doors of these female prison houses be opened, and that the captives be set at liberty. Christianity is from heaven. It came into the world, not to derange and break up the institutions of man's social nature, but to hallow and purify them. Did the God of nature make woman for society, or to shut her up in a nunnery? Let the advocates of nunneries read the second chapter of the first book in the Bible, if they have any; and they will learn that woman was made for man, not to be shut up in prison. Revelation, therefore, is against nunneries.

Reason still presses the inquiry, why should inoffensive and un-suspecting young ladies be decoyed from the path of life, which Christianity prescribes, and be intombed for life within the walls of a convent? *Young ladies*, I say, for the priests will have no others, unless it should be some who were very rich, and received for the sake of their wealth. This fact proves to a demonstration, that the object cannot be of a religious character; for if it were, then the aged and the infirm, who are now excluded, would, of all others, be received. I am aware of the fact, that a religious profession is the bait, by which young females are enticed, by the priests and their panders, into nunneries. They are made to believe that the moment they enter a convent, they are thenceforth removed from all worldly temptation and are, during the remainder of their lives, to be devoted exclusively to the holy duties of religion. But that this is untrue, is evident, not only from the testimony of eloped nuns, and others, but from the above-named fact, viz., that the aged and infirm, to whom such retirement and religious employment might possibly be desirable, are the very persons who are excluded.

Nor can the object be for purposes of charity, such as educating poor children, and nursing the sick. I am aware that the latter is connected with the Hotel Dieu—that there is a fine hospital there, and that many of the sick have reaped essential benefit from it. But, I ask, what necessary connexion there is between this charity, and the imprisonment, for life, of scores of young and tender females? Cannot the sick be taken care of, without doing such violence to the laws, both of God and nature? The sick are nursed, and the poor are educated, to say the least, among Protestants, who have no occasion for nunneries, as well as they are among Catholics. The truth is, this charity business is a mere outward garb—fair to appearance, like a "whited sepulchre"—designed, in connexion with a "religious profession," to conceal from the public eye the real object which the priests have in view, in sustaining cloistered convents. Roman priests are required by their religion, habitually to violate a primary law of the human constitution, in being required to live a life of celibacy. But nature protests against the requisition, and determines on seeking relief from some other source. But concealment is requisite, in order to give external consistency to their professions of chastity. How then can gratification and concealment be secured? A cloistered nunnery, under the colours of peculiar sanctity and charity, presents itself as affording both the requisites. Concealment, however, requires something more than the most arrant deceit and hypocrisy. Children and refractory nuns must be disposed of; and to secure this, habitual murder is necessary, as well as a system of the most severe and tyrannical discipline. Sin, in its progress, being downward, where will it stop? What bounds can you set to it, when unbridled as in a convent, concealed from the public eye? The Hotel Dieu is of long standing, and has grown ripe in iniquity. Hence but a small portion of its diabolical abominations can be disclosed by Maria Monk to the world. There are others which ought not to be "once named as becometh saints."

It seems, then, that the real object of cloistered nunneries is, so far as they respect the priests, their own licentious gratifitation. Now I do not say that this was their original intention. I think it was not. But they soon degenerated into it. Hence the ultimate design of the scores of incipient nunneries in these United States. Oh, that they were rightly understood by mothers and by daughters! Then we should hear of no more taking the veil.

The conclusion, therefore, of the whole matter under this head is this,—That the disclosures of Maria Monk are just what might rationally be expected, from the nature of the case; from priestly celibacy in connexion with cloistered females. How futile, then, is the following question of the priests: "Now we ask the ten thousand readers of the book, (Awf. Disc.,) if the deeds therein alleged are not incompatible with human nature,—if anything that is known of man's capacity for crime can render them credible?" What is the history of Popery, but to a great extent a history of just such incompatibilities?

Before closing this chapter, perhaps something should be said, respecting the order of "sisters of charity," as they are called. These females have, no doubt, done much to mitigate the sufferings of the sick and destitute; as also to impart papal instruction to poor children. This is natural to the kind and sympathizing nature of the female sex. But does this argue anything in favour of this order of women, who are required to live in a state of celibacy? Are these amiable female qualities confined to this mode of life? Must woman live a single life in order to be kind and generous to the needy and the helpless?

But the question is, what is the object of the priests in having these unmarried women clustered about them, as they always have, especially in the absence of cloistered nunneries? Let Miss Monk's narrative in the subsequent pages, respecting the Black Nuns' Island, answer the question. It would seem that the object of the priests, with reference to this order of females, was substantially the same with that of convents. Let, then, the lovers of good order and chastity frown upon this order of women, until it shall be broken up, together with convents. And let young women avoid this vow of celibacy, as they would avoid impurity and wretchedness. It is death to all that is lovely in the female character.

CHAPTER V.

HISTORIC CONFIRMATION OF MISS MONK'S TESTIMONY.

ABSENCE of historic information a cause of disbelief in the "Disclosures"— Spirit of popish history agrees with that of the "Disclosures"—Of murder—The Inquisition—Uncondemned by papists—Slaughter of French Protestants on the eve of St. Bartholomew's day—Murderous spirit with which the news of it was received at Rome—More than 6000 heads of infants found in the Pope's fish-pond—Licentious character of the Roman priests—Golden means to be observed in speaking of it—Extract from Da Costa—Illustrates the character of priests and of the Confessional— One object of the Confessional—Catholic girl in New York—Practice of confessing to a priest should be discountenanced—Extracts from Scipio de Ricci confirmatory of the "Awful Disclosures"—Object of exposing vice—Jesuit moralists sanction vice—Miss M's character of the priests true, independent of the fact of her having been a nun.

THERE are two things, in the disclosures of Maria Monk, which render them comparatively incredible to the American community. First, the enormity of the crimes which she declares are perpetrated in the Hotel Dieu nunnery of Montreal; and, in the second place, the cool-hearted manner in which they are said to be habitually practised in that establishment. This objection so frequently urged against the truth of Miss Monk's narrative, arises from two sources;—1st, the comparative purity of the American people:—and 2nd, the want of historic information respecting the character of the Roman priesthood, in all former ages. The latter of these is the more prominent obstacle in the way of gaining full confidence in the truth of her statements. Hence the fact, so frequently noticed by the friends of Miss Monk, that those persons, who are versed in popish history, as also those who have sojourned somewhat extensively in popish countries, find no difficulty in believing the "Awful Disclosures" to be substantially true. Hence, too, the fact, that gentlemen of extensive observation, who have been reared in Catholic countries, amidst the vices of Roman priests, not unfrequently ridicule the incredulity of the American people, in reference to this matter.

Roman Catholics glory in the infallibility of their church; and, of course, its immutability. It is, say they, the one church of Christ, the same in every age and in every country. The author of these pages is aware of the fact, that when the consequences of this principle are pressed upon the advocates of popery, they attempt to evade them by some Jesuitical prank or other. Still, it is true, if the tree is one and the same in all ages and in all climes, its fruit must be substantially the same, under all circumstances. Thus, in regard to the spirit of popery, it is one and the same the world over, and in every age; and bears substantially the same fruit, wherever it is allowed to arrive to full maturity. Now, what is this spirit, as exhibited on the impartial page of history? Does it contradict the reigning spirit of the Montreal cloistered convent, as illustrated by the disclosures of Maria Monk? Are the crimes which are divulged by her, such as murder, hypocrisy, and the most unblushing licentiousness, novel things in the history of popery? or are they such as naturally fall in with that history? If the pages of Roman Catholic history could be made honestly to oppose the statements of Maria Monk, the controversy would assume altogether a different aspect from what it has now. But they cannot. Truth is immutable, however much it may be falsified and glossed over. A few statements and extracts from well authenticated history will be sufficient to show, not only that Maria Monk's narrative is no libel on the Roman priests, but also to confirm its truth, so far as the history of the past can do it. And here I wish to be as brief as fidelity to the cause of truth and humanity will admit of, for the subject is painful to every virtuous mind.

1. In respect to the crime of murder.

Perhaps no subject more perfectly illustrates the murderous spirit of Roman priests, in past ages, than the "Holy Inquisition," as papists call it. This "infernal tribunal" originated with the priests—it was introduced into every country into which they had the power of introducing it—and by them it was sustained, as long as they had the power of sustaining it. For cruelty, it stands without a rival on earth, and, I hope, also in the dark domains of Satan below. Thank God, that humanity and the Protestant religion have nearly banished it from the earth, although its dreadful spirit still remains with those who originated and sustained it. The object of the inquisition is the destruction of "damnable heresy," by torturing, in the most cruel manner, even unto death, all such as dare to think and believe contrary to the wishes of the church; that is, the priesthood, from the pope downward, for such is the meaning of the word *church* among Roman Catholics. In Spain alone, its victims, according to the estimate of Llorente, from 1481 to 1808, amounted to 341,021. Of these 31,912 were burned, 17,659 were burned in effigy, and 291,456 were subjected to severe penance. Here, then, were nearly 32,000 men and women burned to death, after suffering imprisonment, and a variety of tortures, simply for resisting the will of the priesthood. What is this but the most cold-blooded murder? It is vain for the friends of popery to attempt to blunt the edge of these facts, by saying that they had occurred in the dark ages. Are not all ages dark where popery reigns? And are not papists loud in their denunciation of the reformation, by which the darkness that covered Christendom was, in some measure, dissipated? Besides, what pope, cardinal, bishop, or priest, has ever been known to utter a sentence of condemnation against their "most holy inquisition?" What, condemn an institution which for ages had the sanction of an infallible church! No, never. They will sooner defend it, as bishops England and Hughes have had the hardihood to do, the one in Baltimore and the other in Philadelphia.

The manner in which the Pope and his court received the intelligence of the barbarous massacre of the Protestants in France, commencing on the eve of St. Bartholomew's day, in a. d. 1572, is another instance which shows the murderous spirit of the priesthood. Perhaps the page of history does not contain a darker spot than this. The principal Protestants of the kingdom were invited to Paris, under a solemn oath of protection from Charles IX., a papist, to attend the marriage of the king's sister. The design of the papists was to destroy every Protestant in France, and they came well nigh accomplishing their nefarious project.

Some ten thousand were inhumanly butchered in the single city of Paris, while the work of death was carried on in almost every part of the empire, until from 30,000 to 100,000 Protestants were slain.

And now, reader, how do you suppose the intelligence of this dreadful slaughter was received at Rome? Did the pope condemn the king for the double crime of breaking his oath and murdering his subjects? Did he grieve because so many human beings had been so fiendishly butchered? No, reader. It was to him and his court "glad tidings of great joy." The following is extracted from "Buck's Theological Dictionary."—"When the letters of the pope's legate were read in the assembly of the cardinals, by the express will and command of the king, it was immediately decreed that the pope should march with his cardinals to the church of St. Mark, and in the most solemn manner give thanks to God for so great a blessing conferred on the See of Rome, and the Christian world; and that, on the Monday after, solemn mass should be celebrated in the church of Minerva, at which the pope, Gregory XIII., and cardinals were present; and that a jubilee should be published throughout the whole Christian world, and the cause of it declared to be, to return thanks to God for the extirpation of the enemies of the truth and church in France. In the evening, the cannon of St. Angelo were fired to testify the public joy; the whole city illuminated with bonfires; and no one sign of rejoicing omitted that was usually made for the greatest victories obtained in favour of the Roman church!!!" Alas! what spirit is here? Is it that of the compassionate Saviour? or that of Satan, "who was a murderer from the beginning?"

Once more, and I have done on the crime of murder.

"Pope Gregory, drawing his fishpond, found more than six thousand heads of infants in it; upon which he deeply repented, and, confessing that the decree of unnatural celibacy was the cause of so horrid a slaughter, he condemned it, adding: 'It is better to marry than to give occasion of death.'"—*Hulderic Epist. adv. constit. de Cleric. Celib.*

Were it not a tax upon the reader's patience, I would here add a few extracts from standard Roman Catholic writers on morals, teaching the lawfulness of murder for a variety of frivolous reasons, such as might easily be offered by priests and nuns, in justification of the murders committed by them. But I forbear.

Respecting the licentious character of the Romish priesthood, but little need be said. If ever the golden mean should be observed on any subject, it should be on this. The subject is disgusting, and requires a skilful pen so to manage it as not to promote rather than destroy its practice. There is, however, a fastidiousness about it which is contrary both to scripture and sound reason. This vice, like every other, in order to destroy it, must be exposed to some extent. Nothing can be more pleasing to the priests than the senseless clamours which are raised against the supposed licentious tendency of Maria Monk's disclosures. None are louder on this point than themselves. They are like the thief, who is first to cry, stop thief! Herein Satan transforms himself into an angel of light, and becomes the staunchest advocate of chastity. See that Canadian priest, so chaste that he cannot even shake hands with his own mother, lest he should receive pollution from the touch of woman! What hypocrisy!

It would seem, really, as if some of our newspaper editors had been under the tuition of the priests on this subject. Such moralists, while they avoid Charybdis, shipwreck against Scylla. The character of Roman priests and convents must be known before they can receive that treatment which of right belongs to them. Ah! how many thousands of unsuspecting and virtuous young ladies have been ruined for ever, for the want of just that knowledge which is to be found in Maria Monk's disclosures! And yet, how strange that good men should be so inconsiderate as to unite with profligate priests and others in the only cry which can prevent its diffusion among the people.

I will here give an extract from Da Costa, a Portuguese Roman Catholic writer, who had suffered in the Inquisition, in consequence of being accused of Freemasonry. It illustrates the adulterous character of Roman priests, as also the abominable character of the Confessional. Pope Paul IV., from some cause or other, was induced to issue a bull, ordering an investigation into the crime of *solicitant*, as it is called— that is, when the confessional is used by the priests for licentious purposes. This had reference to the kingdom of Spain. The following is an extract from the bull:—"Whereas certain ecclesiastics in the kingdom of Spain, and in the cities and dioceses thereof, having the cure of souls, or exercising such cure for others, or otherwise deputed to hear the confessions of such penitents, have broken out into such heinous acts of iniquity, as to abuse the sacrament of penance in the very act of hearing the confessions, not fearing to injure the same sacrament, and Him who instituted it, our Lord God and Saviour Jesus Christ, by enticing and provoking, or trying to entice and provoke females to lewd actions at the very time when they were making their confessions."

"When this bull," says Da Costa, "was first introduced into Spain, the inquisitors published a solemn edict in all the churches belonging to the archbishopric of Seville, that any person knowing, or having heard of any friar or clergyman's having committed the crime of abusing the Sacrament of Confession, or in any manner having improperly conducted himself during the confession of a female penitent, should make a discovery of what he knew, within thirty days, to the holy tribunal; and very heavy censures were attached to those who should neglect or despise this injunction. When this edict was first published, such a considerable number of females went to the palace of the Inquisition, only in the city of Seville, to reveal the conduct of their infamous confessors, that twenty notaries, and as many inquisitors, were appointed to minute down their several informations against them; but these being found insufficient to receive the depositions of so many witnesses; and the inquisitors being thus overwhelmed, as it were, with the pressure of such affairs, thirty days more were allowed for taking the accusations, and this lapse of time also proving inadequate to the intended purpose, a similar period was granted, not only for a third but a fourth time. The ladies of rank, character, and noble families, had a difficult part to act on this occasion, as their discoveries could not be made of any particular time and place. On one side, a religious fear of incurring the threatened censures, goaded their consciences so much as to compel them to make the required accusations; on the other side, a regard to their husbands, to whom they justly feared to give offence, by affording them any motives for suspecting their private conduct, induced them to keep at home. To obviate these difficulties, they had recourse to the measure of covering their faces with a veil, according to the fashion of Spain, and thus went to the inquisitors in the most secret manner they could adopt. Very few, however, escaped the vigilance of their husbands, who, on being informed of the discoveries and accusations made by their wives, were filled with suspicions; and yet, notwithstanding this accumulation of proofs against the confessors, produced to the inquisitors, this holy tribunal, contrary to the expectations of every one, put an end to the business, by ordering, that all crimes of this nature, proved by lawful evidence, should from thenceforth be consigned to perpetual silence and oblivion."—*Nav. &c., by Hippolyto Joseph Da Costa Pereira Furtudo de Mendonea*, vol. i. pp. 117–119.

Here then, are the "holy confessors and the holy confessional" depicted to the life, so far as decency will allow the picture to be drawn. It were an easy task, would decency permit, to prove, and that too, from Roman Catholic historians, that the priesthood of Rome is composed of the most licentious body of men that ever infested human society. And yet, the writers of the "Awful Exposure" have the brazen impudence to make the following declaration, "Now the priests of Montreal and of Canada, do enjoy, at least, public esteem for morality, and if necessary, the testimony of every adult in the province would be gladly yielded to their excellent character." The father of lies could not fabricate a purer untruth than this.*

I have taken some pains to inquire of gentlemen from Canada, respecting the moral character of the priests, out of the nunneries, and the result of my inquiries is, that it would be doing them no injustice to apply to them the above picture given of their brethren, the priests of Spain. I could mention names and particulars, if it were deemed advisable. I will mention the name of one "adult," in whose good opinion the friends of the nunnery appear to place much confidence.

---

* A Canadian, speaking of the priests says—"that he had known a party of priests, with Bishop Lartigue at their head, hold a convivial meeting in his village on Saturday, and carry their revels so far that no one was fit to say mass on the following Sabbath.

The gentleman alluded to, is the Rev. G. W. Perkins of Montreal. In a letter, dated March 18, 1836, speaking of the convent, he says:—"Now that fornication is committed, there is no reasonable question;" that is, in the nunnery.*

According to the above picture, what is the confessional? Beyond all question, one of its grand objects is to secure female victims for the impure indulgence of the priests. Its history affords painful evidence of the truth of this declaration; and were it properly understood, no virtuous family would ever allow its female members to visit it, any sooner than they would allow them to visit a brothel.

For the truth of the following statement of facts, I hold myself responsible. A Catholic young woman, ardently devoted to her religion, by the name of Miss N—, lived in the family of Mr. M—, in New York. In her appearance she was quite prepossessing, and probably of virtuous character, up to the time to which this narrative refers. A short time before good-Friday, which was the first day of last April, she was observed to be uncommonly devoted to the ceremonies of her church. About this time she said to a young lady of the family, "My father Confessor is a going to bestow upon me a wonderful gift, about next good-Friday, if I am faithful to go frequently to confession, and confess all my sins, and answer all the questions which he asks me." "What is it, a new gown?" replied the lady. "Oh, no, not a carnal gift, but a spiritual one; I am to be exalted, and to be made a spiritual sister."

---

* The following is the testimony of one of Rome's best popes, extracted from Baxter's Jesuit Juggling, page 219. "Pius II. was one of the best that the Papal seat a long time had; and yet in his epistle to his father, Epist. 15, who was angry with him for fornication, he saith 'You say you are sorry for my crime. I know not what opinion you have of me. You know what you were yourself. Nor am I an hypocrite, that I should desire rather to seem good, than to be good. It is an ancient and usual sin. I know not who is without it. This plague is spread far and near; though I see it not, seeing nature, which doth nothing amiss, hath bred this appetite in all living creatures, that mankind should be continued.' He who was the glory of the Papacy, knew none of the Hierarchy without this beastly sin."—No man, acquainted with the Romish priesthood, will question the infallibility of this pope's testimony in this instance.

Miss N. increased her visits to the confessional, going more frequently as the time of the *exaltation* drew near. At length the time arrived. Miss N. was to go to confess at that time in the evening. She went, but did not return until early the next morning. Sad disappointment and shame were depicted on her countenance. To the question, asking her where she had passed the night, she declined giving a direct answer. On one occasion she said, that she staid in the church all night; but then it should be known that the house of her father Confessor was in the immediate neighbourhood of the church. Miss N. remained in the family of Mr. M. but a few days after this.

I leave my readers to make their own inferences. But I would ask, if it be not the duty of the friends of virtue and good order, to discountenance a practice so corrupting and so ruinous to all that is virtuous in the female character, as is that of confession to a corrupt priest. Destroy the confessional, and you at once destroy that fatal power, which the priests now have over their deluded followers; and until this is done, all your efforts to enlighten and elevate Catholics, will be thwarted by these enemies of the human race. Let, then, every lawful means be used to accomplish this end, remembering that it is at the confessional those chains are forged, applied, and riveted, which hold in bondage so large a portion of the human family; a bondage more dreadful than that of the African slave, because it is the bondage of the soul, which God made in his own glorious image.

I will now furnish my readers with a few extracts from a standard Catholic author, for the purpose of illustrating the character of convents, and of showing that the statements made by Miss Monk, are in keeping with the past history of these establishments. As the authors of the "Awful Exposure" again and again refer us to the life of Scipio de Ricci, a Roman Catholic bishop, as a model writer on female convents, the extracts shall be taken from his memoirs. And it should be borne in mind, that these disclosures were made by this Roman prelate, not in the dark ages, but some forty or fifty years ago. And it should also be borne in mind, that Scipio de Ricci was not a Protestant or an enemy to convents, but a friend to the latter, and a staunch Catholic. And it should be remembered also, that this prelate, not having been connected with convents, knew nothing of them, save what he learned by report, and in his attempts to reform them; when, instead of the inmates being inclined to divulge their own infamy, they were doubtless disposed, out of regard to themselves, to conceal their deeds of darkness. But the case with Maria Monk is very different. She was an inmate of the convent for years, where she had every opportunity of witnessing its abominations. But my readers will see enough, in all conscience, to confirm Maria Monk's statements, in the subjoined extracts:—

"The Dominican Monks, who were members of one of the most numerous ecclesiastical orders, had been the scandal of all Italy, during one hundred and fifty years, for their total corruption: and their direction of the female convents had degenerated into a scene of the basest profligacy. Long habit had so accustomed them to the greatest licentiousness, that scarcely any respect for public decency remained."—*Memoirs of Scipio de Ricci*, pages 96, 97, vol. i.

The nuns of Pistoia testified that the monks taught them "every kind of vice," and that they should look upon it as a great happiness, "that they were able to satisfy their libidinous desires, without the inconvenience of children."

It was necessary to raze from the foundations a monastery and a female convent of Carmelites, which were in fact joined by means of subterranean passages.—Vol. i. pages 98, 121.

A Hindoo brahmin, having become a Catholic priest, says: "The Roman priests in India are like the bonzes of Japan. The nuns are the disciples of Diana, and their nunneries are seraglios for the monks. They were more often pregnant than married women in general. The Jesuits had become brahmins, in order to enjoy the privileges of that caste; among which were exemption from death for crime; and the right of enjoying the favours of every woman who pleased them, it being commonly received, that a brahmin priest sanctifies the woman whom he honours with his attentions."—Vol. ii. pages 216, 217.

"The monks, confessors of the convents, openly taught the Tuscany nuns atheism; encouraged the most disgraceful libertinism; and filled them with impurity, sacrilege, and debauchery of the foulest kinds.

Immorality was thus added to profanation; and corruption brought forth impiety. By tolerating these crimes, the pope plainly announced his indulgence of them; and by encouraging the commission of those iniquities, he became an accomplice."—Vol. ii. pages 263, 264.

"The false or forged virtues of the monks and nuns, are but a tissue of hypocrisy, and a stimulant to the most odious vices. The institutions called *Virginales*, were schools of corruption and licentiousness: and the *soi-disant* tribunal of *penitence* is the constant source of infamous wickedness, by those impudent jugglers, whose authority depends on the blindness of man. The monks, the nuns, their superiors, and even the pope himself, not only tolerated these disorders, but took no measures to arrest the infidelity and impiety of those who were daily adding new victims to their atheism and inordinate voluptuousness."—Vol. ii. pages 276, 277.

But enough of such filth; for it is filth of the darkest dye; and such as ought not to be named, did not the cause of humanity, virtue, and religion, demand it, for the same reason that the Son of God divested the ancient scribes and Pharisees, the embryo prototypes of Romish priests, of their hypocritical robes, and thus enabled the people to see that they were "full of dead men's bones, and of all uncleanness."—Matt, xxiii. 27. The Saviour knew that there was no other way to destroy the superstitious veneration with which the Jews regarded their priests, just as the Catholics, only in a much higher degree, regard theirs. The naming of such vices, should be regarded as an evil, the object of which is the removal of a much greater one; just in the sense in which many a medical prescription is an evil, absolutely necessary, however, to be administered, in order to remove disease, and secure health. The unqualified condemnation, therefore, of this moral medicine, on the ground that some writers deal in it too freely, is as absurd as it would be to condemn the "healing art," because unskilful men abuse it.

Before leaving this subject, I wish to add a single remark further. And that is this: That all the vices spoken of by Maria Monk as practiced in the Hotel Dieu, (yea, and more too,) are abundantly inculcated by the standard writers on morals of the order of Jesuits. If any man wishes proof of this assertion, I would refer him, among others, to Paschal's Provincial letters, a work of undying celebrity. Paschal was himself a Roman Catholic, but opposed to the Jesuits.

According to these moralists, a priest may commit lewdness on the ground of self-gratification; and then on the ground of self-defence, or defending his reputation, he may lawfully murder, deceive, lie, and swear falsely, or employ others to do the same for him. I know that these principles are horrid beyond conception. But they are true; and I hold myself pledged to prove them, giving chapter and verse, if the priests, in any responsible manner, have the audacity to deny them.

Who, then, after reading the preceding part of this chapter, can seriously question the general truth of Maria Monk's statements respecting the character of the Canadian priests and nuns? Especially when it is recollected, that a large portion of these priests are foreign Jesuits, expelled from foreign countries, as an order of men too infamous to be tolerated by civil governments. They have been expelled, as an order of men, from almost every country in Europe, by Catholic as well as Protestant governments. Hence they come in swarms to the North American continent, bringing along with them their ill-gotten gain, by which they build colleges, churches, nunneries, &c. The "disclosures" of Miss Monk, therefore, are unquestionably true, and they would be substantially true, even if it should be proved that she had never been a nun in the Hotel Dieu. This is the opinion of the mass of the Protestant people in Canada. It is to be hoped, therefore, that the testimony of Maria Monk will no more be disbelieved on the ground that she discloses practices so abominable, as to cause virtue to hide its blushing face at the very mention of them.

In conclusion, I will mention two facts, which ought not to be forgotten. 1st. A large number of the Canadian priests are Jesuits, from France: and 2nd. The fact that when Bonaparte broke up the convents in France, bones of murdered infants were found in great abundance. Can it then be supposed, that the French Jesuits are any better in Canada, than they were in France?

DESCRIPTION OF NUNS' ISLAND, AND THE BUILDINGS ON IT.

NUNS' ISLAND, (that is, the Black Nuns' Island,) lies in the St. Lawrence, not far, I think, from the middle of it, a little below Lachine. The wall encloses a considerable space, but yet leaves an extensive pasture outside, with fruit trees scattered about it, and room for two or three small buildings. It is so high as to shut out the view of the edifices from any near point, except, perhaps, the roof and some small part of the upper stories. It has but one gate, which is generally closed, and sufficiently watched by three or four yardmen, to keep out all persons not allowed to enter, viz. such as bring no permits from the Bishop, or the Superior of the Seminary and Hotel Dieu Nunnery. The yardmen, as at the nunnery, are never allowed to enter the buildings, unless it be such parts as are devoted to the stable, fuel, &c.

The buildings are three in number. The largest stands in front, the second behind it, and the third at right angles, on the right, as you enter the first; and the last is that which I first entered. Entering the first building by the front door, you find yourself in a hall, with several doors. The first story rooms along the front are sleeping-rooms, and two of those in the rear are spacious and elegant sitting-rooms, with windows that open upon a gallery, which extends along the rear, and one end of the building on the left hand. With it a door communicates from one of them, and this is the only way of access to it from this side of the building, which looks towards Montreal. In the gallery we sometimes walked for exercise.

The first large room had elegant blue merino curtains with tassels. There was an ottoman in it, of blue cloth, bound with black velvet, with raised corners, so formed as to afford a distinct seat on each side, being the most elegant thing of the kind I ever saw. In one corner of the room was a sofa. The walls are pink, and the cornice is of rich alabaster work, a piece of which I picked up one day on the floor.

Adjoining this apartment is the dining-room, which, like it, is carpeted. The walls are colored blue, and the windows without curtains.

Except during meal times, a table commonly stood in this room, with papers on it. From this room is a door opening, (like the windows,) upon the piazza, which is the only direct access to it from any of the rooms.

Beyond the dining-room is a large spare-room, and another of some kind beyond that.

The staircase to the second story leads on from that below, as well as up to the garret. Near it is a large stove for warming the second story in the winter; and doors open on several sides. One of them leads into a place which I thought very singular, and the use of which I could not imagine. It is a large room without furniture, with a stone floor, lighted, I believe, only by a small grated window, with about four panes of glass. In the midst of this room is a small one, capable of containing about twenty persons, entirely unfurnished, and perfectly dark. The partitions are so thin, that I think a conversation might be overheard through them, even if conducted in a low voice.

At one end of this story are four bed-rooms, each with two windows, a bed, and other plain furniture. These rooms are warmed by one stove, placed in the middle partition, pipes from which extend both ways through the other partitions.

The entrance to the basement is at one end. The second room in it is the kitchen, with a large baking furnace and roasting jack, and several small furnaces, in a corner. A large table used to stand in the middle, and the steps lead up outside to the gallery, which is supported by timbers. The next room has a stone floor, and the remaining one on that side of the basement, a wooden floor. On the front side, and adjoining, is a small cellar with only a little light admitted through a narrow window, which I have peeped through from without. The remainder of the front cellar is all one room, and used for storing fuel.

The second and smallest building, which is in the rear of this, I was in but three times. It has two stories, with a number of small rooms, and little furniture. It appeared to be principally devoted to the priests, when I was there, as I recollect seeing a number of priests there, and several musical instruments lying about.

The third building has a staircase leading up from the visitors' room, which I first entered, into the second story, which is occupied by sleeping-rooms, with a passage on one side into which they open.

I have been in the garret of the third building. It is not partitioned off into rooms, but all thrown into one, if I except a small part towards one end, where pigeons are caught. There is a large looking-glass, so placed that the birds may see themselves in it as they fly by; and, some wheat being scattered near, considerable numbers are caught, most of which are killed, and sent to market in Montreal. The pigeons, being deceived, and taking their own shadows for other birds, are induced to stop, and are then attracted in by the food, until they cannot escape. This is a very common way of taking them in Canada. While in the garret, I sometimes looked out of the windows, and enjoyed a fine view. I could see the river St. Lawrence for a considerable distance, with boats of Canadians or Indians passing down, or crossing to the village of Caughnawaga, which was also in sight, as well as the river's banks for some miles. According to my recollection, there are windows only at one end, and on one side of the garret.

They have a ciergerie, or candle-room in one of the buildings, where, however, only tallow candles are manufactured; there is sometimes a good deal of work to be performed in that branch of business.

One day Father Phelan met me in the Pink Room, and informed me that he had something for me to do. I of course did not dare to object, much less to disobey, after the solemn obligations of my oath, and the hazard, or rather certainty of punishment. I felt myself to be no less in the power of others there, than when I was in the nunnery, and believed that disobedience would be as surely followed with a heavy penalty. Besides, I believed that all authority was vested in the Priests, by the divine law; and was disposed, on this account, (at least a great portion of the time,) blindly to follow their commands and indications, without presuming to question the propriety of them.

Father Phelan told me that I should meet with L'Esperance in the other building, that is, the second, in an apartment which he mentioned; and he wished me to take him to a chamber, which he described, and give him a glass of wine. I should find two bottles, he informed me, in the cupboard in that room, one of them marked with a paper, and that I should pour out for him a tumbler full from that, and might drink some from the other myself. Now I knew that L'Esperance was much addicted to drink, and always ready for wine. I might, under other circumstances, have questioned the object of the step required, or inquired what was the reason for proceeding in such a manner; whether there was anything mixed with the wine in either bottle, and if so, what, and in which. But how could I dare to do so in my present situation? I can hardly think that any consideration would have induced me. I therefore proceeded to the place indicated, and met L'Esperance, invited him to take some wine, and led him to the apartment. On opening the cupboard, I found two bottles, as I had been told I should, one with a paper upon it; and filling a tumbler from it with red wine, and another from the other, I presented the former to L'Esperance, and taking the other, began to drink. Suddenly it occurred to me, with an impression of horror, which I cannot describe, that if there was poison in the wine I had given to the priest, I should be the cause of his death. Phelan had threatened, in the Convent, to give him a dose that should be his last; and was not this the way in which he intended to accomplish his purpose? My feelings were entirely too strong to be restrained. I became in an instant overpowered with the conviction of the truth; and I believe that no threat or punishment in the power of those around me to inflict, would have induced me any longer to pursue the plan on which I was proceeding.

I turned round to look at the priest, and saw that he had not hesitated to take off the draught I had presented to him, and was then drinking the dregs of the cup. What I felt, it would be useless for me to attempt to describe. I put down the glass I held in my own hand, a considerable portion from which I had swallowed, and hastened out of the room without speaking, in a state of mind distressing beyond endurance. I left the house, ran across the yard to that from which I had proceeded, rushed into the room in which I had left Father Phelan, and threw myself upon the sofa. A new thought had occurred to me on the way. Perhaps my wine had been poisoned, either by design or accident: for how did I know that the paper had not been put upon the wrong bottle, or what reason had I to confide in the honour of any person who would treat another as I supposed L'Esperance had been treated? In my extreme agitation of mind, I did not stop to reason: but my fears led me to believe the most dreadful thing which suggested itself. I therefore at once embraced the idea that I was poisoned, and was soon to die in agony. I began to cry, and soon to scream with horror, regardless of everything around me. Some of the old nuns came to my assistance, and first asked me to be quiet, and then commanded me, lest others should learn the cause; but for a long time they found it impossible to pacify me. From some remarks which fell from them, I plainly understood that they had been watching me while I was giving L'Esperance the wine, probably through a glass door.

My health was seriously affected by the occurrences of that day, so that I was removed to a bed, and there was confined about ten days, suffering for a time great pain. My strength became gradually restored, but it was long before I could prudently leave my room.

OCCUPATIONS OF MEN AND WOMEN ON NUN'S ISLAND.

IT would be impossible for me to form any estimate, on which I could place reliance, of the number of men or women I saw on Nun's Island. There was no regular time for breakfast, dinner or supper. No bell was rung, no notice was given for meals, any more than for retiring at night, or rising in the morning. Food was always prepared and ready, when any of us were disposed to eat; and we went when we chose, alone or in company, to the eating-room, at one end of the building, and helped ourselves in true Canadian style.

Many of my readers may not be aware of the style of eating practised among many of the lower Canadians. So many of the priests are of Canadian origin, that their meals in the nunnery, and on the island, are often disposed of in a rude and unmannerly way, with but little use of knives and forks. We often ate standing, while on the island, and it was common to take even meat in the fingers.

As there was no general call, or occasion for assembling at any time, the inmates resorted to their rooms, or lounged about the galleries, yard, or sitting-rooms, as they pleased; so that it would have been impossible to count them all, even if I had been disposed. But I did not ever think of doing so.

Some of the priests, as I understood, were there on penances. This was indeed a merely nominal thing. Priests who have been complained of by their parishioners, in a formal manner, are sometimes sent by the bishop to Nun's Island, and sometimes to the Priests' Farm, to satisfy their accusers with the form of punishment. I have reason, however, to believe that they generally suffered no privations, and were far from regarding their residence as a place of punishment. On the contrary, I often saw them partake of indulgences. The edifice numbered 3, was specially devoted to the priests: but they enjoyed much liberty, and where allowed to go wherever they pleased.

Among their occupations, some occasionally spent a while in reading; and I saw a number of books lying about in several rooms, which the women were not expected to look at. Some played flutes and sang. I have sometimes heard several of them play together. Most of their music, however, was vocal; and while I was on the island I heard a variety of songs sung, particularly those which were most popular in the nunnery.

The women, that is those whose health would permit, had a variety of work to perform, particularly with the needle. Sometimes an order would come from the Superior of the nunnery, to make a number of towels or sheets, and sometimes six or eight shirts were ordered for some priest, in great haste. The old nuns would call upon us to assemble, and gave us no peace till they were done. Orders sometimes came from the Seminary, Nunnery, Priests' Farm, and Bishop. It commonly happened, however, that the greater part of the job was performed by a few of the most industrious or good-natured ones: for the cross and indolent would contrive to get off their part on whoever would do it. At certain seasons of the year large quantities of soap were made, and then old Aunts Margaret and Susan are sent from the nunnery to manage that department. Butter and cheese are made from the milk of the cows kept on the island; and several of the nuns most expert in making them, are employed in the dairy.

I had often noticed a young woman, apparently rather older than myself, with a peculiarly unhappy and depressed countenance; but I had never spoken with her. One day I was set to sew with her on the same piece—a sheet which was to be made. We sat together sewing a whole afternoon, during which little or nothing was said by either of us. When it grew too dark to do any more, and our work was laid aside, we kept our places, and she began to converse with a degree of freedom which I had not expected. We were at the end of the long gallery in the building No. 1, near the window where I often sat, and knew that we could not be overheard.

She began by saying that she was lonely and unhappy; and spoke of the wretchedness of such a situation, to which I replied with equal freedom, and in such a manner as to lead her on to say more. Indeed, she must have known, that if she gave me opportunity to accuse her of complaining, and to get her subjected to severe penances or punishment, I equally committed myself.

She then went on to speak of her early life, and the place of her former residence, which I do not recollect, although she named it. I have the impression that it was somewhere in Upper Canada, a retired and pleasant spot. She said that she longed to get away from the nuns and priests, but knew not how. She was a nun in some Convent, I do not know where; and her Superior was very harsh in her treatment, and had put some dreadful penances upon her. Once in particular, she had nearly destroyed her life; for she made her lie, for several weeks, upon a bed made of ropes, which weakened and injured her so much, that she was unable to sit up for six weeks. If we could contrive any way of escaping from the Island, we might find our way to her native place, where she would be certain of getting a good and comfortable residence, for me as well as herself. At the same time she spoke of it as utterly hopeless, shut up and watched as we were. She spoke of the penances she had endured, with a kind of horror: and said it was hard for her to believe that it was by means of such sufferings that anybody could get to heaven. Indeed, she said heaven must be a dreadful place, if such trials as she was subject to were the way of introduction to it.

She did not speak particularly of the occasion of her visit to the Island: but, from the state of her health, and other circumstances, I had no doubt that it was similar to that which had brought many others there.

I found that her melancholy was that of despair. While speaking of her home, she seemed, indeed, to forget, for a moment, that it was impossible for her ever to see it again, and exclaimed, "O, how happy we should be, living there together!" But then, when recurring again to her actual condition, she assured me that she constantly prayed for death, and sometimes thought seriously that she would take her own life.

I felt very much for her, and once told her I would almost venture to attempt an escape with her. She said that would be entirely useless—we had no chance at all. I afterwards trembled to think how I had exposed myself, and that she might possibly inform against me: but this she never did.

I was not particular in noticing the number of days I spent on Nuns' Island: but I believe I was there very nearly three weeks. I am certain, at least, that three Sundays passed while I was there. One evening an old nun told me I was to return to the nunnery; and that night I set out in company with three priests, and several nuns, after putting on a black cloak and hood, as before. Savage was one of the priests, and Bruneau another. The latter was then confessor at the nunnery. Sainte Mary, I remember, was one of the nuns in company, and two others were old nuns, who expressed much regret at leaving the place, saying, that if there was anything to be done in the nunnery more than common, they must always be sent for.

We proceeded from the gate of the wall on foot to the shore, where Jacques and Pierre were ready with their boat; and having entered it, they rowed across to the river's shore, where we found a charette waiting for us, in which we rode to the city. The driver stopped at the nunnery gate, from which I had started with L'Esperance, and having alighted and rung, we were admitted into the nunnery through the chapel, the sacristy, and the long passage I have more than once alluded to, in my former work. Proceeding to the Superior's room, she received me; and, having made me take off my cloak and leave it there, she conducted me into the nuns' sleeping-room, where I retired to bed.

The next morning, when Jane Ray met me, she addressed me with a sarcastic look, saying—"Well, so you've been to the White Cats' castle?"

I never heard the name of L'Esperance mentioned after this, except on two occasions. Father Phelan one day remarked, "So you gave him a good dose!" thereby confirming my belief, that he was dead with poison, if evidence was wanted to make me feel certain of it. A considerable time afterwards, while I was in the sick-room, I was called to attend a mass, to be celebrated in honor of L'Esperance; so that his death was then no longer to be doubted.

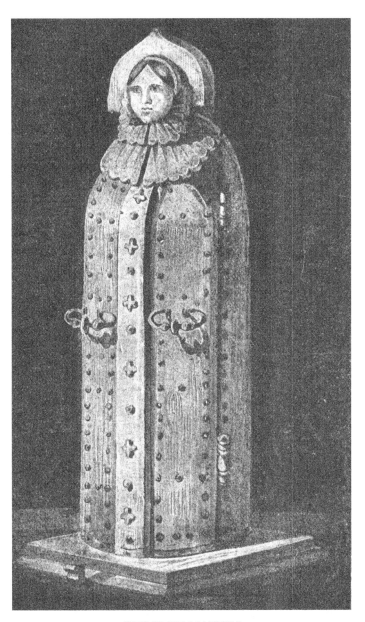

THE IRON MAIDEN

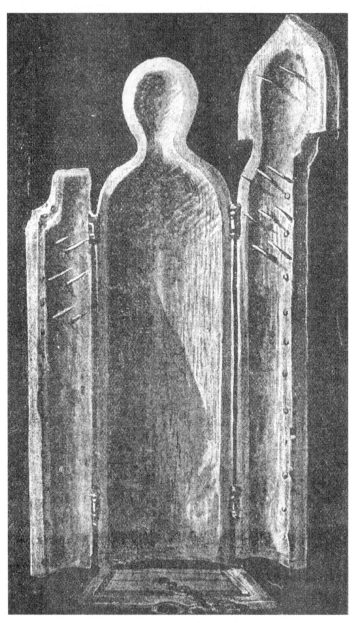

THE IRON MAIDEN—(OPEN.)

CONCLUSION

I HAVE now concluded all the "further Disclosures" which I deem it important to make, in relation to the Hotel Dieu Nunnery. There are many incidents which have been brought to my memory, while I have been employed in preparing the preceding pages; and I might name and describe many other persons with whom I had some acquaintance, or of whom I heard particulars of different kinds. It is necessary, however, to put some limits to myself; and, although I may not be the best judge of what is most important to be known to my readers, I think I have not kept back anything indispensable to them.

So far as I have been able, consistently with truth, and the interests of many, I have endeavoured to avoid giving pain to individuals, by exposing what I know, even though they be culpable, and some of them highly so. My object has not been wantonly to destroy peace; and of this I think several persons will be convinced when they find that I have not mentioned in this book things which they know I am acquainted with.

The public will easily understand why I did not allude in my first volume to the fact that I saw American females at Nuns' Island, under the circumstances in which I have here described them. I was afraid of the consequences at that time, because I thought that was one of the last things the priests would be willing to see published; and that something coming so near home, would embitter some against me, more than anything I could say about deeds done at a distance, and in a different country.

I now take leave of my readers, with a belief that I have done all that can be required of me, and with a sincere wish, that while my disclosures may save some innocent and unsuspecting females from sufferings like my own, I may be enabled to spend the rest of my life in retirement and peace, amongst those who will protect a feeble woman and her harmless child, and in the midst of the blessings of virtuous society.

SIX MONTHS IN A CONVENT

NUNS KISSING THE FLOOR

THE NUN;

OR,

SIX MONTHS' RESIDENCE

IN A

CONVENT

By REBECCA THERESA REED,

LATE INMATE OF THE URSULINE CONVENT, MOUNT
BENEDICT, CHARLESTOWN, MASSACHUSETTS.

PREFACE.

TWO or three facts, of importance to a clear understanding of the following narrative, should be kept in view by the reader, and are therefore stated briefly in a preface to this edition of the work. The chief subject of it, Miss Rebecca Reed, now of Boston in the United States, is not responsible for the publication as would at first on the face of the narrative appear. The manuscript was prepared by her, from copious notes which she took as she had opportunity: of this there can be no doubt. But it may be doubted whether she would at her own instance ever have sent it to the press. It was first published by a number of her friends in that city, who united their persuasions to overcome her reluctance to its appearing in print; partly to shield her from the reproaches that her escape from the convent, and her subsequent conversations and correspondence about its discipline, were bringing upon her; but principally to counteract the prevailing passion among Protestants in favour of a convent education for their daughters, which, among other things, appeared to be giving an impulse to the advances of Popery in that quarter of the world.

In little more than two years after Miss Reed's escape, the convent was destroyed by fire. It had become so unpopular and unsightly an object, that a mob at length assembled and burnt it to the ground. It was to be expected that its proprietors and advocates would charge this outrage on the efforts of Miss Reed and her friends to bring the institution into contempt. Hence the Superior, in her answer to Miss Reed's narrative, represents her as saying that her brother-in-law and another friend declared that *the convent should come down.* As no saying of this kind occurs in the narrative itself, and as Miss Reed protests against having ever uttered anything like it, the calumny has been imputed to the Superior's desire to confirm suspicion against her brother-in-law, who was then under indictment on a charge of abetting the incendiarism.

The fact is, whatever influence the narrative had upon the public judgment and feeling against the convent, no unbiassed person could imagine anything like a conspiracy in the family, or among the friends of this young lady to destroy the property of the establishment and hazard the lives of its inmates. The outrage was owing to a more extended and less recent prejudice against such institutions generally, and that more particularly. Their reported and acknowledged abuses—their inconsistency with the spirit and letter of American laws—their tendency to foster political and moral corruption, and to shelter criminals while they produced crime—were sufficient to account for violence, which yet every friend to good order must deplore.

SIX MONTHS IN A CONVENT.

IN the summer of 1826, while passing the Nunnery on Mount Benedict, Charlestown, Massachusetts, in company with my schoolmaster, the question was asked by a young lady, who I think was a Roman Catholic, how we should like to become Nuns. I replied, after hearing her explanation of their motives for retirement, &c. "I should like it well;" and gave as my principal reason, their apparently holy life, my love of seclusion, &c. The conversation which passed at that time made but little impression upon my mind. But soon after, the "*Religieuses*"* came from Boston to take possession of Mount Benedict as their new situation. We were in school, but had permission to look at them as they passed. One of the scholars remarked, that they were Roman Catholics, and that our parents disapproved of their tenets. The young lady who before asked the question, how we should like to become nuns, and whose name I have forgotten, was affected even to tears in consequence of what passed, and begged them to desist, saying, "They were saints, God's people, and the chosen few;" that they "secluded themselves, that they might follow the Scriptures more perfectly, pray for the conversion of sinners, and instruct the ignorant† in the principles of religion." This conversation, with the solemn appearance of the nuns, affected me very sensibly, owing probably to the peculiar state of my feelings. The impression thus made remained on my mind several months; and at the age of thirteen years and four months, I asked my parents if they were willing I should become an inmate of the convent. This proposition my parents were inclined to treat as visionary; but they soon discovered themselves to be in an error. Nothing of consequence was said on the subject; but soon after, owing to the delicacy of my health, and other reasons, it was deemed expedient for me to visit my friends in New Hampshire; and being fond of retirement, this arrangement accorded very well with my feelings.

---

* By the term "*Religieuses*," I mean those who constituted the Ursuline Community.
† By the word *ignorant*, is meant what they term heretics.

While in New Hampshire, I spent many pleasant hours, which I think of with delight. Memory oft brings to view, and faithfully delineates those hours of retirement and happiness which I imagined I should spend, were I an inhabitant of a cloister.

While writing this narrative, I often lament my little knowledge of history; for, had I been more acquainted with it, I do not think I ever should have united myself to an institution of this nature. But to proceed; I never could prevail on my parents to say much on this subject. I kept silence, resolving in my own mind to become acquainted with some one who would introduce me to the Superior of the Ursuline Community, but did not ask any one till after the death of my mother. Previous to that event, I had become acquainted with Miss M. H., a domestic in Mr. H. J. K's family, near my father's house, in Charlestown.

After my mother's decease, while residing with my father, my sisters being absent, Miss H. came to our house, and begged me to keep her as a domestic a little while, as she had no place. She had walked a great way for the purpose of seeing Mr. K., who had moved away. This was in the fall of 1830. After consulting with my father, I concluded to let her stay. She found me in great trouble and grief, in consequence of the absence of my two younger sisters, whom I very dearly loved, and who had gone to reside with my sisters in Boston. After family prayers were over, and I about retiring, I stepped from my room to see if Miss H. had extinguished her lamp, when, to my surprise, I found her kneeling, and holding a string of beads. I asked her what she was doing. She did not speak for some time. When she did, she said she was saying her "Hail Marys."* I asked her what the "Hail Marys" were, at the same time taking hold of the beads. She then said, "I say my prayers on these to the Blessed Virgin." My friends will, of course, excuse my curiosity at this time, for I had never before learned their manner of praying to saints and angels. Before I left her, she showed me

---

* *Catholic prayer, translated from the Latin.*—"Hail, Mary! full of grace; our Lord is with thee: Blessed art thou among women, and blessed is the fruit of thy womb, Jesus! Holy Mary, mother of God, pray for us sinners, now and at the hour of our death. Amen."

an *Agnus Dei**which she wore to preserve herself from the temptations of Satan. I cannot remember all the conversation which passed the next day on the subject; but I learned that she had been acquainted with the nuns in Boston, and was also acquainted with the Superior.

The first pleasant day, I asked her to accompany me to the Superior, which she did, and appeared, by her questions, to know my motive. She introduced me to the Superior in the following manner:—We were invited by a lay sister† to sit, who, after retiring, in a few moments made her appearance, requesting Miss H. to see her in another room. Soon after, the Superior came in, and embraced me with much seeming affection, and put the following questions to me:—How long since the death of my mother? Whether I ever attended the Catholic Church, or knew anything of the principles of their religion? What I had heard respecting them—of their order—my views of it? What progress I had made in my studies? Whether I had attended much to history—knew anything of embroidery, drawing, or painting, or any other ornamental work? Whether I had ever assisted in domestic affairs? After which questions, taking my hand, she said, "O, it feels more like a pancake, than anything else."‡ She inquired in what capacity I desired to enter the institution?—whether as a recluse or a scholar? Whether I had done attending school, &c.? I replied, that I did not consider my education complete—that I wished to go into the school attached to the nunnery, on the same terms as other pupils, until I had made sufficient progress to take the veil, and become a recluse—that my father was averse to my becoming a nun; but I was of opinion, that he would concur with my episcopal friends, in not objecting to my becoming a pupil. In the course of the interview, the

* Lamb of God;—a small piece of wax sewed up in silk in the form of a heart.

† Those nuns who are occupied in domestic affairs.

‡ This may appear laughable; but as I intend to publish all which will be for the benefit of the reader, I cannot refrain from mentioning this, in order to show the course of flattery, &c., made use of by the Superior and those connected with the establishment, to draw the inexperienced into their power, and make them converts to the religion of the Pope.

Superior conversed much upon the Scriptures, and intimated, that I ought to make any sacrifice, if necessary, to adopt the religion of the Cross—repeating the words of our Saviour, "He that loveth father or mother more than me, is not worthy of me, &c."

At a subsequent interview, the Superior desired me to see the Bishop or Clergy, remarking, she believed I had a vocation for a religious life, and the Bishop would tell me whether I had or not. She also asked if I was acquainted with a Catholic friend who would introduce me to the Bishop, and mentioned a Mr. R. who would introduce me to him. I was unacquainted with Mr. R., but had seen him at my sister's house in Boston. She said that the Bishop or Mr. R. would also discuss the matter with my father, and reconcile him to Catholicity. After consulting some friends who were in favour of the Catholic religion, I consented to see Mr. R.; who, being requested, called at my father's, gave me some Scripture proofs of the infallibility of the Romish church; as "Thou art Peter, and upon this rock I build my church, and the gates of hell shall not prevail against it;" and "Whose sins ye retain they are retained, and whose sins ye remit they are remitted." "He that will not hear the church, let him be to thee as an heathen man and a publican." He (Mr. R.) desired I would secrete the paper upon which the texts were quoted. He then took his leave, saying he would call to see me in town soon at the Misses S., when he would introduce me to the Bishop.

I will here remark, that previous to my joining the community, I heard of many miracles wrought by Catholic priests. Mrs. G. brought a lady one day in a chaise, to show me her eyes, which were restored by means of a priest, Dr. O'F. She, as Mrs. G. stated, was totally blind; but having faith in miracles, she knelt to her confessor, requesting him to heal her. After touching her eyes with spittle and holy oil, she immediately "received her sight."

Before the next interview with the Superior I visited my Protestant friends, the Misses S., when Mr. R. called and proposed to introduce me to the Bishop. He accordingly accompanied me to the Bishop's, and introduced me as the young lady who wished to become acquainted with the tenets of the Church, and recommended to him by the honoured Mother the Superior, with directions for his ascertaining my vocation as a fit subject for a recluse. The Bishop asked me if I knew the meaning of the word "Nun;" how long I had thought of becoming a nun; my opinion, and the opinion of my friends in regard to Catholicity; and as my feelings were easily wrought upon, more particularly at this time, questions were put to me, which more mature deliberation leads me to think were put under the impression that I was very ignorant, and which were very unpleasant for me to answer. He even went so far as to judge my secret thoughts, saying he knew what was then passing in my mind. I then took my leave, undecided what course to pursue, and very little edified by the conversation of the Rt. Rev. Bishop. The Bishop gave directions to Mr. R. to purchase a catechism of the Catholic Church in the diocese of Boston, published with the approbation of the Rt. Rev. Bishop Fenwick, which I refused to accept.

About a week afterwards, I called upon the Superior, and made her acquainted with my conversation with the Bishop, likewise with my refusal of the catechism. On learning that my desire was still strong to become an inmate of the convent, she smilingly said, that for one so young as I was to wish to seclude myself from the world, and live the life of a *religieuse*, was impossible. I remarked, I did not like the Bishop as well as I expected. She exclaimed, "Oh! he is one of the servants of God; he did so to try your vocation and said that I should like him the better the next time I saw him.* After recommending me to pray for grace, she caused me to kneel down and receive her blessing; after which she embraced me, and I returned to my father's house. I shortly afterwards visited the Misses H. in Charlestown, and was introduced to Mrs. G., who was acquainted with the tenets of the Catholic Church, and also with Mr. B. the Catholic Priest. After a short acquaintance with her, I was requested to converse with Mr. B., the priest, which I did, and liked him very much. He also supplied me

---

* I did like him the next time that I called upon him, for he conversed in the most solemn manner, and after learning my name, said, "Is it possible that you have a saint's name!" and gave me St. Teresa as my namesake, a beautiful wax figure habited as an Ursuline nun.

with books, from which I learned that I ought to venerate and receive the religion of the Catholic Church as the *only one and true religion*.

On Good Friday evening, I heard the most affecting Catholic sermon* I ever listened to, upon the Passion of our Divine Redeemer. I soon after visited at Mrs. G's, where I saw a fine drawing, exhibiting the peaceful and flourishing condition of the Holy and Apostolic Church, until the time of the Reformation, under Martin Luther. Mrs. G. recounted the sufferings of the Catholic Church in consequence of this "pretended reformation." My friends will understand, that by this time I had become a constant visitor at the convent. On being sent for at one time by the Superior, I met the Bishop at the convent, who was playing with the dogs; at the same time, the Superior, hastily approaching, embraced me in the most affectionate manner; as she did ever afterwards, when I visited her at the convent. She introduced me to the Bishop again, who did not appear to recognize me, and said I was sister to the lady who visited him in Boston. At this time I thought the Superior and Bishop the most angelic persons living, and, in one instance, gave way to anger in consequence of hearing a few words spoken against them. On being told that my mind remained still the same, the Bishop remarked, "I will pray for you;" and recommended to me the advantage of continuing under the instruction of the priest, and said he should like to see my father or sister.

After the interview with the Bishop, I returned to my father's, who was much displeased with the steps I had taken, and bade me renounce all connection with the Catholics, or leave my friends. (This he said in a moment of excitement.) But being so much attracted by the apparent holiness of the inmates of the convent, and viewing this as the only true church, I wished to become a member of it.

Perhaps it will be proper to state some of Mrs. G's conversation. After hearing from her a pleasing account of the life a nun, &c., I mentioned I should like to become one, and would, if I could prevail on my father and friends to consent; but unless I could, I must despair, as they would not be willing to advance the *money* which would be

---

* I had before attended the lectures in Boston, at the time of the controversy between Dr. Beecher and the Catholics.

needed to go there. She replied, "It is not *money* that will ever induce them to take you; it must all be the work of God." She asked me what my church friends* said upon the subject. On my telling her that they were reconciled to my entering the institution, particularly as a scholar; that they liked the seclusion of a convent, &c., Mrs. G. stated that she could not see the least objection to my following my own inclination. I then took my leave, promising to see her at my friend Mrs. H.'s. The next time I saw her, she advised me to leave my father's house and all, for the sake of Christ. She said she would procure me ornamental work, which would support me, independent of my relatives, &c., which she did. I thanked her most heartily, and told her I thought I should be happy if I were certain of going to a cloister. She gave me her word that I should. I then took up with her advice, and left my friends, I thought for life, as I had no doubt but that I should soon enter the Convent, resolving to leave all for the love of God and to consecrate the remainder of my days to his service. I believed Mrs. G. to be my sincere friend, and an Episcopalian, as she had always told me she was, and placed myself under her protection. After visiting some Protestant friends, I found means to procure my clothing, &c., and went immediately to reside opposite the Catholic church. I employed myself while there in doing ornamental work, for Catholic friends, and also in working lace for the Bishop, the altar, &c. About this time I was offered compensation, but refused it, and received a present of ten dollars, a crucifix, a pearl cross, and two books, with my name stamped upon them in gold letters, which presents I received as tokens of kindness and friendship.† And wishing to deny myself of any thing worldly, I gave up what jewellery I had, telling

---

* My friends of the Episcopal Church thought I could have the privilege of writing when I desired to see them.

† I wish to have it understood, that the lettering on these books was my new name, "Mary Agnes Teresa." My baptismal name, it will be recollected, is Rebecca Theresa. The books were given me by Mrs. G., who said they were from the Bishop; and he afterwards, in the convent, confirmed the statement, saying, he knew at that time of my vocation, and for that reason sent me a religious name, which was a saint's name.

them I knew of no greater sacrifice I could at that time make, than to give up all the treasures my dear mother had left me. I also gave my globe and gold-fish, which were a present to me. At that time I thought I was *holy*, and could hardly speak to a Protestant. I had read many Catholic books. My time was wholly employed in working for the Catholics, except my hours for meditation and prayers.

The ordinance of baptism* was administered to me by Mr. B., himself and a Mrs. P. standing sponsors for me—my former baptism being considered by the Catholics *invalid*. While in Charlestown, I stood sponsor for Mrs. G's daughter, of whom I shall speak in the course of this narrative. I would here remark, had I taken up with the advice given me by many of my friends, I should not now have the unpleasant duty of relating these facts. But so it was: I had imbibed a relish for what I supposed to be "real pleasures," but which, alas! I have found, by sad experience, to be like the "waters of Marah." At an interview with the Superior, I was introduced to two of the "chosen Religieuse," the mother assistant and Mrs. Mary Benedict. The first question asked was, what word I brought from my friends. On my hesitating to give an answer, she insisted upon knowing what they said; on which I told her all they had said, word for word, as nearly as I could recollect; also the advice I received from a Mr. E., which appeared to displease her much; and although she strove to suppress her feelings, it was evident she was much displeased.

After some questions respecting Mr. E., the Superior remarked, he was none other than the man who made children's books. She also questioned me with regard to a conversation which took place between my brother and myself on Charlestown bridge (which was published in the "JESUIT,"† highly exaggerated,) and appeared greatly pleased with the language of my mother, saying, with peculiar emphasis, "O,

---

* At the time of my baptism I was anointed with oil; a piece of salt was put in my mouth, the priest breathing three times upon it, and touching my eyes, ears, and nose with spittle, speaking Latin all the while. They profess to take these ceremonies from the Scriptures.

† I afterwards asked priest B. to explain what it meant: he said Dr. O'F made a mistake in writing it for the press; and he promised it should be corrected.

you will die a martyr to the cause of truth, should you die under persecution." I took my leave of her, promising to call again when she should desire.

After this, she wrote a letter to my father, of the contents of which I was then ignorant, but have since learned it contained offers of two or three quarters' schooling, free of expense. My father says he treated it with contempt; and his answer by the bearer was briefly this—"He wished me to have nothing to do with that institution; that my friends would prefer my going to a Protestant seminary." At my next interview with the Superior, she however told me, my father had become reconciled to my remaining with them two or three quarters, after which time, he would inform them whether he could consent to have me stay there longer as a teacher of music."* She previously presented me with some slate pongee, which was the uniform dress worn by the scholars in the public apartments, telling me at the same time to prepare myself, and have my things ready by such a day. She asked me, if I should come without the consent of my Boston friends, if I supposed they would insert anything in the public papers, or make any disturbance, or come there for me? to which I replied, I thought not. After preparing myself for a public reception, I visited the Superior, when she said, if I would place myself under her care from this time, she would protect me for ever, and particularly from the persecution of the "heterodox," and she looked to heaven above for her reward.†

---

* I attended music because the Superior desired it; and she assured me there was no need of assistance from my friends, even if my father had consented, for I could with my needle be of sufficient use to the community to support myself without their assistance. She also told me I should study when I chose, and might have the privilege of coming into the Religieuse Community to recite to her.

† I wish it to be understood, that being influenced by the Superior and Mrs. G's advice, after hearing Romish preaching and reading their books, I went to board at Mrs. H's., opposite the Catholic church, where I employed my time in ornamental work, visited the Convent often, and informed myself as much as possible of a recluse's life; lived as retired as the "Charity Sisters," except visiting some of my relatives three times, twice accompanied with Romish friends.

She then stated that the Bishop had concluded to receive me, not as a member of the public department, but as a "Novitiate," which would screen me from the questions of the Protestant scholars. She also added, that I should be received as the other sisters were, and that we were to support ourselves by our talents and industry. The names of the sisters were, Mrs. Mary Ursula,* Miss Mary Magdalene, Miss Mary Joseph, and Miss Mary Austin. The latter was both teacher and pupil. I answered that I should like those conditions best. She then desired me to kneel down and take the following obligation:—"I do, with the grace and assistance of Almighty God, renounce the world for ever, and place myself under your protection, from this day, to consecrate myself to his honour and glory, in the house of God, and to do whatever obedience prescribes, and tell no one of this obligation but Mr. B., in confession." After this, the Superior summoned two of the "Choir Religieuse," who conducted me to the garden, where they left me to amuse myself. Presently the Superior joined me, wishing to know how I liked the garden, the flowers, &c. Observing a pocket album in my hand, she asked what I had hoarded up there—some worldly goods? She took it, and examining it desired to know if I wished to keep some money I had in it (fifteen dollars.) I replied no; as I was going to join them, I would intrust it to her care. She also requested me to sing one tune; I complied, and sung "There's nothing true but heaven." Her observation was, she should wish me to commence immediately with music. I then left the convent, and attended the sacraments of Confession and Communion; and on Sabbath morning, August 7th, 1831, I was attended to the gate of the

---

* Mrs. Mary Ursula came from New Hampshire, and was received as *Choir Religieuse*. She was the eldest in the community: this I learned from the Superior, who often reprimanded her for saying many words in an uncouth rustic manner, (such as *daoun* for *down*, &c.) telling her of her ignorance, &c. She never refused complying with the rules, but, when reprimanded, would kneel at once, and kiss the floor. I often wished to ask if she was happy, but dared not speak (without permission) to her. Their proceedings appeared so strange, that I was in continual fear. The novices frequently trembled when approaching "the Mother," particularly at confession.

Convent by my friend Mrs. G. I was shown into the public parlour by the lay sister, and was required to kneel and continue my devotion until the Superior made her appearance. She soon came and made a sign for me to follow her. She led the way into a long room, darkened, at one end of which stood a large crucifix, made of bone, which I was afterwards informed was made of the bones of the saints. The Superior told me, in a whisper, it was the time of silence. But after arranging my dress, she took from her toilet a religious garb, which she placed upon my head, and bade me kiss it, saying it had been blessed by the Bishop. She then pronounced a short Latin prayer, while I was kneeling, at the same time giving me her blessing. After this, she conducted me into another apartment, where was a stranger whom she called a Postulant,* and giving me permission to speak, she left the room. A lay sister then entered the room with refreshment, after partaking which, we had permission to walk in one particular path in the garden. This stranger picked up a pear and began to eat it, and invited me to do the same, which I declined, being acquainted with the rules of the convent, which were very strict, as will be learned in the course of the narrative. She did not regard the rules so strictly as the Superior required, who, being made acquainted with her conversation by separately questioning us, sent her away, as she said, to another order;† but I now know that this was not the case.

To return to our walk in the garden. The bell rang, when we were immediately conducted to the Religieuse Choir; and here the Superior caused me to kneel three times, before I could suit her. After the performances were over, which consisted of the office of adoration to the Blessed Virgin, and prayers to the saints, repeated in the Latin tongue, of which I knew nothing, we proceeded to the refectory, where we partook of our "portions." After saying Latin, we kneeled and kissed

---

* Candidate for a recluse.

† I believed she had gone to another order; and after returning to my sisters, told them so (together with my pastor,) that she was with the Sisters of Charity; when, to my surprise, she called upon me, said she had never thought of going to another order, and that the Superior had not done by her as she agreed.

the floor, at a signal given by the Superior on her snuffbox. Before eating one of the Religieuses said, "In nomine Domini nostri Jesu Christi,"* all making the sign of the Cross, and responding, "Amen." After receiving our portions we performed several devotions, such as kissing the floor and repeating Latin, while the "Angelus" was ringing. We then went immediately to the "Community." On entering this room, the "novices" kneel and repeat the "Ave Maria,"† kiss the floor, and seat themselves for recreation, according to the rules given by the Superior, entitled, "Rules by the Reverend Mother." The following are the rules which were enclosed in a gilt frame, and suspended in the community; and it is the duty of every novice to read them at least once a week:—

1. To rise on the appearance of the Superior.

2. When reprimanded to kneel at once and kiss the floor, until the signal be given to rise.

3. When speaking *of* the Superior, to say our Mother; when speaking *to* her, and to the professed Choir Religieuse, Mamere; to say Sister, when speaking *to* the Novices; *of* them, Miss; and *of* the professed Choir, Mrs.; to say *our* or *ours*, instead of *my* or *mine*.

4. To say "Ave Maria" every time we enter the community.

5. Before entering any room, to give *three* knocks on the door, accompanied by some religious ejaculation, and wait until they are answered by three from within.

---

* In the name of our Lord Jesus Christ. When opportunity offered, I asked the Superior to explain the meaning. She said, in a very solemn manner, "You must not, my dear sister, give way to *curiosity*. Do you not recollect it is against the *rules* for a Religieuse to do so?" I answered, "Yes, Mamere!" and complied at once (by kissing the floor,) when she observed: "A Religieuse should never have a will of her own; as she grew in perfection in the order, she would understand what these words mean; it will be revealed to you when you are deserving." She taught me to believe that the "Office of the Blessed Virgin," (which was in Latin, and which we all repeated, without understanding it), was none other than that chanted in heaven by the saints around the throne of the Almighty, and called the sweet communion of "All Saints."

† Hail Mary.

6. Not to lift our eyes while walking in the passage ways; also, never to *touch* each other's hands.

7. To stand while spoken to by the Bishop or Superior, and kneel while speaking to them; to speak in a particular tone.

8. If necessary to speak to the Superior during a time of silence, to approach her kneeling, and speak in whispers.

9. Never to leave a room without permission, giving at the same time our reason.

10. To rise and say the "Hour"* every time the clock strikes, except when the Bishop is present, who, if he wishes makes the signal.

The following are the written "*Rules and Penances of our Holy Father, Saint Augustine*," together with those of Saint Ursula, as near as I can recollect. They are read at the refectory table every week:—

1. To kneel in the presence of the Bishop, until his signal to rise.

2. Never to gratify our appetites, except with his holiness the Bishop's or a Father Confessor's permission.

3. Never to approach or look out of the window of the Monastery.

4. To sprinkle our couches every night with holy water.

5. Not to make a noise in walking over the Monastery.

6. To wear sandals and haircloth; to inflict punishment upon ourselves with our girdles, in imitation of a Saint.

7. To sleep on a hard mattress or couch, with *one* coverlet.

8. To walk with pebbles in our shoes, or walk kneeling until a wound is produced. Never to *touch anything* without permission.

9. Never to gratify our curiosity, or exercise our thoughts on any subject, without our spiritual director's knowledge and advice. Never

---

* "*The Hour.*—O sacred heart of Jesus! always united to the will of thy Father, grant that ours may be sweetly united in thine. Heart of Mary! an asylum in the land of our Captivity, procure for us the happy liberty of the children of Jesus. May the souls of the faithful departed, through the merits of Christ and mercies of God, rest in peace. Amen."

The above is what is called *an Hour;* there is a different, though similar one, for each of the twenty-four hours in the day. They are written, and placed in two gilt frames over the mantel-piece; twelve over the heart of Mary in one, and twelve over the heart of Jesus in the other. Every time the clock strikes, the one whose turn it is to lecture rises and says one of them.

to desire food or water between portions.

10. Every time, on leaving the community, to take holy water from the altar of the Blessed Virgin, and make the sign of the cross.

11. If a *Religieuse* priest in disobeying the Superior, she is to be brought before the Bishop of the diocese, and punished as he shall think proper. Never to smile except at recreation, nor even then contrary to religious decorum.

12. Should the honoured Mother, the Superior, detect a *Religieuse* whose mind is occupied with worldly thoughts, or who is negligent in observing the rules of the Monastery, which are requisite and necessary to her perseverance and perfection in a religious life, she should immediately cause her to retire to her cell, where she could enter into a retreat.

I shall now continue my narrative of the remainder of the first day. At recreation, the Postulant and I had permission to embrace in a new form, the *Religieuse*. After that, they congratulated me on my success, saying they had ever prayed for me since they had heard of my vocation. The evening bell for the Latin office now rang, and we assembled at the choir, where we performed such ceremonies as I before named, until the time for retiring. As we were strangers, the Superior conducted us to the infirmary, where other Novices were preparing to retire, and before leaving it, bade us not to rise until we had orders. Next morning being holy-day morning, the bell rang at three, instead of four, as it usually does, for meditation in the choir. While the *Angelus** was ringing, at five A. M. we were called to attend Complin and Prime, until half-past six; then Litany to the Saints. After Litany, the bell rang for diet in the refectory, every morning, except Friday; on which day we assembled for confession to the Superior.

The manner of confession to the Superior is as follows:—The room is first darkened, and one lighted wax taper placed upon the Superior's throne; and she is considered as filling the place or station of the Blessed Virgin. After taking their places in the greatest order and silence, the Religieuses respond. Then the lecturess reads from a book, called Rules

---

* The Angelus is the bell rung while repeating the three salutations and three Hail Marys.

from the Ursuline Order, by Saint Ursula, about complaining of the
cold, our clothing, food, &c., &c. They sit on their feet during the
reading, a posture *extremely painful.* The reading finished, the Superior
whispers to the sisters to approach her separately, which they do; each
one in her turn approaches, and repeats the following: "Our Mother,
we acknowledge that we have been guilty of breaking the rules of our
Holy Order, by lifting our eyes while walking in the passage-ways; in
neglecting to take holy water on entering the community and choir;
failing in respect to our Superior, and veneration to our Father; failing in religious decorum, and in respect to our vows—poverty and
obedience; for which we most humbly ask pardon of God, penance
and forgiveness of you, our Holy Mother." As each one finishes, the
"Holy Mother" gives her advice and penances, and her blessing; they
then kiss her feet and sometimes make the cross with their tongues
on the floor; then making their inclination, they retire to the choir
to perform the penances.

After they are all assembled in the choir, the Superior says, *Kyrie
eleison,* and they all answer, *Kyrie eleison;* the Superior says, *Christe
eleison,* and they answer, *Christe eleison,* &c., &c. She then says Litany
to the Saints in Latin beginning with "Sancta Maria," and they respond, "Ora pro nobis," &c., &c. This ceremony is very solemn. It
is performed until eight o'clock, a. m., when we receive our portion
sitting on the floor. The bell rings at half-past eight for young ladies'
recreation. Then we attend to study until a quarter before eleven;
then private lecture until eleven; then bell rings for the examination
of conscience till a quarter past eleven; then for diet.* The services

---

* Our diet consisted of the plainest kind of food, principally vegetables
and vegetable soups, Indian puddings, and very seldom meat. Our tea was
made of herbs, sometimes of the bitterest kind. We partook of this diet in
imitation of the Holy Fathers of the desert to mortify our appetites. Pump-
kins, stewed with molasses and water, served us sometimes as a dessert. Occasionally we had mouldy bread to eat. A very insignificant piece of butter
was sometimes placed on our plates. The Superior's diet was far better than
ours; sometimes it was sumptuous, wine not excepted. I ascertained this, as
I occasionally, in turn, went round to gather the fragments. She sent me, on
two occasions, some apple-parings to eat, as a part of my portion. Some-

at diet are after repeating Latin:—first, they seat themselves in order upon a bench, first crossing themselves in their appointed places, on one side of a long narrow table; before each one lies a small linen napkin or servet, rolled round another small cloth, containing a knife and fork; beside each servet is a plate containing the "portion;" then the Superior enters and passes along to her table, at the head of the room, the nuns making their inclinations as she passes. She then makes a signal on her snuff-box, and the "Religieuse," whose turn it is to speak, says, *"Benedicite;"* the Superior answers, *"Benedicite;"* and so it continues, in a similar manner, from one to the other, the "Efficient"* repeating a Latin prayer. The Superior then makes the signal for the lecturess to read from the lives of the Saints and martyrs, while the others are eating. When the signal is given, each one rolls up the knife and fork in the napkin, and lays it as she found it—(they also open it at a signal;) and the one whose turn it is to do so, after kissing the floor, as a token of humility, takes from the drawer a white apron and a basket containing a napkin, and after putting on the apron, brushes the fragments from the tables into the basket, and takes the servets, making her inclination to each one. She then takes the articles off the Superior's table, one by one, in a napkin, in a solemn manner. If any eatables fall on the floor, they must be taken up in a napkin, and not by any means with the bare hands.

After this, the Superior makes a signal, and the lecturess and before-mentioned *religieuse* kneel in the middle of the floor and kiss it, and immediately rise and join the others in repeating the Latin prayers; after which the lecturess rings the Angelus. During this ringing, they all kneel and repeat it, then assemble in the community for "recreation."

---

times the Religieuses deny themselves any diet; prostrate, kiss the feet of those who remain at table, performing various kinds of penance, while the others are eating and listening to the reading. Those who have permission to deny themselves in the morning, take their work-baskets as they pass to the refectory, where they sew by candle-light, as the lecturess is reading. This has a solemn and impressive appearance.

* The Efficient is one who repeats prayers, and officiates during the office, and serves at Mass.

During this they are permitted to converse with one another, but in a particular and low tone, and only on such subjects as the Superior shall give them. If she be absent, the conversation is usually on the subject last read at the table; and they work during the time.

After recreation, public* lectures take place, and at one o'clock the bell rings for "visitation" to the altar, which, with the Vespers, occupy us an hour and a half. Then the Rosary is said. On hearing the bell again, we all assemble in the community, where there is a "point of prayer" read. Then lessons occupy us until five; meditation and reflection half an hour longer; then the bell rings again for diet, where we go through the observances before named; then recreation forty-five minutes: then the *Miserere*, during which the bell rings; then public prayers in the choir; then the *Benedictus* rings, and the lay sisters† come up into the choir. Matins, lauds, and prayers continue from seven until nine o'clock, when we retire while the bell is ringing, except those who attend lessons and penances. This concludes a day and its services. The same course was pursued every day, except Fridays and Sundays, when there was some variation.

I had become in about a week, apparently so great a favourite of the Superior, that although remiss in duties, it was in a great measure overlooked. She would even reprimand the religieuses for my example and my faults, one instance of which I will give. Failing to arrange the Superior's toilet, and seat, and cricket, it being my turn, one of the religieuses was reprimanded in my stead, and immediately knelt and kissed the floor. After this I was sent for to the Bishop's room, where the young ladies assemble on mass morning, and after kneeling, &c., the Superior asked me how things appeared; if they appeared as I thought they would; if I liked my food, &c. Feeling a repugnance to answer her, she said "Recollect yourself." I told her I liked all pretty well, except my couch. She left, telling me to beg the intercession of St. Teresa. The next day my couch was exchanged for a better, and the

---

* Public Lecture means a subject read aloud by the lecturess.

† One lay sister remains kneeling in the entry until we get to the psalm called Te Deum, when she rings while we are saying it. The Religieuses bow or kneel, &c., but do not join in saying the office.

image of St. Teresa put near it for my use.

Soon after I became an inmate of the convent, the Bishop came into the community and said, "How does that little nun? And what have you done with sister Stimson?" The Superior answered, that she was not fit for the order, and she had sent her to the Sisters of Charity. (See note on page 286.)* He then addressing me, asked how I liked Mount Benedict. I said, "Very well, my Lord." He then said, "O, but you will have to strive with the temptations between the good and evil spirits;" and he then explained all the horrors of Satan, and asked me where St. Teresa my namesake was, and if I had read her life; and told me to say, as she did, these words:—"Now come, all of you; I, being a true servant of God, will see what you can do against me," by way of challenge to the evil ones, and beg her intercession. He told me my sister had been to see if I had taken the veil, or had any thought of taking it; and he said I might rest contented, as my friends would trouble me no more.† He then told me the difference between a holy life and a worldly life; said, the devil would assail me as he did St. Teresa, and make me think I ought to go back to the world, and make me offers of worldly pleasures, and promise me happiness. In order to prevent this I must watch and pray all the time, and banish entirely worldly thoughts from my mind, and throw holy water at the evil spirits, and challenge them to come if they dare. Perceiving the unpleasant effect this had on my feelings, he pourtrayed in lively colours the happiness which would flow from my resisting the evil spirits, and what a crown of glory would be placed upon my head by the angels.

According to my confessor's orders, I took upon myself many austere penances, &c.; but the Superior noticing my exhaustion from this cause, released me from my austerities for a time, saying, I was a favoured one; and she gave me permission to rest while the others rose to say *midnight matins*‡ and to hear mass. On the exaltation of

---

* Page 299 in this edition (Editor).

† I have since learned it was my sister and another lady. They say he told them I had not taken the veil, but hoped I soon would do it.

‡ Midnight mass and midnight matins are said at night during Lent, and midnight mass always on Christmas. This is a time of special humiliation

the holy cross, the Bishop gave us his blessing, we all kneeling in the community. In conversation with the sisters, he remarked one had not a very pleasant countenance; and he asked me how I was pleased with my teacher, saying, he hoped she put a more pleasant countenance on while instructing me.

Once, while walking with the Bishop and Superior, we met a stranger, upon which the Superior required us to turn our backs while she conversed with him. After he left the garden, the Bishop and Superior held some conversation together apart from us, of which I overheard the following words of the Bishop:—"I fear he did not come here accidentally, as he stated, but for some particular purpose." Immediately the Mother-assistant came to me, saying, that gentleman looked very much like me, and asked me if he was not my brother; and having permission to look, I answered, "No, he is not." We then retired within the convent. The Bishop observed to me, just before we went in, that that gentleman looked no more like me than one of the dogs of the convent.

I was particularly hurt in witnessing the austerities put on a religieuse, named sister Mary Magdalene, who came from Ireland. Once, while reciting the offices, she, by accident, or losing breath, spoke in a lower key than she should. At a signal from the Superior, she fell prostrate before her desk, and remained so for one hour, until the office was finished, when she had permission to rise. This was the first time I thought the Superior had done wrong.* Soon after this, in private confession to the Superior, she appeared determined to know my thoughts, and put many questions to me that were hard to answer. I would here remark, that this is the practice at auricular confession. She told me to beg the intercession of my patron saint, of the Blessed Virgin, and Saint Ursula. I complained to her of my strength's failing, and of my diet not being such as I was used to. She replied, that a religieuse should have no *choice*, and that I should

_____

and prayer.

* The Superior often made mistakes in repeating the office, by endeavouring to repeat it without the book. And I learned afterwards from Mary Francis, that the Superior did not understand it.

have left my feelings in the world; and she immediately imposed the following penances;—to make the sign of the cross on the floor with my tongue, and to eat a *crust* of bread in the morning of my portion. The first of these penances I did not fulfil to the letter, making the sign of the cross with my hand instead of my tongue.*

After this, a daughter of my friend Mrs. G. came to the convent, and was permitted to spend some time with me in private. I also had some trifles given me as presents from this little girl, and leave to send what word I wished to my friends. This girl told me at the time, she was coming there to school soon; I therefore sent by her my love to my friends, informing them that I liked the convent very well, and should be very happy to see them, if they would not speak against my religion.†

Soon preparations were made for my taking the *vows* of a Religieuse, a Novena (nine days' devotion) being said for me, and for my perfection in a religious life, and prayers for the conversion of my friends. About this time my sponsor, the priest, visited the convent, and talked, as I then thought, like a godlike person. My reception was to take place *privately*, because we wished to keep my father ignorant of the manner in which I had been received, and because he might hear of it, should it take place publicly; as he before said, I was not eighteen, and he could prevent my going there. They said he could not prevent me, as I was now of age. I was perfectly happy at this time, and presented the Superior with some lines of poetry, which gave her proof of my sincerity and contentment.

She appeared very much pleased with the verses, embraced me very affectionately, and expressed her hearty approbation of my perseverance in performing the duties of the order, and said the request for her entreaties that I might persevere in a religious life should be granted, and she would show the lines to the Bishop. She accordingly did so,

---

* I would state to the reader, that those things were received on my part with great repugnance; but the Superior said they were to prove my vocation, and I submitted without a murmur.

† This message my friends never received, as I have since learned. I was deceived in regard to the friendship of Mrs. G.

when he was present one day, and he said he must write my conversion, for it was so much like St. Teresa's, my namesake. After this, she gave orders to have all my worldly dresses, being ten in number and other articles of wearing apparel, altered for those young ladies whom she clothed and educated; and for me she ordered a long habit to be prepared, which was to be blessed by the Bishop; also a veil which they said denoted purity and innocence.

One time I failed in rising at the Angelus,* which was not noticed by the Superior. The next morning a Religieuse did not rise until the ringing of the Angelus, and when she came into the refectory we were at diet. She brought her pillow, and kneeling, kissed it, and said as follows:—"I have neglected to obey the commands of the Superior, and have not risen until the Angelus, which I am most heartily sorry for; and I humbly ask pardon of God, and penances of you, our holy Mother." The Superior said no one who disobeyed her commands should be permitted to remain in this monastery. Her penance was to kiss the floor, and remain kneeling until lecture and diet were over.

The Bishop, about this time, came to examine our work, &c. After hearing us sing, he complimented us; said he should hardly have thought that I could have learned of heretics to sing and work so well; and desired me to learn him to work lace, as he feared I should not finish his *robe* for Christmas. After being presented, as usual, with wine, he retired. The Bishop's wine is presented in a golden cup. The religieuse who presents it remains kneeling until he has drank it.

As was usual on Saturday evening, after signifying our obedience to the Superior, by prostrating and kissing the floor, we received permission to visit the "*sanctum sanctorum*" on Sabbath morning, to receive the Eucharist, all of us except my teacher (the one who the Bishop said did not look pleasant, and whom I saw in tears on Sunday morning.) The Superior made a signal for me to follow her into the Bishop's room, when, first inquiring into my feelings, as she usually did, she asked me what I thought of my teacher; if she had put any questions to me while at my lessons, and how long before I thought I should

---

* My time was to rise at Angelus, which was rung at five, while the Religieuses rose at four, except on holy-day mornings, when they rose at three.

314 SIX MONTHS IN A CONVENT

be able to pronounce my vows, and take charge of a class in music. She asked me, at another time, what I thought was the reason of my teacher's crying—(her name was Miss Mary Francis). I replied, I did not know. She said it was the operation of the Holy Spirit, and her devotional feelings were very deep.

The next day, while we were at our recreations, Miss Mary Francis appeared in great distress from some cause, and in tears. She soon after pencilled a few lines, and approached the Superior kneeling, &c., and presenting the paper. She appeared confused and very angry, and bade her take a seat. After this, the Superior thought it necessary for me to retire to the infirmary and take an emetic, which I did the next day. The day after this I had orders to take medicine, which I was averse to; and on my declining, the infirmarian* made the sign of the cross a number of times, and told me it was the Superior's orders, and I could not avoid taking a part of it. I remained in the infirmary two days without a fire, and the weather was very cold. I had then permission to go to the choir, where I immediately fainted, at which the Superior was angry, and said in a whisper, she had told me *I ought not to have any feelings.*

For a while, sister Mary Francis was not present at the office and recreations as usual, and the Superior gave as a reason for her absence, that she was ill. But it will be necessary for me to leave for a moment Miss Mary Francis, and speak of Miss Mary Magdalene. The latter was put over me as a teacher, in the room of Mary Francis, whom I then supposed to be sick; but I afterwards learned that she was confined, that she might have a better opportunity to clear herself of the temptations of Satan. Sister Mary Magdalene told me she was about to leave this world, and wished to give me some advice. She said she thought it was God's will to take her to himself. After reminding me of the respect due to the Superior, and of my negligence in not kissing the floor in the choir, and of my looking up while walking in the passages, she then spake of sister Mary Francis; she said she would soon be able to give lessons as before; but wished to know which of

---

* The Infirmarian is one who tends upon the sick. I was as well as usual when I took the emetic.

the novices I thought had the best vocation for a religious life, and which one would be most likely to return to the world. To the latter I replied, "Sister Mary Francis." She asked why. I said she did not appear to observe the rules so strictly as the others. She asked me if that would be any inducement for me. I replied, "No, not *that*." She appeared quite unable to talk, but notwithstanding her weak state and trembling hands, she sewed all the time. I told her it gave me pain to see her distress herself so. With a peculiar emphasis she said, "Sister, *obedience!*" and in a very affecting manner made the sign of the cross.

While at my lessons one day, in the hours of silence, the Superior and Mother-assistant came wishing me to tell them where Miss Mary Francis was. I replied I had not seen her. They left the room, and soon Miss Mary Francis entered, in tears. The Superior followed, and seizing her by the arm, shook her violently, threatening to punish her for disobedience, and wished she had a *cell austere enough* to put her in, and exclaimed "Shame! Shame! you 'disedify' Miss Mary Agnes."* She then told her not to feign sickness again, but to show by her appetite her illness. After the penance of kissing the floor, &c., she gave her a number of prayers to copy for the Protestant scholars. And from that time we were watched with the strictest scrutiny. The next day the Superior gave me permission to write to my father. She said Miss Mary Francis was crazy, and she should not keep her in the convent more than a month longer, if she did not reform. Mary Francis' grief will be well recollected by those in the public apartments. The next day I wrote to my father. The letter† was corrected by Miss Mary Francis, who was not crazed, as stated by the Superior. I then whispered to her (it being the time of silence,) and asked the cause of her grief. She wrote on a slate, "she could not." A religieuse was in the room, watching us very narrowly, and to mislead the religieuse, she reminded me of making false syntax. We next met in the community for recreation. The Superior gave the Mother-assistant permission to speak (Miss Mary Francis was absent.) She began by asking how she did. The Superior

---

* All the nuns have the name of Mary, and added to it is the name of some canonized saint. Miss Mary Agnes was my name.

† This letter was never received by my father.

answered, "She goes on in her old way and observed that she was unfit for the order. The Mother-assistant said, "O, Mamere, let me pray, at least, a month longer for her;" and turning to the novices, asked them to join with her. The Superior granted her permission, but handed her a letter to read. The Mother-assistant turning to us, said, "Sisters, pay attention. This letter is from Miss Mary Francis' aunt, Miss I, of New York." The substance of it was, that she had received her (the Superior's) letter, and was sorry to have recommended to her that person, but she thought she had reformed, and would be a suitable member for a monastery; and she begged pardon for introducing one to her who had disturbed the peace of her little community, and hoped, if it were possible, she would not long be troubled with her, &c. The Superior said, after the close of the letter, "Sisters, you may still continue to pray for her, and I will see about this thing, as it may be a temptation of the adversary." Two or three days after this, I met Miss Mary Francis at my lessons in the community, and again asked her to tell me her distress by writing on the slate, or I would tell the Superior I could not learn of her. She begged I would not, and told me she was under a solemn obligation not to make known the cause of her grief. She asked me if I was happy; I told her I was not, to see her unhappy, and again entreated her to tell me the cause of her tears. She said I must not tempt her to break her promise, for if we were detected in conversation, she would be made still more unhappy. I then asked, if she had recovered from her illness, why she did not go to her class, &c. She said the Superior had forbidden her, but she could not answer any other questions. I had formed a strong attachment for this lady, and it gave me pain to see her so distressed.

At next recreation, the Superior sent us word to meet the Bishop in the meditation garden. Sister Mary Magdalene being too exhausted to walk as fast as we did, the Bishop asked who that was; and being told, he burst into a laugh, and said, "Sister Magdalene, when are you going to heaven?" She replied, in a voice scarcely audible, "I have no will of my own, my lord; whenever it shall please God to take me."*

---

* It is here to be understood, that sister Mary Magdalene was in a consumption, and had entered the convent nine months before in perfect health. She

She thought she should not live to see Christmas. We then assembled in the community, and when all were seated, the Bishop inquired, "Where is that sober-faced nun?" Being told by the Mother-assistant that she was giving lessons to Miss F., he took the letter before spoken of, and looking it over, handed it to the Mother-assistant, saying, "Why do you keep her, and why does she not go to her class?" The Superior said the young ladies were not pleased with her as a teacher. He asked if all disliked her. Miss Mary Benedict replied, "No, my lord; some in the French class appear to like her." On which he said, "show them that letter."

At my next lesson, I told Mary Francis, if she did not explain to me the cause of her grief, I should tell the Superior; for I could receive no benefit from her instructions while she was so confused, and the Superior had reprimanded me for not learning my lessons; and I promised, if she would tell me, I would not inform the Superior. She replied that she could not answer me *then*, but would think of it, and give me an answer in the afternoon. Accordingly, in the afternoon, a religieuse being present, watching us, she communicated what I desired to know by writing on a slate,* and desired to know if I was happy. I answered, I did not like the Superior so well as formerly. She then wrote, that while at prayer and meditation, she concluded it was her duty, particularly as I was dissatisfied, to give me some advice, and considered her promise before made as not binding; and receiving from me a promise of secrecy, she proceeded to say that she hoped she should be pardoned if anything wrong was said by her, as my whole happiness depended on the words she should communicate. "I am," says she, "kept here by the Superior, through selfish motives, as a teacher, under a slavish fear and against my will. I have written several letters to my father, and have received no satisfactory answer; and I have for a long time felt dissatisfied with my situation. The Superior has failed in fulfilling her promise, not complying with the conditions on which I was received; which were, that as she was in need of a teacher, particularly in French and music, I might take the

---

was worn out with austerities.

* We were at the piano; she pretended to write notes, &c.

white veil, and leave whenever I choose; and my taking the veil, 'as it was only a custom,' should not compel me: and that my obligations should not be binding. My father thinks I can leave at any time, for I do not believe he has received my letters; and that letter you have heard read as Miss I's. is a forged one."

We were here interrupted by the entrance of the Superior, who made a sign for me to follow her into the Bishop's room. After asking me how I progressed in my lessons, and hearing me read in the "Novices' Directory,"* she observed that I looked melancholy, and commanded me to tell her the reason. I replied that I did not feel well, that my lungs were sore since taking the emetic,† &c. She said that was only a notion, and bade me tell the true reason without any more equivocation. My words were, I did not love her so well then as formerly. She exclaimed, "O my child, I admire you for your simplicity;" and asked me my reason for not loving her, which I declined giving. She commanded *"obedience"* with seeming mildness, and I told her that I thought she did not pay that attention to me she had promised, and that she was not so kind to me as formerly. She then said, a religieuse should have no will of her own; that their Superior put many things upon them, in order to try their vocation. She then recounted the sufferings of a certain saint, and bade me pray to that saint for protection; and showed me a phial, which she said contained some of Saint Teresa's tears; and said, if I would save my tears while in devotion, she could tell by them whether I should ever arrive to the perfection of a saint. She then gave me her blessing, and reminded me of my reception, which was soon to take place.

----

* This is a book which is used only in convents. It directs us to respect the Bishop as a representative of the person of Christ, and in confession as Christ himself; and the Superior as fulfilling the office of Mother of God.

† My lungs were also very sore in consequence of repeating the offices, so much so, that when present at recreation, when I had permission to speak, it gave me pain rather than pleasure. I have, since leaving the convent, consulted several physicians, who have expressed it as their opinion, that the cause of my bleeding at the lungs, which frequently occurs, was originally the repeating the office and other services, in *one long drawling tone*, which any one can know, by trying, to be very difficult.

At my lesson in the afternoon, I again conversed with Mary Francis concerning the letter, and requested her to inform me how my happiness was concerned. She said still that the letter read to the community was a forged one; that Mrs. I. was her aunt and sincere friend; and did her father know her sufferings, and the treatment she received from the Superior, he would prosecute her; that she feared the Superior as she did a serpent. She then advised me not to bind myself after my three months' "test" or trial* to *that* order, by complying with the rules of "reception," any farther than would leave me at liberty to go to another if I chose; and I must not think, because they were wicked, that the inmates of all convents, were so. I assured her, that although I had thought that there was none good but Catholics, I now believed there were good and bad among all sects. She then requested me not to betray her, and told me the Superior intended to keep me there for life, and she thought it her duty to warn me of the snares laid for me. She disliked that order† and wished me to inform her why, and in what manner I had come there. I related to her then, and during the next afternoon, all the particulars. She appeared very much surprised to learn that my friends had been opposed to my coming, as the Superior had told her that they had put me there for life. She said she had been taken from the public apartment, because she had been seen weeping by the young ladies; that should the Superior refuse to let her go, she should, if possible, make her escape; and named a religieuse (Miss Mary Angela) who had made her escape before. She desired me, if she should be so fortunate as to make her escape, to ask, in private confession, permission to see my friends, and consult them

---

* When persons *first* enter the convent, they take an obligation that they will spend the remainder of their days as a recluse, but they are put on a three months' "test," or trial, to see if they have a "vocation" for that particular order; if not, they are generally placed in another.

† Miss Mary Francis was educated, I believe, in the convent of Saint Joseph, Emmetsburg; also known as the order of the "Sisters of Charity." She possessed an amiable disposition and superior talents, and was universally admired by the inmates of the school; and so far as my acquaintance went, she was deserving the esteem of every one.

about going to the "Sisters of Charity;" and if they were willing that I should go, she would procure me a situation, and by letter inform me of it. She was in great distress on account of *that* letter, which plainly unfolded the motives of the Superior. She said she should appear as calm as possible, as it was the only way to blind the eyes of the Superior, and enable her to escape; and requested me to give her all the information respecting the Superior's intention that I could learn, and to listen to her and to the Mother-assistant's conversation in recreation hours.

At recreation, the Superior observed that Miss Mary Francis had a vocation for a religious life, as she had *refused* to attend the offices and prayers. At our next interview, I inquired of Mary Francis if she had *refused* to attend prayers. She replied, no; that the Superior had discovered her intention to escape, and had *forbidden* her attending offices, communion, and confession, for exposing her feelings before the religieuse; and that the Superior had imposed penance upon her, forbidding her to walk in the garden during recreation; and that the presents given her by the young ladies had been, with the Superior's permission, taken by some one from her desk. She remarked, that we were exhorted to love and pray for those who spitefully use us, but she could not love the community generally, they exercised so much cruelty towards her; that the treatment she received was for no other reason than because she had given way to tears, which were a great relief to her. She was happy, she said, to find one who sympathized with her, and who would not treat her with contempt, as the others did. She said also, that the Superior had done wrong respecting her apparel.

I have now come to that part of my narrative in which I must again speak of the sufferings of sister Magdalene. One day she came from the refectory, and being so much exhausted as to be hardly able to ascend the stairs, I offered to assist her, and the Superior reprimanded me for it, saying, her weakness was feigned, and that my *pity* was false pity. She then said to sister Magdalene, after we were seated, in a tone of displeasure, if she did not make herself of use to the "community" she would send her back to Ireland. On which sister Mary Magdalene rose and said, "Mamere, I would like—"* The Superior cut short what she was going to say by stamping upon the floor; and demanding who gave her permission to speak, imposed on her the penance of kissing the floor. The Superior, after this, imposed hardships which she was hardly able to sustain, frequently reminding her that she had but a short time to work out her salvation, and that she must do better if she did not wish to serve in purgatory. The Superior questioned me about my feelings—wished to know why I looked so solemn. I told her I was ill from want of *exercise*, that I was not accustomed to their mode of living, &c. She said I must mention it to my confessor, which I did.

The next time the Bishop visited us, he was in unusually high spirits, and very sociable; and he related several stories, which are not worthy of notice in this place. He again asked Sister Magdalene when she thought of going to that happy place, to receive her crown of glory. She replied "Before the celebration of our divine Redeemer's birth, my lord." He said she ought to be very thankful that she was called so soon.

I will here relate a conversation of the Bishop with the Superior at recreation hour, respecting the Pope, &c. After talking awhile in French, he said he had received a long letter from the Pope, in which his holiness congratulated him on his success in establishing the true religion in the United States, and made him offers of money to advance the interest of the Catholic Church, and more firmly establish it in America, &c. The Bishop then spoke of the orthodox in Boston, and said Dr. B. had got himself in a "hornet's nest," from which he could not extricate himself. The Superior named a sermon delivered in the North Church by an Episcopalian, and said they must look out, or *they* would get themselves into a "hornet's nest." The Bishop mentioned a visit of Dr. O'F. at Dr. B's., and said Dr. O'F. had scarcely an opportunity to say a word, on account of the noise and crying of the children which were in the room, and with which Dr. B. was playing; said he appeared more engaged with the children than with the subjects of religion, &c., &c. Miss Mary John, the Mother-assistant, exclaimed "Is it possible, my Lord, that a man of God is treated in such a way by

---

* This, and other half-uttered expressions, convinced me that she wished to return to her friends.

heretics?" "Yes," said the Bishop; "none but he that is unmarried careth for the things that belong to the Lord, how he may please the Lord; but he that is married careth for the things that are of the world, how he may please his wife." The Superior said Dr. B. possessed very little sense, and had a weak mind. The Bishop said that the doctor, by the course he had taken, had made many converts to Catholicism; "and perhaps," said the Superior, "he is a wicked instrument in the hands of God to bring about good."

At another time, while walking on the convent grounds, a cannon ball was picked up by one of the religieuses, and the Bishop taking it observed, as he gave it to the Superior, "Here is a British ball, that has killed many a Yankee;" and he also made several other similar observations. At another time, the Superior told the Bishop that two ladies met near the convent; the words she used were, "One Yankee met another, and said, "I *guess* you are agoing to *independence*." "I *guess* I be," said the other. Then they laughed heartily about it, and gave us permission to hold our recreation upon it. The Bishop remarked the Yankees celebrated independence-day in honour of *men*, and *appointed* days of thanksgiving, instead of celebrating the birthday of the Redeemer, in honour of God, &c.*

When I was again summoned to the Superior, she inquired as usual, into the state of my feelings; and when I said I desired to see my friends, she replied, "Why, my dear Agnes, do you wish to see *worldly* friends? Who do you call your friends? Am not I your friend? Is not the Bishop your friend? If your worldly friends wished to see you, would they not come and see you?" I replied "Yes." A few days after

---

* We all had permission at one time to walk with the Superior in the meditation garden. The Superior heard a noise behind the fence, and sent her servants to learn the cause; they returned, informing her that two men were looking through the fence. The Superior remarked, The Bishop had said there was great danger to be apprehended from such persons; that if Protestants were to offer any violence to them, the judgments of heaven would fall upon the wicked; and God had founded them upon a rock so firm that it could not fall. The Superior gave orders to the porters not to allow strangers to walk over the grounds without her or the Bishop's permission.

this I was taken very ill, and went to the infirmary. Miss Mary Francis, hearing of my illness, made an errand to come to the infirmary for some thread to mend her apparel, and pretending not to find it, asked me where the religieuse put it, and desired to know if I had any good news for her. I told her I had not: but as we had permission to assemble for recreation in the afternoon, I would, if I heard any, then inform her. At that instant a novice opened the door, and Miss Mary Francis excused herself by pretending that she was looking for the basket of thread. We were not so strictly watched for a few days as we had been; but when Miss Mary Francis exposed her feelings one day before Miss Mary Magdalene and myself, we were again closely watched. I then asked the Superior's permission to write to my friends, and desire them to come and see me, which she granted; and also told me to write whatever I pleased. I prepared a letter accordingly to my sister, stating that I did not wish to return to the world, but was anxious for a visit from them, &c.

I began now to be much dissatisfied with this convent. My views of retirement, however, were the same as ever, and I thought I would go to the order of the Sisters of Charity, where Miss Mary Francis was educated, as she had promised to introduce me there. She told me, that should I be called to the public apartments, as an assistant in ornamental work, if possible, to slip a billet into Miss I's. hand (a scholar from New York,) who would convey it to her; and I must not open my mind to my confessor until I was sure she had left the community. I asked her if she would take a letter for me into the world; she replied, she dare not, as the Superior would examine her, and not permit anything to be carried from the convent into the world. We then laid the following plan, to mislead the Superior in regard to our intentions. Miss Mary Francis was to complain to the Superior that I would not give proper attention when at my lessons, and I was to tell her that I could not receive any benefit from Miss Mary Francis, on account of her grief and absence of mind. This we fulfilled to the letter. We also agreed on a signal, by which I should know whether she was going with or without permission. If she went without permission, she was to tie a string round an old book, as if to keep the leaves together, and lay it upon the writing desk; if with permission, she was to make the sign of the cross three times upon her lips. I had intimated my desire to go with her; but she said it would be more prudent for me to endeavour to obtain the Superior's permission to see some of my friends, and I could then consult with them, and arrange matters to suit me. After our conversation, she knelt at the altar of the Blessed Virgin, and begged God to forgive us if we acted wrong in this matter; and said to me, "May we not hope for pardon in this matter, if the Superior can be so wicked as to approach the holy of holies and yet receive absolution?" She then selected from a book the letters forming her real name, that I might write to her, should I not get an opportunity to give a letter to Miss I. A religieuse entered, and whispered her to come away, and I never saw her afterwards.

When the Bishop next visited the "community," he said he understood that they were rid of that person who had caused them so much trouble. They all then rejoiced because Miss Mary Francis had gone. The Bishop asked whither they had sent her. They answered, "to her friends." Nothing more at that time was said about it.

Not long after this, at private confession, I was questioned very particularly in regard to my views of remaining there for life. I told my confessor that I was convinced that the order was too austere for me, and then I burst into tears. He endeavoured to comfort me, by saying I was not bound to *that* order for life; I could go to *another* order. I asked him if I might see my friends. He answered, "Yes." After receiving a promise from him that I should go to any other order I chose, I consented to take the *vows*. He gave me to understand, that I need take no other vows than I should at the convent of the Sisters of Charity.

My reception took place the next day. I refused the white veil, because the Sisters of Charity did not wear it, and it was omitted. The choir was first darkened, and then lighted with wax tapers. The ceremony commenced with chants, prayers, responses, &c. A book was placed in my hands, which contained the vows I was to take. As near as I can recollect, the following is the substance of them;—

"O, Almighty and Everlasting God, permit me, a worm of the dust, to consecrate myself more strictly to thee this day, in presence of the most Holy Mother and Saint Ursula, and all of thy saints and martyrs, by living *two years a recluse*, and by instructing young ladies after the manner of Saint Ursula, and by taking upon myself her most holy vows of poverty, chastity, and obedience, which, with thy grace and assistance, I will fulfil."

They all responded "Amen," and repeated a long office in Latin. I still continued to wear the black garb,* which the Bishop blessed; also a long habit and a string of Rosary beads, which were also blessed by the Bishop. He wished to know one day, how Miss Mary Agnes did, after taking the *white* vows; to which the Superior replied, "Very well." He then conversed about the establishment in Boston, and said that some Sisters of Charity were coming to constitute a convent either there or at Mount Benedict lower establishment.†

Meanwhile, sister Mary Magdalene was employed in the refectory. According to the Bishop, she was a saint, and he said there was a saint's body in the tomb, (one of the lay sisters) which remained undecayed. I heard the Superior, about this time, tell Miss Mary Magdalene to burn all her treasure,‡ she would suffer in purgatory for her self love, and she was afraid she did not suffer patiently, for she appeared romantic. Mary Magdalene fell prostrate at the Superior's feet, and said she would fulfil any command that should be laid upon her. The Superior gave her a penance, to kiss the feet of all the religieuses, and asked them to say an Ave and a Pater for her; after which, she lay prostrate in the refectory until the Angelus rung. One communion morning, as I rose and was dressing, I took some water as usual to rince my mouth, and all at once Mary Magdalene appeared greatly agitated, and even in agony; made signs and crosses to signify that I should commit a sacrilege were I then to approach the communion;

---

* The apparel of a religieuse is always kissed by the wearer, every time of putting on and taking off.

† The Bishop, in confession, told me I could, if I preferred it, become one of these sisters.

‡ The treasures consisted of written prayers, books, papers, a lock of her mother's hair, &c., which she brought from Ireland, and kept in her desk.

and I then recollected that nothing must be taken into the mouth on the morning before this sacrament. I relate this to show the state of her mind. The Superior one day requested the Mother-assistant to get the keys of the tomb, and to have a good place prepared for Mary Magdalene, who forced a smile, saying, she should prefer her's near the undecayed saint's bed.

As time passed on, the Superior became more severe in her treatment, because I objected to pursue my music. My mind had been in such an unhappy state, that I for a long time found it impossible to study; and further, I did not wish to receive instruction, for I had determined not to stay there. I therefore succeeded in obtaining the Superior's permission to occupy my time chiefly with the needle, and assured her that I would again study when I felt better.

On one of the holy-days the Bishop came in, and after playing upon his flute, addressed the Superior, styling her Mademoiselle, and wished to know if Mary Magdalene wanted to go to her long home. The Superior beckoned to her to come to them, and she approached on her knees. The Bishop asked her if she felt prepared to die. She replied, "Yes, my Lord; but, with the permission of our Mother, I have one request to make." They told her to say on. She said she wished to be anointed before death, if his lordship thought her worthy of so great a favour. He said, "Before I grant your request, I have one to make, that is, that you will implore the Almighty to send down from heaven a bushel of *gold*, for the purpose of establishing a college for young men on Bunker Hill." He said he had bought the land for that use, and that all the sisters who had died had promised to present his request, but had not fulfilled their obligations; "and," says he, "you must shake hands in heaven with all the sisters who have gone, and be sure and ask them why they have not fulfilled their promise, for I have *waited long enough;* and continue to chant your office with us while here on earth, which is the sweet communion of saints." After she had given her pledge, and *kissed his feet*, he told the several members of the community to think of what they should like best. I was first called to make my request. I had never seen anything of this kind before, and my feelings were such as I cannot describe; and continuing silent, the

Superior bade me name it. I then said I lacked humility, and should wish for that virtue. The religieuses then made their requests: one asked for grace to fulfil the vow of poverty; another, for obedience; a third, more fervent love for the Mother of God; a fourth, more devotion to a patron saint; a fifth, more devotion in approaching the altar and host; and so on. The Superior ended it by making the same request as the Bishop, adding, the purpose intended was that the Gospel of our Lord and Saviour might be more extensively propagated, and all dissenters might be made to turn to the true Church, and believe. The conversation then turned upon the Pope, and the Bishop said the Pope would, perhaps, before long, visit this country; and when things were more improved, and his new church finished, he should write to the Pope, &c. He went into a relation of some parts of ecclesiastical history; spoke of the Pope's being the vicegerent of Christ on earth; and that although the wicked one prevailed now, it was designed for good, and the time would come when all would look to the Pope as their spiritual director on earth. He thought that America rightfully belonged to the Pope, and that his Holiness would take up his residence here at some future day.

Not long after this, Mary Magdalene was anointed or death, and took her vows for life, but she continued to wear the white veil. I thought it singular that Mary Magdalene should at that time take her *black vows*, as they called them, because, as I learned in the community, she had not been there a *year*; and her wearing the *white veil* after taking them, appeared still more singular.

I will endeavour to give some idea of the manner in which she took her vows, and of the anointing. After she had retired to her couch,* the religieuses walked to the room in procession. Sister St. Clair had a wax taper blazing at her feet, and the Superior knelt at her head with the vows, which were copied on a half sheet of paper. The Bishop then came in with both sacraments, all of us prostrating as he passed. After putting the tabernacle upon the little altar, which had been placed

_____

* I learned that the usual custom was to place them in a black coffin, covered with a black pall when they were to take the *black vows;* but in this instance it was omitted.

there for the purpose, he read from a book a great many prayers, all of us responding. He asked her a number of questions about renouncing the world, which she answered. The Superior gave her the vows, and after pronouncing them, she was anointed; sister Clair laying bare her neck and feet, which the Bishop crossed with holy oil, at the same time repeating Latin. He then gave her the *viaticum*, and ended the ceremony as he commenced, with saying mass, and passed out, we all prostrating.

She lived rather longer than was expected, but her penances were not remitted. She would frequently kneel and prostrate all night long in the cold infirmary, saying her rosary and other penances, one or two of which I will mention. She wore next her heart a metallic plate, in imitation of a crown of thorns, from which I was given to understand she suffered a sort of martyrdom. This I often saw her kiss, and lay on the altar of the crucifix as she retired. Another penance was, the reclining upon a mattress more like a table than a bed.

A day or two after this, the Superior, Mother-assistant, and Mary Benedict, ridiculed the appearance of Mary Magdalene, because of the dropsy, which prevented her appearing graceful, and because she was disappointed in not going to heaven sooner. The Superior gave her some linen capes to make, and said, "Do you think you shall stay with us long enough to do these, sister?" She took them, and said, "Yes, Mamere, I thank you?"* Notwithstanding the Superior's severity, she sometimes appeared affectionate. One day I failed in ringing the observances at the usual time. I met the Superior, and fearing she would punish me, I burst into tears. She embraced me very affectionately, and wiped my face with a handkerchief, and said I should not be punished that time. She once told me I might sit at meditation hour, instead of kneeling, as it was very tiresome. She frequently called me *her holy innocent*, because she said I kept the rules of the order, and was persevering in my vocation as a *recluse*. She said I should see my friend Mrs. G. before long; but I did not see her while I was there.

---

* She would often ask permission to take a little water, as she was very thirsty; the Superior always refused it; but still the *obedient* Magdalene replied, "Mamere, I thank you."

While in the convent, I asked once or twice for a Bible, but never received any, and never saw one while there. The Bishop often said that the laity were not qualified to expound the scriptures, and that the *successors* of the apostles *alone* were authorized to interpret them, &c.

The Bishop, in one of his visits, spoke particularly of the cholera. He told us we must watch and pray more fervently or "the old Scratch would snatch us off with the cholera." It was recreation hour, but Mary Magdalene was at work in the refectory. When she came to the community, she appeared like a person in spasms; she tried to say "Ave Maria," and immediately fainted. We were all very much alarmed. At that moment the bell called us to the choir for visitation and vespers. When I retired, I felt much hurt to see Mary Magdalene in the cold infirmary, but did not dare to express my feelings. Next day, at recreation, the Superior, Mother-assistant, and Mrs. Mary Benedict, made a short visit to Mary Magdalene, and on returning they told us she was better, and in a spiritual sense well; for she had refused taking her portion, or anything eatable, as she did not wish to nourish her body, because the will of God had been made known to her in a vision. We all had the promise of conversing with her, but we were so constantly employed in our various offices, that we had no leisure.

The next day, it being my turn to see that all the vessels which contained holy water were filled, &c. I had an opportunity of looking at Mary Magdalene. Her eyes were partly open, and her face was purple; she lay pretty still. I did not dare to speak to her, supposing she would think it a duty to tell of it, as it would be an infraction of the rules. The next night I lay thinking of her, when I was suddenly startled hearing a rattling noise, as I thought, in her throat. Very soon sister Martha (the sick lay nun) arose, and coming to her said, "Jesus! Mary! Joseph! receive her soul!" and rang the bell three* times. The spirit of the gentle Magdalene had departed. The Superior came, bringing a lighted wax taper, which she placed in the hand of the deceased. She closed the eyes, and placed a crucifix on the breast. Sister Martha had whispered us to rise, and the Superior, observing my agitation,

---

* The bell was struck *three* times to call the Superior, *twice* to call the Mother-assistant, and *once* to call Mrs. Mary Benedict.

said, "Be calm, and join with us in prayer: *she* is a happy soul." I knelt accordingly, repeating the litany, until the clock struck two, when we all assembled in the choir, in which was a fire and wax taper burning. After meditation, matins, lauds, and prayers, and a Novena (a particular supplication,) that our requests might be granted, we assembled for diet, and for the first time we had some toasted bread. We also had recreation granted in the time of silence. The Superior sent for us, and instructed us how to appear at the burial of our sister Mary Magdalene, and accompanied us to view her corpse. She was laid out in the habit of a professed nun, in a *black veil;* her hands were tied together, and her vows placed in them. The Superior remarked that this was done by the Bishop's request. At the evening recreation the Bishop appeared in high spirits, and rejoiced that so happy a soul had at last arrived in heaven; and commenced the *"Dies illæ,"* on the piano-forte, accompanied by the voices of the others. He told me I should have Miss Mary Magdalene for my intercessor, for she was to be canonized. The Mother Superior permitted me to embrace the sisters, and gave me the Mother-assistant for my *Mother.* She then presented us with the relics of saints, that by their means we might gain indulgences. She mentioned a "retreat" as being necessary for our perseverance in a *religious life.*

The second day after this, the coffin was placed in the choir, and the funeral services were performed in the following manner: Dr. O'Flagherty sang the office, while the Bishop chanted it. Father Taylor officiated at the altar. Four or five of the altar boys were present, and dressed in altar robes, &c.; two of them held wax tapers, a third holy water, a fourth a crucifix. One swung incense in the censor over the corpse, and another, at the same time, sprinkled holy water upon it. We performed our part by saying the "Dies illæ." The coffin* was then carried to the tomb by two Irishmen. The Bishop, priests, and others followed, singing, and carrying lighted tapers and a large crucifix. The corpse was also followed by some of the young ladies from the

---

* My feelings were much hurt to witness the manner in which the lid of the coffin was *forced* down in its place. The corpse had swollen much, and become too large for the coffin.

public schools, while the religieuses remained in the convent. After depositing the coffin in the tomb, the clergy retired to dinner. We were permitted, at recreation, to hear the clergy converse on various subjects. The Superior told us that the customary libera and prayers for faithful souls departed might be omitted, as the Bishop said Magdalene's soul had gone immediately to heaven. The novices were permitted to relate visions of guardian angels, &c.

At the next evening recreation, the Bishop again visited us, and appeared in very good spirits, played on his flute, and sung. He soon went away, and the Superior said he only came to cheer up our spirits.

Having only a few minutes to stay at confession, I had until this time kept the secret of my friend Mary Francis; but the Bishop perceiving that I grew discontented, endeavoured to comfort me, by saying I was not *bound* to *that* order; but he wished to know more particularly my reasons for disliking it, and began to threaten me with judgments; and observing my agitation, said he *must* know what lay so heavily on my mind. He asked me if it was anything connected with the sickness and death of Mary Magdalene. I told him, "No, not that in particular; I do not like the Superior." He said I must tell him instantly all the wicked thoughts that had disturbed my mind, and asked me various improper questions, the meaning of which I did not *then* understand, and which I decline mentioning. I was so confused, that I inadvertently spoke Mary Francis's name, and begged his pardon for listening to her; and he immediately exclaimed, "Ah! I know all; confess to me what she told you, and do not dare to deceive me; you cannot deceive God." I told him *nearly* all that had passed between Mary Francis and myself. He said that Mary Francis was not a fit subject for any order, and they were obliged to send her away; that she was deranged, and I had done very wrong in listening to an insane person. He said I could not go to the order she mentioned, and that I would be more happy with the Sisters of Charity, who were coming to reside there. He said that worldlings hated me for the good part I had chosen, and would ridicule me should I go back to the world, and then repeated some scripture texts. I still persisted in saying it was my determination not to remain in that order, and told him I disliked the Superior; and he gave me a penance to perform. I was desirous at that time to have them think me obedient, or I should not have condescended to such humiliation. My motive was *prudence*, not want of courage, for by this time I had become disgusted with the life I led, and their manner of proceeding. The next time the Bishop was with us, he requested me to sing any favourite tune I chose. I sang the "Ode on Science," which every one knows, is highly patriotic. At the close of the first stanza, he spoke a few words in French to the Superior, who made a signal for me to stop; but not understanding her I continued until she had made several signals, when I perceived she was evidently displeased with my singing, and then recalled the words which I supposed were offensive.

One day the Superior asked me what it was that lay so heavily on my mind, as the Mother-assistant had previously found me in tears while at our examination of conscience. I excused myself by replying, I was thinking of my dear mother, (which, though true, was not the cause of my grief.) She then left me, but not without distrust, the eyes of the community being upon me. The next tine we met at recreation, one of them remarked, she hoped there was not another *Judas* among them. I endeavoured to betray no emotion, but they still mistrusted I had other views; for, while sitting at my diet in the refectory, I observed my food was of a kind that I had never seen before. It consisted of several balls of a darkish colour, about the size of a nutmeg, of a bitter astringent taste; what they were I never knew. I ate them as I did my other diet, and strove to exhibit no fearful sensations.

A few days after the death of Mary Magdalene, her trunk was brought forward, that the Superior might examine it, and distribute its contents to those she considered the most worthy. She gave to each one some little relic, and to Miss Mary Joseph, sister to Magdalene, some letters which she had composed to be read, as the Superior said, after her death. They were quite affecting, and caused Mary Joseph to weep much, for which the Superior reprimanded her.

Some days after this, the Superior sent for me to practice music, and then made a signal for me to follow her into the Bishop's room. This room is separated from the others by shutters, with curtains drawing on the chapel side. When I had kissed her feet, she desired to know why

I cried at my practice in the choir. I rather imprudently answered, "I could not tell; I did not cry much." (It then struck me, she could not have seen me, as I was *alone.*) I said I was very cold,* particularly my feet; and I had been practising "Blue-eyed Mary," and was affected by the words. She said that what I asserted was false, and commanded me to tell her the true cause, *in a moment;* and pulling the handkerchief from my hand, she bade me kneel and tell her at once, or I should be punished. I was so frightened by the threats and manner of the Superior, that I sobbed aloud, and blood gushed from my nose and mouth. She then seized and shook me by the arm, and seated me, saying, "Hush! be calm, or the young ladies may hear you as they pass the door to go to their practice." She asked me again and again to tell her why I shed tears in the choir, and why I felt such a repugnance to communicate my thoughts. I replied, because I had made a *promise* not to tell, and I could not break it. The Superior turned pale, but suppressing her feelings, bade me break that promise directly, and asked to whom I had made it. I replied I could not tell any one but my confessor. Says she, embracing me, "What! my *dear* sister, not obey your Superior?—tell me, my *dear,* and I will stand *responsible* for you before the judgment-seat. To whom did you make the promise?—to Mary Magdalene or Mary Francis." She also asked me if I had related all the cause of my discontent in confession. I replied, "Not all," and began to weep again. She endeavoured to console me, saying, she could not heal my wounds unless I opened my whole feelings to her; and comparing her words to those of our divine Redeemer, took me by the hand, and with seeming affection, told me to unfold all my feelings to her, as to an own mother; and said she should think it her duty to stay by me until I should relate the cause of my grief, that she might pour into my heart a heavenly balm, &c. I told her I had not seen or heard from my friends, to whom I had written.

   She said that was nothing to the point; she was my friend; and asked me if I called persons who insulted the house of God my friends. I replied, "No." She then said one person had been there who called

---

* The rooms were seldom comfortably warmed, and at times I suffered much from the cold.

herself my sister, and who threw pebbles at the convent. She also mentioned another person, who came with my sister, and whom she said she would not take to "*wipe her feet on.*"* After making this observation, she left me for a few moments to compose myself. Returning, she asked if I knew where I was, and if I had concluded to obey her, or break my vows of obedience, and be *severely* punished. I answered, "No, Mamere, I will tell all I can remember;" for I judged from her threats and looks that I should be confined in a cellar, or have something more severe than usual inflicted upon me; the rules of the order also led me to think so. But notwithstanding my fears of the Superior, I still kept secret the real name of Miss Mary Francis, and her promise

---

* I learnt from my sister, that while I was in the convent she and another young lady went there to invite me to my sister M's. wedding. She asked the portress if I could be seen at that hour, who replied she would see, and asked her to walk in, inquired her name, &c., went out, and soon returned with the answer that the scholars were not permitted to come to the parlour that day. My sister told her it was important that she should see me, and she could not come away without. The portress left the room, returned, closed the shutters, retired, and presently the Superior entered, walking between two servants, and made signs for my sister to approach, inquiring her and the other lady's names, and their business. On being informed, she mentioned that I could not be seen, but she would deliver any message my sister desired; that the young ladies never violated the rules for the sake of seeing company, and that I did not wish to see any worldly friends, or have any communication with them; that my mind was wholly occupied with heavenly things; that I was perfectly happy, and "*growing as fat as butter;*" that I was fast improving in my studies, learning music, and drawing, (untrue.) In consequence of my sister's weeping, and desiring her to name a time when I could be seen, the Superior said she would go and inquire whether I desired to see her. The Superior soon returned, and told my sister that I did not wish to see her, or any worldly relative; but the Superior told her that if I chose I could come to the wedding. They both left the Convent with the impression that I was a public scholar, and could leave when I chose; and thought it passing strange that I should refuse to see them, as I had, before going to the Convent, requested them to visit me. My sister imagined that I had become so infatuated with the Catholic religion as to lose all sisterly affection for those who were averse to it, and went away weeping.

of writing to Mrs. G. or my friends respecting my situation. She then dismissed me for a while. But my thoughts soon whispered me that our "*Ghostly Father*" (as our Directory taught us to call him) had made the Superior acquainted with what passed in secret confession, because without such knowledge she never could have used such threatening language, and never could have been displeased, as she was, at words which I used in secret confession *alone* with the Bishop. She asked me how I dared to converse with Mary Francis on the slate. Now, she never could have known this, only from the Bishop. I was never fully aware of their arts, in getting secrets by confession, until they became too visible to be misunderstood. I then became more reserved, and the Superior remarked that I did not show so much frankness of manner as formerly; the reason of which the reader will understand to be, that every eye was on me. A different course I could not adopt, having lost *confidence* in my confessor. I did not follow his advice, but resolved to follow, as nearly as I could conscientiously, the advice of Mary Francis, being confident she was my friend.

I felt a repugnance at the idea of returning to the world, supposing that many would believe me a person romantic and visionary, and inexperienced in the ways of the world, and therefore unfit for society. And I was also particularly averse to taking this step, because of the solemn promise of seclusion which I had taken. Nevertheless, I resolved to leave that convent, and to write Miss Mary Francis from my friend Mrs. G's., but was undetermined whether I should return to the world. I had reason to think that my letters were never sent to my friends, and determined to convey one privately. I stole a few moments, and hastily wrote some lines with my pencil, and hid them behind the altar; but the billet was discovered, and I never heard from it.

It was my turn that week to read as "lecturess." A book was placed before me in the refectory, called "Rules of St. Augustine," and the place marked to read was concerning a religieuse receiving letters clandestinely. I could not control my feelings, for what I read was very affecting. At this time we were directed to remain in the refectory, instead of assembling in the community, and to repeat "Hail Mary" before a picture. The Superior and Mother-assistant consented to have me practise music no more during the cold weather. They also permitted me to wear warmer clothing.

One day, as I was sitting alone in the refectory in the time of silence, the Superior came in, after kneeling and extending her arms in the form of a cross, she kissed the floor, and rising, walked towards the door; returning she seated herself on the bench beside me. I asked her if I should bring a chair; she answered, "No," and inquired how I felt, and why I changed colour while at the table. I replied that my mouth was very sore, and it hurt me to read. She wished to know what made my mouth sore. I told her I thought it was something I had eaten. She said, *laughingly,* it was the canker, and asked if it was not sent as a judgment for some sin. I replied that I did not know; I had not felt very well for some days, and thought it was partly owing to want of exercise. She then sent sister Martha to conduct me into a room at the farther part of the convent, for the first time, called a *"mangle room."*

There were some sisters there kneeling in devotion, and one turning a machine used for pressing clothes, instead of ironing them, called a *mangle.* She presented me with some altar laces, and told me to have them prepared for the altar the next day at the ringing of the bell. While there I was watched very narrowly; but as I had gathered from the Superior's conversation, at different times, that the gates were watched by the porters and dogs, which were of great value to the convent, I did not dare, then, to make my escape, but appeared very happy, it being a day of recreation in the community, and the celebration of some great saint. The Superior, as she passed her portrait, remarked, that she never looked at it but that it reminded her of smiling. She appeared in unusually good spirits, and gave us permission to wish each other happy feasts, not of luxury and feasting, in the common acceptation of the terms, but of prayers to the saints to free us from purgatory. In the course of the Superior's conversation, she said she had read in the newspapers of a new law which had been passed that no person who was under the age of twenty-eight or thirty years should be allowed to keep any school. The Mother-assistant approved of this law, and said it was good, as it would remove the difficulty which overseers had with young teachers who were unfit to take charge of a school, particularly the discipline.

I would here confess my fault (if a fault it was) of not acknowledging all my obligations in secret confession, and of *pretending* to think Mary Francis deranged; and also of acquiescing in the Superior's commands in her presence with feigned humility. I did this, that my design should not be suspected.

A letter was read to the community, that was addressed to the Superior, from Bishop P. of Emmetsburgh. In it he rejoiced to learn that the "community" was set free of *that* person who was deranged, and whose disposition he had known to his sorrow from her youth. He lamented the departure of Magdalene, who no doubt was a saint reigning in glory, after what she had been willing to suffer to gain Salvation.* I was sent for to attend to the Superior in the Bishop's room, after mass. She was folding his cassock and robe. When I entered, she bade me do as my directory taught, and said I had let *trifles* make an impression upon me, and weak minds only allowed trifles to affect them. Giving me the letter, she bade me tell her what I thought of it. I read it, and said, I could not believe what Mary Francis told me, if she were deranged, but yet I had rather go to the convent where she was educated than stay at that on Mount Benedict. She asked me if I thought of going without protection. I begged of her to let me see some of my friends *there,* or permit me to return to the world. After saying she had sent my letters† to my friends, who, if they wished, could come there and see me, she told me not to trouble myself, for the Bishop would soon be there, and I could talk with him about it.‡

One Sabbath after mass, while we were in the choir repeating the examination of conscience or monthly review, I was called in a whisper into the community with the rest of the sisters, but pretended not to

---

* Since leaving the Convent, I have written to Miss Mary Francis for information in regard to this letter, but have received no satisfactory answer. I have, however, received from her three sisters.

† My friends never received any letter from me.

‡ I cannot remember all that passed in confession, for I was at this time much confused; however, the Bishop asked me how I should like to go to a convent in Canada, which I objected to.

hear. The others went in while I remained. I heard the Bishop speak to them as they went in; but I had absented myself from confession and communion that day, and did not wish to see the Bishop on account of his previous language. After the doors had been opened several times, one of the religieuses (sister Martha)* came in and knelt with me. The bell then rang, and I went into the refectory, waiting as usual for the Mother-assistant's instructions in the Latin office. Sister Martha soon entered, and asked me if I knew where the Mother-assistant was, and whether I had been in the community since mass. I replied, No, but was waiting for the Mother-assistant. After saying office, I went down to the refectory to string some rosary beads, and afterwards returned to the choir, where the novices were telling their beads. The Superior came in to join in devotion, and remained until diet. As we were proceeding to diet, I accidentally *touched* the Superior; she looked at me, and appeared much displeased. At recreation the religieuses were very desirous to learn the state of my mind. I strove to appear unembarrassed, and answered their questions with seeming ignorance. I was not censured for my transgression of the rules, nor was any remark made upon it.

In the evening we were permitted to sit in the community, which had been warmed. After repeating the offices, and during the time of silence, a dog barked in front of the community, and we heard a noise like some one thumping upon the doors. The religieuses fell down before the altar and appeared much frightened. I kept my seat, but at that moment heard the window raised, and the Superior ask who was there. No answer was made to her inquiry. I then felt somewhat alarmed, but endeavoured to betray as little fear as possible. What this

---

* I will not presume to say much about sister Martha, as I never conversed with her, and therefore was not so able to judge of her sufferings, &c. She was a professed lay religieuse, and I believe an American. She was called the porteress, and one of those, I learned, who choose rather to be a door-keeper than to dwell among the wicked. She, together with three of the choir religieuse, lodged in the infirmary with me. While she slept there, she, as did Magdalene, coughed at intervals during the night. Sister Martha often approached the Superior kneeling and weeping.

noise was, or for what reason it was made, I never could learn, but I have supposed it was done to see if I was easily alarmed. The like had several times occurred.

About this time the martyrologies of some saints were read at table; also the history of saints who had been tempted by Satan. Perhaps it may be well to relate one or two. A certain saint, who was strongly tempted by Satan, retired to a desert, and confined himself to a cell scarcely large enough for him to lie at ease. He retired here for pious purposes. After mortifying his body for a long time, he prayed for rain that he might quench his thirst, which was granted; for a bird came and brought him food, which renewed his strength, and he returned to his monastery and was never more troubled with the temptations of Satan.

Some noblemen once invited a poor wandering monk, who was begging for the monastery, to dine with them on Friday. They helped him to meat; he made the sign of the cross, refusing to eat it. They asked the reason; and drawing their swords, threatened his life unless he did eat it. He told them if they would allow him a few minutes that he might pray, and give him a pewter plate to cover the meat, he would eat it. After praying a few minutes that the meat might become fish, he took off the plate, and behold it was fish; and he then sat down and ate, and they believed him an inspired man.

Many accounts of those who had become saints were so disagreeable and even revolting, that I will not attempt to relate or describe them.

As several of my friends desire to learn something concerning the scholars, I will relate what little I know. I never had permission to enter any of the rooms in the recluse apartments, except those before named, and never to the public apartments, except on examination days, when the Superior and Bishop were present. During one vacation, the young ladies who remained were permitted to visit the community to give the members presents.* I never spoke to them but to thank them for a present. They were sometimes at vacation permitted to enter the community and embrace the religieuses.

Complaints were often brought to the Superior while at recreation,

* Although we received presents, we were not allowed to keep them.

and sometimes repeated aloud. They were generally violations of the *rules*, which were very strict. They were sometimes punished for refusing to say prayers to the saints, which they said their parents disapproved of: also for refusing to read Roman Catholic history. A Miss T., of C., was brought to the Superior, and reprimanded for writing her discontents to her friends. The Superior destroying one half the letter, and gave me the blank leaf to write a prayer on. Another was reprimanded severely because she had said to the other young misses, she should be glad when the time came for her to leave the convent, &c. The Superior, shaking her severely, obliged her to kneel and perform an act of contrition by kissing the floor, and saying that she was very sorry that she had offended her teachers, and begged the forgiveness of all.

Some of the young ladies were apparently great favourites of the Superior and Bishop. They sometimes sent for them to bestow presents and caress them. One young lady, of whom the Bishop was guardian, was treated very ill. I often saw her in tears, and once heard the teacher tell the Superior that it was because she had no dress suitable to wear when she went into the world to see her friends. She was designed, as I learned, to be a teacher in a convent in Canada.

A number of the young ladies were unhappy, whose names I have forgotten. I learned that they disliked the discipline.

After this, the Superior was sick of the influenza, and I did not see her for two or three days. I attended to my offices as usual, such as preparing the wine and the water, the chalice, host, holy water, and vestments, &c. One day, however, I had forgotten to attend to this duty at the appointed hour, but recollecting it, and fearing lest I should offend the Superior by reason of negligence, I asked permission to leave the room, telling a novice that our Mother had given me permission to attend to it; she answered, "O yes, sister, you can go then." I went immediately to the chapel, and was arranging things for mass, which was to take place the next day. While busily employed, I heard the adjoining door open, and the Bishop's voice distinctly. Being conscious that I was there at the wrong hour, I kept as still as possible, lest I should be discovered. While in this room, I overheard the following conversation between the Bishop and Superior:—The Bishop, after taking snuff in his usual manner, began by saying—"Well, well, what does Agnes say? how does she appear?" I heard *distinctly* from the Superior in reply, that "According to all appearances, she is either possessed of *insensibility* or great *self-command.*" The Bishop walked about the room, seeming much displeased with the Superior, and cast many severe and improper reflections upon Mary Francis, who, it was known, had influenced me; all which his lordship will well remember. He then told the Superior that the establishment was in its infancy, and that it would not do to have such reports go abroad as these persons would carry; that Agnes must be taken care of; that they had better send her to Canada, and that a carriage could cross the line in two or three days. He added, by way of repetition, that it would not do for the Protestants to get hold of those things and make another "fuss." He then gave the Superior instructions how to entice me into the carriage, and they soon both left the room, and I heard no more.

The reader may judge of my feelings at this moment; a young and inexperienced female, shut out from the world, and entirely beyond the reach of friends: threatened with speedy transportation to another country, and involuntary confinement for life, with no power to resist the immediate fulfilment of the startling conspiracy I had overheard. It was with much difficulty that I controlled my feelings; but aware of the importance of not betraying any knowledge of what had taken place, I succeeded in returning to the refectory unsuspected. I now became firmly impressed, that unless I could contrive to break away from the convent soon, it would be for ever too late; and that every day I remained rendered my escape more difficult.

The next day I went to auricular confession, not without trembling and fear lest I should betray myself; but having committed my case to God, I went somewhat relieved in my feelings. At a previous confession I had refused to go to Canada; but at this time, in reply to the Bishop's inquiry, I answered that I would consider the subject; for I thought it wrong to evince any want of fortitude, especially when I had so much need of it. I did not alter my course of conduct, fearing that if I appeared perfectly contented, I should be suspected of an intention to escape.

It was my turn during that week to officiate in the offices. While reading I felt something rise in my throat, which two or three times I tried to swallow, but it still remained. I felt alarmed, it being what I had never before experienced.* At recreation I was asked what ailed me, and replied that I could not tell; but I described my feelings, and was told I was vapourish.

They were very desirous that week to know if my feelings were changed. I said they were, and endeavoured to make it appear to them that Satan had left me; but in reality I feared I should never escape from them, though I had determined to do so the first opportunity.

I was in the habit of talking in my sleep, and had often awoke and found the religieuses kneeling around my couch, and was told that they were praying for me. Fearing lest I should let fall some words which would betray me, I tied a handkerchief around my face, determining, if observed, to give the appearance of having the tooth-ache, and so avoid detection. For some days I was not well, and my mind, as may be naturally supposed, sympathized with my body, and many things occurred that were to me unpleasant, which I shall pass unnoticed.

But what I have now to relate is of importance. A few days after, while at my needle in the refectory, I heard a carriage drive to the door of the convent, and heard a person step into the Superior's room. Immediately the Superior passed lightly along the passage which led to the back entry, where the menservants or porters were employed, and reprimanded them in a loud tone for something they were doing. She then opened the door of the refectory, and seemed indifferent about entering, but at length seated herself beside me, and began conversation, by saying, "Well, my dear girl, what do you think of going to see your friends?" I said, "What friends, Mamere?" Said she, "you would like to see your friends Mrs. G. and Father B., and talk with them respecting your call to another order." Before I had time to answer, she commenced taking off my garb, telling me she was in haste, and that a carriage was in waiting to convey me to my friends.

---

* I have since named the circumstances to a physician, who says it was *fear* alone.

I answered, with as cheerful a countenance as I could assume, "O, Mamere, I am sorry to give you so much trouble; I had rather see them here first." While we were conversing, I heard a little bell ring several times. The Superior said, "Well, my dear, make up your mind; the bell calls me to the parlour." She soon returned, and asked if I had made up my mind to go. I answered, "No, Mamere." She then said I had failed in obedience to her, and as I had so often talked of going to another order with such a person as Mary Francis, I had better go immediately; and again she said, raising her voice, "You have failed in respect to your Superior; you must recollect that I am a lady of *quality*, brought up in opulence, and accustomed to all the luxuries of life." I told her that I was very sorry to have listened to anything wrong against her dignity. She commanded me to kneel, which I did; and if ever tears were a relief to me, they were then. She stamped upon the floor violently, and asked, if I was innocent why I did not go to the communion. I told her I felt unworthy to go to the communion at that time.* The bell again rang, and she left the room, and in a few moments returning, desired me to tell her immediately what I thought of doing, for as she had promised to protect me for ever, she must know my mind. She then mentioned that the carriage was still in waiting. I still declined going, for I was convinced their object was not to carry me to Mrs. G. and priest B., to consult about another order, but directly to Canada. I told her I had concluded to ask my confessor's advice, and meditate on it some time longer. She rather emphatically said, "You can meditate on it if you please, and do as you like about going to see your friends." She said that my sister had been there, and did not wish to see me. Our conversation was here interrupted by the entrance of a novice. The Superior then gave me my choice, either to remain on Mount Benedict, or go to some other order, and by the next week to make up my mind, as it remained with

* My eyes were opened: I found myself in an error, and had been too enthusiastic in my first views of a convent life. I was discontented with my situation, and was using some deception towards the Superior, and the religieuses in order to effect an escape; therefore I did not feel worthy to attend communion.

me to decide. She then gave me a heavy penance to perform, which was, instead of going to the choir as usual, at the ringing of the bell, to go to the mangle room and repeat "Ave Marias" while turning the mangle. While performing my penance, sister Martha left the room, and soon returning, said she had orders to release me from my penance, and to direct me to finish my meditation on the picture of a saint, which she gave me. But instead of saying the prayers that I was bidden, I fervently prayed to be delivered from their wicked hands.

They appeared much pleased with my supposed reformation, and I think they believed me sincere. The Superior, as a test of my humility, kept me reading; that is, made no signal for me to stop, until the diet was over, when a plate of apple parings, the remnant of her dessert, was brought from the Superior's table, and the signal given for me to lay down my book and eat them.* I ate a *few* of them *only*, hoping they might think my abstaining from the remainder self-denial in me, and not suspect me of discontent or disobedience. I performed all my penances with apparent cheerfulness.

The Bishop visited the convent on the next holy day, and on their remarking that he had been absent some time, he made many excuses, one of which was, he had been engaged in collecting money to establish the order of the "Sisters of Charity" where the "Community" once lived; and he spoke of the happiness of the life of a "Religieuse" of this order. After he played on the piano, "Away with Melancholy," the Superior asked me to play, and the Bishop said, "By all means." I complied, but my voice faltered through fear, when Miss Mary Benedict apologized for me, by saying I had not practised much lately, on account of the Mother-assistant's engagements, and the young ladies occupying all the instruments. She showed the Bishop a robe which I had been busy in working for him. He said I must not on any account neglect my music. After telling one of his stories about a monk, who had disobeyed the rules of his order until Satan took possession of him, he left us, saying he hoped "Old Scratch" would not take possession of our hearts as he did that monk's, and hoped

---

* This was the second time I had been presented with apple parings by the Superior.

that we should never have another Judas in the community.

Some days after the conversation which I heard between the Bishop and the Superior while behind the altar, I was in the refectory, at my work, and heard the noise of the porters, who were employed sawing wood, and I conjectured the gate might be open for them. I thought it a good opportunity to escape, which I contemplated doing in this manner, viz. to ask permission to leave the room, and as I passed the entry, to secrete about my habit a hood which hung there, that would help to conceal part of my garb from particular observation; then to feign an errand to the infirmarian from the Superior, as I imagined I could escape by the door of the infirmary. This plan formed, and just as I was going, I heard a band of music playing, as it seemed, in front of the convent. I heard the young ladies assembling in the parlour, and the porters left their work, as I supposed, for the sawing ceased. I felt quite revived, and felt more confident I should be able to escape without detection, even should it be necessary to get over the fence. I feigned an errand and asked permission of Miss Mary Austin to leave the room,* which she granted. I succeeded in secreting the hood, and the book in which Miss Mary Francis had left her address, and then knocked three times on the door which led to the lay apartments. A person came to the door, who appeared in great distress.†

I asked her where sister Bennet and Sister Bernard were; she left me to find them. I gave the infirmarian to understand that the Superior wished to see her, and I desired her to go immediately to her room.

---

* Sister Martha (the sick religieuse) was scouring the floor at this time, which I saw was quite too hard for her. Not long after I left, I inquired after her, and learned she was no more.

† This was Sarah S. (a domestic,) who appeared very unhappy while I was in the convent. I often saw her in tears, and learned from the Superior that she was *sighing* for the *veil*. When I saw my brother, I informed him of this circumstance, and he soon found who she was, and ascertained that some ladies in Cambridge had been to see the Superior, who used to them pretty much the same language she did to my sister. I have since seen her. She is still under the influence of the Roman Church, but assures me that she did not refuse to see the ladies, as the Superior had represented to them, and she wept because of ill health, &c.

These gone, I unlocked and passed out by the back door, and as the gate appeared shut, I climbed upon the *slats* which confined the grape vines to the fence; but they gave way, and falling to the ground, I sprained my wrist. I then thought I would try the gate, which I found unfastened, and as there was no one near it, I ran through, and hurried to the nearest house. In getting over the fences between the convent and this house, I fell and hurt myself badly. On reaching the house, I fell exhausted upon the door step; but rising as soon as possible, I opened the door, and was allowed to enter. I inquired if Catholics lived there; one answered "No." For some time I could answer none of their questions, being so much exhausted.

As soon as they understood that I requested protection, they afforded me every assistance in their power. I had been only a few moments there, when I heard the alarm bell ringing at the convent. On looking out at the window, we saw two of the porters searching in the canal with long poles. After searching some time, they returned to the convent, and I saw their dogs scenting my course.

While at that house, I looked in a glass, and was surprised, nay, frightened, at my own figure, it was so *pale* and *emaciated*.*

Notwithstanding my wrist being sprained, I wrote a few lines to Mrs. G., whom I still supposed my friend, begging her to come to my relief, for I did not wish my father and sisters to see me in my present condition. I thanked God that he had inclined his ear unto me, and delivered me out of the hands of the wicked. But here was not an end of my afflictions. Mrs. G. came in the evening to convey me to her house. She would not allow me to say anything about my escape at Mr. K's., and wished me to return to the convent that night. I resolved not to go. After whispering a long time to me about the importance of secrecy, she left Mr. K's., but she soon returned, saying she at first intended to leave me at Mr. K's., but had concluded to take me home with her, as she desired some further conversation. Her manners appeared very strange, yet I did not distrust her friendship. Before leaving Mr. K's., she requested me to obtain from them a

---

* It will be perceived that this does not correspond with what the Superior told my sister.

promise not to say anything about my escape, which I did.

After I arrived at Mrs. G's., I showed her my wounds, and my feet, which had been frozen, and told her I did not find the convent what I had expected. She seemed to sympathize with me, and to do all in her power for my recovery. She did not then urge me to say much, as I was quite weak.

The next morning the convent boy on horseback came galloping up to the house, and delivered to Mrs. G. a letter from the Superior, and was very particular, as he said he had orders not to give it to any one except to her. She refused to tell me its contents, and sent directly for a chaise to go to the convent. She took with her the religious garb I had worn on my head, and the book containing Miss Mary Francis' name.* Meanwhile I endeavoured to compose myself, and wrote to Miss Mary Francis, agreeable to my promise, informing her of my afflictions, and of my reluctance to return to the bustle of the world. I proposed to her some questions, and requested her advice. I wrote that I could not think otherwise than that the Superior and Bishop were very wicked. I did not write much, thinking her confessor might advise her not to answer it, as it was probable that the Superior would write to him; and I was anxious to convince Mrs. G. that Mary Francis thought as I did, for Mrs. G. would not permit me to say one word against the Superior or Bishop; and I was resolved to ascertain if Mary Francis was living and happy. When Mrs. G. returned from the convent, she said the Superior had too exalted an opinion of me to think I would say anything against the institution, and she had sent me a *present*, as she still considered me one of her flock; and if I had gone astray, she should do everything she could for me, in a temporal as well as in a spiritual sense, if I would repent. My words were just these: "I cannot receive any present from the Superior; she is a wicked woman, and I do not believe her friendship pure." At this moment Priest B. drove to the door, and desired to see me. I did not think myself in danger, and conversed with him; but I soon found that he

---

* This book I brought away, because Mary Francis had pricked hers and her father's real name out in it, and I wished to refer to it, in order to write her. I took it from my writing desk and slipped it into my pocket.

had seen the Superior and Bishop. He said, that as he was my sponsor, he considered it his duty to advise me, and hoped I was not going to break my *vows* to God, and *expose* myself to the world; because, if I did, I should be ridiculed and laughed at. He said he had before conveyed a novice to the "Sisters of Charity," and would carry me to them, or to some other retired place which I might choose, and that he was deeply concerned for my welfare. I told him I could not think of going anywhere then, as my health would not allow any exposure to the cold, and that Mrs. G. thought it best I should remain with her until I was better, when I should visit my father. He then exclaimed, "what letter is this?" taking up and reading the one I had written to Mary Francis. After reading it, he appeared surprised, and desired to know how I came in possession of her name. He said he should have seen me at the convent had he known I was discontented; and that if the Superior had done wrong, it was no reason I should do so, by speaking against the convent or those connected with it. He then shook hands with me, and said he would converse with me again when I was more composed, and left the house.

I soon began to suspect, by Mrs. G's. manner, that she was not my friend, and that if she had an opportunity she would deliver me into the hands of the Catholics; for I learned from her little daughter, that her mother had given her to the Catholic church, because the Superior had offered to educate her free of expense, and that her mother was acquainted with the Superior before I went to the convent. Now, this I did not know before, and I began to be more guarded, and to fear that all belonging to the Romish church were alike. When I gave Mrs. G. the letter to send to the post-office, she asked if I was afraid she would break it open; and at another time afterwards, she told me I was afraid she would poison me, because I refused to take medicine, which I thought I did not need. Such thoughts did not occur to my mind.

In a day or two, Priest B. again came, and after much persuasion from Mrs. G., I consented to see him. At first he appeared very pleasant, said he had come to render me assistance, and begged me, as I valued my religion and reputation, to take his advice. I told him that I wished none of his assistance or advice; that I should go to my brother's, at East Cambridge, as soon as possible; that as respected my religion, I did not believe in one which justified its followers in doing wrong; and that I was not at all apprehensive that my reputation would be injured on that account by returning to the world. He affected considerable contempt for my aged parent, and ridiculed many things which he said he had heard of my father, and he said,* "Is it possible that a young lady wishes to have her name made public?" I answered, "You very well know I should shrink from such a thing, but I should rather return to the world and expose myself to its scorn, than remain subject to the commands of a tyrant." "Then," said he, "if you are determined to return to the world, you may go to ruin there for all I can do; and rely upon it, you will shed tears of blood in consequence of the step you have taken, if you do not repent and confess at the secret tribunal of God." I told him I should confess to none but God, and that my conscience prompted me to do as I had done. He asked me if I would go with him to the Superior, as she wanted to see me. I replied, "No, I will not, for I believe you or any other Catholic would (if directed) take my life, were it in your power, as truly as I believe I am living, and I will not trust myself in your clutches again." At these words he turned pale, and asked me what I had seen or heard at the convent that made me think so. I refused to say more, and retired at his exclamation that it would be *death* to me. Mrs. G. endeavoured to console me with the assurance that he meant right, and that it would, they feared, be death to my soul.

Mrs. G. afterwards accused me of endeavouring, at the time of my escape, to induce sister Bernard to leave the convent. The Superior sent some articles of wearing apparel, which for a time I was obliged to accept. My sister called; she had been at the convent, and was informed that I was at Mrs. G's. She was overjoyed to see me, but much grieved because (as she thought) I had refused to see her at the convent. I endeavoured to calm her, and promised to explain all another time, assuring her my affection was not diminished and that I should soon visit her. I did not then explain to her the manner of my leaving the convent. It being late in the evening, she soon returned

---

* He informed me I should be anathematized publicly, if I did not repent.

home. The Misses K. also called, and by their conversation I feared they would inform my father of my situation before I should be well and prepared to see him; and I did not wish to grieve him with a knowledge of what had taken place. Mrs. G. said she expected my father would rave at her for having advised me as she had done, if he should find me at her house.

A Catholic lady, who had stood my sponsor, and who brought a letter from Miss Mary Francis,* called, and conveyed me to her house in Charlestown, where my father and brother soon found me, and desired I would return to my friends, which I did in the evening. Before leaving, however, I called on Priest B., and told him that I could never think of again attending the Romish Church, giving my reasons, adding I had been deceived in their religion, and in those who believed it; that I wished to take my leave of him, with the hope that he would not think I indulged any wrong feelings towards them, or that I desired to injure the Romish Church, but sincerely hoped they would reform. I told him this while he sat in the confessional. He remained unmoved, and would not allow that I had been treated ill. He said that I could not but know that the step I had taken would be a great injury to the convent. I assured him that it was not to be charged to me, but to the Superior and Bishop, who by their conduct had compelled me to take that step. I also told him that I believed it had been his intention to deliver me again into their hands, but I had broken the chains which bound me, and felt free; and that I should always be thankful that I had delivered myself from the bondage of what I consider to be a *Romish yoke,* rather than the true cross of Christ

After I had returned to my brother's, Mrs. G. sent to me by her little daughter some money, which she said I had given to the Superior. Five dollars of this sum, and some wearing apparel, I considered as not my own, and sent them back with a note to Madam St. George, stating that I declined receiving anything from them as *presents*, but if they would return what wearing apparel, &c. *belonged* to me, it would be properly acknowledged.

And now I have endeavoured, to the extent of my ability, to give a

---

* This letter had been broken open.

true and faithful account of what fell under my observation during my sojourn among the Catholics, and especially during my residence at the monastery on Mount Benedict. And I leave it with the reader to judge of my motives for becoming a member of the Ursuline Community, and for renouncing it.

If in consequence of my having for a time strayed from the *true religion,* I am enabled to become an humble instrument in the hands of God in warning others of the errors of Romanism, and preventing even *one* from falling into its *snares,* and from being *shrouded* in its delusions, I shall feel richly rewarded.

SUPPLEMENT TO SIX MONTHS IN A CONVENT.

SUCH is the interesting and affecting narrative of Miss Reed, and, assuming its truth, excepting those few parts of it which she acknowledges in her notes to have been hastily and inaccurately recorded, it must be considered, *in its class,* as one of the most powerful appeals to the Protestant world against the absurdities and blasphemies of Popery that ever appeared in print. It has been generally objected to in America, and will no doubt be so in England; that the artifice which the writer in her noviciate frequently practised, according to her own confession, on her Superior, the Bishop, and others, especially as her sufferings increased and her doubts of the good of the system multiplied, argues against the credit due to the narrative. That reader, however, must have little sympathy with a young sufferer, conscious of having been betrayed into a course of suffering by those who pretended to be her best friends, and who even assumed to be the agents of heaven for her good; who can hastily impeach her general veracity upon this slight ground, and suppose that because the persecuted child now and then attempted to relieve her pains by misrepresentation, the free and independent woman can deliberately mature such incipient deceit into a volume of falsehood.

But more of this hereafter. Whether the book now put into the hands of English readers is one required by the state of the times—is one rendered necessary by any increase in the monastic system and spirit—forms a question of much greater importance. Convents once were seats of superior learning, if not scenes of superior devotion: and there may be individuals within their walls now, who cultivate the heart as well as mind with more industry and to better effect than could have been expected in any other mode of life. This argument, however, has lost its force in the altered condition of society, especially in England and America. The freedom of the press, and the unfettered state of literature at large, forbid the thought that from the cells of a monastery any effort of mind can proceed that shall rival or approach the production of modern letters. Then, with regard to religion—who does not perceive that the present age differs as widely from the age of prosperous convents as any two periods of history on this subject can do. We are apt to forget that divine Providence materially diversifies the direction and operation of religious principle at different periods. At one time the passive and at another the active graces of the Christian are called forth. At one season private exercises of godliness, and at another its public effects are excited and required. Winter leads the sap down to the roots, while Summer calls it up into the branches, and displays it in the blossoms and the fruit; and it is now Summer in the religious and the literary world, at all events in the two distinguished nations of the earth in which this book is making its wonderful way.

Admitting, as we perhaps must admit, that the more private and retired influence of religion in convents of their best days was superior to the devotion of the generality of modern Christians, we still avow with confidence, that modern Christians excel in public spirit and active zeal and charity. If it be said that these are qualities put forth by the Catholic advocates of convents, as well as the Protestant opponents of them, we answer that while the zeal and charity of the former are exclusive even to bitterness, these qualities in the latter are as expansive as the wants of mankind, as diffusive as the limits of the inhabited world. When the river spreads wide, or flows in various fertilizing currents, it cannot be expected to roll so deep. Among even Protestants of a century and half ago, and farther back, we discover a strong propensity to exclusion, almost to the degree of the Catholic world; and if the Catholics had any of the glory of true devotion shining around them, it became excelled by the greater glory which encircled the heads of the recluse Puritans. At the same time, how little do we find even in them of the active and wide spreading benevolence exemplified by the best men of modern times! Their own souls—their own families—their own particular churches—these drew forth their concern, while it too much narrowed and restricted it. But the present day exhibits a remarkably altered scene; and from a thousand public assemblies, convened for the very purpose, and evincing their sincerity and fervency by their sacrifices and efforts, we hear the exclamation—"Let the whole earth be filled with his glory."

These reflections are perfectly in accordance with the object which Miss Reed, strives, by the seasonable publication of her striking little work, to accomplish. Did the catholics of America and England, to say nothing of those of other countries, fall in completely with this altered state of society, and strive by open and public efforts alone to diffuse their system and multiply their proselytes, all would be well. But in addition to such efforts they are aiming to perpetuate, or rather to revive, the very worst parts of a system which they are constrained to acknowledge has for ages, if not centuries, been declining in public favour. In addition to public efforts, as zealous as any that are made by Protestants, though much more Sectarian, they are privately endeavouring to fill the convents with inmates, after striving with too much success to multiply the number of those worse than doubtful institutions. All the priests of America and England could not have effected one quarter of the advantage which the Papal system has recently gained in these countries, had it not been for this simultaneous movement of private and public zeal. A recent writer informs us that whereas in America somewhat more than forty years ago, there was only one Romish church; there are now twelve Catholic sees, and a Catholic population of six hundred thousand, worshipping in about four hundred churches! Could this vast increase, so far beyond the ratio advance of inhabitants in the United States, have taken place without the exercise of an influence much more powerful than an open and candid appeal to the judgment of the people by public discourses and printed arguments?

This success will the less surprise every reader who considers the great influence of females, especially religious females, in society, and who remembers that this is the sex for which the institutions now denounced and deplored are very chiefly established. For one individual of the other sex induced to spend his days in the seclusion of a monastery, one hundred females may be found willing or constrained to enter the precincts of a convent. When we call to mind the powers which mothers have over their children, in connection with the depth and strength of the impressions made upon them at that early and tender age, it is impossible not to look with fearful apprehension on any material increase of establishments tending to remove the rising race of females from society, and accustom them to habits utterly unfitting for domestic life. This must even be felt in reference to such as may be expected, after a conventual course, to forfeit their rash and early vows, and enter the state for which God and nature designed them. With reference to the rest, who either spend their lives in seclusion, or emerge with a determination to adopt as few of the maxims and manners of general society, even of a Christian character, as possible, we entertain a different set of feelings; at the same time feelings involving even greater regret, that the fairest portions of God's image on earth should be marred and rendered almost totally useless by mistaken notions of his own will.

To return to Miss Reed's publication, and the credit to which that lady is entitled. Catholics of former ages, and in countries which so far as religion is concerned they almost claim as their own, were seldom anxious to refute or to answer anyone who might happen to impugn their proceedings. But in such countries as England and the United States this silence is neither politic nor safe; and a work like Miss Reed's left unanswered to make its way in society, would be a dangerous foe to the Catholic system, especially to that mysterious department of it which she has witnessed and denounced. It is not often, that, when answers are published to attacks like this, they are put forth by the individuals personally and immediately concerned in the affairs in question: some other scribe, well instructed in the mysteries of the system is generally employed, who discovers deep and sorrowful indignation that those whom he holds in such reverence for their superior wisdom and piety should be the objects of wanton assault. But in the present case, from its nature and peculiarities, it was necessary that the person most complained of—the Superior of the convent—should appear in her own defence, and step for once from her rigid seclusion into the arena of controversy.

This she has done; and at some future time we may possibly give to the public an edition of her little work. But at present we must confine our attention to Miss Reed, and while we examine her general claims to public confidence, must take some notice of what she advances in defence of her bold and approved assault. It must be manifest to every one that much was said by the Superior and the Bishop, when Miss Reed first entered the convent, tending apparently to leave her at perfect liberty to make her own deliberate choice. In some portions of the narrative those great and grave personages even seem to throw early discouragements in her way, and almost to dissuade her from becoming a recluse. How far this was done to prepare for such a contingency as her escape, and for the defence of a system against an attack like hers every reader must judge. On a comparison of her early indulgence and the candour of her first treatment, with the gradual harshness she met with, and the severities she soon found practiced on such as had been some time in the convent, we are constrained to infer that the Bishop and Superior had long been convinced of the necessity of such art to constrain young females of the present day to submit themselves to their control.

Feeble instruments, as they appear, have often been the occasion of great and important changes in society. Miss Reed, should she prosper, as she has to some extent already, in diminishing the influence of the system she denounces, is not the first female of obscure origin and slender resources and talents, whose efforts to overthrow tyranny and unmask bigotry and hypocrisy, have been crowned with signal success. Yet there is nothing in the face of the narrative which would imply her expectation of any great and important result. She is charged with an attempt to destroy the Benedictine convent, and it is quite possible that her book may lead to its ultimate dissolution; but nothing like a design or a hope of this sort appears in the book itself; and in a statement since published in defence of the work she expressly disclaims all such motives in publishing it.

Supposing the narrative respecting Miss Mary Magdalene to be correct, what must be said of the cold and heartless cruelty with which that meek creature was treated! Unless the Superior is prepared with something more direct and circumstantial than a fierce and flat denial of the whole affair, to repel this part of Miss Reed's accusation, no doubt can be entertained of this alone going very far towards bringing down the public indignation upon the system generally as well as the institution in particular.

In a supplement to Miss Reed's Narrative there is a passage, in which she is represented as accounting in a very rational manner for her first disposition to enter the convent, and in which, also, she candidly disclaims all intention to injure that institution, except as a plain statement of facts experienced and witnessed by herself may have that tendency. "I have never wished to conceal that I was no doubt mistaken in thinking a romantic spirit, and the grief and affliction which followed the death of my mother, were a religious zeal for seclusion from the world. My feelings have from infancy been easily affected, and in going into the convent as I did, every one must see that I was influenced more by imagination than by judgment. I now wish others, who may be influenced as I was by false views of things, to understand the real nature of convents. I am sure I have only told what took place there, and have in no case exaggerated it. If what takes place in a convent ought to be approved, and induce Protestants to send their children there, then I have done nothing that could injure it, but would help it with the public. I would merely ask whether, if what I saw and heard was wrong, and yet was concealed from the public by the Community, I have done wrong in telling it in the manner I have, and in allowing it to be published, after my name was brought before the public in order to condemn me. This reflection relieves my mind from the pain I should otherwise feel at the reproaches of the Superior in her answer. I do not feel that I have deserved them. While I was at the convent at first, my imagination was wrought up to the highest; and believing the Roman Catholic to be the only true religion, I was zealous to persuade all others to embrace it; but I never wished to take a cross, and go through the streets of Boston, making known the true faith, as the Superior represents. I believe my friends will admit that I never, on any occasion, conducted, or wished to conduct myself, in that manner."

It appears that one great inducement to Miss Reed's early determination to enter a convent, was her accidental intercourse with a French gentleman, of the name of Rodique, who boarded at the house of a married sister whom she was in the habit of visiting at Boston. She candidly confesses that "he had much influence on her mind in inducing her to join the Catholics." He seems to have met her in another Catholic family she was accustomed to visit—to have resorted to her father's, to give her instruction in the principles of the Catholic faith and discipline—to have adopted some questionable methods to preserve her attention fixed on what he deemed an important object—and to have done all this in the face of a knowledge that her father and family were adverse to any change in her religion. It is scarcely to be wondered that a naturally romantic and susceptible mind should, under such tuition, and immediately on the death of her mother, have turned her affections towards a convent—especially as her dying parent appears to have left this as her last request, that if she could discover any other church more holy than the Protestant, she would unite herself to it. She thought the Papal church more holy, and acted accordingly.

The officious interference of M. Rodique is a sample of the minute, individual, incessant zeal, exerted by Catholics of all classes and countries, to increase, if but one insignificant individual, proselytes to their community. Very seldom would it be found that a Protestant gentleman of any denomination, accidentally lodging at a citizen's house, would take much pains, or any pains at all to convert a young and inexperienced relation of his hostess to the peculiarities of his own faith. But here we have a Catholic gentleman, availing himself of the first intimation that a young Protestant girl might be induced to become a convert to Popery, if not, industriously endeavouring to excite the first disposition towards such a change in her immature mind!

This conduct was the more reprehensible as well as remarkable on account of the studied secrecy with which it proceeded to its purpose. The father of Miss Reed, it is incidentally admitted, knew of his visits to his daughter, and disapproved of them; while he either feared or felt himself unable to prevent them. M. Rodique was a lodger, and we believe a boarder, at the house of his married daughter, and he might hesitate to do anything that should offend him. At all events, though he once threatened to forbid him the house, if not turn him out of it, he never appears to have adopted either the milder expedient or the more formidable extremity. But even these visits were unknown to the sister of Miss Reed, at whose house the officious emissary dwelt; and though in his conversation with her and her husband, the subjects of Catholicism and Convents often arose, he was cautiously silent about them in reference to their young and romantic sister.

Now what would be said, even by such an one, of a Protestant gentleman thus searching out the retreats of a young girl, and keeping his movements as secret as possible from those who were likely to prevent them? No imputation beyond a religious motive ever seems to have been entertained against this Catholic zealot; and yet such conduct, had he been a Protestant, would scarcely have failed to bring down the reproach, the execration, due to a purposed seducer—even though he had pleaded zeal for the conversion of the object of his pursuit to the important peculiarities of his creed, and observances of his religious worship.

Another ingenious device employed by the Bishop (Fenwick, we believe, was his name), to proselyte this young female, must not be passed over. It should be observed that she had an elder sister already with the Catholics, named, either in her first Protestant or her second Popish baptism, Theresa, after the patroness saint of the order to which she belonged; and this circumstance must have greatly encouraged both the Bishop and his agent M. Rodique to hope that another of the family might yield to their sway. In this hope the Bishop obtained—likely through his lay friend's influence with the family—an interview with Rebecca. Then he addressed her in terms of solemn admonition, which she acknowledges very deeply impressed her conscience and heart, and in parting with her, said—"We shall make a good Catholic of you,"—lending her two volumes containing a *Tale,* with which the Catholic peculiarities of faith and worship were artfully blended. These volumes were almost immediately taken back to the Bishop by Mr. Pond, her sister's husband—a circumstance that goes far to prove that the *Novel* they contained was not deemed quite proper for a young girl to read. Very reluctantly did she consent to their being returned.

Even these devices, however, skilful as they were, would in all probability have failed, but for an early and avowed predisposition to Popery and to a convent life in Rebecca's mind. On the other hand, we cannot wonder, that, having heard of this disposition and the frank and public avowal of it, the Bishop should make the usual effort of his fraternity to gather this feeble unsuspecting lamb into the Catholic fold. But who can overlook the character stamped on the system of proselytism, by the almost infancy of the age, amidst which even a Bishop and an elderly lay gentleman deem it their duty to beat up for recruits. Did we find them labouring in their vocation exclusively, or chiefly, among those whose years enable them to judge for themselves, and to embrace with calm deliberation, if they embrace at all, the mysterious discipline of the Romish Church, little of animadversion would be left for a critic of their proceedings to publish. These grave personages, however, in despair of success among adults, are seen casting their baits among mere children; and by craft, when they cannot do it by force, removing them from parental control, shutting them up in a prison, and interposing their assumed authority between them and all their natural protectors, and their most faithful and affectionate friends. All efforts to render others religious and moral are best made at an early age.

> "Children like tender osiers take the bow,
> And as they first are fashion'd always grow:"

But the efforts before us are made to change the religion of children, and that at the expense of at least one branch of moral obligation—to the breach at least of one precept of the moral law—the one standing at the head of the second table, and what is emphatically called *the first commandment with promise*—"Honour thy father and mother." Such efforts should, in all candour and conscience, be reserved for an age in which parental authority is about to cease, and the individuals assailed are becoming masters of their own judgment as well as persons.

In the narrative of Miss Reed's seclusion, mention is frequently made of Mary Francis, thus named after she entered the convent; but before known as Miss Kennedy, and spoken of in an earlier part of the volume as having moved from Boston, on the arrival of a domestic at the house of Rebecca's father in search of her. We have read certain letters of this young lady addressed to Miss Reed, never intended for publication, but which the latter has been constrained to publish in her own defence against the reproaches of the lady St. George, the Superior of the convent. There is not only an apparent breach of confidence here on the part of Miss Reed, but she becomes by this act the instrument—a reluctant one she confesses—of exposing her young friend to the Superior's vengeance—if such an evil emotion can find place in the devout bosom of a lady Abbess.

"Tantæne animis cælestibus iræ?"

We are not anxious either wholly to justify, or severely to censure this part of Miss Reed's conduct. The sufferings of Mary Francis in the convent, like her own, had already been great, and could scarcely be increased by any further infliction of the Superior's anger or malice. But this anger and malice always appear to have been completely under the control of a mind of singular potency and policy. The Superior could behave towards her pupils, whenever she pleased, and it would better answer her chief purpose, with well dissembled kindness and great condescension of manners; and the probability is, that this more gentle and winning character became assumed towards Miss Kennedy, the better to sustain the trembling reputation of the convent amidst the storm which Miss Reed was evidently able to raise against it. There is reason to believe that Miss Kennedy, on the appearance of her letters, was removed to another convent, if not afterwards to a third. Her name, too, was changed from Mary *Francis* to Mary *Paulina*—for what motive the reader must judge, and with what success may be inferred when it is known that her parents were Catholics, and therefore not only disposed to approve of her treatment, but also to acquiesce in these pious artifices to deceive the public respecting her.

Miss Kennedy writes like a good Catholic as well as a friend to Miss Reed. Her admission of what was wrong in the convent is an admission of abuse of what in itself she considers perfectly right. "Do not"—she says—"let anything you have seen disgust you with our holy religion." "Has not our Lord said that scandals must come? can ought but a good thing be abused, or a holy thing profaned?" "Forgive me for presuming to preach; I am so anxious for you to make the best use of your sufferings." "May they make you more pleasing to the divine Saviour of mankind." "You have, my dear Agnes, unfastened the golden link which rivets, more closely than any other, soul to soul and heart to heart; but you are still loved and interesting to me. Oh, dear one, what has during these few months made such sad ravages in your heart. Reflect on your observation to me. 'I am convinced that the Catholic religion is the only true one.' Can you bury in oblivion this your own fervent protestation? and also the happy moments passed before that religion's hallowed altars? Have you abandoned it because you found crime and deceit in some of its professors and in some of its ministers? Was not one of the chosen apostles of our divine Redeemer a traitor? Did not our Lord say 'scandals must come?' Come, where? In the church, undoubtedly?"

A remark or two on these extracts. The letters from which they are made are deemed by Miss Reed's Protestant friends remarkably confirmatory of all her charges of severity against the Superior, and of abuses and cruelties in the convent. We confess we see no such confirmation in them. We should have believed Miss Reed's charges to the full without them, and perhaps our faith in her plain statement would even have been more implicit. We do not mean that they weaken our confidence in her special accuracy any more than in her general integrity; but they put so sacred a construction on her sufferings—they throw such an air of mystery and even sublimity over the scene of her trials—they evince so profound an attachment to the institution amidst all its abuses—they show so clearly what one young person may revile as in itself evil, another may advocate as only sustaining occasional evil abuse,—that we are inclined to think that Miss Reed's friends, and that young lady herself, would have done her cause quite as much good by withholding as by publishing them.

It is also next to impossible for us to look over these letters and not ask—*Is not the hand of Joab in all this?* May not even the Superior's influence, if not the Bishop's aid, be detected in most of what Miss Francis writes? The fine turns of expression which the letters contain—the clever appeals they made to Miss Reed's judgment and conscience as well as heart—the vague indefinite language in which some abuses are admitted—the opening left for a stranger to infer that these abuses regarded the system of Popery generally rather than convents in particular—the insinuations that while the Catholic religion admits abuse, *as the purest system on the face of the earth,* its conventual holy places furnish a retreat from the danger, and involve no other suffering than what is calculated to obviate the far worse evil of sinning,—these go far towards convincing us that whatever apprehension the chiefs of the convent entertain from Miss Reed's statement, they cherish not a moment's fear from the letters of her more Catholic and consistent friend.

This view of her letters, however, enhances the indignation with which we contemplate the discipline of these nurseries of superstition. They are not conducted and controlled by ignorant zealots who know not what they do; but by shrewd and discerning politicians, who are capable of turning almost every incident into an occasion of defence. Their motto is—The end justifies the means; and having given their end the most exalted character—having settled the point, at least with themselves, that their system is infallible and divine—they stop at no expedient however crafty, they withhold no effort however humiliating and censurable, to advance a cause paramount to every other upon earth. Their settled duty to God is, the furtherance of the Catholic religion; and to man is, his conversion to this religion and this furtherance of it; and to these two branches of what they deem divine and infallible legislation, all human connections and courtesy, propriety and feeling, give way, and they boast of an honourable victory in triumphing over and trampling upon them.

Another resort for sustaining the integrity of Miss Reed, and the fidelity of her evidence against the convent, has been made by her friends. Sometime before she entered it, she had been at a school in Boston, under the care of two sisters whose names do not appear further then in their initials—the Misses S...... There can be no doubt of their respectability as superintendants of an accredited and talented seminary, and also as members of the episcopal church in Boston, of which the Rev. Dr. Crosswell is the esteemed pastor. It is to be regret-ted that the instruction of Miss Reed in this school was restricted to embroidery and needle-work, for which she had a superior taste, and in which she became an acknowledged proficient. A little volume is now before us which says that "she was particularly expert in making lace, then much in fashion; but while under the care of the Misses......, she took no lessons except in needle-work."

This, we repeat, is to be regretted. It is acknowledged that "she was far from being ignorant: appeared as intelligent as most young ladies of her age, and always conversed with correctness and propriety. "Her mind"—the volume goes on to say—"appeared very capable of im-provement." Why then, we naturally ask, was not her mind improved in this Protestant school, and by teachers so capable of effecting the desirable and easy work? why was it left in its imperfect incipient state to receive its improvement, if such it might be called, in a Catholic Seminary, and through the discipline of a convent? Why was this tender sapling removed from a garden of free air, in which it already grew and flourished, to be transplanted to a foreign forcing house amidst all manner of stunted, and crooked, and useless exotics? "She often expressed a wish," we are told, "to enter the convent that she might *complete her education.*" Now, without putting any bar upon her entering a convent, when she came of an age to form an enlightened and deliberate judgment, let us ask why did not her numerous and zealous friends somehow contrive to let her *education be completed* before her entrance, and thus give her the chance, at least, of choosing not to enter at all?

The testimony of these Protestant sisters, whose tuition of Miss Reed was so strangely limited to manual ingenuity to the neglect of intellectual studies, and so far as it appears even of religious lessons, expressly confirms all that has been said of the influence of M. Rodique over her mind in favour of Catholicism. This gentleman, they acknowl-edge, "met her at their house at the time she was talking of going into the convent, and proposed to introduce her to the Bishop!" Nay, he appears to have taken her from their house to the Bishop's residence!!

We should not lay the stress we do on these circumstances, were not the ladies volunteers among those who rejoice in her escape from the convent, who testify in favour of her charges against it, and who thus far appear on the stage as adversaries of the institution. We applaud their zeal in all this; but why did their zeal slumber so much and so long at an earlier period, when they ought to have been awake and active in preventing the six months suffering that Miss Reed underwent, to say nothing of the Catholic reproach that will now follow her to the grave, and perchance somewhat hasten her arrival there. They pleaded, indeed, for her being allowed to take her Bible and prayer book with her into the convent: but when told that her prayer book must not accompany her, and that she must have no other than the Catholic version of the Bible, they discover no emotion, they make neither opposition nor protest. Nay, they seem wantonly or wilfully to neglect an opportunity peculiarly favourable for changing her mind and arresting her progress. Her first intercourse with the Bishop was not satisfactory to herself. "She was not pleased with his conversation;" and "she appeared less disposed to go to the convent after that interview than she had done before." What a favourable juncture this for a strong and united remonstrance from her Protestant friends? What a tide in her affairs which they might have taken at the flood? where was Dr. Crosswell at this time, when M. Rodique and the Bishop were so near at hand and ready for action?

We ask these questions more in sorrow than in anger, and with the purpose of warning other parents and teachers, other patrons and friends of young females who are exposed to the insidious snares of Popery, either from the restless vigilance of its emissaries, or the romantic disposition of their own minds. The entire affair before us shows, what must often have appeared on other evidence before our readers, that Catholic ceremonies and sentiments have a remarkable tendency to impress in their favour, minds of this cast. In Protestant countries we daily witness the effect of religious display and parade on such persons, and how much more powerful is *their* attraction than that of the simple and solemn performance of Christian worship! In Protestant and enlightened England, what multitudes are attracted by public meetings and platform exhibitions, and how delighted they are with those parts of the chequered affair in which the ridiculous forms the nearest possible coalition with the sublime! Urge them more frequently to attend the usual week-night services of their several ministers, and they will plead their want of time; but let some more novel and exciting scene be advertised, at another and distant place of worship, and time can easily be found for attendance an hour earlier, and two hours later! Moreover, money can be spared for the collection, and every kind of sacrifice can be endured for the sake of witnessing the show and listening to the speeches of such an occasion, by multitudes who have no sympathy with their own *dear* deserted minister, and no taste for his plain week-night sermons and prayers!

Is the success of Catholic zeal, then, a matter of wonder in the present day in England any more than in America—in London any more than in Boston and Charlestown? Can we be surprised at the rapid increase and effort of that zeal, amidst a people so well prepared for its meretricious embrace by the weak inventions of Protestant folly? Are we astonished to hear that so many, trained for the natural transit at a gay and noisy Protestant chapel, not a hundred miles from Finsbury, should so eagerly pass over to the still more pompous and enchanting temple that modern Popery has furnished, to receive and welcome such butterfly saints? A most remarkable instance of this Protestant Popery, if we may thus associate terms of sworn opposition, took place in a city distinguished by its enlightened institutions and inhabitants, a few years ago. It is not mentioned here with any other motive than to confirm the truth of what has been advanced, and illustrate the views which are taken of the tendency of much that takes place in Protestant assemblies to further the Catholic cause.

An impostor of singular attractions in person, costume, and speech, gained access to several respectable families as the heir of a noble title and estate; which have since, by the death of the then possessor, descended to their rightful expectant. His public addresses, first from the balcony of his hotel, and afterwards in almost every public room of the city in which he had taken up his temporary abode, created such an interest in his favour, that a large portion of the constituency hailed with rapture his announcement at the eve of a general election, to become a candidate for the representation, in opposition to two excellent members, who expected to be returned for the third time without opposition. While his popular talents and speeches, with a large share of assumed philanthropy and seeming condescension of manner, gained him several thousand followers among the lower orders, no small number of religious and respectable persons of all denominations, were delighted with his warm avowals of attachment to religion; and some were even willing to make any sacrifice in their power for his advancement to the very head of the political and religious institutions of the place.

Among his admirers was a lady who conducted a respectable boarding school, and who had deemed it an honour to receive a poor child under her protection, which he had just before, for some reason of his own, thought fit to receive as his own *protegee*. The little girl was placed among her scholars, and the patron was always a welcome visitor at the school. In fact, he became the idol of the institution, and the venerated friend of its respectable conductress. Special and extraordinary visits were at length arranged, and one took place marked with peculiar importance, not only by its religious character, but by the solemn preparations that preceded, and the novel scenes and ceremonies that attended it. A central seat was elevated and adorned for the distinguished guest: and report says that a splendid canopy was placed over it. On either side, but on a level with the floor, were chairs tastefully arranged for the governess and her mother, on the left and right hand of the presiding genius of the evening; and for their inferior visitors and the teachers of the school, on the right and left of them. The other parts of the room were occupied in most admired order by the several scholars and their young friends; while the young protegee, beautifully dressed, was placed on an ottoman at the feet of her illustrious benefactor and adopted father, who was saluted by his assumed title of Sir William, and congratulated as an expectant earl! Before him was a handsome table, an elegant cushion, and a superb Bible; and after the refreshments of tea and coffee, he delivered addresses and offered prayers, which were listened to with more profound attention and fervent applause, than any one of the forty clergymen of the city ever received. What ceremonies or amusements followed, beyond a little sacred and profane singing, we are not with certainty informed. Rumour spoke, at the time, of a dance, but we mention it as a rumour, and not as a reality.

And why have we described the scene at all? Not certainly to dwell upon, still less to rejoice over the fate of the individual thus exalted and honoured. The assumed Sir William was soon after convicted of swindling and perjury, and escaped transportation by a successful plea of insanity; which has, however, given him a place in a lunatic asylum, at least for the period of his intended transportation, and perchance for life. But the scene is described for the purpose of admonition and remonstrance. Where there is a disposition among Protestants, and Protestants of education and respectability, to make on any occasion this use of their religion—this parade of a system whose motto is that *the kingdom of Christ is not of this world*—are not all the young people, especially the young females, who witness such scenes, and behold their parents and teachers, and even *pastors,* delighted with them, more than prepared at the first opportunity, if not to enter a convent, to become members of the so called holy and infallible community of Rome?

To return, perhaps for the last time, to our first subject. Miss Reed's narrative is said to have acquired a vast and increasing circulation in America, and it will no doubt be very generally read in this country. Let it be so—not merely or chiefly to remunerate a spirited publisher, or the publishers of any other edition, for their cost and care; but, above every other consideration, to render the fair authoress as general a benefit as she can become to the rising age of the Protestant world. Her primary object appears to have been the justification of her conduct in clandestinely escaping from the convent; and the purpose of her friends, in the support they have come forward to give her testimony and character, is chiefly the refutation of what they deem the selfish and slanderous answer which her narrative provoked from the Superior. But let our principal purpose, in giving a British circulation to these interesting facts, and by which we are aiming to illustrate them, be the benefit of those churches, and families, and individuals, to whom we are united by a common bond of Protestant sentiment and feeling. Far, very far, let our thoughts be removed from the least intention to inflame the public mind—already, perhaps, too much heated—against the Superiors or subordinates, the priests or the people, of Catholic churches. But this evil may be shunned without proceeding to the other extreme of indifference to the danger of Protestant youth, especially of the sex, from the restless ambition of a once rampant, but now fallen hierarchy, to substitute in their warm affections the traditions of men for the undefiled gospel of "the blessed and only Potentate, the King of kings, and Lord of lords."

For let it never be lost sight of, that the contest between the Romish church and the various evangelical communities which *protest* against it, is not one of mere circumstance and ceremony—of mere discipline and authority—but of religious principle, of sacred and essential truth. The foundation of Popery and the faith of Papists stand, not in the power of God, but in the wisdom of men—not in the merits of Christ, but in the works and virtues of those who borrow in order to blaspheme his name—not in the blood of the Covenant, but in the penances and prayers of those, who profess indeed to be his disciples, but deny him the glory of their purification and redemption. Without attributing to Catholics the absurd and besotted idolatry which the objects they bow before would seem to deserve for them, it is sufficient to support the charge of their departure from the true faith of the gospel, and the spiritual worship of God, that they claim in any sense and in any degree a merit for human doings, super-added to, or independent of, the merit of Christ—"His obedience unto death, even the death of the cross." There is no such thing in existence. The thought is exploded in scripture, and the assumption in whatever form must be abhorrent to all right Christian feeling.

Specious advocates for convents have pleaded thus—"The works performed in those retreats of piety, at all events, bear no resemblance to the pharisaic works censured by our Lord, which were wrought ostentatiously *to be seen of men.*" Still they may partake, and we fear do partake, of the fullest essence of a self-righteous character, being done for a purpose, if possible, more adverse to Christian principles, and therefore more displeasing to God, than ostentation and display—to propitiate divine favour and purchase heavenly blessedness. Those whose religion ostentatiously invites the public gaze, and whose chief object is human approbation and applause, excite pity for their weakness and vanity, and are finely satirised and dismissed by the only encouragement that divine liberality can bestow upon them—"Verily, I say unto you, ye have your reward." But those take more presumptuous ground, and are guilty of greater impiety, who conclude that, by an ingenious system of penance and seclusion, they can either effect that for themselves which the death of Christ alone accomplishes, or can add by their own sacrifices to the value and virtue of his atoning death!

Such efforts to expiate human guilt, and mortify the passions of a corrupt nature, supposing them to be approved or tolerated by God—which is impossible—have no utility, and consequently no moral worth, as public examples tending to the general good. The ostentatious self-righteous man may, in many respects, be an useful one in society. While the principles of his conduct are concealed and do no injury, his actions may do considerable good—often more good from the forward zeal with which they are multiplied and forced as it were on the public attention. But the system of monastic seclusion, while its presumption and self-confidence are offensive to God, has none of the subordinate qualities of utility among men. Nay, it robs society of the benefit which all personal religion is designed, and adapted, and required to render; while its only relative effect is, from its very nature and necessary operation, painfully injurious, in promoting some of the worst feelings in both the governing and governed towards each other—inducing the one to a severity at variance with both Christian and natural feeling, and the other to resistance and reluctant compliance whenever resistance would not prevail or dare not appear.

This is remarkably manifested from the first to the last of Miss Reed's narrative. The six months of her conventual life was one continued contest, more or less in action, between her and those to whom in an evil moment she had yielded up the control of her conscience and conduct. Nor was the evil confined to *her*—who soon felt the yoke too heavy for her to bear, and resolved on an escape from the intolerable

thraldom; but it appears in a more affecting form in the private complaints of her less resisting companions—in their secret sighings and
murmurings, who had not the hope and dared not cherish the wish to
escape from the melancholy prison house. In these less courageous and
more submissive disciples, we see another evil tendency of the system,
not elicited and experienced, at least for any length of time, by Miss
Reed. She early broke the yoke and burst the bonds asunder, and now
appeals openly to the world for the justification of her conduct; but
they privately complain of hardships and cruelties which they have not
the courage to surmount and scarcely the conscience to disapprove.
Without charging them with direct hypocrisy, in professing to submit
with Christian patience to what their heart and soul must sometimes
think strange, if not evil, it is enough to show that they are restless
and unhappy—that, however they may be striving to "learn of Him
who was meek and lowly in heart," they are far from feeling the yoke
they wear as *His* to be *easy,* or the *burden* they are told *He* imposes
upon them to be *light.*

We look on these, and other *moral* evils that wider space would
enable us to record, as some of the worst tendencies of the system
which we cordially unite with Miss Reed in denouncing. At the same
time, it is impossible to be silent on the pernicious influence which
the education of Protestant children in Catholic schools must have on
their present and future *religious* character. The writer of these pages
has witnessed, in different parts of Europe, what the American friends
of Miss Reed apprehended is widely diffusing its baneful consequences
in that country. He has seen, in France and Flanders especially, the
modern *rage,* as it may be called, of Protestant parents for the education of their sons in the colleges and their daughters in the convents
of the Romish church. At Bruges, Ghent, and St. Homer especially,
he found large numbers of Protestant English children availing themselves, under their parents' sanction, of these opportunities, and thus,
for the sake of a good French education, resigning at once all their
native patriotic and Protestant feelings. To attend the routine of such
schools, and not imbibe daily and hourly the very spirit of the religion
they are established to propagate, is impossible. Either, therefore, our

Protestant countrymen and countrywomen are indifferent to what religious character their children acquire, or they calculate too confidently on their ability to counteract, in after life, youthful prepossessions in favour of Popery.

Can it be expected that the Superiors of these establishments will forego their favourite ceremonies? or that they will allow exemptions and innovations at variance with the assumed pre-eminence of their system? or that they will neglect the opportunities thrown in their way by thoughtless Protestants, who have not the same zeal for their peculiarities, and often no zeal at all, of adding to their converts? What then is the consequence? The children thus transferred become regular attendants on the singular frequency of Catholic worship, and thus early converts to the system; or, after six days' attendance on weekly ceremonies, they spend the sabbath with their parents, either in the total neglect of all religious worship, at which they are taught to shudder, or being allowed one reluctant attendance on a Protestant service, always cold enough in England, and on the continent proverbial for its heartless formality and its worldly indifference!

Here the reader is conducted most unwittingly to a prolific spring of the evil now deplored. If human ingenuity had tasked itself to devise a plan for exhibiting Protestantism in an unpopular light, it could not have succeeded better than our countrymen, both lay and clerical, have done in their ecclesiastical arrangements. More dull uninteresting services of a religious nature never were witnessed, than those of the English in the several continental towns in which they congregate. It has been matter of some surprise that French vivacity could ever tolerate the dull music of Catholic worship—that a people so volatile, and fond of the liveliest airs and movements in all other places, can listen for hours together to the droning monotonous tones of the best cathedral choirs. But in the English churches there is no music at all; neither instrument nor voice is heard in the praise of God; nor is there anything else adapted to kindle in the bosom a single spark of appropriate cheerful devotion.

Contrasted with these lifeless services, Catholic churches all around present scenes of stirring attraction to the eye if not to the ear, and young persons especially, are not backward in acknowledging the difference, nor anxious to forego seasons of cheap and welcome excitement, for the mere sake of perpetuating a formal respect for the religion of their own country. Through this cause alone, not a few English young ladies residing on the continent annually become decided and acknowledged converts to the Romish church; and many more renounce Protestant services altogether, and, if they observe public worship at all, observe it in a Catholic temple.

Aware of this continued chance of winning our children "to the obedience of *their* faith," Catholic priests, in towns to which English families resort, are ever on the watch. Without imputing to them improper motives, every one on the spot must observe them evincing a politeness of behaviour, joined with official zeal and vigilance, which Protestant ministers would do well in a better cause to imitate. The writer of these pages resided in a large French city about twelve months, for the improvement of his two daughters in the language, and he had occasion to notice the watchful temper of the priesthood in this respect. His younger daughter, a mere child, heard much from her French teacher of the excellence of a certain young priest, who, in fact, was universally esteemed by Protestants as well as Catholics. The teacher also had spoken to him of what she was pleased to call her favourite pupil. A respectful message was one day delivered by the teacher from the priest, requesting that on her next visit to his house her little scholar might be allowed to accompany her. The child herself was anxious to go, and was highly delighted with his addresses and presents. She has now been sometime in England, but continues to speak with rapture of her reception at the house of Monsieur M—. Nor can her parents forego this opportunity of bearing their testimony in his favour. They are persuaded that he never would have sanctioned the severity of which Miss Reed complains, and would have been the first to lift up his voice against the cruelties inflicted on Miss Mary Magdalene.

Here, some will plead, there is the greater danger; and that families are more safe from innovation amidst evils like those which Miss Reed has exposed in America, than from the more plausible and pleasant way chosen by the French to effect the same purpose. Supposing this to be admitted, the duty of Protestant families in defeating that purpose is, to imitate the amenity of our European neighbours, rather than retaliate on the harshness and inhumanity of the Catholics of the new world. While caution and restraint, to promote our children's fidelity to the Protestant faith, are conducted with a temper like that which marked Monsieur M—'s efforts to conciliate them in favour of Popery—while they are unallied with the bitterness and unstained by the vice, which are bad enough in Catholics, but worse in Protestant zealots—such caution and restraint cannot be exercised with too much vigilance and wisdom, too much decision and perseverance.

In this light Miss Reed's interesting narrative will bear the strictest investigation. It is not a recompensing evil for evil. It is not measuring to the Catholics the measure which they have too often been ready to mete to the Protestants. Her candid admission of all the good treatment she received, and her equally candid admission of the respect and even reverence, with which those young inmates of the convent who suffered much more than herself, returned to those who so cruelly treated them, shows a temper in this young writer vastly superior to that with which Catholic vices and crimes are too often recorded, especially by those who have suffered under them. The very worst thing we have heard spoken of Miss Reed—always excepting the vindictive and vituperative answer of her Superior—was a remark to this effect. "Perhaps this young lady was averse to remaining in an institution which would compel her to continue in single blessedness. Perhaps she had "examined well her blood," and discovered that she could not long "endure the livery of a nun;"

> "For aye to be in a shady cloister mew'd,
> To live a barren sister all her life,
> Chanting faint hymns to the cold fruitless moon."

Perhaps she had identified herself with Milton's lady, and heard the fine and fascinating address of Comus—

> "List, sister, be not coy, and be not cozen'd
> With that same vaunted name virginity.

Beauty is nature's coin, must not be hoarded,
But must be current, and the good thereof
Consists in mutual and partaken bliss,
Unsavoury in th' enjoyment of itself:
If you let slip time, like a neglected rose
It withers on the stalk with languish'd head."

Should this surmise of our heroine's motives be just, we will not censure her—we dare not cast either the first or the last stone upon her. To violate a vow—supposing her to have taken it, which is itself a violation of nature and religion—is a virtue to be extolled rather than a vice to be reproached and condemned. To assert the supremacy of the divine will—clearly intimated in creation—forming an essential part of the machinery of divine Providence—and sanctified as well as sanctioned by every dictate and design of Christianity:—to assert the supremacy of the divine will, thus commended, over every edict of human authority, is acting a noble Christian part, which, however it may have a direct aspect on our own comfort, ought not to be laughed or frowned to silence, as though the selfish feature of it robbed it of all its goodness and beauty, and reduced it to a mere paltry subterfuge for individual private interest.

Should Miss Reed require support under such an insinuation, greater than this argument or argument of any kind can furnish, she may appeal to no less an example than the wife of Martin Luther—nay, to that of the great reformer himself. The young lady that he married—Catherine Boren—had been a nun, and had escaped from a Saxon convent; and Luther himself, by his marriage, especially with such a lady, gave pointedness and force to all his previous arguments against the Catholic law of monastic celibacy, which had then reached the consummation of its immoral abuses, as well as of its lofty pretensions to religious authority.

This accidental allusion suggests a few remarks on another feature of the *expose* of Miss Reed. The most fertile source of moral evil is indolence, especially when it becomes systematic and secluded. It is on this account that great examples of vice as well as virtue are not so productive of imitation as might at first be expected. The fact is, there are hundreds that want energy, for one that wants ambition, and sloth has in this respect prevented vice in some minds as well as virtue in others. Idleness is the grand pacific ocean of life, and in that stagnant abyss the most salutary things often produce no good, and the most noxious no evil. Abstract vice, however, may be and often is, engendered in idleness; though the moment it becomes efficient it must quit its cradle and cease to be idle. In monasteries and convents, therefore, all who admit our nature to be radically corrupt will expect to find the seeds and roots of evil to abound—to be feeble in their strength owing to a restricted mode of life, and the want of space for expansion and exercise—still to abound in luxuriance and variety.

Amidst this evil of monastic seclusion, there is no substantial good to compensate or counteract it. Admitting it to have some salutary influence on those who submit to it, "not by constraint but willingly, not for filthy lucre, but with a ready mind," that influence reaches not beyond a narrow circle. There are undoubtedly some to be found in all ages and in most countries, who have experienced all the calm delight and satisfaction they expected and professed—whose feelings have been raised and kept above the world by perseverance in strict and solemn devotion—who have "sat in heavenly places," and have partaken of emotions and enjoyments beyond the power of language to describe. All this is possible, and by no means improbable.

But how narrow has been its widest range, and how insignificant its greatest influence on society! Private and secluded devotion is of infinite value as the main spring, the moving cause, of an active piety and a wide spreading beneficence: but such piety as this—never coming forth into public action, and scarcely known by the mass of mankind to exist—is as restricted in its social influence, as it is productive of personal superstition, and surrounded and sustained by local corruption. Were this piety in itself as undefiled as its names and pretensions would imply—were it always the vestal inviolable devotion which it assumes to be—were it holy as the fires of heaven, whence alone it professes to be inspired and inflamed—its limited and concealed character would not be nicely weighed against it: but its evil accompaniments, so generally attending it as to prove almost essential to its existence, will always prevent its being held in very high reputation, and render an immense majority of the wise and good as averse to encourage it in others as to adopt it themselves. As in agriculture, he that can produce the greatest crop for himself is not the best farmer, but he that can render his crop the best at the least expense; so in the Christian church, they are not the most valuable members who can acquire for themselves the greatest good, but those who can accomplish this with the least admixture of concomitant ill. For let none presume to think that they can devise any plan of producing good unalloyed and unadulterated with evil. This is the prerogative of God alone.

Apart from the moral evils, more or less corrupting the best religion of convents, there are ridiculous customs and ceremonies which, to say the least, debase that religion, and tend, in the view of young converts to the system, to make it appear a perfect caricature of that sublime reality which the scriptures render it. One of the pupils of the Boston convent thus describes its discipline in which Miss Reed's previous account is perfectly borne out. "The usual punishments of the school were making a young lady sit on the top of a high pyramid, or flight of steps, in a conspicuous place; putting their feet in the stocks, and kissing the floor. All these punishments I have seen in the school. The kissing the floor I particularly remember seeing in three cases. One case was my little sister, whose fault, I believe was making up a face to a young lady. She was ordered to kiss the floor, and complied. Another was a niece of one of the teachers, a Catholic; and the third a little Protestant girl about six years old. These punishments were inflicted in the presence of all the school. Kissing the floor was considered to be one of the punishments to mortify those who had broken the rules."

One or two remarks on this quotation. It is acknowledged that such was the discipline of the convent *schools.* It is, however, manifest that, so far as was practicable, it was the discipline of the entire convent. Its early exercise on the youngest scholars, Protestant as well as Catholic, was evidently intended to prepare them, in the event of their re-entering or remaining in the convent as *religieuses,* for submission either to the same rules, or to rules still more ridiculous and severe. A second remark suggested by the quotation regards the powerful hold which, with all its known evils, the system must have held of the good opinion of surrounding parents. This young lady acknowledges that she "went there with reluctance, because her elder sister, who had been a pupil for a long time, had left it several times, and came home much dissatisfied; but her friends persuaded her to return!" Yet, amidst this dissatisfaction and these escapes of an elder daughter, and the consequent and natural reluctance of a second daughter to enter the forbidding place, not only did the latter enter and continue there three months longer than Miss Reed, but a younger sister also was sent to kiss the floor, in token of her subjection to a scholastic plan, as absurdly redundant in punishments, as it was glaringly deficient in imparting sound tuition in letters, morals, or piety. Such was the infatuation of parents in favour of the convent, that their children were thus successively forced into it, and compelled to remain, notwithstanding they themselves were forbidden to witness the manner in which they are treated. Thus stands the record of the same young lady.

"The whole time I was in the convent I never saw my friends anywhere except in the visiting parlour, which was separate from the school-room and from the community of nuns. No visitors on any occasion were allowed to go into the school-room. My sister and another lady once called expressly to see the school-room, but they were refused. The only persons I ever saw in the school-room, except the pupils, were the Superior and nuns, the Bishop frequently, two priests, Dr. O'Flaherty and Mr. Tyler, and I think our other priest whose name I do not recollect. The school-room was sufficiently large to accommodate a number of visitors. The young ladies all knew that they could not invite their parents into the school-room on any occasion. I never knew any of the parents to visit either the sleeping-rooms or the dining-hall."

Nor is this all. There can be little doubt, not only that letters from their parents sometimes never reached the pupils, but that letters from the pupils were in greater numbers withheld from the parents. It was a rule of the convent for every pupil to write to her parents in the middle of every month; but as each letter thus written was placed unsealed in the hands of the Superior, much uncertainty prevailed about their being despatched, and no small number never reached their destination. This young lady remarks, "it was against the rule to receive a letter which did not come through the Superior. It was understood that all letters addressed to the pupils were opened and read by the Superior, before they reached the persons to whom they were addressed. It rested with the Superior whether any letters we had written should reach our friends or not."

We find it time to bring these desultory, yet we hope appropriate and seasonable reflections to a close. Their object has been to preserve the reader, especially the young reader, from those errors of the day which are most likely to "corrupt them from the simplicity that is in Christ." If those alone who, by countenancing and scattering these corruptions, "sow to the wind, reaped the whirlwind," our regret would not be so great, nor our anxiety for the rising youth of the land so intense. But the mischief is, that the blindness of bigotry seeks its victims chiefly amidst the innocent and unoffending. The cottage is sure to suffer for every error of the church. When corruption occupies the seat of authority, whether ecclesiastical or political, and proceeds from sources to which the young are taught in their earliest lessons to look with respect, it may be compared to that torrent which originates in the mountain, but commits its devastations in the vale. One important rule should perpetually govern us—to bring everything, antiquity as well as novelty, to the light of revealed truth. Mystery magnifies danger, as the fog does the sun. The hand that unnerved Belshazzar derived its most horrifying influence from the want of a body; and death itself is not so formidable in what we know of it as in what we know not. Had Miss Reed understood these things in early life, she had never entered the Ursuline Convent.

Printed in Great Britain
by Amazon

47608407R10215